SOVIET NATIONAL SECURITY POLICY UNDER PERESTROIKA

MERSHON CENTER SERIES ON INTERNATIONAL SECURITY
AND FOREIGN POLICY

Series Editor: Charles F. Hermann, *Director, Mershon Center, The Ohio State University*

Editorial Board:

Alton Frye, *Council on Foreign Relations*
John L. Gaddis, *Ohio University*
Raymond Garthoff, *The Brookings Institution*
Alexander L. George, *Stanford University*
Ole Holsti, *Duke University*
Robert Jervis, *Columbia University*
Arnold Kanter, *RAND Corporation*
John G. Ruggie, *University of California at San Diego*
Enid C. B. Schoettle, *The Ford Foundation*

MILITARY EFFECTIVENESS

Edited by Allan Millett and Williamson Murray
1988

Volume I: The First World War
Volume II: The Interwar Period
Volume III: The Second World War

Volume IV: SOVIET NATIONAL SECURITY POLICY UNDER
                    PERESTROIKA

                    Edited by George E. Hudson
                    1989

SOVIET NATIONAL SECURITY POLICY UNDER PERESTROIKA

Edited by

George E. Hudson

Mershon Center Series on International
Security and Foreign Policy, Volume IV

Boston
UNWIN HYMAN
London • Sydney • Wellington

© 1990 by the Mershon Center

Unwin Hyman, Inc.
8 Winchester Place, Winchester, Mass. 01890, USA

Published by the Academic Division of
Unwin Hyman Ltd
15/17 Broadwick Street, London W1V 1FP, UK

Allen & Unwin (Australia) Ltd,
8 Napier Street, North Sydney, NSW 2060, Australia

Allen & Unwin (New Zealand) Ltd in association with the
Port Nicholson Press Ltd,
Compusales Building, 75 Ghuznee Street, Wellington 1, New Zealand

First published in 1990

Library of Congress Cataloging-in-Publication Data

Soviet national security policy under perestroika / edited by George E. Hudson
     p. cm. — (Mershon Center series on international security and foreign policy)
    Book began as a Mershon Center faculty seminar at Ohio State University between Dec. 1986 and Oct. 1987.
    Includes bibliographies and index.
    ISBN 0–04–445532–1 — ISBN 0–04–445535–6 (pbk.)
    1. Soviet Union—National security. 2. Soviet Union—Foreign relations—1975–
I. Hudson, George E. II. Mershon Center for Education in National Security.
III. Series.
UA770.S6672 1989
355'.033547—dc20
                                            89–32086
                                                 CIP

British Library Cataloguing in Publication Data

Soviet national security policy under perestroika.
  (Mershon Center series on international security and foreign policy)
1. Soviet Union. National security
I. Hudson, George E.   II. Mershon Center   III. Series
327.47

ISBN 0–04–445532–1

Typeset in 10 on 12 point Times
Printed by The University Press, Cambridge

For Anne,
David, and Ted

Contents

PART FIVE
Conclusions and Implications

List of Tables

List of Figures

Preface and Acknowledgments

During the 1970s and early 1980s it had become something of a homily in the West to claim that Soviet national security policy equated to Soviet military policy. The homily was true. The USSR distinguished itself in the international arena primarily through the acquisition of a dizzying amount of nuclear weapons, the possession of large numbers of conventional forces, and the invasion of another communist nation—Afghanistan. The first two factors granted the Soviet Union military parity with the United States; the last served to emphasize the reactive nature of Soviet policy. Given that the Soviets possessed a weak economic arm and often poor diplomatic finesse to complement their military might, it was probably no exaggeration to say that the bulk of Soviet foreign policy was reactive and military oriented.

Yet as the 1990s approach, we are entering a period when the Soviet leadership is questioning past assumptions and when there is consequent change and a potential for more change in Soviet foreign and national security policy. The promises of "radical reform," collectively known as restructuring, thereby merit investigation.

As this book demonstrates, the interaction between the restructuring program and Soviet national security policy places the Soviet Union at a policy crossroads. How far in the direction of change can the Soviet Union proceed? Although this volume cannot provide a definitive answer, behavioral and policy manifestations of promised changes are becoming apparent. The Soviets have entered into an important arms control agreement, for the first time eliminating a whole class of nuclear weapons and permitting American investigators on Soviet soil to verify compliance. They have withdrawn their troops from the quagmire of Afghanistan and have announced they will unilaterally reduce large numbers of troops and conventional military equipment in Eastern Europe, in Mongolia, and at home. The USSR is also encouraging its industries to compete more vigorously in the world market and is more sensitive to global issues, such as the environment and the demands of Third World nations for fairer economic and political treatment. These areas of Soviet declaratory policy have become part of the Soviet national security calculus. Increasing changes in this direction could make the USSR a more formidable competitor for influence in the U.S.-Soviet competition by making Soviet policy more initiatory and less military in orientation.

An implication of a more vital policy, therefore, is the challenge it poses to the United States. How shall the United States respond to a USSR that seeks to defuse some of the past elements of military competition and conflict while at the same time charts new paths for its economic and political security? This book examines this question. It is apparent that the United States, too, is at a policy crossroads in its own foreign and national security policy.

This book began as a Mershon Center faculty seminar at The Ohio State University (OSU), which met four times between December 1986 and October 1987. Convened to study whether there was an emerging "third revolution" in Soviet national security policy, it evolved into an effort to examine the relationship between *perestroika* (restructuring) and change in Soviet policy. Except for the chapter by John E. Tedstrom and the concluding chapter, the contributions contained herein were presented to and critiqued by the members of the seminar. I initially organized and then directed the seminar, edited the chapters for publication, contributing two of my own, and put the book into its final form.

The seminar and other work toward this book were generously supported by the Mershon Center. Many individuals contributed to this collective task. I thank, first, Charles F. Hermann, director of the Mershon Center, for his generous support in funding the seminar and for his valuable remarks on the substance of the investigation. The Center for Slavic Studies at OSU, through the good offices of Miriam G. Schwartz, also provided some financial assistance for the initial seminar meetings.

Special thanks are also due to Philip D. Stewart and Margaret G. Hermann, who helped to provide the essential directions for this project and who, with Charles Hermann, offered excellent and patient criticism of my work. Raymond L. Garthoff and Alexander L. George read the entire manuscript and provided numerous beneficial suggestions for its improvement.

John A. Willieme, the good-natured and efficient project coordinator during the seminar's first year (and now an officer in the U.S. Air Force), ensured that our meetings would proceed properly and wrote useful summaries of each session. Saundra L. Jones, project coordinator for the second year (now an advanced graduate student at OSU), used her organizational skills to great effect and gladly lent invaluable assistance to much of the tedious work associated with editing.

Others who contributed to our understanding at the seminar sessions include Robert W. Campbell, Maurice Ernst, B. Welling Hall, Richard K. Herrmann, Marita Kaw, James M. McConnell, Olga Medvedkov, Yuri Medvedkov, Bruce W. Menning, and Thomas W. Robinson. Joseph Kruzel provided helpful comments on the first chapter, and Thomas F. Remington supplied useful criticism of the project at a panel discussion during a meeting of the Section on Military Studies. I express gratitude to the Hudson Institute for lending its conference facilities to the seminar for its second meeting.

Wittenberg University played an important role in the completion of the book. It provided sabbatical support for me and the services of Barbara A. Korn, who produced the manuscript for the publisher. I greatly appreciate Barbara Korn's cheery efficiency and her efforts to help meet deadlines. John S. Abma also assisted by translating various word-processing languages into the proper format. Members of my winter 1988 Soviet foreign policy class at Wittenberg read a draft of the book as part of their work and made useful comments about it.

Last and certainly not least, I thank my wife, Anne Barry Hudson, for her patience and efforts at a time when she had her own important work to complete. It is to her and our two boys that this book is gratefully and affectionately dedicated.

GEH
Springfield, Ohio
April 1989

• PART ONE •

Introduction

• CHAPTER ONE •

Conceptualizing Change in Soviet National Security

George E. Hudson
Wittenberg University and the Mershon Center

When Mikhail Gorbachev became general secretary of the Communist party of the Soviet Union (CPSU) in March 1985, he faced a panoply of difficulties left over from the irresolution of the last years of the Leonid Brezhnev era and from the political instability caused by two rapid successions to Brezhnev. Three months prior to his appointment Gorbachev marked the criticality of the time in a confidential report delivered to Party and government officials. Reform was necessary, he noted, to correct problems of "vast dimensions." At stake, he claimed, was the possibility of "increasing working people's prosperity, ensuring the consolidation of the USSR's position on the international scene, and enabling it to enter the new millennium in a manner worthy of a great and prosperous power."[1]

Economic prosperity and international power, Gorbachev recognized, were inextricably intertwined. He was determined to make reforms in both, starting with economic and social policy. The problems confronting him in domestic affairs were enormous and included at least four key concerns:

1. *Declining rates of economic growth.* According to PlanEcon statistics, the average annual growth for the net material product showed a

steady decrease to 3.4 percent during the Eleventh Five-Year Plan (FYP 1981–85), down from 5.6 percent and 4.2 percent in the 9th and 10th FYP, respectively ("1986 Panel" 1986: 4–5). Growth in industrial production and retail trade turnover demonstrated similar declines.

2. *Gross economic inefficiency,* stemming in part from a slowing of real income per capita, labor productivity, and technological lag. Soviet economist Tat'iana Zaslavskaia's public writings demonstrated the importance of income incentives as a stimulus for productivity. Without higher incomes—and goods other than alcohol to purchase with them—Soviet workers could not be expected to produce well. Gorbachev strongly supported these comments, attacking "wage leveling" in favor of incentives and noting the importance of increasing the availability of consumer goods.[2] Economic inefficiency also stemmed from the low level of technology in the Soviet economy generating the necessity to rebuild the machine-building industry.

3. *The general structure and managing of the economy.* Gorbachev identified managerial change as a key component to economic and social reform in the June 1987 Plenum. "We must realize that the time when administration boiled down to orders, bans, and appeals is over," Gorbachev stated.

> It is now clear to everyone that it is impossible to work under such methods. They are simply ineffective. To create a powerful system of motives and incentives, prompting all workers to reveal their abilities to the utmost, and to work fruitfully, utilizing more effectively productive resources—these are the imperatives of our time. (Gorbachev 1987b: 43)

4. *Nationality problems.* Soviet statistics indicated differential growth rates in the population of Soviet republics, which helped to indicate the emergence or decline of various nationalities. For instance, between 1940 and 1986 the population of the RSFSR increased by 30 percent, while the Uzbek SSR increased by nearly 300 percent and the Azerbaidzhan SSR, over 200 percent (*Narodnoe Khoziaistvo* 1986: 8). According to one Western estimate, "by the end of the century, between 20% and 25% of the country's total population and almost 40% of its teenagers and young adults will be 'non-Europeans,' of whom the vast majority will be Central Asians" (Azrael 1984: 608). This would likely demand new policies on the allocation of goods and services, new plans for locating Soviet industry in the areas of greatest population growth, and a general political willingness to hear out the demands of nationalities, such as the Tartars, a group of which received considerable press coverage and even a meeting with Soviet

President Andrei Gromyko in 1987. At the January 1987 Plenum Gorbachev called for the analysis of nationality relations in the wake of nationalist rioting in Alma Ata (Gorbachev 1987a: 28).

These key concerns interacted strongly with areas related to national security policy. One of the ironies of the nuclear age was that although Soviet defense spending continued to account for about 12 to 15 percent of gross national product and thereby consumed resources that could have been used elsewhere, the Soviet ability to defend itself from nuclear attack actually decreased, given the Reagan administration arms build-up, lack of progress in arms control, and Western European cooperation in increasing intermediate-range nuclear missiles in Europe. In addition, the Soviet realization that any nuclear war could bring nearly total disaster to the USSR lent force to new propositions that changed the emphasis from nuclear weapons in future war planning to concern with high-tech conventional forces (Ogarkov 1982). High technology in the military demanded a restructuring of the closely related civilian economy for success, including heightened investment in the civilian sector, personnel changes, and better training for members of all nationality groups.

Other national security policy areas presented problems, ranging from the lack of Soviet appeal in the Third World, to little progress in healing key issues of Sino-Soviet relations, to the necessity to improve relations with both Eastern and Western Europe. Events demanded a rethinking of fundamental national security policy.

Transformations, in fact, are beginning to occur in the Soviet security arena. The Soviets have agreed to eliminate intermediate-range nuclear missiles, to allow intrusive measures to verify arms control agreements, to examine the priority that the military has enjoyed in Soviet economic planning, to withdraw their troops from Afghanistan, and unilaterally to reduce troops and military equipment from Eastern Europe, Mongolia, and the western military district of the USSR. In looking at military change from a slightly different perspective and at an earlier time, William Odom depicts the changes he sees in Soviet national security policy as a "third revolution" in Soviet military affairs. He states, "the Soviet General Staff has embarked upon a third revolution in military affairs in its history. . . . Each [revolution] has had a major impact on Soviet economic, social and scientific policies. Each to date has received priority over virtually all other aspects of public policy in the Soviet Union" (Odom 1985: 1).

Is a so-called third revolution or perhaps even more radical change occurring in Soviet national security affairs? Significant evidence would support the proposition that important transformations are taking place, none more compelling than the campaign of self-criticism occurring since the demise of Leonid Brezhnev, the CPSU general secretary responsible for a Soviet military build-up of large proportions. Known currently as *perestroika,* or the restructuring of Soviet society, this effort seeks to correct the unidimensionality of Soviet superpower status through internal economic reforms and changes in military doctrine that have profound implications for the assumptions underlying Soviet national security and, over the long term, for the conduct of Soviet national security policy in the years ahead. Only now are we beginning to understand that the third revolution may be much more far-ranging and consequential than Odom suggests.

This book intends to uncover the emerging relationship between restructuring and Soviet national security policy by investigating a number of traditional Soviet policy areas to determine the extent to which basic change has occurred—that is, change in Soviet national security assumptions, policies, and behaviors. It endeavors to explain why these changes have taken place in terms of shifts in the Soviet domestic sphere and to draw out the implications of change for the conduct of Soviet politics and foreign policy and for U.S. relations with the USSR. In doing so the work poses the following questions: Are we witnessing a "revolution" in Soviet national security policy today? If so, what is its nature? Is it of equal consequence across the various subareas of Soviet national security policy? How does it relate to the restructuring of Soviet society and to changes in Soviet military doctrine? What are the divisions within the Soviet political elite over the direction of Soviet national security policy, and what implications do these divisions have for change in the future? How does Soviet national security policy respond to external pressures? What are the implications of change for the contexts of Soviet domestic politics, Soviet foreign policy, and U.S. policy toward the Soviet Union? Are the patterns of change clear enough to delineate an explanation about change in Soviet national security policy?

In probing what appears to be a broad "revolution" in Soviet national security policy, this chapter investigates, first, the varying propositions that may be offered to explain why Soviet national security affairs may be changing; second, the major concepts of the study; third, the framework and organization of the book; and, finally, the overall significance of the study.

This chapter introduces readers to the relationships among several different elements of Soviet national security: the "change agents," those factors of leadership, economic policy, external conditions, and intellectual ferment and upheaval that seem to create change in Soviet national security affairs; the changes in security assumptions and ideas.

national security policy, and behavior, what are called the "elements" of Soviet national security affairs; and the "rate of change" for the elements of national security, from stability to incremental change to significant change to radical change. These topics, in addition to a definition of national security and a fuller discussion of restructuring, are discussed in the next two sections of this chapter. Their relationships may be portrayed as in Table 1.1.

Alternative Propositions: The Change Agents

There are at least four sets of alternative propositions one could attach to explanations for change in Soviet national security affairs. As we shall see, these are examined in many of the chapters in this book, particularly in Part Three.

The first set centers on *leadership* as a change agent. The death of Brezhnev and the emergence of Gorbachev has made a crucial difference in the shape of Soviet national security to come. Without Gorbachev—the dynamic, politically astute leader—change in Soviet policy, both domestic and foreign, would be impossible. He has recruited a key cadre to help him set in motion the program of profound social change called perestroika, has encouraged radical forces for change in the intelligentsia and has created important institutional changes.

A variant on the impact of leadership states that there has been an evolutionary change in leadership and that Gorbachev himself is simply part of a pattern that found its genesis under Brezhnev. Key Brezhnev speeches, such as the one at Tula in 1977 (Brezhnev 1977), demonstrate that national security was undergoing change anyway and that most of Gorbachev's suggestions today are merely elaborations of earlier notions along a predictable path. This perspective regards Gorbachev as mainly a conduit for change, not an initiator. A related view goes further to state that the system does not allow leaders to alter policy very much because the leaders are captives of the system. No matter how radical Gorbachev may sound, the omnipresent bureaucrat will successfully oppose him, thwarting the best efforts for progress. Under this schema leadership makes little difference. The Soviet military, a powerful bureaucracy, is in charge of military policy; if change occurs at all it is because the military wants or permits it.

The second set emphasizes *economics*. Stagnating economic conditions have forced the leadership to address many fundamental areas of the economy and to assess national security in terms of the well-being of the whole economy, not just a portion of it. Thus changes in economic conditions permit transformations in the elements of Soviet

Table 1.1

Relationship Among Components of the Book

Rate of Change → ↓ Change Agents	Stability			Incremental Change			Significant Change			Radical Change		
	SIA*	Policy	Beh	SIA	Policy	Beh	SIA	Policy	Beh	SIA	Policy	Beh
Leadership												
Economics												
External Conditions												
Intellectual Ferment and Upheaval												

* Security Ideas and Assumptions

national security. The need to apply high technology to the restructuring of the industrial base demands nothing less than a massive modernization of the Soviet industrial plant. In this effort the military will have to await advances in basic industrial technology before it may modernize itself. Over the long run the military and other instruments of national security will undergo profound alterations because of changes in industry and the economic system.

An opposed perspective on economics as a change agent contends that the Soviet system will retain a strong separation between the military and civilian sectors of the economy. The military will continue to get the best materials and the best management personnel because it is a strong bureaucratic player, an essential dimension of national security. Great technological change can occur within military industry without first happening in the civilian economy. The state of the Soviet civilian economy, then, is not fundamental to enhancing Soviet national security.

A third set of propositions hypothesizes that *external conditions* are a basic change agent for explaining Soviet national security shifts. For instance, the Reagan administration rearmament, the mire of Afghanistan, and the lack of success in the Third World in general have forced the Soviet Union to reassess its position in the world. Gorbachev is seen as retreating in the face of American military, economic, and political might and being forced to rethink his strategy. In addition, the Soviets have looked at their weakened position in the Third World and have by themselves evaluated alternative approaches to gaining influence. Here activities of Third World nations, not the United States, are key to understanding Soviet shifts.[3] Those who perceive external conditions as a key factor in explaining change may also contend that growing world interdependence is a condition the Soviets cannot ignore. The Soviets are dependent for their security on emerging worldwide social, political, and economic conditions and are beginning to develop a stake in international control over pollution, nuclear reactor standards, alleviating world hunger, and international trade. They realize they can no longer retreat into a shell to escape international forces. The USSR must deal with the world society and economy; it cannot institute a new, isolationist policy similar to Stalin's efforts to pursue "socialism in one country" during the 1930s (Hall 1987).

Another view of external forces posits that Soviet ideological commitments continue unabated—particularly the need to expand the communist system, through, for instance, the establishment of friendly communist governments—in the face of a hostile international environment. Far from changing, Soviet national security continues to be defined exclusively in terms of national sovereignty and military security as the Soviet leadership perceives its problems in the world. Any apparent change in Soviet policy, such as the call for more international safeguards for nuclear reactors or a closer relationship between Third World nations and multinational corporations, are just tactical adjustments to take advantage of a political situation that may have developed. The USSR, in this view, continues to be Stalinist in its outlook.

The fourth and final set of propositions underlines the importance of *intellectual ferment and upheaval* behind shifts in national security policy. Ideas drive change in this proposition, much as the theories of Copernicus changed notions of the universe or as Karl Marx's views generated a new understanding of the workings of the capitalist system. Both led to revolutionary change that would have been impossible without the fundamental comprehension of and solution to the problems they posed. The new Soviet policy of *glasnost'*, or openness—in part allowing intellectuals to discuss numerous social and political problems relatively freely in their economics and sociology journals or in their plays, novels, and poems—has made a strong impact. Many of these articles and works have a direct bearing on national security in that they raise new formulations for resolving national security problems. The play *The Peace of Brest-Litovsk* (Shatrov 1987) or the writings of Tat'iana Zaslavskaia (e.g., 1986) are examples.

From this perspective the Soviet leadership believes that allowing the military to dominate national security thinking was a mistake and that it is time to open the ranks for debate and for innovative solutions that can lead to fundamental change, but within the constraints of Party control. Even Marshal Ogarkov has accepted this framework and recognizes, for example, the importance of the arguments that the modernization of the Soviet military demands the prior renovation of basic Soviet industry—a fundamental change in the way the Soviets approach military security. Some are convinced that Soviet discussions of "new political thinking" reject the idea of basing national security on efforts to achieve unilateral military superiority and instead seek mutual security (Primakov 1987: 4).

Alternatively, another assessment of intellectual ferment and upheaval posits that important Soviet leadership cadres realize that new ideas could lead to the very destruction of the Soviet system unless they are stopped. The ideas we hear in Moscow these days will become passing fancies as soon as the implications for such fundamental precepts as Party control over policy become plain to important groupings in the Soviet leadership and bureaucracy, which will put an end to the ideas. In this view it may actually be convenient for the leaders to allow relatively free discourse for a while to expose the free thinkers and then to crush them (Aksenov et al. 1987).

There can be, then, very different notions of the impact of the four aforementioned actors. One extreme perceives them as dynamic change agents; another, as relatively unimportant factors in Soviet politics, given that the USSR is basically resistant to change. This book's assessment of how these change agents behave is discussed in the concluding chapter when they are linked to the major concepts of the study and are woven into an explanation of change in Soviet national security policy.

The Major Concepts: National Security, the Elements of National Security, Restructuring, and Rate of Change

Almost any activity in which a nation engages can be said to contribute to its "security." For what is security but that feeling of freedom from danger that countries constantly pursue through varying instruments under their control? Strong elements of domestic as well as foreign policy are often involved in the national security process. Security involves freedom from physical danger but also from psychological danger, and it is therefore a very subjective term (Snow 1987: 5–6).

Although a subfield of international relations called national security studies has emerged in recent years, there is still no common acceptance of how the field delimits itself relative to, for instance, the fields of military science on one hand and international politics on the other. One of the more compelling definitions of the term notes that the national security field

> is the study of the security problems faced by nations, of the policies and programs by which these problems are addressed, and also of the governmental processes through which the policies and programs are decided upon and carried out. (Smoke 1987: 301)

This definition closely fits the general concerns of the current study.

The literature of national security studies contains works that align themselves across a broad spectrum, from the more narrowly military oriented to those adopting a broad perspective. Three clusters of works may be identified on the continuum. The first looks at national security as the advancement of state interests through military policy. This approach examines the use of military force, threats of coercion, demonstrations of force ("showing the flag"), and arms transfer policy. This method of investigating national security is typical for studying the Soviet Union, given its reliance on the military arm (Booth 1974; Kaplan 1981; MccGwire

1987). The study of national security under this rubric becomes a synonym for defense studies.

A second approach is to examine combinations of military and nonmilitary instruments in the enhancement of a nation's security. Thus in addition to the concerns noted under the first prototype, this one views diplomatic efforts and attempts at alliance building—what we might call the "political instrument" of national security—which have as a direct aim the ensuring of a nation's safety in the international arena. Quite often studies of U.S. national security take this tack, given the vast amount of information analysts possess about U.S. military strength, political infighting in the government, and memoirs of former officials who often record the details of discussions with foreign heads of state (Kennan 1967, 1972; Kissinger 1979, 1982; Talbott 1985).

A third tack incorporates economic policy as a means to advance state security. Economic imperatives help to define national interest. This military-cum-political-cum-economic approach is broad gauging, looking at the panoply of instrumentalities available and used in the enhancement of national security. Some studies of both the Soviet Union and the United States typify this effort (Holloway 1983; Jordan and Taylor 1981).

The classification, though certainly not all-inclusive, helps to point to the different scopes that are involved in national security studies—from the most narrow, military-oriented ones to the very broad. It also helps to identify the agents, both domestic and foreign, used in augmenting security.

This volume represents in part an attempt to clarify the evolving Soviet perception of national security—that is, the development particularly in the last several years of the changing assumptions underlying (a) the breadth of nations and regions the USSR considers essential to shore up or advance its security position worldwide and (b) the varying tools the USSR wishes to bring to bear in this effort. In doing so it allows for an investigation of national security that will place it close to the broadest definition of the term: the military, political, and economic means by which security may be established in the areas of the world Soviet leaders deem essential. The broad view permits authors of individual chapters the flexibility of investigating military and nonmilitary instruments as they contribute to security and of examining the extent to which the elements of Soviet security have undergone change.

The elements of Soviet national security can be visualized as encompassing the three basic subareas indicated in Table 1.1.

1. *Security assumptions and ideas:* a system of views upon which plans for enhancing Soviet national security are founded. This system encompasses notions about the utility of force but also includes views

about diplomacy and international trade as tools to shore up security interests. Military doctrine, the set of ideas upon which plans for wartime and peacetime defense are founded, is an important subcategory given the importance of military thinking in the Soviet concept of national security. Doctrine includes statements about such matters as just war, the inevitability of war, the winnability of nuclear war, the role of nuclear weapons in the future, the role of conventional forces, the importance of surprise, and the significance of morale in war. Efforts to change security assumptions and ideas are key indicators of intellectual ferment and upheaval in political-military thinking and may be responsible for driving changes in national security policy.

2. *National security policy:* the authoritative, declaratory statements by political and military leaders regarding the requirements of Soviet security and the broad means for their realization in the context of the balance of power. Such pronouncements reflect Soviet perceptions of the USSR's relative military potential and capabilities (manifested partly in military expenditures and arms control policy), the political stability of the Soviet regime (including an assessment of the willingness of the population to make sacrifices), the economic health of the Soviet system (its ability both to meet citizen demands and to foster the potential to have an impact on the global economy), and relations with other nations and the maintenance of alliance systems (particularly relations with the United States and the Warsaw Pact countries). These considerations in the Soviet view of the USSR's relative position in the world are called in Soviet parlance the "correlation of forces."

3. *Behavior:* the manifestation of policy in actions designed to utilize the instruments of policy and in efforts to influence Soviet society and/or foreign policy entities to achieve Soviet security needs. Actions and efforts include changes or continuities in behavior, such as the substitution of nonmilitary for military means to conduct relations with essential areas of regions of the world or continuing the production of new generations of weapons.

This book examines the connection between the elements of Soviet national security and the restructuring of Soviet society. Thus the next term to discuss is *restructuring*. Restructuring appears to have two basic meanings. First, it is a *program* for profound social change in all spheres of Soviet life, including cultural, economic, political, and historical affairs. It is probably no exaggeration to state that perestroika encapsulates a new social doctrine—that is, an argument for an allocation of new social values designed to lift the USSR into post-Stalinism. In terms of the four alternative propositions discussed in the second section of this chapter, restructuring can be envisioned as the changes in leadership, economics, external conditions, and intellectual ferment and upheaval that would occur if this program were successful.

Much attention in this book is paid to the economic changes that Mikhail Gorbachev and his allies have developed to transform the Soviet Union into the postindustrial stage of development from its current state of malaise. The changes include in part the design and implementation of technological advance in the Soviet industrial and agricultural plants. Thus Gorbachev has called for the modernization of the machine-building industry, which, if he is to be believed, will accomplish its nearly full restructuring by the year 2000. But change also involves managerial technology, the application of modern techniques of management to be sure economic plans are properly implemented. Technological change also demands the acquisition of modern computing techniques and significant educational advance and personnel replacement.

Thus the second sense in which the Soviet leadership uses restructuring is the *process* by which the program is to be accomplished. The major emphasis of restructuring is its focus on transforming the vast middle-level bureaucracy of the Party and state apparatuses. It is there that the battle for social reconstruction and modernization will be won or lost; for without the bureaucracy's active support a restructuring program cannot be completed.

Restructuring as a process demands, first and most important, glasnost', or the open competition of ideas and criticism of the standard ways in which the Soviet system came to operate under previous administrations, including those of Stalin, Khrushchev, and Brezhnev. Glasnost', normally translated as "openness," is a policy intended to create a machine to drive the forces of behavioral change. In discussing the "democratization" of the USSR as a "decisive condition for restructuring," Gorbachev states that it is important

> to deepen and develop in all possible ways the conditions of openness and publicity that have taken place in the country, which allow each person to reveal his public position, to participate actively in the lively judging and deciding of the important problems of society, and to hasten the processes moving in this direction. (1987b: 82)

For the first time since the early to mid-1920s, security policy ideas are open to broad debate and are manifested through, for example, more open discussions on military doctrine and portrayals in the arts of how security policy discussions may take place (Shatrov 1987).

Openness is intended to foster criticism of the middle bureaucratic levels from below—that is, from the popular level. This strain of governing serves to keep the middle levels sensitized to their everyday interactions with workers and clients. To the extent that the mass level supports Gorbachev's programs, middle-level officials will have to support them or risk being reported and possibly fired. A lack of attention to programmatic ideas on an everyday basis will doom restructuring from the outset.

Openness also involves pressure from Soviet intellectuals through the debating of alternative methods of conceptualizing and instituting programs. The relative liberty of expression is inherently dangerous to those occupying the middle levels who have become satisfied with their lot in life and routine ways of managing their satrapies, so well established under Brezhnev. In this way glasnost' helps to establish a new social contract between the intellectuals and the CPSU: in return for their support of restructuring, the new administration is willing to bestow upon intellectuals new freedoms of expression.[4] There has been an outburst of ideas in treatises about restructuring the economy, such as in Zaslavskaia's writings, and in many other areas of Soviet intellectual life—for instance, in literature and the arts, where the misfortunes of the Stalin period, including its massive bureaucratization, have been exposed, as in *Children of the Arbat* (Rybakov 1987). According to Gorbachev, "democratization" lies at the basis of glasnost', although observers in Western nations should understand the limits to democracy, given the continuing importance of Party control.[5]

Restructuring as a process also subsumes, first, the effort to install in key sectors of the economy bureaucrats trained in more modern managerial skills and to appoint new editorial staff for influential periodicals, such as the CPSU organ *Kommunist* and the literary journal with a new face, *Ogonek*. A large number of effective managers from military industry have been transferred to branches of the civilian economy, supplanting Brezhnev appointees and lending that sector greater expertise and presumably more efficient production methods. Second, to ensure continuing effective leadership and pressure on the bureaucracy, perestroika also encompasses elite change at the highest levels of the Party and government. Third, institutional change, such as the reorganization of certain sectors of the Soviet economy into "superbureaus," generates new settings for policy implementation and presumably facilitates the flow of new ideas essential to restructuring.

Restructuring at this stage is still only an effort by the current Soviet administration to try to drag the USSR, through programs and political pressure, into a more modern and open era. There is significant opposition to perestroika, about which Gorbachev has made reference (1987a: 20; 1987b: 22; 1988:2). The programs and process of restructuring may be conceived as Gorbachev's way to build his authority as problem solver and as politician and to ensconce himself in the general secretaryship for some time to come.[6]

The economic/technological imperative that lies behind restructuring is not the only factor involved in changes in the elements of national security, although there is no mistaking that technology is very significant for explaining change. There are other factors that should be conceived as change agents, including leadership, external conditions, and intellectual ferment and upheaval. These matters will be discussed in more detail later, when the framework of the study is introduced and in succeeding chapters as we consider the substantive areas of Soviet national security.

Finally, perestroika is not some well-conceived and laid out rational plan of action designed by Gorbachev and omniscient advisers. There is sufficient evidence from major inconsistencies in the Twelfth Five-Year Plan, for instance—particularly in the plans for achieving long-term versus short-term goals—that Gorbachev and his collaborators do not yet understand just how restructuring will come about.[7] Policymaking in the Soviet system (and in other political systems, for that matter) is often reactive "ad-hocery" subject to bureaucratic pressures that confound whatever plans the leadership may establish. The shape of policy is evolving; there is still no consensus about its direction; and neither national leader nor analyst can be sure what changes the future will bring.

The concept of change is, of course, relative to the time and society in which it occurs and is difficult to define under the best of conditions. Four basic questions to ask about change deal with the following: Change from what? Change to what? Change when? Change at what rate? The first two will be answered only briefly here. Soviet national security policy appears to be eschewing its overreliance on the military as an instrument of policy and its extreme concepts of national sovereignty. Very different assumptions appear to underline Soviet policy which have the effect of directing the USSR toward examining nonmilitary aspects of enhancing security and toward accepting a concept of mutual security. Subsequent chapters will deal in depth with these two questions.

"Change when?" deals with the period that delimits the study. The emphasis in this book surrounds the changes that have come about since Brezhnev died in November 1982, particularly those since March 1985, when Gorbachev was named general secretary of the CPSU. Nevertheless, change viewed in such a short-term fashion would produce ahistorical statements that would not probe the richness of the process of change in Soviet national security affairs. It is partly to enrich the historical analysis that we include a chapter about military crisis and social change in Russian and Soviet history.

Yet to paint the investigation in too broad a swath would generate analyses of subareas that would not likely capture sufficient detail about restructuring in the current era. Thus the approach to answering the question "Change when?" will take the middling tack of investigating the current of Soviet national security policy and the factors affecting it under the present administration, but with a view to their roots in the past ten to twelve years.[8] The Gorbachev leadership, then, will be envisioned as attempting to produce changes on its own—that is, changes that differ from the thrust of policy under Brezhnev—as providing a flux for changes that began to be instituted under Brezhnev but which, for one reason or another, never reached a culminating point, or as some combination of both.

Perceiving change in this manner will allow the observer to understand change in a context that does not totally depend on the Gorbachev leadership as an explanatory factor for change. It also implies that further shifts may not depend on Gorbachev's presence. Should the Soviet general secretaryship change, many of the security directions described in this volume could continue unabated because they began before Gorbachev came to power and received further support, or because they proved to be fruitful directions for change when Gorbachev introduced them and continue to be buttressed.

Evaluating "Change at what rate?" introduces a significant amount of uncertainty. The policy areas discussed herein do not lend themselves to fine, quantitative definitions and so cannot be measured precisely. Furthermore, even if quantitative measures could be found, it would be unlikely that we would discover common metrics. Thus it would be very difficult to compare the rate of change in one policy area with that in another. Compounding the uncertainty of the discussion is that for a nation experiencing so little change in so many domains during the Brezhnev administration, nearly any current change may be characterized as "radical" or even "revolutionary."[9]

Whether or not we use these terms, it is still important to generate impressions about the degree of change in the elements of Soviet national security, realizing that transformations are not completely comparable from issue to issue. Statements about change will always contain a certain amount of subjectivity.

To lend clarity to answering "Change at what rate?" within categories of Soviet national security affairs, four concepts concerning the rate of change should help to guide our understanding. The first, as indicated in Table 1.1, is stability. Under a condition of stability apparently there is no discernible shift in the national security area: previous security ideas and assumptions are accepted and interpreted as in the past;

no substantive changes in national security policy occur and previous policies are restated; there is no behavioral change either in level of effort expended or in the targets of Soviet activity. The current view of Soviet security is more or less the same as it was ten to twelve years ago. Such change can be graphically portrayed as in Figure 1.1.

Figure 1.1 Stability

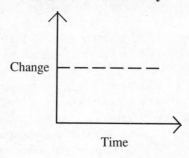

Figure 1.2 Incremental Change

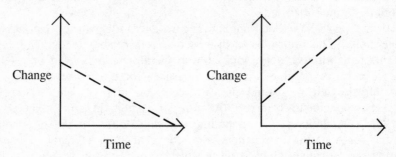

Figure 1.3 Significant Change

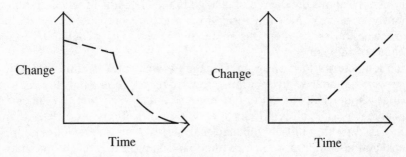

The second type of change is incremental. Under this condition alterations began to occur before Gorbachev came to power, and the direction of change under his administration is more or less the same: Soviet leaders view those security ideas and assumptions that are amended as logical extensions of the past; national security policy experiences a slight reinterpretation, but elites claim it is basically the same as in the past; the leadership somewhat increases the level of effort being directed toward the same or similar targets as before. Although the future may produce sharper shifts, the elements of national security appear to be extrapolations of tendencies under Brezhnev. We represent this type of change in Figure 1.2.

Third is significant change, where there is an increase or decrease in the level of effort. The rate of change is different from the past but in the same direction: security ideas stress changing conditions and the leadership adds new assumptions to existing ones; elites accept the appropriateness of previous policy but explicitly elaborate new goals or means; and Soviet leaders introduce new categories of behavior and add new targets to existing ones. Significant change appears in Figure 1.3.

Radical change is the final category. Radical change concerns an alteration of direction or a step-level shift. We might call it a qualitative or sea change, to use the Marxian terminology. Under this schema Soviet elites reject past ideas and assumptions in favor of other alternatives, perhaps for something totally new or a return to an idealized past; the leadership also condemns former policies and proclaims new ones with new goals and/or means in mind; and leaders change their behavior as well, canceling existing programs and beginning new ones that are the opposite of prior ones. Changes in direction and step-level changes can be portrayed as in Figure 1.4.

If it is true that radical transformations are taking place in key Soviet domestic policy areas and in fundamental Soviet perceptions of the international environment, then a perhaps slow pace of change in Soviet national security policy and behavior today may be accelerated in the future. It is part of the purpose of this work to indicate where such significant or radical changes are currently happening or are likely to take place and then to assess what impact they might have on Soviet politics, Soviet foreign policy, and U.S. relations with the Soviet Union. The concluding chapter will highlight these matters and draw out the implications.

Figure 1.4 Radical Change

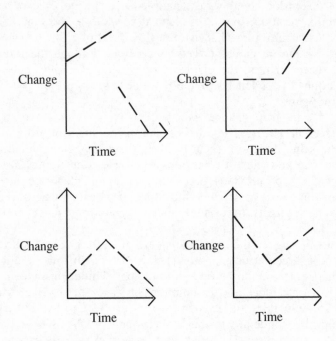

Framework and Organization of the Study

To summarize the discussion so far, this book deals with three inter-related areas for probing shifts in Soviet national security affairs: (a) the change agents affecting the elements of Soviet national security; (b) the elements of national security; and (c) the consequences and implications of change in national security matters. Figure 1.5 depicts these relationships.

The book examines its topics from left to right as portrayed in Figure 1.5. After an overview of the context of change, it addresses the change agents first; the changes in Soviet national security elements second; and their consequences and implications third. Part Two establishes the context of change in Soviet national security policy by examining the key factors for change in Russian and Soviet history, the perceptual underpinnings of current Soviet thinking about security, and the patterns of stability and change in the Soviet economy. Part Three addresses the

Figure 1.5 The Framework of the Study

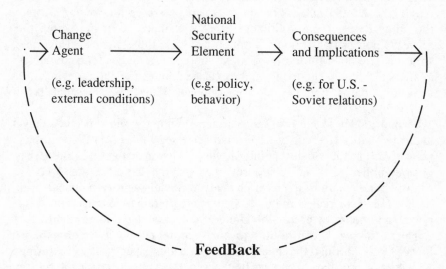

change agents in its analysis of the impacts of modernization and the competition for resources between the civilian and military sectors, changes in technology, domestic politics and leadership change, and institutional change.

Part Four contains a discussion of change in security ideas and assumptions, policies, and behaviors—that is, in the elements of Soviet national security—by observing changes in Soviet military doctrine, particularly the notion of reasonable sufficiency, in Soviet policy toward Western Europe, in Soviet policy toward Eastern Europe and the Warsaw Pact countries, in Soviet relations with the Third World, and in Soviet arms control policy. Finally, Part Five examines the patterns of change, attempting an explanation of change in Soviet national security policy and assessing the implications of change for Soviet national security objectives and U.S. policy toward the Soviet Union.

Significance of the Study

This book helps to address at least four broad concerns of students of Soviet politics and international affairs. First, it aids in understanding the dynamics of change in Soviet foreign policy. All too often casual observers of Soviet foreign affairs assume that Soviet policy will shift only if the United States or its allies exert pressures for change. In fact this study suggests the key importance of changes occurring within the Soviet Union as the primary factors influencing the elements of national security. The book therefore provides support for studies long conducted in the field of international politics that examine the intimate linkages between domestic politics and foreign policy (Bialer 1981; Rosenau 1966; Wilkenfeld 1973).

Second, this book contributes to understanding the substance of change in Soviet national security affairs and clarifies the concept of national security from the Soviet point of view. The investigation, then, has obvious policy relevance for observers from the United States who try to determine whether apparent changes in Soviet security policy are just trickery or have real content. If significant or radical changes in ideas, policy, and behavior occur, the United States may have to respond.

Third, this work contributes to our comprehension of reform in the Soviet Union through the investigation of various aspects of restructuring. Excellent works have been written about the general shape of reform in the USSR (Colton 1986; Hewett 1988), but the time has come for the detailed analysis of reform as it applies to Soviet national security affairs.

Fourth, the significance of this work lies in its relevance for understanding change even beyond the Gorbachev administration. Should Gorbachev fall from grace, the policy tendencies described here will have a profound impact on the next set of leaders, possibly biasing their policies in the direction that Gorbachev has laid down. For as George W. Breslauer demonstrates, succeeding Soviet leadership cadres need to adopt some policies from the immediately preceding administration if they are to legitimize themselves.[10]

Notes

1. A discussion of Gorbachev's "secret report" was published in *La Republica*, March 27, 1985, pp. 1, 9. See Gorbachev (1985).

2. One of Zaslavskaia's works on incentives is contained in a three-part interview with her (see Zaslavskaia 1987). In this piece she says it is all right to have 100–300 percent wage gaps, but not 900 percent or a new class of petty capitalists (called NEPmen) will

develop. Gorbachev's remarks are contained in his June 1987 Plenum report (Gorbachev 1987b: 43–44) and in his January 1987 Plenum report (Gorbachev 1987a: 14). These two reports, in addition to Gorbachev's remarks at the opening session of the June 1988 Party Conference (Gorbachev 1988), contain the most extensive discussion of restructuring and openness to date and should be considered the three most critical documents for understanding the domestic policy directions of the Gorbachev administration.

3. This is one of the basic themes underlying a new, excellent work on Soviet-Third World relations (see Kolodziej and Kanet 1989).

4. I thank Professor Yuri Medvedkov of The Ohio State University for suggesting the notion of the social contract as it relates to glasnost'. For discussions of how Gorbachev's new ideas conflict with the old social contract that stresses egalitarianism, stability, and security, see Trehub (1987) and Hauslohner (1987).

5. See Gorbachev (1987a: 23; 1987b: 23; 1988: 4) on the importance of central Party control. A brief word may be necessary here about the criticism of middle management as the basis of restructuring. At the June 1987 Plenum (1987b: 11–12) Gorbachev leveled strong criticism at high governmental ministers, such as Nikolai V. Talyzin, chairman of GOSPLAN, and even K. S. Demirchian, first secretary of the Armenian Communist Party organization. Gorbachev, in appearing to shift his critical efforts to high levels, seemed to have focused on higher-ups to enhance the pressure on nameless middle-level bureaucrats ("some comrades")—against whom much of the criticism was directed in his speech. The logic seemed to be that if higher officials cannot escape Gorbachev's wrath, then neither can others.

6. For a discussion of how Soviet leaders build authority, see Breslauer (1982: 3–8 and throughout).

7. For a critique of inconsistencies in the 12th FYP, see "1986 Panel" (1986).

8. As of this writing, twelve years takes the analysis back to 1977 and Brezhnev's Tula speech (1977), at which time the shape of Soviet national security policy appeared to be changing. Michael MccGwire asserts that fundamental change in Soviet national security policy began in late 1966 (see MccGwire 1987: Appendix A). By necessity some of the chapters in this book will have to refer to events somewhat earlier than the 1977 period in order for their analyses to be complete.

9. Gorbachev used the term "radical reform" in his speech at the Twenty-Seventh Party Congress in February 1986 and continues to use it. The term "revolution" as applied to perestroika is mentioned in Smirnov (1987: 3).

10. See, for instance, Breslauer's (1982: 27–32) discussion of Khrushchev's approach to consumer satisfaction, as an example of how policies of the past are used in authority-building.

References

Aksenov, Vasily, Vladimir Bukovsky, Edward Kuznetsov, Yuri Lubimov, Vladimir Maximov, Ernst Neizvestny, and Aleksandr Zinoviev (1987, March 22). "Is 'Glasnost' a Game of Mirrors?" *New York Times,* p. E27.

Azrael, Jeremy R. (1984). "Emergent Nationality Problems in the USSR." In Erik Hoffman and Robbin F. Laird, eds., *The Soviet Polity in the Modern Era.* New York: Aldine.

Bialer, Seweryn, ed. (1981). *The Domestic Context of Soviet Foreign Policy.* Boulder, CO: Westview Press.

Booth, Ken (1974). *The Military Instrument in Soviet Foreign Policy, 1917–1972*. London: Royal United Services Institute for Defence Studies.

Breslauer, George W. (1982). *Khrushchev and Brezhnev as Leaders: Building Authority in Soviet Politics*. Boston: Unwin Hyman.

Brezhnev, Leonid I. (1977, January 19). "Outstanding Exploits of the Defenders of Tula." *Pravda*, pp. 1–2.

Colton, Timothy J. (1986). *The Dilemma of Reform in the Soviet Union*. New York: Council on Foreign Relations.

Gorbachev, Mikhail S. (1985). *La Republica*. Translated in Foreign Broadcast Information Service (FBIS), *Daily Report: Soviet Union*, March 28, pp. R1-R3.

——— (1987a). "O perestroike i kadrovoi politike partii." *Kommunist*, 3 (February), 5–47.

——— (1987b). "O zadachakh partii po korennoi perestroike upravleniia ekonomikoi." *Kommunist*, 10 (July), 5–47.

——— (1988, June 29). "O khode realizatsii reshenii XXVII s'ezda KPSS i zadachakh po uglubleniiu perestroiki." *Pravda*, pp. 2–7.

Hall, B. Welling (1987). "The Influence of Global Interdependence on Soviet Security Ideas and Assumptions." Presented at the Mershon Center Seminar, "A Third Revolution in Soviet National Security Affairs?" Columbus, Ohio, October.

Hauslohner, Peter (1987). "Gorbachev's Social Contract." *Soviet Economy*, 3(1), 54–81.

Hewett, Ed A. (1988). *Reforming the Soviet Economy: Equality versus Efficiency*. Washington, DC: The Brookings Institution.

Holloway, David (1983). *The Soviet Union and the Arms Race*. New Haven, CT: Yale University Press.

Jordan, Amos and William J. Taylor (1981). *American National Security: Policy and Process*. Baltimore, MD: Johns Hopkins University Press.

Kaplan, Stephen S. (1981). *Diplomacy of Power: Soviet Armed Forces as a Political Instrument*. Washington, DC: The Brookings Institution.

Kennan, George F. (1967). *Memoirs, 1925–1950*. Boston: Little, Brown.

——— (1972). *Memoirs, 1950–1963*. Boston: Little, Brown.

Kissinger, Henry (1979). *White House Years*. Boston: Little, Brown.

——— (1982). *Years of Upheaval*. Boston: Little, Brown.

Kolodziej, Edward A., and Roger E. Kanet, eds. (1989). *The Limits of Soviet Power in the Developing World*. London: Macmillan; Baltimore, MD: Johns Hopkins University Press.

MccGwire, Michael (1987). *Military Objectives in Soviet Foreign Policy*. Washington, DC: The Brookings Institution.

Narodnoe Khoziaistvo SSSR V 1986 G. (1986). Moscow: Financy i Statistika.

"1986 Panel on the Soviet Economic Outlook" (1986). *Soviet Economy*, 2(1), 3–18.

Odom, William E. (1985). "Soviet Force Posture: Dilemmas and Directions." *Problems of Communism*, 34(4), 1–14.

Ogarkov, Nikolai (1982). *Vsegda v gotovnosti k zashchite otechestva*. Moscow: Voenizdat.

Primakov, E. (1987, July 19). "A New Philosophy of Foreign Policy." *Pravda*, p. 4.

Rosenau, James N. (1966). "Pre-Theories and Theories of Foreign Policy." In R. Barry Farrell, ed., *Approaches to Comparative and International Politics*. Evanston, IL: Northwestern University Press.

Rybakov, Anatolii (1987). "Deti Arbata." *Druzhba narodov*, 4–5, 67–183.

Shatrov, Mikhail (1987, April). "Bretsksii mir." *Novyi mir*, 4, 3–51.

Smirnov, G. (1987, March 13). "Revoliutsionnaia sut' obnovleniia." *Pravda*, p. 3.

Smoke, Richard (1987). *National Security and the Nuclear Dilemma: An Introduction to the American Experience*, 2d ed. New York: Random House.

Snow, Donald M. (1987). *National Security: Emerging Problems of U.S. Defense Policy*. New York: St. Martin's.

Talbott, Strobe (1985). *Deadly Gambits: The Reagan Administration and the Stalemate in Arms Control*. New York: Vintage.

Trehub, Aaron (1987). "Gorbachev and the Soviet Social Contract." *Radio Liberty Research Bulletin*, 37, RL 361/87, September 16.

Wilkenfeld, Jonathan (1973). *Conflict Behavior and Linkage Politics*. New York: David McKay.

Zaslavskaia, Tat'iana (1986, September). "Chelovecheskii faktor razvitiia ekonomiki i sotsial'naia spravedlivost'." *Kommunist,* 13, 61–73.

—— (1987). "The Personality of a Scholar and Restructuring." *Argumenty i fakty*, March 28–April 3, pp. 4–5. Translated in *Current Digest of the Soviet Press*, 39(16), May 20, p. 8.

• PART TWO •
The Context of Change

Part Two examines the context of change in Soviet national security policy. Although there are likely a large number of such contexts that may enlighten understanding of the relationship between restructuring and change in Soviet national security policy (such as geographic or anthropological), three key aspects stand out: the historical, ideological, and economic.

As to the first element, in Chapter Two Steven Merritt Miner addresses whether there are common patterns of reform throughout Russian and Soviet history that may give us clues to the nature and scope of change under Gorbachev. In examining these patterns he notes the particular importance of technological/military lag and a vigorous leadership as stimuli for change in policy and reform under the tsars and early Soviet leaders. In assessing the likelihood of Gorbachev's success as a reformer, Miner reminds us that the past demonstrates that leadership has its limits for change in Russia and the Soviet Union. For past leaders have been unable to resolve the dilemma that radical reform poses: building an effective economic and social system conducive to innovations in security policy and competition in the military sphere while at the same time maintaining political control.

In the second context—the ideological—Philip D. Stewart and Margaret G. Hermann investigate in Chapter Three the maelstrom of intellectual ferment and upheaval surrounding debates over the future direction of Soviet national security policy. Known collectively as the "new thinking," the new ideas emphasize that national security encompasses mutual security and economic security, not just unilateral military security, and demonstrate significant to radical change. Resolution of the debate will determine the basic premises of future Soviet policy. "New thinking" has not yet won out, but one of its strongest proponents is Gorbachev himself, the transitional leader.

Finally, in Chapter Four John E. Tedstrom outlines the economic context, analyzing the dimensions of current Soviet economic reform. The link between Gorbachev's economic reforms and the shape of national security policy should be clear: to the extent that more money is invested in nonmilitary areas of the economy, Soviet growth in defense spending will tend to decrease, signaling and permitting alterations in Soviet policy. While addressing the history of Soviet economic development since 1950, Tedstrom evaluates the capacity of the current regime to change its economic system. He sees the current reforms as yielding potentially significant economic change and constraining growth in the Soviet defense budget in the medium term. In the long run, however, Tedstrom is not as optimistic about the capacity of the Soviet economic system to change in the directions of Gorbachev's long-term policy. More detailed discussions of economic changes and their impact on national security are discussed in Part Three.

• CHAPTER TWO •

Military Crisis and Social Change in Russian and Soviet History

Steven Merritt Miner
Ohio University

Michael Voslensky, a prominent Soviet exile, recounts how he once asked an archivist at the Soviet Foreign Ministry why scholars, even Soviet historians who were presumably reliable, were denied access to critical historical documents. Voslensky said he could understand why records from the postrevolutionary period were closed, but why were tsarist archives also off-limits? The archivist's answer is illuminating: he replied, "Because Russian diplomacy was faced with foreign-policy problems similar to [those of the present], and in certain instances it made decisions identical with our own. We have no interest in publicizing that" (Voslensky 1984: 323).

The archivist's answer may apply equally well to the study of Soviet security policy, and it provides eloquent testimony to the utility of studying Russian history in order to understand the Soviet present. After all, certain key features of Russia's condition, such as climate and geography, do not change at all; and others, such as perceptions, beliefs, or political methods, are shaped in part by historical tradition, or "political culture"(White 1979). This is not to claim that all the problems facing the current Soviet leadership have exact parallels or precedents in the past— it can be argued, for example, that the nuclear question is entirely novel.

But the student of Russian history is continually struck by the persistence of certain continuing, overarching themes in Russian and Soviet history.

Prominent among these is the Russian response to Western military and technological superiority: ever since Muscovy freed itself in the fifteenth century after 250 years of Mongol domination, Russia has attempted to match the skills of the technologically more advanced Western powers. To this end it has undergone several revolutions from above, waves of transforming zeal that have swept and shaken every aspect of Russian life before eventually receding. Several Russian and Soviet leaders strove to transform their nation from above, from Peter I through Alexander I, Alexander II, Lenin, and Stalin. Each hoped to copy or even surpass the Western powers' technical virtuosity without weakening Russia's authoritarian government and hierarchical society. These most ambitious leaders of Russian and Soviet history chased an elusive goal: a society possessing the greater efficiency and inventiveness of the West without the relative decentralization and pluralism that had made these things possible. As Prince Adam Czartoryski once observed of Alexander I: "He would readily have agreed that every man [in Russia] should be free, on condition that he would voluntarily do only what the Emperor wished" (Czartoryski 1987: 25).

Deeply distrustful of *stikhiinost'*, or spontaneity, Russia's reformers have generally refused to countenance the emergence of social and political forces independent of the state that could perpetuate and build on their reforms; as a result, enthusiasm for dramatic change has seldom outlived the great reformers. This pattern of ebbing and flowing waves of reformist zeal was evident even before the advent of Bolshevism. Sir Donald Mackenzie Wallace, a perceptive British observer of Russia at the turn of the century, wrote,

> Russia advances on the road of progress not in that smooth, gradual, prosaic way to which we [in Western Europe] are accustomed, but by a series of unconnected, frantic efforts, each of which is naturally followed by a period of temporary exhaustion. (1984: 139)

We are witnessing another manifestation of this pattern; there can no longer be much doubt that Gorbachev has cast himself in the role of reformer. The purpose of this chapter is to examine earlier Russian and Soviet military-technical leaps in order to discover, if possible, common portents or omens of change that can help us to gauge the likely methods and scope of Gorbachev's changes. In a study such as this, which is concerned with understanding the Soviet approach to current problems, one might question the relevance of historical precedent. Too often, however, Americans have evinced a lack of curiosity about the Russian and Soviet past, which has undermined their efforts to deal effectively with Moscow. To a far greater extent than Americans, Russians are aware that their history has shaped their present; and the Soviet leaders, who after all base their claim to rule on a theory of historical progress, have demonstrated time and again how they draw upon historical example in dealing with the tasks of governance. Indeed, many of the terms that Gorbachev has chosen to define his goals are drawn, perhaps consciously, from prerevolutionary Russian precedent: *Perestroika* or *pereustroistvo,* for instance, are terms Alexander I adopted to characterize his early, halting, and ultimately fruitless efforts to limit the capricious powers of the autocrat. Catherine II and Alexander II both employed the term *glasnost',* which formerly was translated into English as "official publicity." And in a foretaste of the Twenty-Seventh Party Congress, Alexander II called for greater *zakonnost',* or legality, in Russian government.

It is not the intention here to examine specific changes in military doctrine or operations; a detailed look at Peter the Great's extension of Western-style military drill, for example—interesting though this may be in its own right—is scarcely germane to an understanding of Gorbachev's possible methods. Instead, the purpose is to look at Russian and Soviet leaders' general approaches to change, the necessary preconditions for successful large-scale change in Russian and Soviet history, and the limits on such change.

Several prominent Russian and Western historians argue that military demands have been the driving engine behind the great social and political outbursts of Russian and Soviet history.[1] It may not be true of Russia, as Napoleon once said of Prussia, that it was "hatched from a cannon ball," but nevertheless change in the Russian military has always been deeply entwined with wider social and political change. Historians long ago abandoned the notion that a country's military is somehow independent of its social, political, and economic bases. In Russia, at least since the collapse of the Muscovite military service state at the end of the sixteenth century, change in the military has required change in society as a whole. One of the principal conclusions of this book is that Gorbachev, too, must tackle more than purely military tasks if he is to maintain the Soviet Union's military competitiveness.

Russian and Soviet Patterns of Reform

The first significant Western military challenge early-modern Russia faced was the "gunpowder revolution," which came at a time when Russia was ill-prepared to respond. Muscovy had just undergone the most severe period of social chaos in its history, the *smutnoe vremia,* or Time of Troubles, which lasted roughly from 1598 to 1613. Wracked by the consequences of Ivan IV's *oprichnina,* the disastrous Livonian war, peasant rebellion, the dynastic struggles following Ivan's death, the Smolensk War, and numerous other crises, Russia in the early seventeenth century adopted harsh measures in response to the increasing complexity and expense of warfare.

In the two centuries preceding the Time of Troubles, Moscow had risen to dominance among the various contending Russian cities by shrewd diplomacy and the perfection of what has been called the military service state. This was a system by which Muscovy's rulers ensured the loyalty of their principal servitors by distributing conquered territory, in exchange for which the servitors acted both as agents of the crown and as recruiters and officers in the Muscovite army. This was akin to the Ottoman military; both systems were fierce and proved more than a match for their premodern competitors. In both cases, however, the military service system was limited logistically: it demanded constant conquests to replenish the pool of land available for distribution by the crown, and it lacked a supply net sophisticated enough to project power over great distances. In addition, both the Ottoman and Russian service states were shaken by the advent of early-modern European military tactics using accurate gunpowder weapons (gunpowder had long been available, but its use had been limited by the low level of firearms technology). Russia lacked the economic base of the relatively more prosperous Western countries and was forced to expend more of its scarce resources to compete with its Western rivals, at this time primarily Poland and Sweden.

According to one account of the Russian military during this period (Hellie 1971), in order to compensate for the labor shortage and devastated tax base brought about by the social and political chaos of the Time of Troubles, the young Romanov dynasty (founded in 1613) formalized and strengthened the institution of serfdom, which to that time had been customary and not codified. This had the effect of propping up the endangered military service state, as well as contributing to the already growing stratification of Russian society. The early Romanovs also undertook a gradual phasing out of the older militia in favor of Western-style units. This process was drawn out and fraught with political risk; it came to its violent conclusion late in the century under Peter I.

For our purposes there are five points to note in this example of military-social change: (1) Reform was undertaken following an unsuccessful war against a technologically more advanced power—in this instance, Poland. (2) Military-social reform was possible in part because prior social and political upheaval, accompanied by large-scale rural violence, had shaken traditional bonds of authority, enabling the crown to assert its power more deeply. (3) The changes involved a tightening or sharpening of already existing trends, as opposed to entirely radical innovation. (4) The strong measures were enacted by vigorous leadership, which stood in sharp contrast to the weakened central power of the preceding years. (5) These changes demanded greater discipline of society and a further restriction of individual Russians' already severely circumscribed personal liberty.

The better-known reforms of Peter the Great, begun later in the same century, in many respects followed a similar pattern. Most nonhistorians, under the influence of popular accounts portraying Peter as the tsar-transformer, believe that he dragged Russia kicking and screaming into the modern era.[2] It is a view both Peter and his close advisers would have liked, but it is not entirely accurate. As one historian of tsarist Russia has noted:

> The achievement of Peter the Great . . . lay not in turning Russia upon a new course, but in transforming her along social and political lines that preserved at least basic ties to her traditions. Russia's successful transformation in the eighteenth century therefore saw her become successful in competition with the West, while preserving her traditional social and political institutions intact and even strengthening them in the process. (Lincoln 1982:169)

Peter accelerated and gave much greater focus to a process already well under way by the time of his accession to the throne. The great Russian historian Vasilii Kliuchevskii goes even further, claiming that "the whole of Peter's program had been drawn up in outline by the statesmen of the seventeenth century" (1958: 57).

Many contemporary Western observers of Peter noted his extensive borrowing from Sweden, Holland, and England and confidently predicted that Russia would soon come to resemble a Western state. In fact, however, though Peter's goals were certainly sweeping and his programs had an enormous impact on the subsequent course of Russian history, Russia retained its distinct character. The tsar was most successful when forcing the pace of changes already begun under his predecessors or else when instituting programs that accorded with accepted Russian practice. When Peter departed too sharply from Russian tradition, as in his advocacy of primogeniture and his numerous efforts to limit the powers of provincial bosses, either his efforts were thwarted during his lifetime or his hard-won gains dissolved shortly after his death. Early historians, focusing too narrowly on the whirlwind of activity during Peter's lifetime, were insufficiently aware that many of his reforms were ephemeral and in some cases actually further confused governmental affairs, notably the operation of the bureaucracy and the regulation of succession (Plavsic 1980: 19–45). Despite Peter's efforts to create a "well-ordered police state" along Western lines, Russian political life proved remarkably resistant to change and retained many of its essential Muscovite features through the end of the eighteenth century (Ransel 1975). Nor, evidently, did Peter's reforms have a radical effect on social mobility into the higher ranks of governmental service.[3]

Peter's reforms conform to the five points enumerated earlier. Although historians differ about the causes and degree of premeditation behind his transforming schemes, most (such as Kliuchevskii 1910) believe that military demands drove Peter forward. As with the earlier response to the gunpowder revolution, Russia under Peter underwent reforms of both the army and its logistical-economic base following military disaster, in this case the opening stages of the lengthy Great Northern War against more advanced Sweden. Peter's task was eased by the decay of the old Russian political and social order—including the final taming of the Church even before he gained the throne—and the defeat of the *streltsy,* the remnants of the old-style army, when Peter was still a young man. As his predecessors had done when tightening the serf system half a century before, Peter drew heavily upon Muscovite custom and precedent. He certainly qualified as a forceful leader, surviving several early challenges to his throne and carrying out his schemes with little regard for the cost.

Finally, Russian society emerged from Peter's reign more disciplined; the old Muscovite service state had in theory ascribed to each individual his or her place, but practice had been less rigorous than theory. Peter enforced a service requirement for the nobility with a thoroughness unmatched by his predecessors, his rapacious demands for manual labor emptying whole villages for service in the army, industry in the Urals, and the construction of his city on the Neva. Peter strove to focus the economic and human power of the Russian state for the purposes of war by persuasion when possible, more often by force. As he once remarked, "Even if [change] is good and necessary, yet it be novel and our people will do nothing about it until they are compelled" (Kliuchevskii 1910), sentiments that might easily be attributed to Lenin, Stalin, or even Gorbachev.

Peter's military reforms, continued and extended by his successors at a much reduced pace, placed Russia on an adequate footing to compete on roughly equal terms with the other European Great Powers until the Industrial Revolution triggered yet another military crisis in Russia. So long as the pace of technical change remained slow, Russia could maintain its place in the Great Power club; but by the middle of the nineteenth century Russia had once again fallen behind in the economic and technical race, and its backward social institutions—primarily serfdom—acted as a further drag.

Before examining the so-called Great Reforms of the midnineteenth century, however, it is instructive to look at Alexander I's largely still-born attempts to reform his empire. The young tsar called serfdom a "state of barbarism" (McConnell 1970: 146), advocated perestroika of Russian society, and in his first years on the throne discussed numerous constitutional plans designed to limit the despotic powers of the autocrat. Little came of such schemes, however, in part owing to Russia's wars with Napoleon and to Alexander's increasing preoccupation with foreign affairs. Another consideration militating against constitutional reform is of particular relevance to current Soviet problems: reformers around the tsar were reluctant to encourage a constitution, the ultimate effect of which would invariably be to hand greater power to the landed nobility. The nobility, like today's *nomenklatura,* was one of the principal obstacles to reform. Though circumscribing the autocracy was perhaps desirable in theory, at some time in the distant future, the immediate effect of limiting the tsar's power would be to strengthen the natural opponents of change.

Alexander I's Russia lacked one critical precondition for successful reform: before the great Industrial Revolution of the nineteenth century, Russia was a major economic power; its military might and economic resources, especially the Ural iron industry, proved adequate to defeat the French invasion. Serfdom and the autocracy may have been distasteful, but, as the victory over Napoleon showed, they did not yet threaten the power of the state. Even if Alexander desired to reform Russian government and society—and historical opinion is sharply divided on the question of his sincerity—he lacked the requisite social and political consensus to act. Indeed, the great Russian victory and St. Petersburg's dominant diplomatic position following 1815 tended to reinforce the hand of opponents of reform, such as N. M. Karamzin.[4]

By midcentury, however, the Industrial Revolution had transformed the nature of power; sheer numbers were no longer paramount. Despite possessing the largest army in Europe, Russia suffered a humiliating defeat on its own territory in the Crimean War of 1854–56 at the hands of the two leading industrial powers, France and Great Britain. As before, defeat was a spur for change. Historians debate whether the need for military reform was the primary reason for the abolition of serfdom;[5] but many of the Great Reforms initiated by Alexander II were unambiguously related to military change. Once again, as in the previous two instances, the direct agent of reform had been military defeat by a technologically superior Western power—or, in this case, an alliance.

But the reforms of the 1860s and 1870s differed in one crucial respect from the examples cited earlier: although there had been an increase in peasant disturbances during the Crimean War, there had been no social upheaval approaching the scale of the Time of Troubles or the crisis of late seventeenth-century Russia. Instead the governmental structure carried on unshaken during the succession from Nicholas I to Alexander II and in fact played a creative role, actually initiating many of the most important reforms and at times goading on a somewhat reluctant monarch (Keep 1985: 351). Another difference between the Great Reforms and those of Peter is worth mentioning: one express purpose of the Alexandrine reforms was to improve the lot of the average Russian subject, and in some ways this aim was attained. The notoriously long term of service in the army, for example, was shortened. But the unintended overall result of peasant emancipation was a decrease in the peasants' standard of living.[6]

Nor were the purely military reforms of the 1870s a uniform success. As Allan Wildman and others have shown, by creating a modern European-style army in Russia, the Miliutin army reforms required recruits to perform the duties of citizen-soldiers while Russian society denied them the benefits of citizenship (Wildman 1980: 36–40). This was an unstable combination, as would become manifest during the war against Japan in 1904, and even more so against Germany in 1914–17.

Successful peasant emancipation, arguably the most sweeping piece of social engineering in Russia's history (excepting Stalin's collectivization, or "second enserfment" as it was known to peasants), required exceptional force of will on the part of the tsar to outmaneuver social and institutional inertia. Despite considerable foot-dragging by the pervasive but largely unorganized opposition, Alexander was able to quell his own doubts and forge "a unique interaction between enlightened officials, progressive aristocrats and moderate segments of the intelligentsia" (Lincoln 1978: 355) in favor of emancipation and reform. These diverse segments of Russian society were for a time fused together by the promise of enlightened reform and by a relaxation of intellectual controls following the death of the reactionary Nicholas I.

This relaxation took the form of *glasnost'*, openness or official publicity, exposing many of Russia's governmental and social ills. Some prominent figures, such as Prince Petr Dolgorukov, argued for the widest possible application of glasnost'. Dolgorukov wrote that "*glasnost'* is the best physician for the ulcers of the state. . . . A wise use of *glasnost'* is the best weapon for destroying false rumors, secret schemes, absurd and evil hearsay. . . . A reasonable and proper discussion of various questions will supply the government with information about the needs and requirements of Russia" (Lincoln 1982: 185).

Dolgorukov was addressing one of the key problems faced by tsarist Russia—or, indeed, by any authoritarian system: lacking a free press or other extrainstitutional channels for the flow of critical comment, the tsarist government did not receive reliable information about the social problems confronting its own society. It should be noted that *Kolokol'*, Alexander Herzen's dissident journal published in London and smuggled into Russia, was read avidly at this time by reform-minded individuals both in and out of government and partially filled this gap in critical, independent comment. Unfortunately, Russian traditions proved too strong for the flowering of the 1860s incarnation of glasnost' as Dolgorukov envisioned it; instead a more crabbed interpretation prevailed as advanced by O. A. Przhetslavskii, a member of the Main Censorship Administration. He wrote that *"glasnost'* must be in an inviolable harmony with the circumstances of time and place. In other words, it always must have an indissoluble link with, and conform to, the bases and forms of the state and civic structure, it must never work in conflict with them" (Lincoln 1982: 188). The debate over the bounds of press freedom in the 1860s has a decidedly modern ring; the exchanges between Egor Iakovlev and other editors on the one hand and Viktor Chebrikov and Egor Ligachev on the other apparently cover much the same ground. And Gorbachev's Orwellian assertion that "we are for openness without reservations, without limitations, but for openness in the interests of socialism" indicates that, as in the past, the more restrictive view is likely to prevail.[7]

Seen from the perspective of a progressive-minded bureaucrat in today's Kremlin, the Alexandrine reforms may provide an unsettling precedent; for while they aimed to create a more efficient army and better society through orderly, enlightened change from above, they in fact further divorced the regime from society as a whole. Indeed, the history of late imperial Russia can serve to support Tocqueville's adage that there is no more dangerous time for a bad government than when it tries to reform. By using coercion and strengthening state power at the expense of personal liberty, Peter the Great bequeathed to his successors a powerful Russia; by contrast, Alexander II's efforts to reform Russia by loosening the bonds of the state led to spiraling demands for change and the appearance of a violent and irreconcilable revolutionary movement, apparently confirming Karamzin's warnings that anarchy would follow even a moderate weakening of the state's authority in Russia.

The last large-scale attempt of the tsarist regime to effect peaceful reform is in many ways also the most intriguing. Following the disastrous war against Japan and the revolution of 1905, even the slow-witted Nicholas II understood that only fundamental reform could save his dynasty.

Reluctantly he authorized the creation of a duma—although he soon altered the franchise when he found the first election results unpalatable —and he allowed the last great statesman of the Romanov period, P. A. Stolypin, to enact sweeping governmental and economic changes.

Like Gorbachev, Stolypin first sprang into national prominence as a relatively young provincial governor, a background that gave him an intimate appreciation of Russia's agrarian crisis. Again like Gorbachev, Stolypin stood apart from his bureaucratic predecessors, with the important exception of Sergei Witte, in his understanding and mastery of public relations, a skill that prompted one recent historian to call him "an able actor" (Manning 1982: 270). Stolypin was no democrat, becoming notorious as minister of the interior for his ruthless suppression of the 1905–6 peasant Jacquerie and for his merciless attitude toward revolutionaries who would not submit to tsarist authority. At the same time, however, Stolypin realized, as few Russian bureaucrats had before, that the tsarist system rested on a hazardously narrow social base. He supported a sweeping military modernization program and tried to reduce the endemic *proizvol,* or arbitrariness, of the autocratic system. Most significantly, Stolypin promoted legislation designed to break up the peasant commune, hoping thereby to create a class of peasant smallholders that would have a tangible stake in the continuance of the old order.

> I propose that, first of all, it is necessary to create a citizen, a peasant owner, a small landowner and the [agrarian] problem will be solved. Citizenship will reign in Russia. First a citizen and then citizenship. But with us the opposite is preached. (Levin 1965)

The Stolypin reforms conform to the established Russian pattern. As in the past, a disastrous war, all the more shocking for being at the hands of newly industrialized Japan, once again convinced the reigning monarch that drastic governmental, military, and social change was the only alternative to the rapid decline of Russian power. The reforms commonly identified with Stolypin were not novel; they were drawn up before 1905 by his predecessors and only enacted after war and domestic crisis had shaken Nicholas's torpor. Stolypin provided the strong leadership needed to advance his programs, patiently pressing Nicholas to accept change, whereas before 1905 the tsar had been unwilling to dilute his autocratic inheritance. But Stolypin was never his own man; he lacked the legitimacy often instantly accorded a hereditary monarch, and at all times he had to please his tsar. Because of this his peak period of influence was rather short, amounting to only six months according to one historian.

Conservative opponents organized quickly, soon regaining the tsar's ear (Levin 1965).

Historians disagree whether if, given sufficient time, Stolypin's programs would have enabled the tsarist system to survive, or at least to disintegrate gracefully. The most recent study suggests that the centerpiece of his reforms, his attack on the commune, was only modestly successful (Atkinson 1983). But even more seriously, Stolypin sought to achieve contradictory goals. He chased the same elusive chimera that has dazzled Russian reformers since Peter: a populace that, given the proper legal and economic inducements by a strong leader, would display the virtues of a free citizenry while remaining loyal and submissive to the autocracy. The tsars' successors have chased the same shadow.

The Soviet years have seen a repetition of the ancient Russian pattern of military-technical competition with the West. Indeed, one historian has argued for many years that the fundamental significance of the Bolshevik revolution lies in Russia's national quest to compete on equal terms as a Great Power with the Western states. This line of reasoning holds that industrialization and the creation of a modern army could not be as smooth and organic a process in Russia as it had been in the West, owing to Russian backwardness. Having to compete with more advanced powers, Russia could not afford the luxury of time. Stalin's revolution from above, his forced industrialization and collectivization of agriculture, were thus part of a continuous process of crash modernization that began even before the revolution, only to be accelerated by Lenin and the Bolsheviks, who worshiped at the shrine of rapid economic growth. Stalin became "the perfect Leninist" (von Laue 1971: 186) through his realization of the USSR's Great Power dream.

Not all historians accept such a view; many believe that Stalin's forced march to industrial power was wasteful, was not the best course open to Russia, and was not even the best possible outcome of Leninism.[8] The rise of Japan and other Pacific economic powers suggests that different methods, much more humane than Stalin's though equally rapid, can overcome backwardness and produce more impressive results. One need not believe in the historical inevitability of "Stalinism," however, to see that he advanced his radical economic program by stressing the Soviet Union's need to compete with the advanced West. His "socialism in one country," a slogan with powerful nationalist and xenophobic appeal, demanded that the USSR focus the energies of its people, by means of pervasive propaganda, exhortation, and coercion, on the headlong construction of heavy industry with little thought for individual liberties or consumer welfare. Stalin defeated his rivals on the left by playing up the largely spurious "war scare" of 1927; and he and his followers ushered in the first five-year plan with show trials of industrial "wreckers," allegedly the hirelings of foreign capitalist powers (Meyer 1978). Throughout the first five-year plan and the 1930s, the Communist leadership repeatedly stressed that the Soviet Union was surrounded by a hostile capitalist world, that spies were omnipresent, and that time was short before the inevitable armed clash between "imperialism" and socialism (Fitzpatrick 1978).

The Bolshevik and Stalin revolutions shared many characteristics with earlier Russian transformational leaps. Defeat in war, first against Japan and then against the Central Powers, had led to revolution and the demise of the 300-year-old Romanov dynasty. Although the Bolshevik state was certainly revolutionary, in its quest for industrialization and military power it did not follow an entirely uncharted course; it continued a process, by more violent and forceful means, that was already well under way during the late imperial years. Even in the military, although the nature of political controls changed radically, a great deal of continuity linked the Red Army to its tsarist predecessor; indeed, many of the early Soviet military stars, such as Mikhail Tukhachevskii, were former tsarist officers. Stalin's leadership was vigorous and his cult all-pervasive; this stood in sharp contrast both to the hapless Nicholas II and to the chaos of Soviet politics following Lenin's death, and it fits our pattern of strong leadership following a period of uncertainty. Finally, Soviet citizens' lives during the Stalin years became far more regimented than at any period in prerevolutionary history.

Like many of his tsarist predecessors, Stalin sought to surpass Western economic and military power by means of a revolution from above. But as in the previous historical examples, although such methods can produce great results for a time, at a staggering cost, they discourage spontaneity. Stalin's dictatorship bequeathed industrial power to his heirs, but he also left a legacy of a "swollen state [and] spent society" (Tucker 1981–82).

The Heritage of Reform

If indeed there has been a pattern underlying military and social change in Russia's past, what might this tell us about the Soviet present and future? It would be unwise to deduce from a historical pattern an ineluctable course of future events, and few, if any, in the West possess reliable information about Kremlin debates. Such disclaimers aside, however, looking at the pattern of reformist leaps in Russian and Soviet history, one can hazard some comparisons and contrasts with the current situation in the Soviet Union.

The factors militating against sweeping change are formidable: unlike our historical examples, the Soviet Union has not recently suffered a military defeat. On the contrary, accounts of the victory in World War II saturate the Soviet media and historical literature, providing the Communist regime with one of its most important claims to legitimacy. And today's Stalinists have already warned that tampering with the socialist system could weaken the USSR, making it vulnerable to imperialist attack. As it did under Alexander I, victory in war may hinder reform.

One could point to the war in Afghanistan as a goad to change. But by itself the war does not seem sufficient to produce wide-ranging domestic changes. Of all Russia's wars, the Afghan conflict is most akin to the lengthy campaigns against the Caucasus tribes in the early nineteenth century. This conflict dragged on for years, earning the Caucasus the sobriquet "graveyard of the Russian Army," but Russia's travails in this colonial war never provoked a rethinking of military practice, much less did they trigger large-scale social change.

Nevertheless, the price of remaiming in Afghanistan eventually became too high, and the Soviets have now extricated their troops from that country. Afghan guerrillas are being supplied with sophisticated weapons that finally undermined Soviet air superiority to the point that, according to State Department estimates, in 1987 Soviet forces were losing one aircraft per day. This important military failure, combined with the poor showing of Soviet equipment in battle against Israel in Lebanon, almost certainly strengthens the hand of those claiming that radical change in the Soviet system is necessary to keep up with Western technology. It is still too early to tell whether Moscow will leave its Afghan allies to fend entirely for themselves. Nevertheless, Moscow's willingness to pull out of Afghanistan completely has been perhaps the most telling test of the vigor of Gorbachev's changes.

It is difficult to see how Moscow can insulate its vital position in Eastern Europe from admission of defeat in Afghanistan. One should remember in this context that the Polish revolt of 1863 was one of the first events to persuade Alexander II that change should occur at a slower, more carefully regulated pace. Unrest in Poland, or in any Eastern European satellite state, could bring Gorbachev's reforms to a crashing halt.

Perhaps the most important barrier to significant change is the increasingly well-entrenched nomenklatura, which, as a self-defense mechanism, seems determined to resist structural reforms. This is a problem many Soviets freely admit. It has been a long time since the Soviet system was shaken as it was by the revolution, the purges, and the world war, and one can certainly understand Gorbachev's periodic outbursts against the inertia of the bureaucracy. Perhaps he intends to tackle the nomenklatura, but it

is the opinion of several prominent scholars of the Soviet Union that, like
Stolypin, he will be satisfied with improving the operating efficiency of the
existing system rather than unleashing radical change.[9] Even if he did favor
sweeping change of the military and an overhaul of the military's social
and logistical base that this would demand, Gorbachev may simply lack
the requisite power to bring his plans to fruition. He has made numerous
personnel changes, though it is too soon to judge the long-term results.
Simply promoting new faces without addressing the manifest structural
defects of the Soviet economy and government will certainly fail to produce
a reinvigorated economy and society. One also wonders whether Soviet
society as a whole would not prove resistant to stricter discipline now that
Stalin-style coercion and revolutionary exhortation are, for the time being,
played out.

The challenge to change certainly exists in a number of ways: Richard W.
Judy's chapter points out how today, as in the past, Western technological
advances threaten Moscow's hard-won military edge. Economic reform in
China and, even more important, the rise of Japanese economic power is
surely disquieting to those who recall how quickly the latter country once
rose from near feudalism to Great Power status, inflicting a major defeat
on the established Russian empire. The emergence of precision-guided
conventional weapons and the prospect of space-based defensive systems
also apparently disturb the Soviet leadership. If such weapons work a
transformation in the nature of warfare analogous to the first Industrial
Revolution, the Soviet Union must undergo important changes or face
the prospect of falling behind the United States as a military power. As
Hans Heymann points out in his chapter, the Soviet Union may no longer
be able to afford the luxury of insulating its pampered military sector
of the economy from its throttled consumer sector. Even if the Soviet
leadership is not really as worried by the prospect of space weapons as
it sometimes makes out, it may still find the threat of SDI useful as a
means of linking the need for domestic economic reform with the cause
of national security.

The central dilemma of reform in the USSR is, however, that in order
to compete successfully in the military sphere, the Soviet Union must
not only make military changes; it must also address structural social,
economic, and political problems. In short, it must decide between loss
of effectiveness and loss of political control. Surrendering power does not
come naturally to bureaucracies—tsarist, Soviet, or Western. Reform
demands sweeping change at a time when the Soviet Union is more
conservative structurally than ever before in its history. At present despite
much brave talk, the Soviet ruling class evinces little inclination to take
giant strides.

In the past, as the foregoing examples show, Russia had to suffer defeat in war and social dislocation before a sufficiently broad consensus could be built for important change. This was, however, in the years before the mass of Russians was literate; the Soviet leadership may calculate that relative openness, or glasnost', in the Soviet press can patch together a reasonably broad coalition favoring change. Most of Gorbachev's publicly stated goals have historical precedents, and it is difficult to believe that he is unaware of glasnost' under Alexander II. Indeed, it would be a fair guess that he chose to use the term in order to convey a message about the purpose, and limits, of debate. So far it would seem he has chosen to adopt the more restrictive version of this concept: the Soviet press may act as a channel to air the social, economic, and, to a much lesser extent, political ills of Soviet society. It may not, however, question the leading role of the Party or explore other sacrosanct subjects. Muscovites are unlikely, for instance, to read a press exposé on dachas of Politburo members—unless an individual member is already headed for the rubbish heap of history. Linda Feldmann, a *Christian Science Monitor* correspondent, worked for a time as a reporter with *Moscow News,* the flagship of press openness.[10] Her fascinating account is not uniformly optimistic; despite encouraging instances of accurate, critical reporting, Soviet writers still habitually refer sensitive topics to political leadership for prior approval, and certain subjects remain forbidden.

Even in its attenuated form, however, the new relative openness serves two vital functions: not only does it expose shortcomings that the hierarchy wishes to address, but it may also inform the government of pressing social ills. As Soviet sociologist Tat'iana Zaslavskaia has admitted, Soviet leaders lack basic statistical information taken for granted in the West. They frequently have no idea how widespread certain problems are, such as the levels of crime and alcohol abuse. Soviet leaders have thus made ill-informed policy decisions leading to disastrous consequences (Zaslavskaia 1987). As it did under Alexander II, glasnost' may educate more than just the common reader.

Vigorous leadership has always played a central role in previous reforms, and the early indications are that Gorbachev can provide this. Western enthusiasm for the general secretary often seems tinged with wishful thinking—we simply do not yet know enough to gauge with much accuracy his true intentions or, more important, to outline the restrictions under which he operates. Nevertheless, like Stolypin, Gorbachev is a master of public relations, whereas his predecessors routinely managed the marvel of appearing simultaneously cadaverous and surly. Given that the USSR has had neither war nor revolution to focus the national mind, a great deal hinges on the ability of Gorbachev and his supporters to make their case convincingly. But as the example of Alexander I shows, no matter how charismatic, leadership divorced from the essential preconditions for change is unlikely to go far.

Most disturbing is that Gorbachev, for all his energy and optimism, is apparently pursuing the same conflicting goals that confounded his forbears, tsarist and Soviet. He hopes to provide material and social incentives to urge the Soviet people to duplicate and surpass Western achievements, and he is even dispensing limited doses of political freedom as a further inducement. But he still apparently believes that the fruits of economic and political freedom can be grown, like a hothouse plant, in an authoritarian, socialist system. The examples of his predecessors who tried to reconcile rapid economic growth with continued authoritarian rule are not encouraging: to be sure, impressive results can be produced at great human cost through coercion and violence, as Peter the Great and Stalin showed. Conversely, however, the failings of Alexander II and Stolypin stand as a warning that rapid social change without sufficient political liberalization can lead to disaster. Although Gorbachev clearly has numerous admirers in the West, they should perhaps ask themselves this question: If we want to see the growth of genuine social and political pluralism in the USSR, with the economic and technological benefits that might flow from this, is another revolution from above really likely to produce such results? History gives few grounds for hope on this score.

Of course, the shortcomings and failures of past reforms do not ensure future failure. Historians are naturally inclined toward pessimism: it is easy to imagine a historian in the late fifteenth century concluding that the Catholic Church had always been, and would therefore always be, capable of crushing widespread heretical dissent. We may be on the verge of a Communist Reformation that will upset all smug calculations; but so far there seems to be little of Martin Luther about Gorbachev.

Notes

1. One of the most outspoken proponents of this school is Richard Pipes (1974).
2. Such is the argument of, for example, Massie (1980).
3. This is the thesis of Meehan-Waters (1982).
4. See, for example, Pipes (1986). This is a long attack on sweeping, rationalistic reforms.
5. Rieber (1966) argues that military necessity was behind all the Great Reforms, including serfdom, but, in the most recent and thorough study of the prerevolutionary Russian army, Keep (1985: 352) has questioned Rieber's chronology and suggests that military considerations were only one set of motives behind peasant emancipation.
6. See, for example, Robinson (1932: chap. VI).
7. Gorbachev, quoted in the *New York Times,* January 13, 1988.

8. Stephen F. Cohen is the foremost exponent of the school that holds that there was a sharp break between Leninism and Stalinism (1985: chaps. 2 and 3).

9. See, for example, Bialer (1986), Leonhard (1986), and Goldman (1987).

10. *Christian Science Monitor,* September 11–15, 1987.

References

Atkinson, Dorothy (1983). *The End of the Russian Land Commune, 1905–1930.* Stanford, CA: Stanford University Press.

Bialer, Seweryn (1986). *The Soviet Paradox: External Expansion, Internal Decline.* New York: Knopf.

Christian Science Monitor (1987). September 11–15.

Cohen, Stephen F. (1985). *Rethinking the Soviet Experience: Politics and History since 1917.* New York: Oxford University Press.

Czartoryski, Adam, quoted in Andrej Walicki (1987). *Legal Philosophies of Russian Liberalism.* Oxford: Oxford University Press.

Fitzpatrick, Sheila (1978). "The Foreign Threat during the First Five-Year Plan." *Soviet Union/Union sovietique,* 5.

Goldman, Marshal I. (1987). *Gorbachev's Challenge: Economic Reform in the Age of High Technology.* New York: Norton.

Hellie, Richard (1971). *Enserfment and Military Change in Muscovy.* Chicago: University of Chicago Press.

Keep, John L. H. (1985). *Soldiers of the Tsar: Army and Society in Russia, 1462–1874.* Oxford: Oxford University Press.

Kliuchevskii, V. O. (1910). *Kurs russkoi istori.* tom 4. Moscow: Arnold-Tret'iakovskii.

——— (1958). *Peter the Great.* Boston: Beacon Press.

Leonhard, Wolfgang (1986). *The Kremlin and the West: A Realistic Approach.* New York: Norton.

Levin, Alfred (1965). "Peter Arkadevich Stolypin: A Political Reappraisal." *Journal of Modern History,* 35, 445–63.

Lincoln, W. Bruce (1978). *Nicholas I: Emperor and Autocrat of All the Russias.* Bloomington: Indiana University Press.

——— (1982). *In the Vanguard of Reform: Russia's Enlightened Bureaucrats, 1825–1861.* De Kalb: Northern Illinois University Press.

McConnell, Allen (1970). *Tsar Alexander I: Paternalistic Reformer.* Arlington Heights, IL: Harlan Davidson.

Manning, Roberta Thompson (1982). *The Crisis of the Old Order in Russia: Gentry and Government.* Princeton: Princeton University Press.

Massie, Robert K. (1980). *Peter the Great: His Life and World.* New York: Knopf.

Meehan-Waters, Brenda (1982). *Autocracy and Aristocracy: The Russian Service Elite of 1730.* New Brunswick, NJ: Rutgers University Press.

Meyer, Alfred G. (1978). "The Great War Scare of 1927." *Soviet Union/Union sovietique,* 5.

The New York Times (1988). January 13.

Pipes, Richard (1974). *Russia under the Old Regime.* Harmondsworth, England: Penguin Books.

Pipes, Richard, ed. and trans. (1986). *Karamzin's Memoir on Ancient and Modern Russia.* New York: Atheneum.

Plavsic, Borivoj (1980). "Seventeenth-Century Chanceries and Their Staffs." In Walter McKenzie Pinter and Don Karl Rowney, eds., *Russian Officialdom: The Bureaucraticization of Russian Society from the Seventeenth to the Twentieth Century.* Chapel Hill: University of North Carolina Press.

Ransel, David (1975). *The Politics of Catherinian Russia: The Panin Party.* New Haven, CT: Yale University Press.

Rieber, Alfred J. (1966). *Politics of Autocracy: Letters of Alexander II to Prince A. I. Bariatinskii, 1857–1864.* Paris: Morton.

Robinson, Geroid Tanquary (1932).   *Rural Russia under the Old Regime.* Berkeley: University of California Press.

Tucker, Robert C. (1981–82). "Swollen State, Spent Society: Stalin's Legacy to Brezhnev's Russia." *Foreign Affairs,* 60 (Winter).

von Laue, Theodore H. (1971). *Why Lenin? Why Stalin?: A Reappraisal of the Russian Revolution, 1900–1930,* 2d ed. New York: Lippincott.

Voslensky, Michael (1984). *Nomenklatura: The Soviet Ruling Class; an Insider's Report.* Garden City, NY: Doubleday.

Wallace, Sir Donald Mackenzie (1984). *Russia on the Eve of War and Revolution.* Princeton: Princeton University Press. (Originally printed in 1897.)

White, Stephen (1979). *Political Culture and Soviet Politics.* New York: St. Martin's.

Wildman, Allan K. (1980). *The End of the Russian Imperial Army: The Old Army and the Soldiers' Revolt, March–April 1917.* Princeton: Princeton University Press.

Zaslavskaia, Tat'iana (1987, February 6). "Voprosii teorii: Perestroika i sotsiologiia." *Pravda.*

• CHAPTER THREE •

The Soviet Debate over "New Thinking" and the Restructuring of U.S.-Soviet Relations

Philip D. Stewart
Margaret G. Hermann
The Mershon Center

A debate is taking place in the Soviet Union on many of the basic positions and traditional assumptions of Soviet security policy.[1] The outcome of this debate will determine the character of U.S.-Soviet relations for a generation to come. This is a debate in which, sooner or later, the peoples and governments of the West must also engage, as the questions it poses go to the heart of Western security policy and to the most basic assumptions about what is desirable and what is possible in U.S.-Soviet relations.

Given that in the past U.S.-Soviet relations have been based upon the fundamental irreconcilability of ideological, political, and economic differences, the current debate suggests the prospect—even the necessity —of separating ideology from foreign and defense policy. And given that the United States and the Soviet Union have each based their security policy on a largely unilaterally determined, unstable mix of nuclear deterrent and nuclear war-fighting capabilities, the Soviet debate suggests a desire to replace this with a collaborative approach to building mutual security through the drastic reduction of nuclear and conventional military capabilities. Moreover, whereas the dominant Western and Soviet perspective has been to view Soviet and Western interests in the Third World as essentially competitive and fundamentally incompatible, the current Soviet debate poses the necessity of building relationships that promote common interests in Third World stability and development while greatly improving the capacity for managing continuing differences.

So far there are significant signs of the impact of this debate on Soviet policy. Two prominent indicators are the Soviet proposals at Reykjavik and the Soviet acceptance of the so-called double-zero option to eliminate nuclear missiles in Europe. Combined with a Soviet readiness to accept highly intrusive, on-site inspection regimes,[2] these actions are suggestive of major changes in the Soviet approach to nuclear security. Gorbachev's unilateral initiative to reduce Soviet conventional forces by 500,000 men reflects new thinking even in the crucial conventional area (*New York Times* 1988b). Other signs of fresh thinking in Soviet international affairs include greater seriousness in seeking mutually acceptable resolutions of conflicts in Afghanistan and the Middle East.

Although the potential importance of this Soviet debate for American policy was noted by former Secretaries of State Kissinger and Vance following their February 1987 visit to Moscow (Peterson, Kissinger, and Vance 1987), relatively little attention has been paid so far to the assessment of the possible directions and implications of this new Soviet thinking.[3] This chapter is an effort to identify the factors giving rise to this debate and to examine the ideas of the Soviet advocates of new thinking.

The area of change in Soviet thinking with the greatest direct potential for reshaping Soviet security policy is military doctrine, and perhaps military strategy. These changes are not new under Gorbachev, however, but have accumulated over at least the last decade.[4] In essence Soviet military doctrine has increasingly come to recognize that there are no "reliable" scenarios for the employment of nuclear weapons in an East-West conflict. Under every contingency Soviet military planners have come to realize that the probability of the ultimate massive nuclear destruction of the Soviet homeland is unacceptably high.[5]

Gorbachev is pushing for a wide-ranging restructuring of economic life.[6] Significant improvements in productivity and quality are essential to meet minimal requirements for incentive-producing consumption, investment, and defense. Gorbachev has made it clear that he sees a significant and sustained reduction in the level of international tension as essential to this revitalization of the domestic economy. There is evidence to suggest that stabilization, if not reduction, of the military budget is an important component of Gorbachev's strategy for economic modernization.[7] If so, this creates a direct link between his economic objectives and national security policy. Only in a calmer international climate can such a policy be justified, let alone sustained.

The thesis of this chapter is that Soviet security policy under Gorbachev is at the threshold of a possible radical change. We suggest that the basis of this redirection lies in two conundrums: Soviet (and American) inability to achieve security through reliable deterrence while at the same time seeking or being driven by technology toward an effective nuclear war-fighting capability;[8] and the growing inability of the Soviet economy to sustain high rates of military growth while at the same time meeting the material expectations of the Soviet people.[9] It is true that these problems are not new, nor is Gorbachev the first to attempt to address them. But Gorbachev is the first Soviet leader to pursue the creation of a climate in which consideration of radical change is possible.[10] Building on the public recognition of a need for radical change and his own publicly stated commitment to bring about change, he is encouraging others to participate in the development of a new Soviet national security policy.[11] His policy of *glasnost'* (openness) is fostering dialogue and debate in many circles.

The real test of policy change lies in observable behavior, however, not in rhetoric. Why, then, pay attention to the policy debate? We offer two kinds of reasons. First, in contrast to Brezhnev, Gorbachev seems determined to be a transformational leader (Burns 1978). Far from being content with minor adjustments designed to keep the ship of state afloat just a bit longer, Gorbachev has stressed again and again his determination to bring about fundamental changes in Soviet society and foreign policy. And, like a transformational leader, he is spending time bringing important constituents along with him.[12] Although he probably will not achieve all of his goals, we as analysts cannot develop an adequate understanding of present policy, let alone future trends, without a clear grasp of the larger design of which specific acts are a part.

The second reason is that not only the rhetoric but also the substance of Gorbachev's policy raises profound questions about the fundamental assumptions on which Western policy toward the Soviet Union has been based for more than four decades.[13] Maintenance of an effective and sound Western security policy demands a thorough grasp of the assumptions, impulses, and ideas underlying Gorbachev's vision.[14] In fact, we would argue that not only analysts but also policymakers should understand both the roots and the thrust of Gorbachev's vision. The reason is that this "revolution" may create opportunities that have not existed since the end of World War II to transform the U.S.-Soviet relationship, in both its military and political dimensions. The extent to which such opportunities in fact arise will depend in significant part on Western readiness to respond to Soviet initiatives. Such a readiness will require Westerners not only to understand thoroughly what may be possible, but also to debate among themselves what kind of new security and political arrangements may be desirable and acceptable.[15] Understanding the dimensions of Gorbachev's vision is a first step in this process.

Having said all this, we must begin by observing that Gorbachev does not have a "blueprint."[16] There is no clearly worked-out or fully developed conception of a new Soviet security policy at this time. What there is, rather, is an unfolding process whereby under Gorbachev's leadership and protection a thoroughgoing reexamination of past Soviet policy achievements and failures, assumptions, and beliefs has been unleashed. Major participants in this process include officials close or sympathetic to Gorbachev in the top leadership, the International Department, the Foreign Ministry, and the General Staff. In addition, several institutes of the Academy of Sciences have become active and at times influential in this process. Although this debate is less than three years old, already many of the basic elements of a new approach to security and to international affairs are visible. Most of the fundamental ideas of this vision are laid out in Gorbachev's *Pravda* article on a "Secure World," and many of its implications are being worked out and communicated largely in private, oral discourse.[17]

From Unilateral to Mutual Security

The traditional approach to national security is based upon the assumption that each nation, relying on its own resources and those of its allies, must develop military, economic, and diplomatic capabilities sufficient to address present and potential threats from adversaries. A fundamental political issue is always "How much is enough?" The search for a sufficient defense often leads to arms races in which two nations or sets of nations expend vast resources, frequently without altering the basic balance of forces. In the nuclear era security has been sought through attempts to create capabilities to "assure" destruction of the other side in the event of conventional or nuclear attack. To "limit damage" to oneself, each side has sought the capability to destroy as many hardened targets as possible in a retaliatory or preemptive strike. This search for a war-fighting capability, which was a dominant characteristic of Soviet doctrine in the 1960s and probably up to the late 1970s, tends to destabilize deterrence and foster strategic arms races.

From 1945 until the late 1960s the Soviet Union was in the untenable position—at least in its own view—of being subject to assured destruction by Western nuclear forces but of not having a similar capability of its own. The goal of strategic parity was finally achieved and, the Soviets hoped, assured by the signing of the SALT I agreements in 1972. Although this agreement and, to a certain extent, the SALT II treaty, signed in June 1979, did serve to limit certain primarily quantitative dimensions of the strategic arms race, both sides continued to make rapid advances in nuclear war-fighting, or hard-target kill capabilities. The net effect was to create growing doubts on both sides about the durability of nuclear deterrence.

At the same time, however, the drive for more effective war-fighting, particularly at the intermediate level, was having significant political costs. Rather than neutralizing or intimidating Western Europe, deployment of the Soviet SS-20s (Garthoff 1985: 110–19) and the late 1983 collapse of the INF negotiations only served to heighten anti-Soviet feelings in Europe and made U.S. compensatory deployments easier.

Underlying the reassessment of these problems that is taking place under Gorbachev are conclusions in Soviet doctrine to the effect that an unavoidable outcome of any significant use of nuclear weapons would be widespread devastation of the Soviet homeland. Western conservatives argued in the 1970s that the Soviet Union was willing to absorb even very large casualties from a nuclear conflict to achieve its goals, but Soviet leaders now appear to reject a security policy that virtually assures the widespread destruction of the Soviet Union in the event that a major war breaks out.[18]

What alternative approach to security does the Gorbachev leadership espouse? Drawing inspiration from the work of the Palme Commission, Gorbachev calls his new approach "mutual security." Mutual security is the antipode of unilateral security. Mutual security is based on the premise that meaningful, stable, and psychologically reassuring security can never be achieved in the nuclear era through efforts by individual states to attain effective deterrence. Technology and uncertainty will always push each side toward greater war-fighting capability and thus undermine deterrence. Mutual security sees both sides as hostages to the nuclear arms race. The only effective way out of this hostage relationship, the only way to increase the security of either the United States or the Soviet Union is through cooperation on a broad front. Mutual security accepts as a fact that in the nuclear era neither side can achieve security at the expense of the other. If one side feels its security threatened or damaged by actions of the other, such as the threats perceived by the United States from Soviet heavy missiles and by Europe from the Soviet SS-20, or by the Soviet Union from the highly accurate Pershing-II intermediate-range or the MX intercontinental missiles, then it will take compensatory actions that in turn may be perceived by the other side as reducing its own security. Of course these views are not universally accepted in the Soviet hierarchy. The traditional view that collaborative security arrangements through negotiation with the West either do not work or are inadequate means for assuring Soviet security are still discernible (Akhromeev 1987).

The Military Dimension

The implications of mutual security for the military policy and the conduct of U.S.-Soviet relations, as advocated by one side in the Soviet debate, are profound. For example, mutual security suggests that threats should be addressed by mutual actions to reduce their sources and manifestations. Traditional deterrence requires continuous "build-ups" or "improvements" to "maintain" or "extend" deterrence.[19] General Secretary Gorbachev and former President Reagan, though each rejected deterrence for a different reason, agreed that reducing the number of nuclear weapons on both sides should increase the sense of security both countries feel. It is little wonder that Soviet officials who advocate this view describe the transition to a policy of mutual security as involving "a very deep change in attitude, in understanding of the role of military force, of disarmament, and of our relations with other countries, including the United States."

It can be reasonably countered that reducing arms, even nuclear weapons, addresses only the symptoms of the differences between the Soviet Union and the United States, not the causes. Moreover, reducing nuclear weapons—especially in Europe—in all probability will increase the Soviet sense of security by eliminating the U.S. capacity to respond in a limited but nuclear way to a Soviet conventional attack without at all reducing Western fears of overwhelming Soviet conventional superiority. In Gorbachev's vision this problem, clearly recognized by Soviet analysts, is addressed at several levels. At the most immediate and operational level, in response to a Warsaw Pact proposal, new talks have been agreed upon which have as their objective the reduction of conventional forces in Europe through disbanding of units and destruction of equipment. Gorbachev's promise of unilateral reductions of Soviet forces and equipment in the USSR, Eastern Europe, and Mongolia, delivered in his December 1988 UN address (Gorbachev 1988), should add impetus to the talks. While this reduction would still leave a considerable Soviet force in being, it would probably effectively eliminate any Soviet capability for a sudden and rapid conventional attack on Europe.

Indeed, the communiqué of the May meeting of the Political Consultative Committee of the Warsaw Pact affirms the concept of "reasonable sufficiency" as the guiding concept on military force posture. Two elements of this concept are central: the idea that reductions of conventional forces should move toward elimination of the capability for offensive actions by either side, and a readiness for "unequal, asymmetrical" reductions in those forces when one side has more than the other (*Pravda* 1987b: 1–2).[20] As elaborated in private talks, some Soviet analysts envision this approach as resulting in, among other things, substantial asymmetrical Soviet reductions of tank forces down to equal levels at numbers substantially below present NATO numbers. Reductions are envisaged through destruction of equipment and disbandment of military units.[21] Mary C. FitzGerald's chapter delves into reasonable sufficiency in more depth.

The idea of substantial reductions in Warsaw Pact and NATO conventional forces, while central to the acceptability of the concept of mutual security to the West, to date has not found much support in Soviet doctrinal analyses, although a reading of FitzGerald's chapter shows that it is increasing. Indeed, one of Ogarkov's main arguments for shifting away from nuclear weapons is to free resources for more effective Soviet preparation for the "air-land battle," the high-technology conventional war of the future. This same consideration underlies the broader military support for reconstruction of the Soviet economic mechanism. Only an economy that is itself at the level of contemporary world technology can sustain a competitive high-technology conventional capability.[22] Conversely, manpower shortages and investment resource shortages similar in kind but far worse in degree to those that led to Khrushchev's unilateral conventional force reductions in 1955–58 are recognized as critical issues by at least some in the Gorbachev leadership. Clearly the question of conventional forces is rapidly becoming the central issue that will shape Western responsiveness to Soviet ideas of mutual security.

Once again, however, the profound nature of the changes in security policy for both East and West implied by mutual security are evident here. What would be the effects on NATO cohesion and effectiveness of a major reduction in American forces in Europe, say from the current 350,000 to perhaps 100,000 troops? Would an American commitment to Europe remain credible? Could Europe sustain a will to defend itself under such conditions, let alone a capability? These questions have already been raised in the debate. Alternatively, would not such a major reduction and thinning out of forces, combined with the necessary intrusive verification measures, bring about a fundamental transformation in Western assessments of the Soviet military "threat" with which U.S. and NATO forces would have to contend?

On the Soviet side, an equally difficult question is whether the Soviet Union would effectively be abandoning its ability to enforce the Brezhnev Doctrine in Eastern Europe in such an agreement. *Pravda* editor Afanasev's response to a reporter's question about the current Soviet view of its 1968 invasion of Czechoslovakia is suggestive in this regard: "It is an incident worthy of deep study. In connection with the restructuring currently being promoted, it is necessary to have a critical review of the evaluation given then on the 'Prague Spring' movement" (*Asahi Shimbun* September 7, 1987: 7).[23] Although the history of the much less ambitious Mutual and Balanced Force Reductions (MBFR) talks does not provide much encouragement for the success of the new conventional arms talks, Soviet readiness to negotiate a basic reduction in its capacity to challenge the West militarily is suggestive of the introduction into policy of an important element in the new Soviet concept of mutual security.

It is not surprising that under Gorbachev the economics of security also push some in the regime to espouse the idea of mutual security. Although the Soviet leadership appeared ready to "pay any price" to achieve and maintain nuclear parity when it believed that such parity would enhance security, the Gorbachev leadership's doubts about the capacity of nuclear deterrence to bring commensurate security raise deep questions about the value of these economic sacrifices.[24] One well-placed adviser expressed this concern as follows:

> I think each of us is stupid if one country is very proud that it has thrown out one-and-a-half trillion dollars in the last six years on weapons, which it will never use and which will become obsolete in five or six years, or ten years, and the country has acquired a tremendous international debt in the process. It is equally stupid that another country is very proud that they have parity with this. It is this entire enterprise that we have to rethink! (Dartmouth Task Force 1987)

Political Relations and Regional Conflicts

Soviet proponents of new thinking in international relations recognize that an effective policy of mutual security must be more broadly conceived than unilateral security. They freely admit that it must address some of the more basic sources of perceived threats to both sides. One well-known Soviet policy adviser recently stressed his "full understanding" that security is "not a military or technical problem" or one that can be solved "by the best possible defense." In his view precisely this recognition has prompted the new approach to arms control under Gorbachev. In fact he suggests that mutual security must involve changes in four spheres: military, political, economic, and humanitarian. The thrust of policy changes in each of these areas should be to reduce the sense of threat posed to the interests of the other and thus gradually to alter in a positive direction the perceptions each has of the intentions of the other (Primakov 1987: 4). Some Soviet analysts go so far as to suggest that this approach "puts forward" the question of "joint management" of questions of military stability[25] as well as of regional conflicts. Concerned about charges of U.S.-Soviet condominium, Soviet thinkers emphasize that this does not mean any imposition of solutions on others, whether in the Middle East, South Africa, or Central America.

The political sphere involves not only acceptance of "the right of each nation to go its own way" but also recognition of the relationship of regional crises to the security of the United States and the Soviet Union. If this idea were to become widely applied as Soviet policy, it would represent a change of some significance. Throughout the 1970s, notwithstanding the 1972 Basic Principles agreement, the Soviet Union insisted that developments in the Third World—with the possible exception of the Middle East—bore no legitimate relationship to U.S.-Soviet relations or to the legitimate security concerns of the United States. American observers, including Henry Kissinger as secretary of state, attributed much of the decline of détente to the one-sided advantages the Soviet Union achieved through proxy interventions in Third World conflicts. Soviet actions were explained by their leaders as ideologically justified support for the national liberation movement. This perspective remains influential even today in some Soviet policy circles.

Yet partly as a result of the impact of the endless military conflicts in Afghanistan, Angola, Nicaragua, and elsewhere and partly from more honest analysis of the reasons for the failure of Soviet-oriented regimes and movements in the Third World,[26] some Soviet advisers and policymakers seem to adopt a very different view. One Soviet analyst explained this view as follows:

> In the nuclear age there are very rigid limits governing ideologically motivated political policies. That is why, for example, the Soviet Union

is now so cautious not to get involved in any form in revolutionary processes in the Western Hemisphere. This caution arises in spite of the fact that from the traditional ideological point of view, there is some sense in getting involved. (Dartmouth Task Force 1987)

In a somewhat different context, another Soviet analyst expressed the new tendency in Soviet thinking about the Third World powerfully when he said, "The experience of the past two decades suggests that the more deeply we each become involved in regional conflicts, militarily particularly, the greater the damage to our international influence, reputation and prestige." He continued, "you had this experience in Vietnam"; and he was willing to accept, when questioned specifically, that the Soviet experiences—particularly Afghanistan—had helped to encourage this conclusion.[27]

Gorbachev himself has expressed support for these views in his statement, "Any attempts, direct or indirect, to influence the development 'of not our own' countries, to interfere in this development, should be ruled out." Rejecting the former Soviet position that "no one can guarantee the status quo," Gorbachev asserted that all peoples have "sovereignty to choose the roads or forms of development," including "the right to the social status quo" (*Pravda* 1987i: 1). In his own view Gorbachev appears to see Soviet interests as lying in the settlement of regional conflicts through mediation and multilateral peace-keeping efforts, rather than in encouraging turmoil and conflict. He repeated these views in an important speech before the United Nations (Gorbachev 1988). The withdrawal of Soviet forces from Afghanistan is a behavioral indicator of this attitude.[28]

The Economic Dimension of Security

In the Soviet view the economic dimension of security has two aspects: economic relations between East and West and relations between the north and the south. Traditionally Soviet economic policy has been based on the principle of autarky—that is, maximizing economic independence from the outside world. This policy reflected the reality of limited East-West economic contacts in the 1930s and the postwar period, but it also was indicative of an ideologically based concern about involvement with capitalist economies which might provide leverage to the enemy. This view was only partially modified during the 1970s. Even though Soviet foreign trade grew significantly in this period, this growth was governed more by import substitution concerns than by any real effort at participation in an economically driven international division of labor.

Although the leadership toyed with the idea of a significant opening of the Soviet economy to the effects of competition in the global market, this concept was dropped after the failure of the U.S.-Soviet trade agreement in 1974. The massive foreign debts acquired by Poland and other Eastern European countries as a result of their efforts to integrate more fully into world markets only reinforced autarkic tendencies in the last years of Brezhnev's regime.

By early 1987, however, signs of a reassessment were becoming visible. The most important of these is the new law permitting joint ventures with Western firms in the Soviet Union, including equity interest by the Western partners. In a historic departure the traditional monopoly over foreign trade exercised by the Ministry of Foreign Trade was partially broken open by this and other legislation, as John E. Tedstrom discusses in his chapter. The Gorbachev leadership has also shown renewed interest in participation in such international economic institutions as the GATT. In short there are signs that autarky is being replaced by acceptance of the economic interdependence of the socialist and capitalist economies. In a speech designed to stimulate Soviet new thinking, Gorbachev called for "active steps to seek new opportunities for our entry into the world economy" (1987: 4–6). Such a move has the potential for altering Soviet assessments of its own interests in the stability and orderly growth of the world economic system.

Soviet appeals to its Third World clients and friends to stay within the Western economic system are another important sign of this trend. But here the Gorbachev vision is broader. Some Soviet policy advisers under Gorbachev increasingly perceive the growing gap between the rich north, in which they now include themselves, and the poor south as posing a fundamental and growing security problem, not only for the West but for the Soviet Union as well. As one Soviet analyst stressed: "We must recognize that we cannot have really dependable security if it goes on this way, because it destabilizes whole regions." Gorbachev has put it only slightly differently: "A world in which a whole continent can find itself on the brink of death from starvation . . . is not a safe world. Neither is a world safe in which a multitude of countries and peoples are stifling in a noose of debt" (*Pravda* 1987i: 1). In this connection Gorbachev has called for a thorough reevaluation of Soviet economic pledges to the Third World (Gorbachev 1987b: 4–6) and an overall investigation of the Third World debt structure (Gorbachev 1988: 15). The traditional Soviet position on Third World economic problems asserts not only that their economic plight was the sole responsibility of the former colonialists, but that turmoil in the Third World is an inevitable result of neocolonialism and one that will "inevitably" facilitate revolutionary progress.

Now some Soviet thinkers see Third World turmoil as an increasingly probable source of Soviet-U.S. conflict and therefore one that is contrary to the interests of both countries. That these fears may have even deeper, subtler roots is suggested by the comment of another Soviet policy adviser: "Our two countries in perhaps fifty years will be the only ones to whom each can turn in time of need. We live in a very complicated world. We are a minority, a very small minority, 10 percent in a world ridden with problems. We do not think about the real problems which we will have to face in ten years or fifteen years, in one way or another" (Dartmouth Task Force, 1987).

The conclusion Soviet advocates of "new thinking" are now drawing with increasing frequency is that it is in the security interests of both the USSR and the United States to cooperate in alleviating problems of Third World economies.[29]

The Question of Credibility

Thoughtful persons must naturally ask whether the "new" Soviet thinking discussed here presages significant and genuine new directions in Soviet foreign policy or merely one more disinformation or propaganda campaign. Precisely because the ideas in the Gorbachev vision do go to the heart of traditional assumptions underlying U.S. policy toward the Soviet Union, evidence of their introduction into policy and behavior must be particularly persuasive before it should be taken very seriously by the U.S. policy community. We must also recognize that in any major policy debate there are seldom clear winners or losers. Rather, policy in one or another arena may come to reflect more or less fully the ideas supported by one political alliance or another. Particularly in Soviet policy debates, accommodation and compromise have been the norm rather than a clear winner or loser. Judgments about the credibility of Soviet new thinking should be based on three kinds of evidence: ideas and statements of intention, policy declarations, and behavior. Ideas and policy declarations may be sufficient to call forth U.S. interest in exploratory discussions and negotiations. Moreover, they can serve as guideposts identifying behaviors we might expect as evidence of meaningful changes in policy. The more fully the ideas or vision described here is supported by appropriate Soviet behaviors, the more credible will become Soviet assertions of really "new thinking" in foreign policy.

For many Americans the question of the Soviet threat is more than military and goes beyond the question of Soviet involvement in the

Third World. It is difficult not to feel threatened by a Soviet Union that denies its citizens basic political rights. Soviet domestic politics bears most directly on foreign policy precisely on these issues. Questions of Soviet emigration policy and treatment of dissidents were constant impediments to even the modest efforts at détente in the 1970s. Under Gorbachev we are beginning to see a new approach to the treatment of dissidents and at least a partial reassessment of emigration policy. While it is still too early to assess how far these changes will go, more than 12,000 Soviet Jews and nearly as many German and Armenian Soviet citizens were permitted to emigrate in 1987, as compared with only a thousand for the previous year (Goldman 1989). Moreover, reports suggested that only 400 political prisoners were still interred in Soviet labor camps and prisons.[30] As important, an overall review of Soviet criminal procedure and the legal code is under way.

Arms control is an area in which there is already considerable behavioral evidence of a new Soviet approach. Most attention has focused on specific arms reductions proposals, but what may be most indicative of a turn toward mutual security is the shift in Soviet policy on verification. The former insistence on "national-technical means" reflected, among other things, a deep-seated Soviet and Russian paranoia and fear of the "enemy." The level of intrusiveness accepted in the Intermediate Nuclear Forces treaty, in which, among other steps, Western observers are stationed at factory and warehouse sites, represents a sea change in Soviet attitudes toward cooperative verification measures. Similarly, Soviet agreement to eliminate two entire classes of nuclear systems, albeit representing only 4 percent of the total arsenals, adds an increment of credibility to Gorbachev's stated objective of eliminating at least 95 percent of present nuclear arsenals. This issue is discussed in further detail in the chapters by Robert L. Arnett and Robert W. Clawson.

The credibility of the Soviet assertions about its desires to effect a total withdrawal of troops from Afghanistan were demonstrated in February 1989. In sum, the credibility of mutual security must be built step by step through arms control agreements, settlement of regional conflicts, and such changes in Soviet society and politics that the majority of Westerners are persuaded that the Soviets have not simply limited their capability to threaten the West, but do not intend to do so.

Gorbachev's Vision and Soviet Politics

Ultimately the fate of Gorbachev's own vision of mutual security may well be decided by the pace and extent of domestic change. Yet the difficulties of realizing Gorbachev's domestic vision are clearly more formidable than the challenge he faces in foreign policy, for here, in addition to well-placed ideological foes, he must deal with deeply entrenched bureaucracies highly practiced in defending their interests, a highly suspicious political apparatus,[31] and a largely apathetic public (*Mlada Fronta* 1987: 50–51). The obstacles to successful reform of the Soviet economy and society are explicitly recognized by Soviet officials.[32] Valentin Falin, head of the International Department of the Central Committee, stated in an interview, "Economic reforms . . . during the 70 years since the revolution were, in a word, a history of miserable failure." Observing the deep opposition that reform efforts generate, Falin noted that "both Khrushchev and Kosygin, who succeeded him, lost their position, despite their efforts to work economic reforms" (*Tokoyo Shimbun* 1987: 8). Suggestive of the lack of incentive for the bureaucratic apparatus to support reforms is Falin's statement that unless the current staff of "19 million people working in the state administrative organizations in the USSR [are] reduced by 30 to 40 percent, . . . we cannot solve other problems." Concluded Falin, "It is true that strong opposition and resistance exist" (*Tokoyo Shimbun* 1987: 8). Conversely, to fail to bring about a far more efficient economy through far-reaching reforms, as a Soviet economist observed, "would mean gradually descending to the position of an underdeveloped third-rank power" (Antonov 1987: 2).

Prominent among Gorbachev's efforts to broaden his coalition and hem in the opposition is his campaign to introduce some degree of "democratization" or political competition, protected by secret ballots, within governmental deliberative bodies, in the workplace, and even within the Party.[33] At the June 1988 Party Conference, Gorbachev successfully pushed through proposals to formalize limited terms of office and more open electoral procedures. Yet as reflected in frequent press reports, these proposals have encountered bitter and determined opposition from the Party and state apparatus, precisely those opponents whose positions are threatened by democratization. The outcome of this struggle will significantly affect Gorbachev's power and thus the whole reform effort.

The best-known element of Gorbachev's domestic program is the policy of glasnost'. As George E. Hudson suggests in Chapter One, this policy is designed to enlist the intelligentsia, cultural leaders, and the press to Gorbachev's side in the fundamental debates on Soviet foreign and domestic policy he has unleashed. A central component of glasnost' is a far-ranging reappraisal not only of Stalinism but of the institutional and political heritage of Stalin. The political purpose of this reevaluation of the Stalinist past was formulated clearly in a recent letter to *Pravda:* "To learn nothing from those tragic examples means to repeat over and over again the same mistake, whereby we were fed nothing but quotations and promises for many decades" (*Pravda* 1987h: 3). Only by critically rethinking the entire experience of Stalinism, in both foreign and domestic policy, some of Gorbachev's supporters contend, will any thoroughgoing, lasting redirection of Soviet society and policy become possible. It is precisely the effort to critically reexamine the Stalinist period, however, that already has generated open and virulent criticism.[34] A deputy editor of *Pravda,* Dmitrii Valovoi, criticizing Rybakov's anti-Stalinist novel, *Children of the Arbat,* asked, "Who built socialism and who brought about victory in the war? If Stalin were a bad guy and all his close associates were foolish, then who assumed the leadership?" (*Mainichi Shimbun* September 4, 1987). Even Gorbachev has had to say that in reassessing the past it is important that people who lived through those times believe "their life was not in vain" (*Pravda* 1987e: 3).[35]

Although foreign policy was traditionally the prerogative of a very small group within the Soviet leadership, Gorbachev will have to win and maintain the support of a rather broad coalition to implement his own sweeping vision. Such a coalition will need to include significant segments of the military leadership, Party ideologues, and others traditionally hostile to U.S.-Soviet accommodation. This issue is discussed in detail in the chapters by William J. Bishop and Jan S. Adams, but it is worth noting here that some well-informed Soviet analysts feel that Gorbachev's vision is shared only by a minority consisting in part of members of the political and cultural intelligentsia. Ordinarily these people, including members of the Academy of Sciences—particularly those in the foreign policy institutes—have not been seen as an especially influential group. However, when such intellectuals serve a strong and influential patron, and when that patron encourages creative political thinking and is responsive to new ideas, as was the case to a degree under Khrushchev but seems particularly true today under Gorbachev, then such academics may play a critical role. The revitalized Central Committee foreign policy staff, under Secretary E. K. Ligachev's and Valentin Falin's leadership—into which a number of talented, creative intellectuals have recently been drawn—provides a more politically significant reservoir of support for Gorbachev's "new thinking." Moreover the replacement of large numbers of top military officers in the past four years, many of whom are associated with Gorbachev or appear to accept much of his program, suggests that the Soviet leader is moving swiftly to bring the military into his reform coalition.[36]

Where is Gorbachev's strongest opposition? Although it is possible only to speculate, his opposition may well include the traditionally conservative regional Party leaders, parts of the KGB, and a large number of senior military officers, as well as parts of the Party Central Committee and its staff and doubtless even some members of the Politburo.[37]

What factors will determine the course of the debate over Gorbachev's vision for a reconstruction of foreign relations? Gorbachev's greatest chances for long-term success arise from having a series of policy outcomes that are labeled by others as successes. By gradually building practical evidence of the workability of his new approach to foreign policy, Gorbachev can undermine the credibility of those who insist on the continuing validity of traditional Soviet ideas and thereby strengthen his own political influence. This need may, in fact, account for some of the high risks Gorbachev appears to have taken in the search for an early arms control agreement.

The extent to which Gorbachev is able to institutionalize support for his policies, so that those who support his approach occupy the decisive policy and administrative positions and those who are doubters or opponents are rendered powerless to side-track or undermine his policy, will also powerfully influence the long-term prospects for new thinking. Traditionally the literature on Soviet leadership has seen the skillful use of the power of appointment as the central factor in a Soviet leader's power (Fainsod 1965: chaps. 5 and 6). Already this power has been used to reshape the national security policy apparatus[38] strengthening Gorbachev's control over the military leadership, the foreign ministry, and the CPSU Secretariat. However, Gorbachev himself recognizes the importance of winning broad backing not only from the foreign policy establishment but from the public as well. As noted earlier, the policies of glasnost' and democratization are designed in part to encourage supporters among the public to pressure middle-level administrators, including the Party apparatus, to be more responsive to Gorbachev's program. Unless Gorbachev is willing and able to implement democratic institutional reforms that enable the public to express its support in persuasive ways, this may do him little good against entrenched bureaucratic opposition.[39]

At the same time, Gorbachev runs two great risks: that of inertia and that of failure. If Gorbachev does not push his programs with sufficient vigor and speed, the bureaucracies threatened by his programs may feel it safe to ignore him. His policy objectives will then be undermined by the forces of inertia. However, if Gorbachev pushes too hard, too fast, in too many directions at once, he may suddenly find that he has alienated too many essential interests. The danger then is that these interests will coalesce and remove him. Gorbachev's apparent sensitivity to his various constituencies may reflect his attempt to deal with these potential problems. By knowing when a certain group is ready to move, he can see they get some movement; by being willing to hold back implementation until the right people are on board, he can try to forestall failure.

It is important not to believe that American policy can influence these events in any specific, calculable manner; however, the history of the 1970s clearly demonstrates that American behavior can and does have substantial cumulative impacts on the credibility and sustainability of a particular Soviet policy line. Gorbachev's vision contains both positive and negative elements for the West, but he seems determined to transform the nature of the U.S.-Soviet relationship. Whether this will be done in a manner that strengthens Western security and interests as well as Soviet depends in some measure on how well the United States understands the issues in the debate over Gorbachev's vision and how thoroughly and creatively it reevaluates the premises of U.S. security policy.

The United States must be ready to meet the constructive elements of Soviet new thinking halfway. The West must be prepared to test the Soviet commitment to these ideas across the range of issues where change is under way. This will require readiness to go beyond criticism of the weakness in Soviet ideas and the shortcomings in Soviet behavior to creative effective responses that meet the interests of both sides in a more stable, secure world. These issues are addressed in George E. Hudson's concluding chapter.

NOTES

1. Although it can be argued that this debate began at the April 1985 Plenum shortly before Gorbachev's ascension to power, the dialogue appears to have been formally launched within the Soviet foreign policy community by Gorbachev in a speech to leading officials at the Ministry of Foreign Affairs on May 23, 1986, summarized in *Vestnik Ministerstva Inostrannykh del SSSR*, No. 1 (August 4, 1987), pp. 4–6. In this speech Gorbachev called for "a more sober, a broader evaluation of the specific facts, rather than viewing everything only from the point of view of one's own interests." Otherwise, he argued, "without meeting our partners halfway . . . it will be difficult to achieve any improvement in international relations."

2. Examples include intrusive regimes with respect to chemical weapons and the dismantling of INF forces. Related illustrations include the mutual inspection of troop maneuvers, the mutual inspection of chemical munitions factories, the on-site visit by a group of congressmen to the much-disputed Krasnoyarsk radar station, and cooperation in the on-site calibration of nuclear test-monitoring seismic equipment. See Gorbachev's summary of these activities in *Pravda* (1987i), pp. 1–2. For a report on the radar site visit, see *The New York Times*, September 7, 1987, p. 1.

3. William G. Hyland's article (1987) is a thoughtful and informed overview of Soviet new thinking and its implication for U.S. policy.

4. For a review and analysis that sees a "third revolution" in Soviet military strategy, see Odom, (1985). See also the chapter by Mary C. FitzGerald in this book and FitzGerald (1987).

5. See the important statement on the Warsaw Pact Doctrine (*Pravda* 1987c). For a concise Soviet statement of the meaning and implications of this doctrinal change, see the comments of deputy chief of the CPSU International Department, Vadim Zagladin, to a visiting French delegation reported by TASS on September 30, 1987, and printed in Foreign Broadcast Information Service (FBIS), *Daily Report: Soviet Union* (FBIS-SOV-87-190, October 1, 1987), p. 36.

6. The rationale and main directions for reform of the economy are laid out in M. S. Gorbachev's report to the June 1987 Plenum of the Central Committee, reported in *Pravda* (1987d). This report has been followed by a new Law on State Enterprises and new directives on price reform.

7. An explicit recognition of this motivation is made by Major-General Yuri Lebedev, a leading spokesman for the Soviet General Staff in an interview with the Spanish paper *Diario 16,* August 3, 1987. This interview was translated in FBIS, *Daily Report: Soviet Union* (FBIS-SOV-87-161, August 20, 1987), pp. 42–43. See also John E. Tedstrom's chapter in this volume.

8. This point was made in several different ways by Vitalli Zhurkin and Nikolai Shishlin on the radio program "International Observers Roundtable" for May 31, 1987.

9. This point was specifically emphasized by Lebedev in the interview cited in note 7. See FBIS, *Daily Report: Soviet Union* (FBIS-SOV-87-161, August 20, 1987), pp. 42–43.

10. Internationalizing the discussion of approaches to a new system of security is the point of Gorbachev's article on a "secure world" (*Pravda* 1987i), pp. 1–2.

11. This includes both public and less visible efforts to encourage scholars, policy analysts, and practitioners to free themselves from old dogmas and to learn to think "independently" about both basic and particular issues in foreign policy. Two major examples of this effort include an article by Politburo member Alexander Iakovlev (1987), pp. 3–22; and a speech by Politburo member E. A. Shevardnadze (1988).

12. This is part of the function of his highly public visits and "walkabouts" to many parts of the Soviet Union.

13. This is the main point of Hyland's argument (1987), especially in the questions he poses on pp. 20–21.

14. For a Soviet view of the "requirement for the unification of human culture" as a foundation for new thinking, see *Sovetskaia kul'tura,* August 22, 1987, p. 3.

15. A distinguished panel of American policy analysts, convened by the Institute for East-West Security Studies, concluded that America has a strong self-interest in the success of Gorbachev's domestic and foreign policy reforms, describing them as the "most encouraging developments of our era." See the summary report by MacMillan and Ullman (1987), p. 23. Charles Gati (1987), on the other hand, pointing to the fact that the Cold War really arose over Soviet domination of Eastern Europe, cautions that Soviet treatment of that region—that is, the extent to which the Soviet Union is willing to grant real autonomy to this region—should be the real measure of Soviet intent in restructuring international relations.

16. In his article on a "secure world," for example, Gorbachev describes his ideas as taking shape "in the process of evolving the new political thinking" (*Pravda* 1987: 1).

17. The conversations that form the primary source material for this chapter took place from 1986 through 1988 in Moscow and Washington within the framework of the Soviet-American Dartmouth Conference. Founded in 1960 by Norman Cousins at the urging of former President Eisenhower, this forum has held regular meetings for the past 27 years. These meetings are always unofficial and off the record. In January 1986 by mutual agreement a special task force on political relations was formed to exchange

and develop ideas on the most basic questions in the U.S.-Soviet relationship. To the present this task force has met three times. Though under the Dartmouth Conference ground rules it is not possible to associate specific ideas with particular individuals, listing the participants on both sides is permissible. The principal Soviet and American citizens taking part in these discussions are as follows.

Soviet participants: Vitalli Zhurkin (Co-Chair), Deputy Director, Institute of U.S.A. and Canada Studies, USSR Academy of Sciences; Georgii Arbatov, Director, Institute of U.S.A. and Canada Studies, USSR Academy of Sciences; Evgenii Primakov, Director, Institute of the World Economy and International Relations, USSR Academy of Sciences; Nikolai Shishlin, Propaganda Department, Secretariat of the CPSU Central Committee; Vladimir Baranovskii, Head of Section, Institute of World Economy and International Relations, USSR Academy of Sciences; Vitalli Ganzha, Colonel, General Staff, USSR Ministry of Defense; Andrei Kortunov, Researcher, Institute of U.S.A. and Canada Studies, USSR Academy of Sciences; Mikhail Milstein, Senior Analyst, Institute of U.S.A. and Canada Studies, USSR Academy of Sciences; Alexander Nikitin, Senior Researcher, Institute of U.S.A. and Canada Studies, USSR Academy of Sciences; Sergei Rogov, U.S. Representative, Institute of U.S.A. and Canada Studies, USSR Academy of Sciences; and Genrikh Trofimenko, Chief of Section, Institute of U.S.A. and Canada Studies, USSR Academy of Sciences.

American participants: Seweryn Bialer (Co-Chair), Director, Research Institute on International Change, Columbia University; John Buchanan, former member of Congress, Chairman, People for the American Way; Thomas Foley, U.S. Representative, Democrat, Washington; Albert Gore, U.S. Senator, Democrat, Tennessee; Harold Saunders, Guest Scholar, The Brookings Institution, former Assistant Secretary of State for Near East and South Asian Affairs; Paul Simon, U.S. Senator, Democrat, Illinois; Stephen Solarz, U.S. Representative, Democrat, New York; Philip Stewart, Director, Program in Soviet International Behavior, Mershon Center, The Ohio State University, Dartmouth Conference Coordinator; Daniel Yankelovich, Chairman, Daniel Yankelovich Group, Incorporated; and Cyrus Vance, former U.S. Secretary of State, 1976–79.

18. In his *Pravda* article, for example, Gorbachev observes that "dangers have emerged which put into question the very immortality of the human race." This point of view has led to an official Soviet position that denies that nuclear deterrence is either valid or acceptable. In the same article Gorbachev asserted, "It is more correct to say that a world war has been averted despite the existence of nuclear weapons." Until nuclear weapons are eliminated, the Soviet view does seem to accept the concept of minimal deterrence, seen by Gorbachev as achievable with about 5 percent of the present nuclear weapons (*Pravda* 1987i: 1).

19. For a careful analysis of Gorbachev's January 15, 1986 proposals on the elimination of nuclear and other weapons of mass destruction by the year 2000, see Matthew Evangelista (1986); for an illuminating Soviet exchange on the implications of traditional nuclear deterrence, see the dialogue between a Soviet writer and a nuclear submarine commander in *Moskovskie novosti*, March 8, 1987, and the "clarification" in *Literaturnaia gazeta*, May 6, 1987, p. 7.

20. See particularly section 4 of the report. The meaning and implications of these ideas are elaborated in a number of Soviet sources. See, for example, FBIS (1987a, 1987b), *New Times* (1987), Iazov (1987), and Semeiko (1987).

21. There has been opposition in the past to these ideas, and it probably still exists. See, for instance, the interview with the head of the Malinovskii Military Academy of Armored Troops, Colonel General V. M. Gordienko, who stated, "both now and in the forseeable future, there is no alternative to the tank as the leading weapon system of

ground forces, especially in view of the fact that tanks and tank troops are strong not only on the offensive but also in defense" (1987: 1).

22. Some Soviet analysts are trying to provide such a doctrinal basis by arguing that technology now and for a long time to come favors the defense over the offense. See Kokoshin and Larionov (1987). We are indebted to James M. McConnell for bringing this article to our attention.

23. For a more cautious view, see Gati (1987).

24. In recognition of the need to deal directly and openly with the economic costs of its own military policy, the Soviet leadership has given numerous hints about a readiness to publish a full and detailed military budget. Gorbachev recently affirmed this intention in a remark on the "comparability of defense spending." "I think that given proper effort already within the next 2 or 3 years we will be able to compare the figures that are of interest to us and our partners and that would symmetrically reflect the expenditures of the sides" (*Pravda* 1987j).

25. Two manifestations of at least a recognition of the need for greater contacts at the military level as a step toward creating a new security system are the meetings between the Soviet defense minister and the U.S. secretary of defense on March 15–17, 1988.

26. For a careful study of the Soviet experiential and intellectual roots of this reanalysis, see Valkenier (1986). See also the review essay by George Breslauer (1987), and Roger E. Kanet's chapter in this book.

27. One of the often ignored Soviet incentives for rethinking their occupation of Afghanistan is its domestic impacts. Articles in the Soviet press suggest that this is indeed a growing problem. See *Pravda* (1987f) and *Pravda Ukrainy* (1987). On the growing problem of drug use in the Soviet Army, see *Krasnaia zvezda* (1987), p. 2.

28. A significant sign of Soviet willingness to "pay a price" with an important ally as a step toward creating more favorable conditions for a negotiated settlement in the Middle East was Gorbachev's statement to President Hafiz al-Asad of Syria that "reliance on military power in settling the conflict [in the Middle East] has become completely discredited" (*Pravda* 1987a), p. 2. This statement has been followed by a deliberate and visible slowdown in the delivery of Soviet weapons promised earlier to Syria. For a useful Soviet view of its commitment to a constructive role in a negotiated settlement, see the interview with Evgenii Primakov in *Al-Hawadith*, September 25, 1987, pp. 26–27, reported in FBIS, *Daily Report: Soviet Union* (FBIS-SOV-87-190), pp. 27–31; see also the interview by Alexandr Zotov, a Central Committee consultant on the Middle East and one of the architects of the Soviet Union's new approach to the Middle East, in *Al-Watan Al-'Arabi*, June 26, 1987.

29. See Gorbachev's proposals on tying debt repayments to the level of Third World country exports (*Pravda* 1987i).

30. As of the end of September 1987, according to Andrei Sakharov, only about 400 "prisoners of conscience" remained in the Soviet Union. Agence France Presse, September 29, 1987, reported in FBIS *Daily Report: Soviet Union*, (FBIS-SOV-87-188), September 29, 1987).

31. From the tone of their commentaries, many observers have identified Politburo members V. M. Chebrikov, head of the Party Commission on Legal Policy, and Yegor Ligachev, head of the Party Commission on Agriculture, as at best dubious of the scope and pace of the policies of democratization and glasnost'. See, for example, V. M. Chebrikov's address at the one-hundredth anniversary of the birth of Felix Dzerzhinskii (*Pravda* 1987g); and Legachev's warning against "one-sided" interpretations of "individual periods of history," in *Pravda* (1987i), p. 2.

32. For a view from the viewpoint of a plant manager, see *Izvestiia* (1987), p. 2.

33. The policy of "democratization" was announced at the January 1987 CPSU Central Committee Plenum by M. S. Gorbachev (1987a) in his address, "On Restructuring and the Party's Cadre Policy." For an insightful discussion of problems in implementing electiveness of officers in the Academy of Sciences, see the three articles in *Literaturnaia gazeta*, "So What Is More Evident to the Bosses," September 9, 1987, p. 10.

34. For some of the polemics, particularly those who argue that critical reexamination of the past determines Soviet patriotism, see *Pravda,* August 21 and September 7, 1987.

35. See also Ligachev's warning cited in note 31. An important official statement on the Stalinist period is Gorbachev's address on the eve of the seventieth anniversary of the Soviet revolution, reported in FBIS, *Daily Report: Soviet Union* (FBIS-SOV-87-212, November 3, 1987). See also Vodolazhskii (1987–88), pp. 14–15.

36. Also see the chapter by William J. Bishop.

37. Yegor Ligachev, Viktor Chebrikov, and Ukrainian Party chief Vladimir Shcherbitski have all expressed caution or skepticism about significant elements of Gorbachev's program.

38. See the chapters by Jan S. Adams and William J. Bishop in this book.

39. For an excellent analysis of the effects of bureaucratic opposition on Khrushchev's power, see Hyland and Shryock (1968).

References

Akhromeev, S. F. (1987, December 22). *Krasnaia zvezda,* p. 1.

Antonov, M. (1987, September 17). "To Go One's Own Way." *Sotsialisticheskaia industriia.*

Breslauer, George (1987). "Ideology and Learning in Soviet Third World Policy." *World Politics,* 39(3), 429–48.

Burns, James MacGregor (1978). *Leadership.* New York: Harper & Row.

Dartmouth Task Force on Political Relations (1987). Mimeo report of a meeting, December 1986, Washington, D. C. Dayton: Kettering Foundation.

Evangelista, Matthew (1986). "The New Soviet Approach to Security." *World Policy Journal,* 3(Fall), 561–99.

Fainsod, Merle (1965). *How Russia Is Ruled* (rev. ed.). Cambridge: Harvard University Press.

FBIS (Foreign Broadcast Information Service) (1987a). "International Observers Roundtable." In *Daily Report: Soviet Union* (FBIS-SOV-87–104, June 1), pp. CC1–CC7.

——— (1987b). "News Conference on Warsaw Pact Military Doctrine" with V. F. Petrovskii, deputy foreign minister, Colonel-General M. A. Gareev, deputy chief of the General Staff, and others. In *Daily Report: Soviet Union* (FBIS-SOV-87–120, June 23), pp. AA1–AA4.

FitzGerald, Mary C. (1987). *The Soviet Civilian Leadership and the Military High Command, 1976–1986.* RAND Report R-3521-AF. Santa Monica, CA: RAND Corporation.

Garthoff, Raymond L. (1985). *Détente and Confrontation.* Washington, D. C.: Brookings Institution.

Gati, Charles (1987). "Gorbachev and Eastern Europe." *Foreign Affairs*, 65(5), 958–75.

Goldman, Ari (1989, April 5). "4,000 Soviet Jews Migrated in March." *New York Times*, A10.

Gorbachev, M. S. (1987a, January 28). "On Restructuring and the Party's Cadre Policy." *Pravda*, pp. 1–4.

────── (1987b, August 5). "Time for Restructuring." Delivered at the Ministry of Foreign Affairs, May 23, 1986. Summarized in *Vestnik Ministerstva Inostrannykh Del SSSR*, No. 1, 4–6.

────── (1988, December 8). "M. S. Gorbachev's Speech at the U.N. Organization." *Pravda*. Translated in FBIS *Daily Report: Soviet Union* (FBIS-SOV-88–236, December 8), pp. 11–19.

Gordienko, Colonel General V. M. (1987, September 13). "Stronger than Armor." *Trud*, p. 1.

Hutchinson Robert (1987, June 13). "Gorbachev Tightens Grip on Soviet High Command." *Jane's Defense Weekly*, no. 23.

Hyland, William G. (1987). "Reagan-Gorbachev III." *Foreign Affairs*, 66(1), 7–21.

Hyland, William G., and Richard W. Shryock (1986). *The Fall of Khrushchev*. New York: Funk and Wagnalls.

Iakovlev, Alexander (1987). "Social Sciences and the Attainment of a Qualitatively New State of Soviet Society." *Kommunist*, no. 8, 3–22.

Iazov, Army General D. T. (1987, July 27). "The Military Doctrine of the Warsaw Pact Is the Doctrine of the Defense of Peace and Socialism." *Pravda*, p. 5.

Izvestiia (1987, September 13). "A Director's Monologue." P. 2.

Kokoshin, A., and V. Larionov (1987). "The Battle of Kursk in Light of Today's Defensive Doctrine." *Mirovaia Ekonomika i Mezhdunarodnye Otnosheniia*, no. 8, 32–36.

Krasnaia zvezda (1987, September 4). "Hashish in an Envelope." P. 2.

MacMillan, Whitney, and Richard H. Ullman (1987, October 7). "America's Self-Interest in Helping Gorbachev." *New York Times*, p. 23.

Mainichi Shimbun (1987). September 4.

Mlada Fronta (1987). Discussion by *Ogonek* deputy chief editor, reported in FBIS, *Daily Report: Soviet Union* (FBIS-SOV-87-177, September 14), pp. 50–51.

New Times (1987, July 13). "Of Reasonable Sufficiency, Precarious Parity, and International Security," no. 27, pp. 18–21.

New York Times (1988a, April 12).

────── (1988b, September 7).

────── (1988c, December 8). "The Gorbachev Visit: The Problem of Mankind's Survival."

Odom, William E. (1985). "Soviet Force Posture: Dilemmas and Directions." *Problems of Communism* (July-August), 1–14.

Peterson, Peter G., Henry Kissinger, and Cyrus R. Vance (1987). *Report of the Council Delegation Visit to the USSR*. New York: Council on Foreign Relations, February.

Pravda (1987a, April 25).

────── (1987b, May 30). "Communiqué on Conference of Warsaw Pact States."

────── (1987c, May 31). "On the Military Doctrine of the Warsaw Pact Member States." Pp. 1–2.

────── (1987d, June 26). M. S. Gorbachev's Report to the June 1987 Central Committee Plenum. Pp. 1–5.

────── (1987e, July 15).

────── (1987f, August 5). "I Did Not Send You to Afghanistan . . ."

────── (1987g, September 11). V. M. Chebrikov's Address at the 100th Anniversary of the Birth of Felix Dzerzhinskii.

────── (1987h, September 14).

——— (1987i, September 17). "The Reality and Guarantees of a Secure World." Pp. 1–2.

Pravda Ukrainy (1987, September 6). "People with a Particular Destiny."

Primakov, Evgenii (1987, July 9). "New Philosophy of Foreign Policy." *Pravda*.

Semeiko, Lev (1987, August 13). "Instead of Mountains . . . On the Principle of Reasonable Sufficiency." *Izvestiia*, p. 5.

Shevardnadze, E. A. (1988). "Shevardnadze Speech to July Conference Noted." *Vestnik Ministerstva Inostrannykh del SSSR* 15, 27–46. Translated in FBIS, *Daily Report: Soviet Union* (FBIS-SOV-88-184, September 22), pp. 1–24.

Tokoyo Shimbun (1987, August 27). Interview with Valentin Falin.

Valkenier, Elizabeth (1986). "Revolutionary Change in the Third World: Recent Soviet Reassessments." *World Politics,* 38(3), 415–35.

Vodolazhskii, V. (1987–88, December 28–January 3). "Facing Up to the Truth." *Nedelia,* 52(28), 14–15.

Zhurkin, Vitalli, and Nikolai Shishlin (1987). "International Observers Roundtable" radio program. Translated in FBIS, *Daily Report: Soviet Union* (FBIS-SOV-87–161, August 20), pp. 42–43.

• CHAPTER FOUR •

The Soviet Economy: Growth, Decay, and Reform

John E. Tedstrom
Radio Liberty

Although the Soviet economy never achieved superpower status, its size and growth for much of the postwar period has been of a magnitude that supported a commitment to defense and national security virtually second to none. Recently, however, Soviet economic decay has thrown into doubt the ability of the Soviet authorities to maintain their traditional pattern of defense spending and, indeed, the prudence of their traditional national security doctrine and policy.

This chapter assesses the current Soviet regime's capacity to change its system in the face of the relatively recent developments in the Soviet and global economic environments. Toward this end the chapter examines the Soviet economy from three interdependent perspectives. The first section examines the Soviet growth record with an eye toward explaining why the Soviet economy grew so rapidly during the 1950s and 1960s and why it slowed so dramatically during the 1970s and 1980s. The second section presents the Soviet Union's goals for its economic future as Soviet planners have outlined them in the Twelfth Five-Year Plan (FYP) and the Plan to the Year 2000. The third section examines how the Soviet leadership plans to achieve those goals through a "radical reform" of the Soviet economic system. The discussion of Soviet economic performance will necessarily be quantitative in nature. Where possible, official Soviet statistics are used in the analysis. Where Western estimates are believed to be more appropriate, for the sake of either coverage or accuracy I rely on the data base developed by the U.S. Central Intelligence Agency. These estimates, though sometimes controversial, were chosen because of their consistency and comprehensiveness and because the methodology used to generate the estimates is well defined.[1]

The history of Soviet economic performance is uneven. On one hand, the economy grew rapidly in the two decades after Stalin's death. This growth in output enabled the Soviet military to grow to superpower status and enabled Soviet consumers to enjoy increases in their standard of living. On the other hand, Soviet economic growth rates have been generally declining since World War II. As portrayed in Table 4.1 by the mid-1970s annual growth rates of the Soviet economy had fallen to approximately half of the 1960s level with little hope of significant improvement in the foreseeable future. The technological gap between East and West appeared to widen, and improvements in Soviet living standards all but disappeared. In general Soviet society declined to intolerable levels as the incidence of alcoholism, corruption, and black marketeering increased and worker motivation deteriorated.

By the late 1970s many in the Soviet Union recognized that the extensive growth strategy they had been relying on had lost its efficacy. Policy statements began to emphasize resource stringency and the need for increases in productivity. By the early 1980s it appears that even the Soviet military establishment was told that it would have to get by on less so that a larger share of output could go to investment. Many Soviet economists also recognized, however, that merely calling for improved efficiency and reallocating output among end users was no solution to the systemic problems that were causing the Soviet economy to decline. A serious and increasingly public discussion arose among Soviet policymakers and academics as to how best to reform their economic system in hopes of generating long-term economic growth and prosperity.

This discussion has now come to a head in the Soviet Union. General Secretary Gorbachev and his associates are attempting to put the Soviet economy on the rails of intensive growth through what they call a "radical restructuring" of the Soviet economy and society. The fundamental characteristic of an intensive growth strategy is growth through improvements in productivity as opposed to increases in factor inputs (land, labor, and capital). In reality this is the Soviets' only hope for improved economic performance, given the resource limitations they face now and in the future. How far Gorbachev is able to go toward succeeding in these efforts will determine not only the future welfare of the Soviet consumer

TABLE 4.1

USSR: Growth of Gross National Product at Factor Cost, by End Use
(Average Annual Rate of Growth)

	1961–65	1966–70	1971–75	1976–80	1981–85	1982	1983	1984	1985	1986
GNP (CIA)	4.9	5.1	3.0	2.3	1.9	2.6	3.2	1.4	1.1	4.2
National income produced (Soviet)	6.5	7.8	5.7	4.3	3.6	4.0	4.2	2.9	3.5	4.1
Consumption (CIA)	3.7	5.4	3.4	2.5	1.8	0.6	2.3	2.9	1.6	3.0
Investment										
CIA	7.3	5.4	4.2	4.3	3.4	3.6	4.3	1.1	3.1	6.0
Soviet	5.4	7.3	6.7	3.7	3.7	3.5	5.6	1.9	3.0	8.4
Administration, R&D, elements of defense, inventory change, net exports, and outlays (CIA)	4.9	4.1	1.1	−0.4	0.2	6.3	3.9	−1.5	−3.4	4.8

SOURCES: Central Intelligence Agency (1987), p. 66; *Narodnoe Khoziaistvo SSSR za 70 let* (1987), pp. 51, 58.

but, as other chapters in this volume document, the role that the Soviets are able to play in the game of global politics as well.

Soviet Economic Performance: Growth and Decay

During the 1950s and 1960s, resource abundance in the Soviet Union supported an extensive strategy for economic growth. During the 1950s Soviet GNP grew at a rate of 5 to 6 percent per year, and during the 1960s at about 5 percent per year. High investment rates allowed for the rapid development of the Soviet industrial infrastructure, and growth of defense expenditures enabled the Soviet Union to become a military superpower. Although consumption has generally been treated as a residual claimant of Soviet wealth, Soviet consumers also enjoyed improvements in their standard of living during the 1950s and 1960s.

The key to rapid growth in Soviet aggregate output during this period was rapid growth of inputs into the production system. This included rapid capitalization, large additions to the labor force, and relatively high consumption of material inputs. Growth in productivity, traditionally an important component of modern economic growth, while present, was not impressive.

Soviet investment rates since World War II have been high and generally higher than the growth rates of other end use categories, as indicated in Table 4.1. By 1960 investment as an end user comprised one-fifth of Soviet GNP and by 1970, one-fourth of GNP. Industry was the largest claimant of investment resources, annually claiming approximately 35–36 percent of total investment since the mid-1950s.

One of the most important factors in Soviet economic growth during this period was a rapidly growing labor force. As demonstrated in Table 4.2, during the 1950–60 period, employment in the Soviet Union grew by 14.8 million persons and during the 1960–70 period, by about 200 million. In part this growth was attributable to a significant increase in the labor force participation rate, but the bulk of the increments came from an expansion of the Soviet working-age population. Employment in agriculture dropped significantly during this period, from approximately 43 million in 1950 to less than 38 million in 1970. Employment in industry grew rapidly, increasing more than twofold from 1950 to 1970 During this period of extensive growth and rapid industrialization, these large increases in the labor force and shifts from farm to factory were critical to the performance of the Soviet economy.

The Soviet economy has also benefited from the general abundance of many raw materials and natural resources. Even now the Soviets can claim

TABLE 4.2
Soviet Labor Force Growth and Projections (in thousands)

Year	Total Employment	Annual Growth Rate (Avg.)	Nonagricultural	Total Agricultural	Labor Force Participation Rate
1950	80,646	—	37,611	43,035	—
1960	95,398	1.7	55,223	40,165	82.9
1970	118,565	2.2	80,773	37,792	88.2
1980	136,350	1.4	100,854	35,496	88.1
1990	141,500	0.4	—	—	88.0
2000	150,400	0.6	—	—	88.0

SOURCES: Columns 1 (except 1990 and 2000), 3, and 4: Rapawy (1985), p. 8. Columns 1 (1990 and 2000) and 5: Feshbach (1983), p. 99. Total Employment refers to the respective annual averages. Total Agricultural includes state and collective farms and private subsidiary agriculture.

to possess approximately 40 percent of the world's natural gas reserves and 30 percent of coal reserves. They also have vast reserves of crude oil. In other sectors the Soviets calculate that they have about 40 percent of the world's reserves of iron ore and perhaps 20 percent of its forest reserves. They also claim to have the world's largest supplies of manganese, nickel, lead, molybdenum, mercury, and antimony (Rowen 1984: 37). In large part because of the abundance of these and other important resources and their convenient location near many industrial centers in the European part of the Soviet Union, many Soviet industries (for example, the petroleum industry) enjoyed low or even declining marginal costs until the early to mid-1970s.

The Soviets also benefited during this period from favorable global economic conditions. In the late 1960s they began to open their economy to world trade, and by the early 1970s reductions in political tensions eased the constraints on East-West trade. The increase in world oil prices during that period also improved the Soviets' terms of trade vis-à-vis the energy-importing West. These factors gave the Soviet Union access to Western technology that it otherwise had been unable to obtain. This technology both deepened the Soviet capital base and allowed the USSR to avoid many of the inevitable mistakes and false starts involved in the research and design process. Overall the expanded participation of the Soviet Union in the global economy during this boom provided a significant contribution to Soviet economic performance.

In the broadest sense there are three claimants to economic wealth: investment, consumption, and defense. A look at the allocation of resources among these competing claimants and the relative priority assigned to each by the leadership is key to an analysis of the economic-defense policy relationship. Because of conceptual vagueness in Soviet statistics on national income, it is difficult to get a direct measure of the allocation of resources among end users. One way to get a sense of the relative growth of consumption and investment is to examine the distribution of Soviet industrial production. In the Soviet national accounts industry is divided into Group A, which produces the means of production (such as machine tools), and Group B, which produces consumer goods (such as household refrigerators). By examining the planned and actual growth of output in these two categories, we can get a good idea of the leadership's commitment to consumption and investment. In addition, at least for broad measures of investment and consumption, the CIA estimates are generally accepted proxies, and I will refer to both Soviet statistics and CIA estimates here (*Narodnoe Khoziaistvo za 70 let* 1987; Central Intelligence Agency 1987).

CIA estimates indicate that annual Soviet investment rates averaged about 11 percent during the 1950s and just under 7 percent during the 1960s. Even though the decline in average annual growth rates over this period was significant, investment generally grew at faster rates than Soviet GNP. On the other hand, average annual growth rates of consumption were generally lower than the growth rates for GNP. Consumption averaged about 3.7–5.7 percent growth per year between 1950 and 1970. These estimates correspond fairly well to official Soviet statistics on the growth of output in Groups A and B. The figures indicate that from 1950 to 1970 the growth rates of output in Group A were approximately 1.5 to 2.0 times as high as the growth of output in Group B.

The trade-off between allocations to defense and investment is a complex problem with both micro- and macroeconomic aspects. Analysis of this issue is further complicated because both Western estimates and Soviet data on the size and growth of the Soviet military budget are inconclusive and highly controversial. Because Hans Heymann's chapter in this volume deals more directly with this issue, I will not dwell on it here.[2] In general, however, there is less debate over the growth of the Soviet defense budget than over its size, and many analysts accept (with due caution) the estimates calculated by the CIA. These estimates indicate that during 1965–75 the Soviet military budget increased at approximately 4–5 percent per year, roughly equivalent to the rate of growth of GNP for that period (Joint Economic Committee 1983: 230). Despite any statistical vagueness, the important point to keep in mind is that the extensive growth pattern that characterized the first twenty-five years of postwar Soviet growth permitted significant growth of all end users, even though consumption tended to receive less favorable treatment as time went on.

The impact of rapid economic growth on Soviet foreign and military policy, though impossible to quantify, was clearly positive in that it gave the Soviet leadership capabilities and flexibility not afforded to smaller economic powers. Although there are disagreements as to the causal relation between Soviet economic performance and Soviet attempts to expand its sphere of influence, the correlation between the two is clear. At the very least one can link the rapid growth of military strength to the rapid growth of the Soviet military budget. In this sense the status of military superpower would have been even more difficult and painful to achieve had the Soviet economy not performed as well as it did. There is little doubt that this superpower military capability was the critical factor as the Soviets began to increase their role in global politics.

Since the early 1970s this seemingly comfortable situation has deteriorated dramatically. Soviet economic performance has decayed to painfully low levels and has constrained growth in consumer welfare, the development of the industrial base, and the growth of the military budget.

The decline in Soviet GNP growth rates has continued virtually without interruption; from 3 percent per year during the first half of the 1970s to 2.3 percent during the Tenth Five-Year Plan (1976–80) and 1.9 percent during the Eleventh FYP (1981–86). Economic growth thus far in the Twelfth FYP has been mixed (Tedstrom 1988a). There are some indications that at least during the Ninth and Tenth Five-Year Plans (1971–80), consumption had to suffer significant reductions in growth relative to the "productive" sector. During the Ninth FYP, for example, the output of Group A grew by 46 percent whereas the output of Group B grew by only 36 percent, in spite of the fact that Group B was initially planned to grow slightly faster than Group A. This is clear evidence that the Soviet commitment to investment has remained relatively strong throughout this period of resource stringency. By 1986 investment claimed nearly one-third of GNP.

The trade-off between investment and defense was also made more sensitive because of the macroeconomic stringency discussed earlier. This appears to have created some policy dilemmas for the Soviet leadership. Evidence suggests that sometime in the early to mid-1970s resource stringencies and declining economic growth rates compelled the leadership to try to reallocate resources in favor of investment in hopes of generating an acceleration in growth. Although the CIA indicates that investment did increase in size relative to other end users, it is not clear that this growth came at the expense of the defense budget (Campbell 1987; Tedstrom 1988b).

For the Eleventh FYP, however, there is fairly clear evidence that the leadership made a firm policy decision to accelerate the growth of investment at the expense of the military. In preparing the plan investment growth rates were continually revised downward. When the final plan was accepted, investment was to stay virtually flat at the 1980 level. However, over the course of the plan investment was not restrained and grew faster than the planned targets, even though there was no acceleration of economic output to feed this growth. At about the same time a number of other events occurred which would suggest that at least a good deal of the unplanned growth of investment came at the expense of the defense budget. Perhaps most persuasive is the much-analyzed meeting in October 1982 between the top Soviet political and military leaders (*Pravda* 1982). Rebecca Strode convincingly argues that the purpose of this meeting was to explain to the military establishment the necessity to reallocate resources in favor of investment (1986: 55–69). The CIA has revised its estimates of Soviet defense spending since the mid-1970s, stating that since 1976 Soviet procurement rates have been virtually flat and the growth of overall defense spending has dropped to about two percent per year (Joint Economic Committee 1983: 230).

The underlying cause of the declining economic growth rates that have put such a burden on the Soviet defense and consumption budgets is the transition from an economic environment of resource abundance to one of resource stringency. In contrast to the Soviet experience of the 1950s and 1960s, the marginal costs of virtually all economic inputs (labor, capital, and land) have been increasing over the past fifteen or twenty years. Moreover, this scarcity is exacerbated by an economic system that encourages waste and inefficiency at all levels of the production process.

One of the major resource constraints facing Soviet economic planners is the slowdown in the growth rate of the Soviet labor force. Caused primarily by decreases in the growth rate of the Soviet working-age population, the growth rate of the Soviet labor force has been falling steadily since the late 1960s. During the 1980s it has dropped to less than 0.5 percent. The expected growth rate for the 1990s is only slightly better, portrayed in Table 4.2 (0.6 percent per annum), not enough to relax the labor force constraint. Sources of easing the labor constraint, such as shifting workers from low-productivity to high-productivity jobs, drawing on the military manpower pool, or increasing the retirement age will have only marginal effects at best.[3]

An additional problem associated with the declining growth rates of the Soviet labor supply is that virtually all growth in the labor supply will come from the Muslim areas of Soviet Central Asia. This brings its own difficulties because people in these regions tend not to speak Russian and also tend to be less interested in the modern industrial environment. Moreover, most of the new jobs in the Soviet Union will be found in Siberia and in the already industrialized large cities of the European part of the country, where population growth is restricted and which are far from the Muslim work force, which has never exhibited a willingness to move. These problems further compound the labor supply problem in both the civilian economy and the armed forces.

The availability of relatively inexpensive material inputs has also been dwindling. Although the situation in the energy sector has been particularly burdensome, it is more or less representative of the situation with most raw material resources in the Soviet Union. The underlying problem in the energy sector (and in other extractive industries) is geographic and in that respect is not within the control of Soviet economic policy. With the continued depletion of oil, gas, and coal fields that are located in the industrial western regions of the Soviet Union, the Soviets have been forced to move exploring and extracting operations for all fossil fuels to ever more remote and forbidding sites in the east. This involves both higher operating costs and higher investment requirements. In 1970 some 10 percent of total energy produced in the Soviet Union was transported to the European part of the country from the eastern regions. By 1985 that figure stood at more than 42 percent. Soviet estimates of the impact of this geographic shift are that it can increase the cost of energy consumed west of the Urals by two and a half times (Popyrin and Sidorenko 1985: 31).

Nonenergy raw materials are also becoming less accessible and hence more costly. The Soviets have largely depleted their reserves of nickel, bauxite, and copper in the Urals and are now having to explore sites in northern Siberia. In the case of a number of raw materials—especially iron ore and coal—deterioration in the quality of these resources has exacerbated the geographic problem. In both cases the Soviets find themselves forced to transport increased quantities of lower-grade iron ore and coal over longer distances. Moreover, they find it necessary to process or enrich both of these resources before they can be used in production. This is an expensive process and adds significantly to the unit cost of these inputs.

Inefficient utilization of these resources compounds the problem of dwindling supplies. Since the 1950s the productivity of combined Soviet capital and labor has steadily fallen. Although there may have been a slight improvement during the early 1970s, CIA figures show that after 1973 growth rates of productivity were negative. The 1980s have seen a continuation of this trend virtually without respite. As shown in Table 4.3, low and negative growth rates of factor productivity (the efficiency with which labor, capital, and land are utilized) continue to constitute a drag on output growth rates, as measured by growth in GNP.

TABLE 4.3
USSR: Aggregate Factor Productivity
(Average Annual Rate of Growth)

	1961–65	1966–70	1971–75	1976–80	1981–85	1986[a]
Gross national product[b]	4.9	5.1	3.0	2.3	1.9	3.8
Factor productivity	0.5	0.9	−1.3	−1.2	−1.0	1.2
Man-hours	3.3	3.0	1.3	1.1	1.2	3.6
Capital	−3.6	−2.2	−4.6	−4.3	−4.0	−1.2
Land	4.7	5.0	2.9	2.5	2.1	4.2

[a] Preliminary
[b] Based on indexes of GNP (1982 rubles), by sector of origin at factor cost.
SOURCES: Central Intelligence Agency (1987), p. 70; Kurtzweg (1987), p. 135.

Low efficiency and wasteful use of inputs is pervasive in the Soviet economy. Examples of machine tools that contain too much steel, truck engines with low compression ratios which consume too much gasoline, and gas pipelines that are unnecessarily large in circumference abound in both Soviet and Western literature on the Soviet economy. The incentive structure of the Soviet economic system does not induce managers, designers, or production personnel to economize resources. On the contrary, artificially low interest rates that understate the true cost of capital, prices that fail to reflect either scarcity or utility, and the focus on meeting centrally planned output targets at any cost pervert incentives throughout the Soviet economy and actually encourage the wasteful use of resources.

Thus although some of the Soviet economy's problems are beyond the direct control of the leadership (i.e., the availability of human and material resources), changes in economic policy can affect the way resources are used and thus contribute to an improvement in economic performance. Incentives can be restructured in order to encourage efficient use of material inputs and to spur innovation. Management can be freed to make decisions without interference from above, and the consumer can have an impact on product quality and selection without threatening the fundamental authority of the Soviet government or the CPSU.

Goals for the Soviet Economic Future

Gorbachev's economic goals are outlined in the Twelfth FYP and the Plan to the Year 2000 (*Pravda* 1985: 1–6). His overall aims for the economy are intensified growth (*intensifikatsiia*), accelerated growth (*uskorenie*), and economic and technical modernization (*perestroika*).

The various components of Gorbachev's strategy can be logically divided among short-term, medium-term, and long-term efforts. Briefly, the main point of the short-term program is to squeeze as much productivity growth out of the Soviet labor force as possible. This is the critical "human factor" that has received so much attention in the Soviet press since the early 1980s. Although the evidence is far from conclusive, economic growth does seem to have benefited from real increases in labor productivity in 1986 and 1987. The 1988 State Plan results state that virtually all economic growth was attributable to increases in labor productivity (Tedstrom 1989).

In the absence of significant systemic reforms, however, the long-term impact of these improvements is not likely to be great. Unless the traditional relationship between Soviet workers and their environment is changed to allow real increases in living standards, there will be little motivation for labor to continue to perform more efficiently. In addition, management must experience a change in its environment so that it feels motivated to encourage innovation and efficiency.

Some of these issues are addressed in the medium- and long-term components of Gorbachev's program. The Soviets began the transition to the medium term with adoption of the Twelfth FYP. From the evidence found in this plan and in the speeches of Gorbachev and his colleagues, a fairly concrete picture emerges as to how they hope to generate economic growth over the course of the next decade. The key point of the program is to move to the intensive growth model mentioned earlier and to do so within the context of the traditional Soviet economic system. Gorbachev's long-term program, to be discussed later, more concretely addresses systemic reform of the Soviet economy.

On the macroeconomic level, economic growth is to pick up speed to an average 4.1 percent per year during 1986–90 and to average over 5 percent per year during the 1990s (for 1986–87 it averaged about 3.2 percent per annum). Vital to this upsurge in economic growth are planned increases in factor productivity. To achieve the economic growth rate targeted for 1986–90 the plan indicates a growth in labor productivity of 4.2 percent per year, with an average annual rate of 4.6 percent per year in industry. Also important is the reduction of material intensity of economic output. Gorbachev emphasizes the importance of conserving "intermediate inputs." The goal is to get more final output per unit of intermediate input, such as fertilizer, energy, or steel used in the production process. To this end the energy content of Soviet production is planned to decrease by 8.5 percent over the course of the plan and the metal content by 14 percent.

The Twelfth FYP emphasizes the need to reequip the Soviet industrial base and schedules growth in investment to significantly outpace growth in consumption. Capital investment from all sources is to increase by 4.9 percent, slightly faster than GNP. Consumption is to grow a bit slower than GNP, averaging 2.7 percent per year during 1986–90, but is planned to grow a bit faster during the 1990s. Given these figures, it is clear that there is not much room for an acceleration of defense spending.

With regard to investment, the emphasis is to be on reconstructing and reequipping the industrial infrastructure rather than rebuilding it from scratch. Depreciation rates will be nearly doubled with the goal of replacing fully one-third of the total capital stock by the end of the Twelfth FYP. A corollary to this is the plan to raise industrial output to qualitatively new levels. For example, V. Kirichenko, director of the Gosplan Economics Scientific Research Institute, noted that "within machine building, priority is given to machine tool building, production of computer equipment, instrument making, electrical engineering, and the electronics industry" (*Pravda* 1986a: 2). It is Gorbachev's intention that the development of these technologies will have a positive effect on the quality of industrial output in all sectors of the economy. Currently only about 15–17 percent of Soviet machinery meets world standards. Gorbachev's now admittedly overambitious goal for 1990: 90 percent (Gorbachev 1987b: 92–95).

In the Twelfth FYP the emphasis on economic growth over defense has been, if anything, strengthened. Gorbachev, as well as a number of top Soviet military leaders, have begun to stress the concept of "reasonable sufficiency," discussed in depth in Mary C. FitzGerald's contribution to this volume. For example, in a major speech to the Eighteenth Congress of the Soviet Trade Unions early in 1987, Gorbachev declared, "we shall not take a single step in excess of what is required and necessary for a reasonable and sufficient defense [*dostatochnaia oborona*]" (Gorbachev 1987a: 5).

This policy has been supported in practice. Investment growth rates for the Twelfth FYP are well above those in past years and above growth targets for GNP as well. Moreover, the investment plan has been consistently overfulfilled since the beginning of the Twelfth FYP. A portion of this growth comes from reducing the growth rate of consumption, which is part of the Twelfth FYP. But investment rates of the magnitude planned and achieved for the Twelfth FYP also require a cutback in the growth of the military budget (Tedstrom 1988b).

The competition between defense and investment also takes place at a lower level. A key element of Gorbachev's acceleration program is to reallocate investment in favor of the civilian ministries within the machine-building sector. A number of the top Soviet leaders have recently noted the burden of the military budget on economic growth and have publicly called for a shift of emphasis away from defense. For example, Prime Minister Nikolai I. Ryzhkov, in a major speech on the Twelfth FYP, noted that "we need to remind ourselves once again that in the years of the last five-year plan attention to development of the machine-building branch [in its capacity of providing equipment for investment] flagged" (cited in Campbell 1987: 26). Investment in civilian machine building is to grow some 80 percent over the course of the quinquennium. This is in stark contrast to the 20 percent growth it experienced during the Eleventh FYP.

At an even more disaggregated level, there has been increasing pressure on the VPK (Voenno-Promyshlennaia Komissiia, or Military-Industrial Commission) ministries to better serve civilian needs. Any number of articles in the Soviet press have addressed the issue of poor performance in the production of, for example, consumer electronics by VPK ministries such as Minelektronprom, Minradioprom, and Minobshchemash.[4] In the fall of 1988 major resolutions on improving the consumer sector called on the VPK industries to step up their production of consumer goods.[5] In addition, the Ministry of Machine Building for the Light and Food Industries and Domestic Appliances (Minlegpishchemash) has been abolished and its interests divided up among a number of VPK ministries. This is an obvious attempt to draw on the efficiency and quality of the military sector for the development of consumer goods production. This evidence, together with the emphasis on growth in the civilian over the VPK ministries noted earlier, makes it clear that the leadership recognizes the drag that the military budget represents for economic growth. My overall conclusion is that in the medium term at least, the resource scarcity issue is so constraining and the pressure to improve economic growth and living standards so great that it is highly unlikely that we will see any acceleration in Soviet defense spending, and may even see a reduction.[6]

The Long-Term Reform Plan

The long-term reform program as set out by Gorbachev is a comprehensive and complex set of measures designed to enhance the efficiency of economic activity on all levels. A full analysis of such a broad-gauged program is beyond the scope of this chapter, but it is possible to examine the fundamentals of what Gorbachev has in mind[7] and to make a few educated guesses about the impact of the economic reforms on the Soviet defense effort.

First, we can be certain that the Soviets will not allow defense spending to drop below a level required to maintain rough parity with the West. The economic pressures in the Soviet Union are not of the magnitude that would dictate such a sacrifice. Second, economic pressures in the Soviet Union are strong enough to dictate a more careful approach to the allocation of defense resources — more rumble for the ruble. This could include a shift of resources away from procurement and toward military research and development, a strategy of quality over quantity. Finally, it is likely that for the most part the defense industries and enterprises will be insulated from many of the more radical economic reforms. Their supplies will be guaranteed, prices will be centrally controlled, and the pressures of *khozraschet* (decentralized decision making), though applied formally on the defense industries in January 1989, will be buffered by strong interests in the defense and Party apparatus.

The economic reorganization and restructuring is to be generally completed by the end of 1990 in order that the Thirteenth FYP may be drawn up under the new economic mechanism. Despite a good deal of resistance, a number of the reforms have already been implemented. Major examples are the Law on State Enterprises, which took effect in January 1988, and the Law on Cooperatives, which took effect July 1, 1988. Over the course of the Twelfth FYP other important reforms will be legislated and implemented in order to develop gradually the new economic system along the lines Gorbachev has outlined. Still, even Gorbachev now admits that the planned pace of the reform was too ambitious and that the leadership underestimated the degree of resistance to the reforms which can be found at all levels of Soviet society (Gorbachev 1988).

The Soviets now consider the enterprise (whether state owned or cooperative) to be the primary economic actor in the Soviet economy. The creation of "the most favorable economic environment for the enterprise" is the foundation upon which the restructuring of the economy is predicated. Essentially this means giving the enterprises more economic independence than they have heretofore enjoyed.

Independence for these enterprises includes transfer to full cost accounting and self-financing, providing effective internal incentives for workers, stimulating work aimed at the consumer, all-around resource savings, and broad use of science and technology. Further, the enterprises are charged with independently drafting their own five-year plans based on state orders, direct orders from enterprises, and consumer demand. These orders and contracts are binding, and, according to the Basic Provisions, "fulfillment of orders and contracts serves as the most important criterion for evaluating the activities of enterprises and providing material rewards for employees." In fact we now see more emphasis on these criteria as success indicators in plan fulfillment reports. Finally, enterprise work collectives are to hold elections of their leaders based on broad competition for those positions.

An essential complement to the independence of the enterprise is reduction of the role played by the central economic bureaucracy. Instead of involving itself in the micromanagement of the economy as it did before, the USSR State Planning Committee will focus its efforts on "strategic directions of the planned guidance of economic and social development, the formation of major national economic proportions, the realization of main scientific and technical achievement, the refinement of the structural investment policy, and the insurance of the balanced nature of the national economy." One implication of this reduction in the role of the central bureaucracy is a commensurate reduction in the size of the bureaucracy and its staff. For example, the number of ministries is to be reduced and many of their duties are to be reallocated to superministries, which will again focus on broader questions of economic planning and management.

The reform program targets four aspects of the centralized planning mechanism for improvement: planning methodology, provisions for material and technical supply, price formation practices, and financial and credit-granting policies.

As before, annual, five-year, and longer (usually fifteen-year) plans will form the framework for the development of the Soviet economy. The five-year plans are to be created with input from the enterprises, ministries, State Planning Committee, and Council of Ministers and are to be ratified at a CPSU Party congress. The main development in the planning process is to be the transition to "economic methods of planning the activities of enterprises on the basis of planned targets, long-term stable economic standards, and state orders, and allocations." Further, the Basic Provisions specify that "planned targets should not be directive in nature and should not restrain the work of the collective in the elaboration of the plan, giving it wide scope for the choice of solutions and partners when concluding economic contracts."

One of the most significant components of the reform package is a "radical reorganization" of the means of material and technical support. Essentially this entails a transfer to wholesale trade arrangements (*optovaia torgovlia*) between organizations in which central allocation now exists. Wholesale trade is to be carried out through "free buying and selling based on direct contracts (*po priamym dogovoram*) between producer and consumer." This is designed to enhance the influence of the purchaser in the economic relationship and to accord enterprises more flexibility in obtaining material and technical support. This transition to direct, wholesale trade relations is scheduled to be completed within four to five years. It is worth noting, however, that special provisions are made for the filling and support of state orders. Such provisions will likely lessen the impact of this element of the reform program dramatically.

Prices have long been one of the weakest links in the Soviet economic system. Gorbachev's program calls for prices to be integrated at all levels of production, from research and development to retail sale, in order to reflect more accurately the cost and societal value of each commodity. However, it is clear that price reform is such a sensitive issue that a consensus could not be reached by the time of the June 1987 Plenum. The Basic Provisions thus called for the broadest discussion of the pricing issue on a countrywide basis and charges the USSR State Committee for Prices to concentrate its activities on preparing and carrying out a radical reform of the price formation system. Although that discussion is complex, most of the economic policymakers advocate some kind of price control system to overcome the tendency of increasing prices based on the growing powers of enterprises, to eliminate the tendency toward monopolism, and to shield the producer from consumer pressure under the new conditions of self-financing.

The finance and credit system is also to be restructured to facilitate the economic activities of enterprises and to eliminate financial waste and pilfering. Specific developments in the spheres of finance and credit include making finance and credit one of the major instruments of the plan-based economy; making five-year financial plans an integral part of the state plans for economic and social development; charging the USSR Ministry of Finance to develop a fundamentally new financial policy based on combining the interests of the state and enterprises (to ensure, in part, control over the efficiency of management by using monetary levers); making credit-granting institutions more fully interested partners in the economic activities of enterprises; increasing the role of the State Bank of the USSR as overall organizer and coordinator of all credit-granting arrangements; improving radically the consumer insurance and money-saving banking services; introducing new kinds of insurance and increasing its quality as well as the availability and quality of consumer savings banks; and enhancing the influence of the financial and credit-granting mechanism in the sphere of foreign economic activity. Within this restructuring a systematic process of making the ruble convertible, first within the Council for Mutual Economic Assistance (CMEA) and later (by implication) with other currencies, is to be undertaken.

Reforms in the agricultural sphere are still not fully formulated despite the efforts of the CPSU Plenum on agro-policy of March 1989. Thus far three major elements of the agricultural economic system have emerged. First, in November 1985 the State Committee for the Agro-Industrial Complex (Gosagroprom), a superministry, was created through the merger of five ministries and a state committee. The charge of Gosagroprom is to manage the production, marketing, and processing of farm output on a higher level with the hopes of reducing the inefficiencies caused by ministry-level meddling. At the March 1989 Plenum on agricultural policy Gosagroprom came under strong attack for inefficiency and bureaucratic resistance to reforms, and its responsibilities will surely be trimmed, if it is not dissolved entirely (*Ekonomicheskaia gazeta* March 1989: 1–7). The second major step in the restructuring of Soviet agriculture was a decree adopted in March 1986 which was designed to allow farmers to sell a larger portion of their produce privately at market-determined prices. Related to this, Gorbachev has emphasized the use of "private" contract groups that are responsible for the entire process of agricultural production and are paid according to their output. Finally, the concept of leasing contracts as of March 1989 has received official sanction by the CPSU. Under this program land can be leased to individuals, groups, or families. This is a major step and one that directly contradicts the traditional socialist concept of ownership. Although no legislation has passed, the intent seems to be to allow leases to last for the lifetime of the leaseholder and for the leases to be inherited by the leaseholder's children. Still, there are a number of problems—notably the allocation of productive land and scarce equipment which need to be resolved if the full potential of this measure is to be realized.

Gorbachev has also addressed the foreign trade system and has taken steps to decentralize decision making and increase flexibility within the system. Several relevant changes have been made. First, the State Foreign Economic Commission was created as a superministry that has general oversight responsibilities for all foreign trade activities. Along with this the Ministry of Foreign Trade was abolished and its responsibilities transferred to other ministries and agencies (Hanson 1988: 2–3). As of January 1, 1987, a number of ministries and seventy selected enterprises were permitted to engage directly in foreign trade activity, and a new special Bank for Foreign Economic Activities of the USSR replaced the old Foreign Trade Bank. The new bank is to coordinate the finances of virtually all foreign economic activities, not just foreign trade. This is in keeping with the overall effort to streamline the central bureaucracy. Finally, Soviet enterprises and ministries have both been sanctioned and encouraged to enter into joint venture deals with both CMEA and Western firms.

Conclusions

The underlying point of this chapter is that the Soviets have been confronted by severe economic problems that have threatened their claim to be a successful example of a Marxist-Leninist state and their ability to compete militarily with the West. The question examined in this chapter concerns to what extent the Gorbachev leadership has been able to restructure the Soviet economic mechanism in order to redress these problems. After sifting through the evidence we have so far, it cannot be concluded that he has in fact been able to change many of the fundamentals of the system which have been such a weight on economic development. To be sure, the level of discussion and the degree of innovation in Soviet economic thinking is more exciting and meaningful now than any time since the early 1960s or perhaps even since the New Economic Policy.

Gorbachev has targeted a number of areas for change that are certainly in the right direction and could indeed contribute to economic growth. In the short run his approach to the personnel issue has made many people at all levels of the system insecure enough about their jobs to be concerned about performance and productivity issues. The Nineteenth Party Conference in June 1988 and the Extraordinary Party Plenum in September 1988 serve to underline this aspect of Gorbachev's strategy. In the medium term his restructuring of the traditional Soviet investment strategy is in theory a very positive step. By focusing on renovation instead of rebuilding, new technology instead of standard equipment, and the civilian sector rather than defense, it is possible that he can extract some additional growth out of the old system.

I cannot be so optimistic about the long run—say, the next fifteen or twenty years. The proposals embodied in the main reform programs, such as the Basic Provisions, do not redress the fundamental systemic obstacles to economic efficiency that plague the Soviet economy. On the whole central management of the economy through planning, financial control, and personnel policies will remain intact. Any deviation from that historical trend will occur only at the margins. The slow and difficult development of the cooperative sector and the individual labor movement speaks clearly to this.

It is worth repeating that the reform package Gorbachev has produced so far is only part of a complex and lengthy process. Dramatic changes in the Soviet economic system and Soviet economic performance simply cannot come overnight; the economic obstacles are too complicated and the political opposition to reform is too great. One should be careful, then, not to judge Gorbachev's long-term program too quickly. We should not expect it to create a totally new, decentralized Soviet economic system or by itself to generate a new national security policy. Instead, its success should be gauged according to how well it moves toward those goals within the tumultuous economic and political dynamics of the Soviet system.

Notes

1. I gratefully acknowledge the support of the Hudson Institute, under whose auspices I composed the first draft of this chapter, and the contribution of Dr. Robert Campbell, who read earlier drafts of the chapter. The problems associated with Soviet statistics are well outlined in Treml and Hardt (1972). For an explanation of the CIA methodology, see Joint Economic Committee (1982). A systematic and authoritative treatment of converting Soviet national income data to comparable Western concepts is in Campbell (1985).

2. See also Campbell (1987) and Tedstrom (1988b). Burton (1983) effectively documents the thrust of this debate among Western analysts.

3. For an excellent analysis of these issues, see Feshbach (1983) and Goodman and Schleifer (1982).

4. See *Pravda*, June 3 and 10, 1986, for example. The ministries have a number of responsibilities. In this context I refer to their oversight of the production for electronic components; radio and computer technology and other finished electronic goods; and missiles and rocketry, respectively.

5. See *Izvestiia* August 21, 23, and 24, 1988. For an analysis see Tedstrom (1988c).

6. This case is argued more thoroughly in Tedstrom (1988b).

7. For a more complete analysis of Gorbachev's long-term reform program, see Tedstrom (1987a), upon which this section is based. Quotations in this section refer to the text of the "Basic Provisions for a Radical Restructuring of the Soviet Economy," *Ekonomicheskaia gazeta*, No. 27, July 1987, pp. 11–14 (hereafter Basic Provisions). For recent books on Gorbachev's economic strategy, see Hewett (1988) and Goldman (1987).

References

Burton, Donald R. (1983). "Estimating Soviet Defense Spending." *Problems of Communism*, 32(2), 85–93.

Campbell, Robert W. (1985). *The Conversion of National Income Data of the USSR to Concepts of the System of National Accounts in Dollars and Estimation of Growth Rates*. World Bank Staff Working Paper Number 777. Baltimore, MD: Johns Hopkins University Press.

—— (1987). "Resource Stringency and the Civilian-Military Resource Allocation." Unpublished draft chapter for a Center for Strategic and International Studies book on Soviet civilian-military relations.

Central Intelligence Agency, Directorate of Intelligence (1987, September). *Handbook of Economic Statistics, 1987*. Washington, DC: U.S. Government Printing Office.

Feshbach, Murray (1983). "Population and the Labor Force." In Abram Bergson and Herbert Levine, eds., *The Soviet Economy to the Year 2000*. Boston: Unwin Hyman.

Goldman, Marshall I. (1987). *Gorbachev's Challenge: Economic Reform in the Age of High Technology*. New York: W. W. Norton.

Goodman, Ann, and Geoffrey Schleifer (1982). "The Soviet Labor Market in the 1980s." In U.S. Congress, Joint Economic Committee, *Soviet Economy in the 1980s: Problems and Prospects*, Part 2. Washington, DC: U.S. Government Printing Office.

Gorbachev, Mikhail (1987a). "Speech to the 18th Congress of Trade Unions." Reported in *Ekonomicheskaia gazeta*, no. 10 (March), 1–5.

――― (1987b). *Perestroika: New Thinking for Our Country and the World*. New York: Harper & Row.

Gorbachev, M. S. (1988, June 29). "O khode realizatsii reshenii 27-ogo s'ezda KPSS zadachakh po uglubleniiu perestroiki." *Pravda*.

Hewett, Ed. A. (1988). *Reforming the Soviet Economy: Equality vs. Efficiency*. Washington, DC: The Brookings Institution.

Joint Economic Committee, U.S. Congress (1982). *USSR: Measure of Economic Growth and Development, 1950–1980*. Washington, D.C.: U.S. Government Printing Office.

――― (1983). *Allocation of Resources in the Soviet Union and China—1983*. Washington, DC: U.S. Government Printing Office.

Kurtzweg, Laurie (1987). "Trends in Soviet Gross National Product." In Joint Economic Committee, U.S. Congress, *Gorbachev's Economic Plans*. Washington, DC: U.S. Government Printing Office.

Narodnoe Khoziaistvo SSSR (various issues). Moscow: Finansy i Statistika.

Narodnoe Khoziaistvo SSSR za 70 let (1987). Moscow: Finansy i Statistika.

Popyrin, L. S., and V. A. Sidorenko (1985). "The Role of Atomic Thermal Energy in the Centralized Fuel Supply." *Vestnik, Akademii Nauk SSSR*, December, 30–42.

Pravda (1982, October 28).

――― (1985, November 9).

――― (1986a, June 19).

――― (1986b, July 5).

Rapawy, Stephan (1985). *Civilian Employment in the USSR: 1950–1980*. CIR Staff Paper no. 10. Washington, DC: Bureau of the Census.

Rowen, Henry S. (1984). "The Soviet Economy." In Erik P. Hoffman, ed., *The Soviet Union in the 1980s*. New York: Academy of Political Science.

• PART THREE •

The Change Agents

Of the many factors contributing to change in Soviet national security policy, those having the most important impact are the mix of economic reforms, institutional changes, and leadership alterations that have been occurring over the past several years. Building on the analyses of the previous section, the next four chapters begin by examining the nature of change in the economic realm. Given that national budget priorities reflect policy, the basis of Soviet national security policy can change through economic shifts.

In Chapter Five, Hans Heymann, Jr. illuminates the issue by analyzing the nature of the defense burden and its weight on the Soviet economy. He highlights the military's dilemma: in making up its mind whether to support economic reform, it must choose between desiring more power now (upholding the current system) or more power later (submitting to reform). In making the shift to the latter choice, Heymann asserts Gorbachev should design innovative policy responses that will satisfy the need to change the economy and satisfy the military at the same time. These changes should occur carefully and, Heymann concludes, incrementally if they are to have a chance of success.

Richard W. Judy examines the relationship between technology and national security policy in Chapter Six. He also sees incremental change occurring. Soviet technology, particularly computer technology, is far behind the West, placing the USSR in a weak position. But can the Soviets catch up? Judy's analysis suggests that this will be a very difficult task because the nature of the computer revolution demands responses from the Soviet political and economic systems which are very different from other Soviet efforts to make up technological lag. Unlike Soviet responses to building the atomic bomb, only radical economic reforms, including establishing dynamism as an inherent part of the economic system, are prerequisites for creating the technology necessary to change Soviet national security policy in the ways the Soviets desire.

Part of reform in national security policy includes the installation of new leaders throughout the Soviet political and economic systems. William J. Bishop analyzes the current changes in Soviet leadership in Chapter Seven and notes the significant changes that have already taken place in the Party and the military. Change has led to the assertion of more Party dominance in military affairs. Yet because of the nature of Soviet coalition politics, Bishop maintains, Gorbachev will have to deal with important constraints imposed by the process of governing the Soviet Union. Although there appears to be a consensus in principle for changing Soviet foreign and domestic policy, the counterweights of Soviet politics make radical change very difficult and incremental change likely in most policy areas.

In Chapter Eight, Jan Adams' interpretation of institutional change in the USSR contrasts with Bishop's views on leadership. In perceiving more conflict than consensus at the top, she asserts that Gorbachev's role as leader involves more than being beholden to a coalition; Gorbachev is probably dominant and is using institutional change to forge his policy preferences. She notes significant to radical change already in many institutions that help to create conditions for significant alterations in security policy. The military-industrial sphere shows the least institutional change (incremental change).

• CHAPTER FIVE •

Modernization and the Military-Civil Competition for Resources: Gorbachev's Dilemma

Hans Heymann, Jr.
Defense Intelligence College

The principal task of this chapter is to attempt to clarify the issues and difficulties facing Gorbachev as he tries to break down the barriers and rectify the imbalances between the military and civilian segments of the Soviet economy that he has inherited from his predecessors—barriers and imbalances that now seem to threaten the very foundations of Soviet national security.

Defense Bias in Resource Allocation

The implantation in the Soviet economy of a systematic bias in favor of production of the instruments of military power goes back almost sixty years to the launching of Stalin's forced draft industrialization drive. In the interwar years of the 1930s, the policy focused on the single-minded pursuit of a heavy industry base and a weapons mass production capability that was vindicated during World War II by the nation's remarkable performance in containing the *furor teutonicus* and saving the Soviet empire.

Following the war the security paranoia that so notoriously afflicted Stalin persisted among his successors. The high-intensity pursuit of military prowess continued to be the hallmark of Soviet economic development in the immediate postwar decades, even though increasingly the need to improve living standards (to provide a richer and more varied diet, make available desperately needed housing, and offer a wider range of consumer durables) was recognized by the Soviet leaders as politically essential if worker productivity was to be stimulated and the legitimacy of the regime preserved. This was the case especially during the Khrushchev reform era of the late 1950s and early 1960s, and continuing even during the succeeding largely stagnant Brezhnev years through the end of the 1970s. But the primacy of the defense claim to resources was never seriously questioned.

The persistent defense-favoring Soviet resource allocation policy inevitably resulted in what Ed Hewett (1987) calls "a partitioned economy," in which one segment—a privileged, high-quality island—became capable of turning out (although not necessarily efficiently) some of the world's most advanced and sophisticated weaponry while the rest of the production system, chronically disadvantaged and neglected, remained barely able to provide for the rudimentary needs of the populace. In essence, the predominant Soviet aim was to increase the power of the state with a minimum level of consumer welfare being accepted as a necessary contraint. It now appears that this narrow focus, and the resulting state of affairs, is no longer tolerable to the leadership. Gorbachev at least views it as a serious threat to the long-term national security of the USSR—a threat not merely in the narrow sense that a weak economic base will be progressively incapable of supporting a strong defense but in the broader sense that the nation needs more than a formidable military posture to sustain its superpower status: it needs a respectably functioning economy and the legitimacy-enhancing political benefits that such an economy bestows upon the regime.

Redressing the Balance

How did the Soviet leaders arrive at this inescapable conclusion, and how have they been trying to deal with the problems it poses? Robert Campbell addressed these questions in an unpublished paper contributed to the February 6–7, 1987 session of the Mershon Seminar on Soviet National Security Policy and reviewed the available evidence more fully in a subsequent draft contribution to a larger ongoing study on Soviet civilian-military relations (Campbell 1987).

Campbell argues persuasively that in an environment of steadily decelerating economic growth beginning in the mid-1960s, the massive Soviet military buildup that took place in the 1960s and 1970s imposed increasingly heavy burdens on the economy. It gave rise to a severe three-way tension between the demands of the military for precious high-tech resources, the need to invest to restore a satisfactory rate of growth, and the need to improve consumption to provide work incentives and meet minimal consumer expectations. That massive Soviet defense effort gained for the leadership an epochal trophy: strategic parity with the United States. But the trophy was won at very high cost in terms of a badly neglected basic production plant and a pitifully weak consumer infrastructure.

In Campbell's judgment the Soviet leaders probably sensed the severity of the defense burden—in terms of its opportunity cost to the civilian economy—by the second half of the 1970s, but their attempt to put a lid on defense spending during the Tenth Five-Year Plan (1976–80) appears not to have been sufficiently forceful or effective to succeed. Although Western intelligence analysts observed a distinct slowdown in the volume of Soviet military procurement beginning in 1976, the reduced volume of procurement quite likely did not ensue in lowered real procurement costs. The reasons for this dichotomy are complex; they include institutional, technical, and statistical factors that in combination may well limit the leadership's ability to constrain the flow of resources to the military-industrial establishment. (One of these factors is discussed further in a later section.) In any event, Campbell notes that whatever budget restraints may have been imposed on the Soviet military in that period, it failed to yield any perceptible release of resources to investment or to consumption. The leadership's efforts to put the brakes on military spending evidently became more serious during the Eleventh FYP (1981–85), when a reordering of priorities must have taken place. The weight of Campbell's evidence implies that during that period military expenditure growth was effectively capped to permit a substantial growth in investment, aimed especially at reequipping the civilian economy and renovating the capital stock. But the sluggish performance of the civilian machine-building sector during this period strongly suggests that the leadership had little to show for its substantial investment boost.

The real effort, however, to reallocate resources toward restoring the civilian economy (especially the machine-building sector) to proper functioning only began under Gorbachev, as John E. Tedstrom details in the preceding chapter. Implicitly if not explicitly, Gorbachev's program—as revealed in the Basic Provisions presented at the June 1987 Party Central Committee Plenum *(Osnovnye polozheniia* 1987: 2–3) and in the general secretary's report to the plenum (Gorbachev 1987)—mandates a modest though by no means inconsequential shift of resources (both human and material) from the defense to the civilian sector of the economy.

Although there are great uncertainties about precisely how the program will unfold, the resource shifts foreshadowed in its provisions represent a wholly new trend. It raises a host of questions that deserve closer examination.

One question worth probing is the attitude of the Soviet military toward the task of revitalizing the civilian economy, and particularly whether it feels totally threatened by that undertaking or whether it recognizes, however reluctantly, that it has a vital stake in revitalization.

Military-Civil Linkages

We in the West seem to have made some progress in recent years in recognizing that there are crucial linkages between the civil and military parts of the Soviet economy. One area of greater awareness is a rejection of the long-held notion that the Soviet "dual economy" is functionally divided—that there is a civilian sector where nothing works and a military sector where everything works superbly, because it enjoys "absolute priority," and that the two can coexist in splendid isolation from each other. A corollary of this notion is that Soviet military power could be made ever more formidable while the economy limped along—as an embarrassment perhaps, but not as a fatal constraint.

For a long time this view persisted despite mounting evidence that the Soviet military have in recent years become less and less insulated from the stringencies affecting the rest of the economy while their open-ended access to resources steadily eroded. Moreover, it is axiomatic that in any economy—even one that treats national security as a supreme political-economic good—the production of weapon systems rests on a pyramid of basic and intermediate industrial production that feeds both the civilian and military sectors. Indeed, we know from U.S. experience that as weapon systems evolve toward ever more sophisticated technological stages, military production becomes more dependent on the state of the art of the industrial base. Investment in that base then becomes not an alternative to defense outlays but an essential companion piece.

Western scholars are now paying serious attention to what George Weickhardt calls the "integration and interdependence of the civilian and defense sectors" (1986: 197–99). Julian Cooper speaks of the "manifold interrelations" between the two sectors (1986: 221); and the U.S. intelligence community, in its most recent public issuance on Soviet economic performance, characterizes the civilian machine-building sector as "the primary source of manufacturing technology and equipment" for modernizing the industrial base upon which defense production ultimately rests (Central Intelligence Agency 1987: 6).

There seems to be a consensus now that the Soviet defense sector's industrial supplier base is no longer capable of delivering to weapon assemblers the qualities and quantities of sophisticated inputs (microchips, digital switches, electro-optics, special metals, composite materials) that modern systems increasingly require. In part this is the consequence of many years of penurious investment in the less glamorous but still essential parts of the supporting supplier base. But it can also be traced to a persistent and systematic usurpation by the military of critical high-tech outputs of that base—outputs that should have been ploughed back in large measure into the modernization of the base. In microelectronics, for example, the Soviet military has largely monopsonized the output of advanced integrated circuits (ICs) while these were still in their early stages of series production. This has enabled the military to get advanced ICs quickly into new weapon systems, but it has also had long-term deleterious consequences for the evolution of the industry. Not only did it deprive the rest of the economy of a flow of advanced chips but, more important, it short-circuited the development of a large civilian semiconductor market. Thus the industry was prevented from achieving the kinds of ultra-high-volume production runs that have done so much in the West to develop high manufacturing skills, raise product yields, and vastly improve quality.

How clearly does the Soviet military perceive its current predicament? Although the evidence on this is still somewhat murky, there are ample indications that the key military leaders are not oblivious of the present state of affairs. They are unmistakably aware of their heavy dependence on the civilian economy and are fretting over the extent to which they are affected by its shortcomings. Most widely publicized, perhaps, are the views of Marshal Ogarkov, chief of the Soviet General Staff, expressed repeatedly until his demotion in September 1984. His statements leave no doubt about his concern over the Soviet qualitative lag in the information-based technologies. As Mary C. FitzGerald points out elsewhere in this volume, Ogarkov recognized the serious implications of this lag for the Soviet ability, in the longer run, to meet the U.S. competition in conventional arms. Ogarkov's perspective, moreover, is shared by other leading members of the military-industrial complex, as FitzGerald also notes.

A Soviet major general writing in the armed forces Party organ makes the point of the military's dependence on the industrial-technological base quite explicitly:

> In the matter of strengthening military-economic potential, it is difficult today to overestimate the party's concern for cardinal acceleration of scientific-technical progress—the further priority development of machine-building, particularly machine-tool-building, robot technology, computer technology, instrument-making, and electronics—are simultaneously the basic catalysts of military-technical progress.
>
> Today what is required for serial production of contemporary weapons and the newest combat equipment is not usual or ordinary equipment but the most modern and frequently unique equipment—new in principal instruments, numerically-controlled machine-tools, robot equipment, latest generation computers, and flexible manufacturing systems. In other words, the present stage of the military-technical competition that has been imposed on us by imperialism demands a high level of development of those branches of industry with the best prospects, of the most modern technology, and of a highly qualified workforce. (Iasiukov 1985)

There can be little doubt that the determined pursuit of high-tech weapons systems, coupled with the current high-intensity effort to modernize the industrial base, has generated formidable claims against scarce resources. Just how formidable has long been a contentious matter among Western analysts of the Soviet scene. It is now becoming increasingly apparent that not only the West but Soviet leaders themselves may lack an accurate measure of the extent of the burden that these demands now impose on the Soviet economy.

Assessing the Weight of the Defense Burden

It is sometimes useful to remind ourselves of the tenuousness of the measurements upon which we depend for our economic assessment of Soviet defense activities, given that the Soviet leadership's passion for secrecy and its Byzantine price system conspire to make this task a virtually unmanageable one.

I shall not attempt to describe the rather sophisticated but unavoidably "heroic" dollar-costing methodology used by the CIA to reconstruct synthetically the magnitude of Soviet defense activities each year. In essence its aim is to aggregate, in a common denominator (U.S. dollars), the basket of goods and services made available to the Soviet military in any one year so that it can be compared with U.S. budget outlays for similar purposes. Although the resulting artifact provides some sense of the relative size of Soviet and U.S. defense programs at a point in time, and some notion of trends in these magnitudes over time, it also has some serious limitations. The two most important are that, first, it tells us nothing about Soviet military *spending*, because it spends rubles, not dollars. The dollar estimates reflect U.S. rather than Soviet resource costs. Second, the methodology prices Soviet defense goods and services at the point where these items pass into the hands of the military. That is, it prices the *outputs* of the defense industries, not the resource *inputs* into those industries; hence it fails to capture the full input costs. (In a market economy this would not create much of a problem; in a "command economy," with its fabricated price system, it can make a big difference.)

These two limitations pose severe problems for interpreting the real cost implications of changes in the level of procurement. For example, when U.S. intelligence observed a reduced rate of Soviet defense industry output (procurement of military equipment) in physical terms beginning in 1976, it appeared, when translated into dollar equivalents, as "reduced spending" on procurement. But it is highly probable that real Soviet procurement costs during this period in fact went up because the sharply rising technical complexity of newly introduced weapon systems depressed factor productivity; that is, it lowered the efficiency with which the defense industries were able to use their combined factor inputs (labor and capital) to produce weapons output. If that did happen, the dollar-costing methodology would not have caught these increases in real costs.

Although this matter remains somewhat conjectural, it seems entirely consistent with scattered evidence that during this period of dramatically rapid weapons modernization the Soviet economy experienced large, unanticipated cost overruns brought about by design flaws and long delays in the development cycle, faulty and interrupted production, idled or underutilized work forces, and overhead costs that remained fixed in spite of a reduced scale of output.

If that in fact occurred, it would have meant the worst of both worlds for the Soviet military: a lower volume of weapons procured but higher real procurement costs. Such a situation would not have been captured in our dollar estimates.

In principle we might expect such a cost escalation eventually to be reflected in higher ruble prices, and an accurate valuation of Soviet defense spending in ruble terms might pick up these escalating costs. But whether Soviet price formation in the military sector actually captures these surging costs and whether the limited sample of ruble prices available to us is adequate to reflect these costs is highly dubious. Indeed, it is quite likely that the Soviet military itself does not fully appreciate the real costs of its weapons programs, inasmuch as the procurement prices paid to the defense industries may grossly understate real costs of production (because of budgetary subsidies, budgetary grants for R&D, shifting of costs to the civilian sector, and so forth). In fact, uncertainties about the "real" cost of defense could well give rise to sharp contention between military and civilian leaders, with the latter looking at a different set of cost data compiled at so-called comparable prices. Such cost indexes would appear much higher, insofar as they are notoriously "pushed up" by inflationary price increases that are widely condoned in the defense industries.

In sum, the question of how fully aware the Soviet military leaders— or, indeed, Soviet political leaders—are of the extent of the burden their defense programs have imposed on the rest of the economy must remain moot. But a consciousness of the military's dependence on critical civilian inputs is surely there. Gorbachev has been vocal on the subject, and the issue, though only occasionally addressed in the military press, must be a troublesome one for the defense establishment as well.

The Military's Dilemma

Recognizing the indivisibility of military power from its economic base is one thing; accepting its implications is quite another. One implication for the military is that they are now faced with a crucial trade-off between more military power *now* and more military power *in the future*. If the deficiencies of the civilian underpinnings are such that large new investments will be required in a wide range of lagging industries over many years before the momentum of modern defense production can be restored, it means that their weapons acquisition process must settle for a lower rate of new hardware accessions in the interim. It means putting limits on the number of new weapon developments that can be pursued concurrently, and it means having to rely on more retrofitting of older systems instead of building new ones—all bitter pills to swallow. Moreover, the medicine would not be so hard to take were it not for the virtually open-ended time horizon of the prescription. The antiquated capital stock supporting Soviet defense production evolved over the decades. Its renovation will take a long time. How long before the soldiers' patience runs out?

We have here a military establishment that has been pursuing the goal of strategic parity tenaciously for decades; through much of the 1970s it had gloated over a trend in the "correlation of forces" inexorably in its favor, and it had basked in the sunshine of world recognition of Soviet "essential equivalence" in the superpower competition. Now this establishment must face the prospect of its hard-won trophy being snatched away by developments largely beyond its control.

Seemingly overnight the leadership has become painfully aware, first, that the technological-industrial base of Soviet weaponry is critically deficient and that its technological lag is widening rather than narrowing, and, second, that they are now being powerfully challenged by the (arch-rival) United States to a long-term military-strategic duel in a sphere (high technology) in which that rival enjoys an unquestioned comparative advantage.

As regards the technological lag, this is hardly a new phenomenon. Western assessments of that lag have been surprisingly consistent over the years. A milestone British study of Soviet industrial technology published in 1977 found no evidence of any diminution of the technological gap over the previous fifteen- to twenty-year period in the key Soviet industries it examined (Amann, Cooper, and Davies 1977: 66). U.S. intelligence and Defense Department studies reach similar conclusions for later periods (Joint Economic Committee 1976: 54; Department of Defense 1980: 82; DOD 1986: II). A recent study (Central Intelligence Agency 1987: 4) reveals a rather striking pattern of U.S. leads over the USSR in the key informatics technologies: in such vital areas as microprocessors; mainframe, mini-, and supercomputers; computer-controlled machine tools; flexible manufacturing systems; and the all-important domain of software, the U.S. lead over the USSR is estimated at between seven and twelve years.

The significance of such leads-lags comparisons is, of course, always questionable, particularly in areas of economic activity where the technologies may be *applied* quite differently in the two countries. Soviet weapon systems design practices are notable for building on their relative strengths and engineering around their weaknesses—and Soviet priorities are different from those in the West. Richard Judy makes this point quite persuasively (Judy 1986: 354–67; 1987: 162–70), contrasting the vastly different "information societies" emerging in the United States and the USSR. He also describes other unique aspects of Soviet technology policy in the next chapter of this volume. Still, the informatics technologies have been developing at such an explosive rate in the advanced industrial West and represent such fundamental building blocks to the vast array of scientific, economic, and social activities in any modern or would-be-modern society, that the prospect of steady retardation in this realm must be profoundly disturbing to the Soviet leaders.

As regards the U.S. high-tech military-strategic challenge, this is surely at the cutting edge of Soviet concerns. The challenge is epitomized by the Strategic Defense Initiative (SDI), but it would probably exist even without it. The innovativeness of the American science and technology

(S&T) effort, and its formidable potential when effectively harnessed to its defense effort, has been a source of enduring anxiety to the Kremlin. The specter of SDI thus poses a massive threat, even if in the long run that initiative is supported only half-heartedly by the American public. SDI arouses Soviet fears in at least three dimensions (listed in ascending order of intensity of arousal): (1) as a potentially deployable, space-based ballistic missile defense system; (2) as the leading edge of a broad-based U.S. military research, development, testing, and evaluation (RDT&E) effort featuring sensors, computer programs and applications, signal processing and exotic kill mechanisms that will have an impact on the entire spectrum of military roles and missions; and (3) as the technological centerpiece of a global U.S. challenge to the Soviet geopolitical gains of the past two decades that threatens its very superpower status.

Gorbachev's Policy Response: The Imperatives

If this is a fair approximation of the way Soviet leaders assess their strategic situation, it raises a host of considerations—both imperatives and constraints—for a Gorbachev policy response if it is to have any chance of success. Crucial among these are the need to create a broad consensus in the country that the USSR faces a national security challenge in the most comprehensive sense of that term; the need to proceed sequentially to avoid attacking too many sacred cows while generating the necessary momentum and support to overcome bureaucratic inertia and the social resistance of a wide spectrum of powerful interests and factions; the need to correct long-standing disproportions in the economy without being able to afford massive resource shifts among the basic GNP allocation categories of investment, consumption, and defense—because all three will have to be nurtured; and, consequently, the need to mount the effort in a very long-term perspective—that is, in the context not of a five–ten year but a twenty–thirty year time horizon. It would appear that the *perestroika* strategy that Gorbachev has been pursuing so far reflects an astute recognition of precisely these imperatives.

His first emphasis on revitalizing the "human factor"—getting rid of incompetence by a shakeout of top personnel, creation of a climate of disciplined effort, adoption of a new approach to social mobilization through calls for *glasnost'* and *demokratizatsiia*—is aimed both at building a broad consensus and at overcoming passivity and cynicism. It seeks to engender enthusiasm among the modernizing intelligentsia, including the sizable army of young, educated technicians and ambitious tech- nocrats, and to "demobilize" the forces of resistance (the entrenched bureaucracy and the traditional working class) who seek, understandably, to protect their privileges and preserve the existing "social contract."

Further, Gorbachev's early concentration on relatively "safe" reforms of the *decision hierarchy*, aimed predominantly at strengthening central authority (setting up super-"biuros," commissions, and complexes) and only half-heartedly at enlarging enterprise autonomy, suggest a conservatism and political caution befitting a new, power-consolidating leader. The more fundamental and controversial reforms of the economic *information system*—the crucial price-setting principles, the financial/banking sinews of the economy, and the "policy guidance" planning system—are infinitely more complex and were left to a later period. They are now beginning to be tackled, but much more gingerly. The ten reform decrees that were released following the June 1987 Plenum (*O korennoi perestroike* 1987) are a case in point: though their scope appears to be sweeping, the decrees are largely descriptive and conceptual in nature, providing little by way of implementing guidance. And the most critical and sensitive reforms of the *incentive/motivational system*—eliminating obligatory targets, providing effective differential rewards, and fostering integral, systemic recognition of high-quality performance and independent initiative—are at best only ambiguously embedded in the measures promulgated so far. And yet, as John Tedstrom shows us in his analysis of the reform program in the previous chapter, it is impressive to see how far the campaign has come since its initiation.

A critical look at the first wave of Gorbachev reforms two years ago led some observers to conclude that they were little more than slightly warmed-up versions of previous failed or abandoned attempts at reform instituted under Kosygin in the 1960s and Brezhnev in 1979. Gertrude Schroeder, for example, judged these early measures as "neither radical nor a reform, for they do not re-form (restructure) the economic system in any essential way" (1986: 300). That judgment was no doubt warranted at the time. The net effect of those early initiatives on economic performance could only have been small. But the assumption was that the measures introduced then stood as a complete package. In a recent, painstaking assessment of the more sweeping reform program revealed in July 1987, Schroeder takes a more respectful view of its significance and possible impact, preserving, however, a considerable skepticism about its ultimate benefits (1987: 219).

Many observers tended also to look upon the early measures as if they were the outcome of some kind of coherent blueprint or "grand design," when they should more properly have been viewed as a piece of "pragmatic incrementalism"—the first installment of a succession of measures of gradually rising scope and consequence—a process rather than a fully formed strategy in which the personal dynamics of the leader and the atmospherics he creates tilt the political climate of the country in favor of effective combat with the forces of resistance. That seems to be precisely the kind of process Gorbachev has been pursuing; hence judgments about the parts of his package instituted at any point in time are almost certainly premature. The whole becomes more than the sum of the parts, and the parts are still evolving.

Gorbachev's Policy Response: Impact on the Military

Securing the military's acquiescence and participation in the reforms poses a continuing, severe challenge to Gorbachev. From the perspective of the military leaders there can be little doubt that they feel seriously threatened by a prospective transformation of the established system, the effect of which will be the breaking down of the wall that protects their privileged access to resources. It will dilute their priority status and make them vulnerable to the economic chaos that the reform process can be expected to engender. How deep their anxieties run is probably a function of their expectations as to how rapidly and comprehensively the reforms will be applied to *them*. On this matter Gorbachev seems to be making an effort —at least in the short run—to reassure them.

Reassurance is certainly called for, considering how radical the alterations appear, at least on the surface. In barest outline, the alterations include the elimination of obligatory plans and their replacement by nonbinding five-year "control figures" that are aimed only at "orienting" the enterprises as they draw up their own plans. Enterprises are to be granted a considerable measure of economic autonomy: they will be largely "self-financing"; they will be expected to buy their inputs and sell their outputs in a wholesale trade network at "contract" prices to be agreed upon between buyer and seller; and they will be permitted to fail under specified insolvency procedures. In parallel with the greatly enhanced enterprise autonomy, the operational role of the center is to be sharply curtailed. All this, at least on the face of it, adds up to a radical change in the way the economy operates and a drastic constriction of the manipulative control long exercised by the Party and the bureaucracy at the center.

On the other hand, such sweeping changes will not be put into effect all at once; they are to be phased in gradually over a number of years. Even more to the point, the decrees make ample provision for shielding the defense sector from the decentralizing and decontrolling effects of the measures being introduced. Most prominent among these provisions is the continued reliance by the center—although, assertedly, on a gradually diminishing scale—on central direction and allocations, but henceforth in the form of "state orders" (*goszakazy*) that enterprises are obligated to fulfill and that will cover the most crucial outputs. These state orders will carry with them guaranteed supply of materials and higher prices than could be obtained through the newly created channels of bilateral contracting and wholesale trade. True, over time these state orders are to diminish in volume and, by the optimistic target date of 1992, are to cover only a small fraction (20–25 percent) of total output; but initially they will cover up to 80 percent of industrial production—and, of course, defense production is prominently included within this rubric.

In short, there is reason at this point for the military to feel somewhat reassured: central management of the economy is being preserved; the pillars of the traditional economic system remain prominently in place— the capacity and institutions for planning, management, rationed distribution of materials, price setting, and so forth are being retained at the center; and, of most immediate relevance to the military, the system of state orders provides a vehicle for keeping the defense sector almost entirely and indefinitely insulated from the decentralized, "reformed" economy and hence unaffected by whatever efficiency-generating impact the reforms may have on the economy at large.

But there's the rub: if the military industries are permitted to remain outside of the reformed system, with their priority status and privileged access to resources essentially intact, the reform would almost certainly atrophy. The civilian sector would be choked off as the scarce high-quality resources needed for civilian modernization would continue to be preempted by the weapons programs, and the military sector would be sheltered from having to operate more competitively or efficiently, with the result that no qualitative transformation would occur in either sector and economic performance would continue to deteriorate.

Gorbachev has no intention of letting this happen. The reform decrees give him ample weapons for depriving the military of their protective cover. They empower the central agencies to issue fewer military state orders, thus limiting the "protected" sphere; to reduce the proportion of state orders awarded to a single producer, putting out a larger share for competitive bid; to limit centralized material allocations to the truly scarce items, requiring the enterprises to seek their other needed inputs in the wholesale market; and in other ways to expose military production to a less protected environment.

Gorbachev has not so far used any of these weapons, and it is not at all clear at this point how the military would fare in such a more contested environment. With his characteristic ambivalence between audacity and caution, he seems to be focusing his attack on squeezing the military for resources—capping the growth of their programs and cajoling them into making larger contributions to the modernization of civilian machine building. His impatience with military foot-dragging in this latter area has surfaced in a Council of Ministers' decision to dissolve an important civilian machine-building ministry (the Ministry of Machine Building for Light and Food Industry and Household Appliances) and to transfer all of its enterprises, lock, stock, and barrel, to the defense sector. The purpose, clearly, is to put these long-neglected, disadvantaged civilian enterprises under the privileged defense umbrella and compel the defense industrial ministries to assume formal responsibility for their modernization—a straw in the wind, perhaps, but also a potentially significant innovation. Calls for "reasonable sufficiency" in the level of Soviet military power (discussed later in this volume by Mary C. FitzGerald) seem to interact strongly with this economic squeeze on the military.

The Outlook

What does Gorbachev's astute combination of boldness and circumspection, of innovativeness and conventionality, of iconoclasm and conservatism, portend for the likely success of his undertaking?

Looking at the sequential nature of his campaign, one suspects that he is operating under the star of Napoleon's famous strategic dictum: "*On s'engage et puis on voit*" (Engage and then watch what happens). Abraham Becker argues that "Gorbachev became a 'radical' reformer in spite of himself, led on by the force of events" (1987: 3). But if so, he may discover that a sequential, escalatory approach is a difficult strategy to implement, in that it tends to arm the resistance. One wonders whether at some point Gorbachev will not need to develop something more of a conceptual framework for his reform architecture, including a more coherent vision of the kind of functioning economic system that his policies and programs are supposed to create. Most important, there is the overarching concern as to whether he will be able to garner enough political support and clout to implement an internally consistent strategy. When one looks around within the present Politburo or among the high Party elite, one does not readily identify the sort of dynamic, politically powerful personalities upon whom he could confidently lean in this daunting venture.

An even more worrisome aspect is the fact that resource stringencies throughout the Soviet economy now are such that there are no large "hidden reserves" or idle resources that can be readily extracted from the system and put to work, or major shifts engineered from one GNP sector to another.

In the area of investment, large additions to and renovations of fixed capital are going to be necessary for modernization, no matter how hard Gorbachev tries to stress an intensive rather than extensive development strategy. Truly massive investment growth is going to be required to upgrade the capital stock throughout the "fuel-energy complex" and in a wide range of basic industries. But neither defense nor consumption can yield up the kinds and quantities of resources that could begin to quench the investment thirst.

On the defense side, putting a temporary damper on the growth of defense spending in order to free investment resources for upgrading the country's industrial base may be possible for the next several years. But given the current Soviet assessment of the threat to its relative military standing, and given the fact that the ongoing weapons development programs have a dynamic of their own, it will not be easy, in the Soviet political setting, to cap these programs over the long pull, even if U.S.-Soviet tensions were to become significantly more relaxed.

On the consumption side Gorbachev, like his predecessors, has shown some political sensitivity to the need to meet at least minimal consumer expectations and to provide tangible incentives to the work force. The fact that he has boosted investment in consumer durables and housing, is making a strong push for individual and cooperative enterprise in the production of consumer goods and services, and that he has, at least so far, shied away from raising food prices and utility rates suggests that he recognizes the imperatives and constraints under which he must operate in this sector. But in time he will have to move much more drastically in this and other potentially explosive areas.

In sum, given all the impediments cited and the legacy of decades of economic mismanagement, it would seem that genuine modernization in the present Soviet environment can only be a slow and agonizing process. The economy is very large and complex; the power structure administering it and the rules under which it operates are root-bound and encrusted; and the ideology that originally inspired it still has an aura of inviolability about it. Gorbachev surely recognizes all that but seems driven by a conviction that nothing less than the legitimacy of the Soviet system is at risk and that the modernization of Russia can no longer be put off.

The point here is simply to suggest that short of revolutionary upheaval, change in long-established systems can only come at the margin and should not be expected to yield rapid or even benign results. The process of reform is more likely to be marked by contention, confusion, and instability than by coherence, consistency, and steady purpose. Even if the process is implemented with an enthusiasm that we have not heretofore witnessed in any socialist society, its course will have to be measured in decades rather than years.

References

Amann, R., J. W. Cooper, R. W. Davies (1977). *The Technological Level of Soviet Industry*, New Haven, CT: Yale University Press.
Becker, Abraham S. (1987). *Gorbachev's Program for Economic Modernization and Reform: Some Important Political-Military Implications*. RAND Report P-7384, September 10. Santa Monica, CA: RAND Corporation.
Campbell, Robert W. (1987). "Resource Stringency and the Civilian-Military Resource Allocation". Unpublished draft for Center for Strategic and International Studies book on military-civilian relations.
Central Intelligence Agency, Defense Intelligence Agency (1987). "Gorbachev's Modernization Program: A Status Report." Submission to the Subcommittee on National Security Economics, Joint Economic Committee, U.S. Congress, March 19. Washington, DC: U.S. Government Printing Office.
Cooper, Julian (1986). "Comments on George Weickhardt's Article," *Soviet Economy*, 2(3), 221–27.
Department of Defense (1980). *The FY-1981 DOD Program for Research, Development and Acquisition*. Washington, DC: U.S. Government Printing Office.
—— (1986). *The FY-1986 DOD Program for Research, Development and Acquisition*. Washington, DC: U.S. Government Printing Office.
Gorbachev, Mikhail S. (1987, June 26). "O zadachakh partii po korennoi perestroike upravleniia ekonomikoi. Doklad General'nogo sekretariia TsK KPSS M. S. Gorbachev na Plenume TsK KPSS 25 Iuniia 1987 goda." *Pravda*, pp. 1–5.
Hewett, Edward A. (1987). "The Soviet Economy and Soviet National Security." Presented at the Kennan Institute Conference on The Dynamics of Soviet Defense Policy, The Wilson Center, Washington, DC, September 22.
Iasiukov, Major General M. (1985). "Voennaia politika KPSS: Sushchnost' soderzhanie." *Kommunist vooruzhennykh sil*, October 20.
Joint Economic Committee (1976). Hearings, *Allocation of Resources in the Soviet Union and China, 1976*, Part 2. Washington, DC: U.S. Government Printing Office.
Judy, Richard W. (1986). "Computing in the USSR: A Comment." *Soviet Economy*, 2(4) 354–67.
—— (1987). "The Soviet Information Revolution: Some Prospects and Comparisons." In Joint Economic Committee, U.S. Congress, *Gorbachev's Economic Plans*, Vol. 2. Washington, DC: U.S. Government Printing Office.
O korennoi perestroike upravleniia ekonomikoi: sbornik dokumentov (1987). Moscow: Gospolitizdat.
Osnovnye polozheniia korennoi perestroiki upravleniia ekonomikoi (1987, June 27). *Pravda*, pp. 2–3.
Schroeder, Gertrude E.(1986). "Gorbachev: 'Radically' Implementing Brezhnev's Reforms." *Soviet Economy*, 2(4), 289–301.
—— (1987). "Anatomy of Gorbachev's Economic Reform." *Soviet Economy*, 3(3), 219–41.
Weickhardt, George C. (1986). "The Soviet Military-Industrial Complex and Economic Reform." *Soviet Economy*, 2(3), 193–220.

• CHAPTER SIX •

Technology and Soviet National Security

Richard W. Judy
The Hudson Institute

The symbiosis between technology and military affairs is ancient. Russian history, perhaps more than that of any other major power, provides palpable and repeated evidence of the mutual dependency between the state's technological and economic policy on the one hand and its military and national security policy on the other.

Military considerations have long been recognized as "change agents" carrying profound consequences for Russian economic policy and life.[1] In the Soviet period, just as in the time of Peter the Great, the impact of military considerations on economic policy and society has been manifest. Alexander Gerschenkron described the Stalinist variation on this ancient theme in these classic words:

> There is very little doubt that, as so often before, Russian industrialization in the Soviet period was a function of the country's foreign and military policies. . . . the combination of ancient measures of oppression with modern technology and organization proved immensely effective. All the advantages of industrialization in conditions of backwardness were utilized to the hilt: adoption of the fruits of Western technological progress and concentration on those branches of industrial activity where foreign technology had the most to offer; huge size of plant and the simultaneity of industrialization along a broad front assuring large flows of external economies. (Gerschenkron 1962: 148–149)

This chapter explores some implications of technological advancement for Soviet national security policy in the years ahead. An important underlying proposition is that the reverse impact of technical and economic factors on Soviet military doctrine and national security policy (taken in its broadest meaning) is no less real and significant than the "direct" impact illuminated in the quoted passage by Gerschenkron. The relationship between technology and policy is fully symbiotic, and the arrows of causality run in both directions. The two sets of variables, technological and political, appear as both causes and effects, as change agents and agents changed.

This relationship between technology and national security policy is anything but simple; rather, it is a dynamic, multidimensional, multistaged process wherein reverberations of cause and effect are echoed and amplified through the passage of time. When that process is observed within a single dimension, such as strategic weapons, over a short time interval, the causal linkage may appear straightforward; a particular technological development precedes and appears to "cause" an alteration of policy. In other cases the reverse linkage appears to hold; a particular policy necessitates development of a certain technology for its success. Over a somewhat longer time frame, we observe a classic "chicken and egg" relationship in which new technologies, sought to implement existing policy, so alter military thinking and practice that pressures mount for modifications in policy whose optimal implementation requires new technology, and so on.

When thinking about militarily relevant technology, it is essential to distinguish between military technology per se and military industrial technology that girds the loins of a nation's economy to produce weapon systems and otherwise support the forces. Furthermore, "technology" is hardly some inexorable, stateless force. Militarily relevant technology in the modern era is a quarry caught only after organized and purposeful pursuit. Without doing great violence to reality, we may resolve that pursuit into two principal phases. In the first phase, research and development (and sometimes espionage) attacks and, when successful, solves the basic scientific and engineering problems. Then comes the second, or implementation, phase in which newly developed technology must be "debugged" and incorporated into the military force structure or, in cases of industrial technology, into the fabric of the economy. Changes in national security policy as well as broader policy consequences may arise in either of these phases.

Research and development to produce new weapons or to refine old ones is done by the organized science and technology establishments of nation-states. For the purposes of this chapter, I concentrate on the USSR but compare Soviet developments to those in the United States to facilitate the argument. For the Soviets, the national origin of new or improved military technology—that is, whether it is *nasha* (ours) or *chuzhaia* (theirs)—often has much to do with the manner in which it is incorporated into the force structure as well as its implications on military doctrine and national security policy. A discontinuous and potentially threatening leap forward in military technology by the United States historically has brought about the following Soviet response: (1) intense pressure on Soviet military research and development (R&D) to match or counter the U.S. move; and (2) diplomatic moves either or both to stonewall and obfuscate until Soviet military R&D can redress the "position of weakness," or to forestall or delay deployment of the new technology by the United States. The point to note is that the anxious Soviet response to the adversary's (chuzhaia) technological advance is qualitatively different from the measured response to their own (nasha) gains. For example, the Soviets' crash program to match the United States in nuclear weapons contrasts with the step-by-step march of their space program.[2]

This chapter is concerned with Soviet policy responses to technology of foreign origin. A major point of the essay is that the policy responses to discontinuous change in foreign technology with obvious military applications have been more pronounced than more continuous change in technology with broad civilian as well as military applications, even when the pace of that change has been rapid. This is probably only natural. A sudden leap forward of the military technology of a foreign power seems far more likely to concentrate Politburo attention than the rapid but smooth development of a new technology, even if it has profound military implications.

To explore these points, two case studies of symbiotic interaction between technology of foreign origin and Soviet national security policy are offered. One is historical—the case of nuclear weapons—and the other is contemporary—the development of computer-based technologies. What makes these cases interesting and instructive is that in the case of nuclear weaponry, the centrally directed campaign to close the gap proved successful, whereas in the case of computer-based technologies, it has not and almost certainly will not. What has changed, and what implications flow therefrom?

Soviet Reaction to American Technological Innovation in the Early Postwar Period

The pattern of "foreign technological action/Russian reaction" is a familiar paradigm. The period since World War II illustrates it well. Given that since the beginning of the Cold War the United States has been largely successful in pursuing a strategy of compensating for numerical inferiority by maintaining technological superiority in weapons, the Soviets have frequently found themselves playing catch-up. The case of the atom bomb is a classic example.

Nuclear weapons were first deployed by the United States in 1945. Swiftly, via the doctrine of massive retaliation, they became a centerpiece of American national security policy. The Soviet superiority in numbers and location in Europe was countered by the American threat to deal a devastating blow at Russia should it dare to move against war-weary Western Europe. The import of this nuclear threat was apparent to everyone and most grievously to the Soviets.

What were the consequences for Soviet national security policy of the American monopoly of nuclear technology? On the question of building their own bomb, the Soviets had two basic options: to do it or not do it. Because the idea of ceding global dominance to the Americans was abhorrent to Stalin, it was natural that the Soviets should have spared no effort to master the technology and to develop their own nuclear capability (Josephson 1987: 36–39).[3] David Holloway described the situation as follows:

> But it is clear that the existence of the U.S. programme [to build the atom bomb] was an important factor in the evolution of the Soviet effort. The decision to embark on building the bomb was taken in 1942 only after reports had been received that the United States and Germany were already pursuing this goal. The dropping of the bombs on Hiroshima and Nagasaki demonstrated that the bomb could be built and that it was extremely powerful. Before 1945 many Soviet physicists had doubted that the bomb could be built; now the Soviet effort was intensified. Work on the fusion bomb was stepped up after the US explosion of November 1952. (Josephson 1987: 37)

As the Soviet nuclear capability evolved toward parity with that of the United States, military doctrine and national security policy evolved as well. That an acrimonious atmosphere of cold war should have accompanied the frantic Soviet effort to produce the bomb may not have been inevitable, but Stalin's determination to hold and subjugate the territory overrun by the Red Army made it virtually so. Lacking real power to resist Western insistence that he abide by the Yalta and Potsdam agreements, Stalin sent the obdurate Molotov to bluster and stonewall, to substitute bellicosity for power.

Breaking the American nuclear monopoly and even development of thermonuclear technology did not negate the American doctrine of massive retaliation. The Americans had, in the form of the Strategic Air Command and forward bases, a credible means and a doctrine of delivering a nuclear strike to the Soviet homeland. The Soviets, with nothing comparable, had no nuclear delivery system without which the bomb was a mostly psychological weapon. So the Soviet feeling of vulnerability and the policy of glower persisted well after they mastered nuclear technology. But the other part of the policy, that of neutering the American nuclear threat, dictated creation of a delivery system. This policy imperative came together with existing Soviet momentum in missile technology and German technology captured at Peenemunde in 1953 to produce the decision to develop the SS-6, the first ICBM and launcher of *Sputnik*. The SS-6 first flew in August 1957, though it was not militarily operational before 1960 and was elbowed aside in deployment by the newer SS-7 and SS-8 (Josephson 1987: 39). Nonetheless, by the early 1960s the Soviets had broken the American monopoly on technologies, enabling the attacker to strike the enemy homeland. With the publication of Marshal Sokolovskii's *Voennaia strategiia*, the early 1960s also saw the articulation of a new Soviet military doctrine, what William Odom called the "Second Revolution" of that doctrine, that took account of nuclear and ICBM technologies.[4]

Soviet policy on the home front during those atomic catch-up years is properly considered a part of national security policy given that the USSR was truly a garrison state at that time. The fundamental features of Stalinist economic and social policies are well known: forced draft industrialization; sacrifice of consumer sectors of the economy for heavy industry and military production; centralization of economic decision making; suppression of all forms of dissent; isolation of the Soviet citizenry from the world community; state coercion raised to an art form. In Gerschenkron's words, "the combination of ancient measures of oppression with modern technology and organization proved immensely effective."

What does this case show us? Does it show technology to be an exogenous factor determining the development of Soviet national security policy? Of course not. Absent the unyielding Soviet doctrinal tenet that no adversary should be permitted to wield strategic superiority over the USSR, the postwar American technological superiority need not have been resisted. Absent the legacy of Russian absolutism, the Stalinist state could not have persisted. Rather, the case demonstrates the interaction of technology, historical tradition, and national security policy as the Soviet Union grappled with the problem of military and economic backwardness. In this particular equation only historical tradition and the foreign technological lead were exogenous; both Soviet technological response and national security policy turned out to be endogenous to the system.

Contemporary Interplay between Technology and National Security
Policy: The Case of Informatics

With many of the same variables present, we again set up the equation;
this time for the case of computer- and communications-based technologies,
or "informatics," as the Soviets now call them. Again we have an American
technological innovation and early lead. Again the technology carries
profound implications not only for military power but for economic
power as well. But for various reasons to be explored, the Soviet policy
response and the probable implications thereof have been very different
from those of the previous case.

The first difference arises in the fact that informatics technology at first
disguised itself as "mere" scientific computing machines and hid its wider
applications from everyone. The earliest applications of computers were
to compute ballistic trajectories for artillery personnel. Indeed, it was for
that purpose that the ENIAC, the first electronic computer, was built
in the United States. The motivation for the MESM, the first Soviet
computer, was similar. The second class of applications consisted of
scientific calculations in nuclear physics and a third again concerned
ballistics, this time for missiles. In all of these cases computers played
the role of scientific equipment operated by scientists in a few laboratories.
Few (if any) of the early computer scientists in any nation had a vision of
the widespread diffusion of computer technology into the general economy
that has occurred since midcentury. Should it surprise anyone that no
nation's political leaders were more clairvoyant than their scientists?

A second difference stems from the circumstance that the military impact
of informatics technologies has come gradually and more subtly than
that of nuclear weaponry. The explosions at Hiroshima and Nagasaki so
alarmed Stalin that he gave *carte blanche* to Igor Kurchatov as well as the
NKVD to create the Soviet atomic bomb (Emelanov 1979). The need for
a delivery system was equally obvious to the Soviet political and military
leadership. The spread of computer technology throughout the American
economy and the development of a user-oriented computer market was
driven not by military requirements but by the aggressive and unrelenting
marketing efforts of companies such as IBM, NCR, and Burroughs. Those
efforts converted latent demand for information-processing systems into
orders for equipment and software. Without those marketing efforts
many computer users would never have realized that they had a need
for computers, nor could they have learned to use them productively.The
sellers' market that has prevailed in the Soviet economy combined with the
very structure of the Soviet economic system to preclude the emergence of
a marketing-driven push toward informatics.

Finally, development of modern information technologies requires support from an industrial base in other manufacturing and service sectors that is much broader than that which proved necessary to develop the nuclear weapons and their delivery systems. In the early postwar period the interaction of technology and Soviet national security policy was one that could be worked out in the sector of society specializing in such matters —for instance, certain institutes of the Academy of Sciences as well as the ministries responsible for defense, foreign affairs, security, and the various defense industrial ministries. Indeed, Soviet society frequently has been regarded as a two-sector society, the first consisting of the defense sector ("Sector D") and the second consisting of everything else ("Sector E"). The problems of achieving nuclear parity with the United States were solved in Sector D.

The early, narrowly military applications of computers in the USSR (for example, ballistic calculations and scientific number crunching) could be and were done on a few machines (such as MESM and BESM) designed and largely built in institutes of the Academy of Sciences. But solving the problems posed by the subsequent explosion of informatics technologies and the information revolution could not be solved solely within the walls of Sector D. A broader infrastructure became necessary. However distinct the walls between Soviet Sectors D and E may once have been, they have become increasingly anachronistic. The logic that dictates their dismantling becomes increasingly apparent as the century wanes. In fact, one result of Gorbachev's *perestroika* may be to erode those walls asymptotically to the point of disappearance. Nowhere is this more evident than in the area of informatics.[5]

As in the case of nuclear weapons, the informatics technology originated in the West, largely in the United States. Beyond doubt, Soviet computer technology is more derivative than Soviet nuclear technology. American nuclear technology was protected by tight secrecy, and the contribution of espionage to eventual Soviet successes in the field remains debatable. But in the case of computer technology, the Soviet indebtedness to U.S. forerunners is openly (albeit infrequently) acknowledged. The technological borrowing is so widespread as to be called ubiquitous.

The Soviet ES family of mainframe computers derives directly from IBM 360/370 predecessors that appeared between 1965 and 1975.[6] The Soviet SM family of minicomputers derives directly from DEC's PDP-11, which first appeared in 1970.[7] The Elektronika series of microcomputers, which has been widely used in Soviet military applications, also derives from the PDP-11. The most widely used Soviet microprocessor, the KR580 series, is a functional copy of the Intel 8080 first marketed in the early

1970s. The Agat, BK-0010, PK-1, PK-20, and other Soviet "personal computers" trace their ancestry directly to the Apple II, PDP-11, Intel, and IBM predecessors. And so it goes.

To be fair, the existence of indigenous Soviet computer designs must be acknowledged. During the 1950s and 1960s various Soviet research institutes, mainly within the Academy of Sciences, designed a variety of computers. The technology that they embodied was derivative even if the specific designs were Soviet originals. But the results were highly unsatisfactory except to those with a stake in their design. After the formation of the State Committee for Science and Technology in 1965, responsibility for computer design was removed from the Academy of Sciences and transferred to industry. Eventually three ministries became computer producers; the Ministry of Radio Technology (Minradioprom), the Ministry of Electronics (Minelektronprom), and the Ministry of Instrument Building, Automation, and Control Systems (Minpribor). Of the three, Minradioprom and Minelektronprom are classified as defense (VPK) ministries.

The entire history of the computer era in the Soviet Union has been one of playing "catch-up" to American technology in both quality and quantity. The technological time lag between the appearance of machines of comparable capacity in the two countries hovers in the range of five to seven years. The difference in performance capacity between state-of-the-art computers in the two countries must be reckoned by factors of five to ten or more, and the differences have yet to show signs of narrowing. These qualitative differences are combined with vast quantitative differences: the magnitude of installed computer capacity in the United States is on the order of sixteen times greater than in the Soviet Union, whereas the annual output of computers in the United States is roughly ten times greater than in the USSR (Judy 1987: 161–75).

A critical difference between nuclear technology and informatics technology in its consequences for Soviet policymaking is the qualitatively different impact that the two made on the minds of those in the Kremlin. The implications of the atom bomb struck Stalin with great force. In contrast, awareness of the importance of the informatics technologies dawned but slowly in the minds of the top Soviet leadership over the course of four decades. Little more than occasional and perfunctory exhortation is available to indicate that the top leadership had the remotest clue of the importance of these technologies until the 1970s. By the end of that decade the senior technical intelligentsia was completely aware of the informatics gap, although the message seems not to have been grasped fully by the Brezhnev Politburo.[8] Then, in quick order the torch was passed from Brezhnev to Andropov to Chernenko to Gorbachev.

On January 4, 1985, *Pravda* announced that the Politburo had "considered and basically approved a state-wide program to establish and develop the production and effective utilization of computer technology and automated systems up to the year 2000." Raising economic productivity and efficiency by accelerating scientific and technical progress, particularly in machine building and electronics, was said to be an overarching objective of this new program.

Gorbachev, reporting to the Central Committee in June 1985, put the matter in the following words:

> Machine building plays the dominant, key role in carrying out the scientific and technological revolution. . . . Microelectronics, computer technology, instrument making and the entire informatics industry are the catalyst of progress. They require accelerated development. (*Pravda* 1985b: 2)

The new informatics program, which has not been publicly disseminated, is said to call for acceleration of production, improved quality, and the introduction of new models of computer equipment (Vinokurov and Zuev 1985: 18–29). Applications of informatics technology—especially computers and microprocessors—and automation are to lead to a "comprehensive intensification of the national economy." The program specifies scientific research, machine building, metallurgy, power engineering, natural resource exploration, and "a series of other sectors" as the main foci for the new technology.

Although they remain implicit among the "series of other sectors," military applications clearly have top or near-top priority. Systems employing sophisticated microprocessors as well as other computer and communications technologies are the technological fountainhead of the "third revolution" in Soviet national security policy. Soviet political leaders and civilian spokespersons in the computer field have made no secret of the critical importance they attach to the military application of high-tech information systems (Hershey 1986: 21–28; Voinov 1986: 22–25).

Research and development applications of information technologies occupy an extraordinarily high position in the current list of priorities. This is apparent not only from official rhetoric but from the backgrounds of the people recently appointed to senior positions in the Soviet scientific establishment. One of Gorbachev's most senior advisers on scientific matters, Evgenii Velikhov, heads the Department of Informatics, Computer Technology and Automation of the Academy of Sciences.[9] The newly appointed president of the academy is Gurii Marchuk, a computer scientist who was the founder of the Computer Center of the Academy's Siberian Section in Novosibirsk.

The application of computers to all aspects of production automation stands with military and R&D applications at the top of the Soviet priority pyramid. The Soviet drive for production automation has numerous objectives. One derives from present and anticipated future labor shortages. Another stems from a conventional concern to lower costs by harnessing technology to the production process. An important subset of those objectives, however, flows directly from considerations that have national security implications. These will be addressed here.

Computer-aided design (CAD) enjoys one of the highest priorities among civilian applications of high technology. It is an application that spans the informatics and production automation objectives of Soviet science and technology (S&T) policy. It also spans a broad domain of military and civilian applications. CAD's high priority dates to the Eleventh Five-Year Plan (FYP 1981–85) although it rose farther during the early Gorbachev years.

Soviet CAD technology lags seriously behind the American, but it nevertheless has reached the stage of being very valuable for electronics and mechanical design work. Various problems attend the introduction of CAD into Soviet design organizations that are endemic to the Stalinist system of centralized economic management. The core problem is that system's perverse incentive structure. Not only do organizations lack incentive to improve designs, but the system actually gives designers greater rewards when they create more expensive designs. High barriers between Soviet design bureaus and production organizations also impede the fullest implementation of CAD.[10]

Rapid progress in CAD is a critical Soviet necessity from the standpoint of national security. The complexity of modern weapon systems is beyond what conventional methods of manual design can achieve within acceptable constraints of performance, time, and cost. The same generalization holds with only slightly reduced force to the entire technological base upon which high-technology defense systems rest. As Marx or Lenin might have said, CAD is an objective necessity for a sustainable third revolution in Soviet national security policy.

Industrial applications of informatics have long been among the top Soviet priorities.[11] The pace of implementing automated process control systems surpassed that of management information systems as long ago as the Tenth Five-Year Plan.[12] The new emphasis being given to microprocessors, computerized numerically-controlled machine tools (CNC), robotics, and other "smart" machinery represents a stepping up of the already high priority accorded industrial applications. The marriage of these various technologies makes possible flexible manufacturing systems (FMS), computer-integrated manufacturing (CIM), and other kinds of computer-aided manufacturing (CAM).

Soviet robots and machine tools are generally less sophisticated than their American counterparts, but two points should be stressed. First, the Soviets are making a determined effort to close the qualitative gap; and second, if Soviet statistics are to be believed, new computer-aided manufacturing technology is being produced at a rapid clip. Gorbachev et al. are betting that sooner or later these efforts will pay off.

Just as CAD is a prerequisite for the *design* of high-tech military systems and their electronic and mechanical components, so CAM is a prerequisite for their *production*. High-precision, very specialized manufacturing regimes with rigorous quality standards, more characteristic of specialty job shops than mass assembly lines, are the rule in the high-tech production environment. The rub comes from the fact that the unit cost of production in specialty job shops is exceedingly high. Flexible manufacturing systems, with their ability to reconfigure and retool under computer control, are a virtual necessity if precision job shop results are to be achieved at something beneath astronomical costs of production.

A major difference between the case of the atomic bomb and the case of informatics technology is that the Soviet policy response was clear-cut in the first case and highly complex and even confused in the second. When Stalin learned in 1942 that the Americans and Germans were working on the atom bomb, he pulled a top Soviet nuclear physicist, Igor V. Kurchatov, away from work on tank armor and set him at the head of a crash program not unlike the American Manhattan Project. In short, it was possible and highly effective to focus the effort narrowly within Sector D.

In contrast to the case of nuclear technology policy, an official Soviet policy for informatics technology can hardly be said to have existed until 1985. Even then the technology and its multiple applications were so disparate and pervasive that the conventional Soviet method of centralized control has proved extraordinarily difficult to implement. In an attempt to bring this unwieldy sector under a single roof, the Soviets have established one after another "coordinating" entity. The State Committee for Science and Technology has traditionally held senior responsibility for technical leadership in the informatics field. In 1983 came Velikhov's Informatics Department (*otdel'*) of the Academy of Sciences whose charter gives it wide coordination responsibilities within and outside the academy. In late 1985 the Soviets created the Intersectoral Scientific and Technological Complex (MNTK) for Personal Computers with wide-ranging duties in its given area. Then in early 1986 a new State Committee for Computer

Technology and Informatics was established, apparently with broad powers to direct the industry. Beneath all these coordinating bodies are the computer-producing ministries, Minradioprom, Minelektronprom, and Minpribor. At the lowest level of the Soviet informatics industry are myriad hardware and software research institutes and production enterprises of the ministries. Under conditions of perestroika, wherein enterprises are supposed to have much greater power to determine their own destiny, the confusion is considerable.

The *Pravda* report of the 1985 Politburo discussion of the fifteen-year plan for informatics technology stated that the plan was "basically approved" (1985a: 1).[13] The clear implication here that *not all* of the plan was approved is reinforced by the plan's nonappearance in print. It is reasonable to infer that one locus of disagreement was the manner in which the industry was to be organized. The persisting organizational confusion since January 1985 suggests that the bureaucratic battles over who controls the informatics industry remain unresolved.[14]

Two additional informatics topics of great controversy that appear to have been addressed but only partially resolved by the January 1985 Politburo meeting are those of personal computing and computers in the schools. Both areas of computer application carry potentially profound implications because they involve the wide diffusion of computer technology to the population at large.

Until 1985 the existence of personal computers was hardly recognized. The topic was almost totally ignored in the Soviet press despite the fact that PC technology was burgeoning in the United States, elsewhere in the West, and in Japan. Soviet efforts to design and produce PCs had been little, late, and lamentable. The question is: why did the Soviets dither so? Theories abound. In early 1984 Professor Loren Graham of MIT speculated that "it is becoming increasingly clear that these machines and their associated culture are challenging some of the basic principles of the Soviet state—state control over information and secrecy about vital data" (Graham 1984: C1-C2). Dr. Olin Robison of Middlebury College opined, "The Russians can't easily accommodate computer technology because it gives too many people too much information" (*Time* 1985: 85).

Although the PC issue may have been one of the topics upon which there was incomplete agreement, the January 1985 Politburo meeting appears to have adopted a major decision to proceed vigorously (by Soviet standards) with personal computers. The decision was foreshadowed in August 1984 in a key article by Academician Velikhov (1984: 3–9). Since then glasnost' has come to personal computing. No topic in the whole field of informatics has been hotter since January 1985.

How Soviet PCs will be used is a question offering even richer possibilities for speculation than those of why it took so long to decide to build any and which PCs eventually will be built. Some early Western speculation held that PCs would be kept under lock and key like copiers. Others said the PCs will be out and available for use but the printers will be locked away. As of late 1988 the weight of evidence appeared to be that glasnost' was prevailing and that the new Soviet PCs would be out and available for professional and educational use. Some Soviet informatics visionaries now anticipate a full-blown, PC-based information society *on American lines.*[15]

The momentum of personal computers, even in the Soviet Union, seems to be so great that they cannot be locked away. Conversely, their scarcity will confine PCs mainly to official desks except for those that find their way into private ownership by way of *blat* (pull), luck, and the second economy. PCs bode to become valuable productivity tools in Soviet workplaces as well as coveted status symbols.

Education computing long was stuck on the bottom rung of Soviet informatics priorities. But this area also found its way into the long-run plan discussed and "mainly approved" by the Politburo in January 1985. The new crop of Soviet leaders appears to recognize that the right kind of human capital formation is no less necessary than computer hardware to the realization of their informatics dream. Considerable energy and talent recently has been infused into the world of Soviet educational computing. A multistage plan exists for getting computers into Soviet schools over the next fifteen years.

The plan calls for about 400,000 PCs to be shipped to the schools during the Twelfth FYP. This is enough to equip about 30,000 schools, or one of every two Soviet secondary schools. The number of computer-equipped classrooms is supposed to reach 100,000 by 1995 and 120,000 by 2000. All of this implies a plan to put about 1.3 million computers into Soviet schools by 1995 and about 1.6 million by the end of the century. These numbers compare with over 3.0 million computers in American schools in 1986.

Even if Soviet plans are fulfilled completely—something that depends upon their success in spurring PC production—Soviet educational computing will for some time be much less "hands on" and much more theoretical than educational computing in American schools. But the pressures are building fast in the Soviet educational community to extend the use of educational computers to other disciplines and applications. The widespread use of computers in Soviet schools now appears to be only a matter of time.

The Gorbachev leadership clearly has adopted policies intended to redress the informatics lag behind the United States. But the structure of Soviet society continues to restrict development of the informatics technologies and the industries based on them. To break those bonds to the extent necessary to design and produce state-of-the-art informatics hardware and software will necessitate more radical measures of economic and organizational reform than the Soviets heretofore have been willing to contemplate. Similarly, the process of applying informatics broadly across Soviet society will carry implications that are only beginning to be foreseen.

Implications for Economic and Organizational Reform

The characteristic policy response of the Soviet leadership to perceived problems in science and technology has been to centralize organizational responsibility. The model, of course, is Kurchatov's task force to create the Soviet atom bomb. In Soviet theory a high-priority, centralized effort brings the best people and other necessary resources together with the power to crack bureaucratic heads together and make things happen. This ability to focus energy and resources on high-priority objectives has long been conceded, even by Westerners, to be an advantage of the Soviet command economy.

It should hardly be surprising, therefore, that when the Gorbachev leadership finally recognized the importance of the informatics technologies, its policy response was to try to centralize responsibility for their development. The various intersectoral coordinating bodies previously described were created to overcome lofty ministerial and other bureaucratic barriers. But the results have been highly disappointing. Design bureaus retain stubborn pride in their local design efforts and resist cooperation with others. Ministries with turfs to protect and many other obligations to meet resist "coordination" and seek to produce what is easiest for them. Flexible and rapid action is frustrated by the multitude of players, each of whose assent must be obtained. Gosplan and Gossnab, the state planning and supply committees, retain a firm grip on the power to allocate resources. The lockstep of the five-year planning process imparts great rigidity. The centralized agencies, such as state committees and research institutes entrusted with responsibility to lead the charge, have proven powerless to mobilize and direct this bureaucratic rabble. Occasionally the "lead organization" has become more a part of the problem than of the solution.[16] A prominent Soviet computer scientist recently put it in the following terms:

> One of the impediments to unleashing creative initiative and forging new knowledge is, in my view, the institutional assignment of responsibility for

one or another sector of the national economy: for example, as in the designation of lead organizations that "answer for" progress in a particular area of science. The consistent pursuit of this principle at all levels of the management hierarchy breeds monopoly, the obsequiousness of so-called sectorial science, and the unwillingness or inability to understand others' ideas. Society needs a mechanism for circulating new knowledge, no matter where it may originate or who may be its messenger. (Ershov 1988: 92)

Centralized management of science and technology may work satisfactorily when there is but a single great objective, such as the creation of an atomic bomb, to be achieved. It cannot work well when there are many projects because not all of them can enjoy top priority. When, as now, more than twenty MNTKs claim top priority for resources and ministerial attention, the power of selecting which "top priority" to recognize reverts to the ministries, which defeats the original intent. The Soviets now are desperately seeking new institutional forms to promote science and technology. Within the constraints of their system, however, that is anything but an easy search. Academician Velikhov spoke of recent Soviet institutional experimentation in the following rather wistful terms:

But all of these [institutional] forms still do not accomplish the unimpeded movement of our scientific developments to industrial production. It is well known that in the rest of the world, especially in the United States, the most widespread form of innovation is through the medium of "entrepreneurial" firms which are small firms in which the originator of one or another system or idea follows it from the beginning to the final product. The encouragement of such small groups whose work is of such great value is extraordinarily important for us. This is how the personal computer and many other innovations first appeared on the world scene. Alas, we still lack such entities. Today, if a scientist attempts to cross the border between science and industry he lands in an unfriendly and hostile environment. (Velikhov 1987: 20)

In the Gorbachevian grand strategy, *urskorenie* (economic acceleration) and *intensifikatsiia* (raising the technological level of production) are seen by the Soviet leaders to depend upon perestroika—that is, the package of Gorbachev's economic reforms. It is therefore relevant to ask: How may perestroika affect the Soviet system's receptivity to technological change?

The core of perestroika that will effect both the supply of and demand for technological innovation is the imposition of full financial accountability and independence upon the basic decision-making unit of the Soviet economy, the enterprise. Much remains to be learned about how in actual

practice this will be accomplished (Will enterprises really be on their own
without petty tutelage from above?) and under what conditions (Will prices
be allowed to reflect relative scarcities? Will taxes and other exactions from
enterprise revenues reward or penalize technological innovation?).

For perestroika effectively to promote technological innovation in the
Soviet economy, it must be radical. In concrete terms, that means ensuring
the following six components:

(1) *Financial independence:* Enterprises must become truly independent,
free to prosper or fail in accordance with their own efforts, decisions,
and luck.
(2) *Merit pay:* Individual remuneration must be proportional to the value
of a person's contribution to his or her enterprise's financial health.
(3) *Freedom of entry:* The legal and bureaucratic obstacles to new
enterprise creation must be cleared away.
(4) *Unfettered exchange:* Produced goods and services must be bought
and sold only with the mutual consent of buyer and seller and
without undue societal constraints. The state must contract for goods
and services like any other buyer.
(5) *Rational prices:* Price formation must be flexible enough to respond
to changing relative scarcities, and prices of goods and services must
approach market-clearing levels and/or be freely contracted between
buyers and sellers.
(6) *Neutral taxes:* Exactions from individuals and enterprises must not
discriminate against risk taking, hard work, or innovation.

Acceptance by the Soviets of a perestroika sufficiently radical to include
these six provisions would merit the term "revolutionary." In the near
future, however, they are likely to prefer less radical reform. Proportional
to their timidity will be their failure to achieve their aspirations to make
technological dynamism an inherent attribute of their system.

Implications of Applying New Technology

Historically the adoption of significant new technologies produces different
classes of effects. The primary effects are simply the benefits sought by the
decision to adopt the technology in the first place. Secondary effects result
from the adjustments necessary to accommodate to the new technology and
are transitional in nature. Tertiary consequences are manifest in the longer
term and are largely unanticipated and diffuse in their societal impact.
Both the secondary and tertiary effects may be judged by different people

to be either favorable or unfavorable. By way of illustration, here are a few anticipated secondary and conjectured tertiary effects of a widespread Soviet adoption of the information technologies.

The massive introduction of new, computer-aided design and manufacturing technologies (CAD/CAM) will bring organizational and individual trauma. For example, the change from conventional manufacturing to CAM has serious implications for the work force. Many workers and skills are rendered redundant. Those workers remaining on the production floor must perform a wider range of duties, and they normally require substantial retraining. The nature of work changes qualitatively. Workers' attributes of attentiveness, diagnostic acuity, initiative, sense of responsibility, and concern for quality assume preeminence. Narrow job classifications, which may have been suitable for traditional manufacturing, become irrelevant or a hindrance to the adjustments required for CAM.

Flexible manufacturing systems and computer-integrated manufacturing, if they are to be successful, necessitate an entirely new and integrated approach to product and manufacturing process design. If a product is to be "manufacturable" by robots and made movable by computer-controlled materials-handling equipment, its assemblies, its components, and the product itself must conform to constraints imposed by the specifications of the robots and equipment. Product designers must bring manufacturing considerations into their work at the earliest stage. Standardization of components and subassemblies for different final products becomes very important.

Piecemeal introduction of the more sophisticated types of CAM, such as flexible manufacturing and computer-integrated manufacturing, is hardly feasible. In an existing organization the old manufacturing line usually must be shut down, the area gutted of old equipment, and new equipment installed. Obviously much careful planning must precede this step or the new system will work poorly, if at all. The various components and other pieces of equipment must arrive in a timely fashion so that they may be installed by skilled workers. Missing links in an automated line typically mean that the line cannot operate or must do so with "inserts" of manual labor at the missing links. This is usually an expensive expedient and often quite unsatisfactory.

Full realization of the potential benefits of CIM require that the control of inventories at both ends of the manufacturing process be integrated into the system. At the input end, the computerized system should maintain stock records of all purchased and manufactured components and subassemblies. From these and from usage data captured while the computers monitor the production processes, the system should trigger orders to suppliers, preferably on a computer-to-computer basis via telecommunications linkage. At the output end, the CIM system should interface its inventory of finished products with sales and shipping information, again on a computer-to-computer basis.

The integration, under computer control, of a broad range of functions from material input to manufacturing to product distribution creates the conditions for highly integrated data collection, storage, and processing. The experience of American firms is that a preponderance of the payoff from CIM comes at this stage, where the CIM system interfaces with the management information system. Great savings of personnel costs and improvement of function become possible at middle management levels as the system takes over responsibility in functions such as ordering, receiving, inventory, shipping, and accounting. Two important points need to be stressed. First, profound innovation is unsettling in all societies, but the specific circumstances and traits of the Stalinist socioeconomic system exacerbate the difficulties. Second, Soviet enterprise managers will consider the costs of implementing new technology prohibitive the more they are concerned with short-term versus long-term performance, the more they face conditions of a sellers' market, and the more they face inflexible labor conditions and unresponsive suppliers. Because these features characterize the traditional Stalinist form of Soviet industrial organization, the Soviets will encounter very serious difficulties so long as they retain that form. If the incentive structure that Soviet enterprise managers confront continues to reward fulfillment of a plan based on historical performance levels, those managers are likely to see few benefits to balance the risk and expense associated with the introduction of new technologies.

Conclusion

The technological level of modern weapons is rising very rapidly. It follows that a nation's ability to mount and maintain a superpower military establishment depends on a broad technological base and a dynamic economy capable of incorporating new technology into both production processes and end products. The Soviets have neither.

In the early 1980s advances in computer technology that originated in the United States—especially the development of sophisticated micro-processors and other integrated circuits—presented the Soviet leadership with a classic case of technological and economic backwardness that threatened to lose their hard-won military position vis-à-vis the West. Responding in characteristic fashion, the Soviets have tried a variety of centralized catch-up measures. But these have not worked. No longer is it sufficient to respond to perceived lags behind foreign adversaries with crash programs to catch up as the Soviets were able to do in the case of nuclear weaponry.

The conclusion that emerges from the foregoing is that radical economic reform, perestroika and more, is a condition for the successful implementation of Soviet dreams to develop and implement new technology in general and informatics in particular. Glasnost' and perestroika are logical conditions if the Soviets wish to overcome the increasing lag that separates the way in which the informatics and other technologies are developed and implemented in the USSR from the way they are in the West. And these new technologies must be developed and exploited or Soviet military prowess will decline relative to that of the United States and other potential adversaries. In short, perestroika is necessary to build the kind of economy that is necessary to build the kind of weapons that can compete in the high-tech military game.

But perestroika cannot succeed without providing greater incentives to producers. Merit pay means nothing when money buys nothing. Given that the fruits of perestroika will not be realized for some time, the Soviet leadership needs to channel resources from the military to the civilian sectors to buy that necessary time. That, in turn, requires a respite from the exhausting military confrontation with the West. "New thinking" (*novoe myshlenie*), with its restructuring of Soviet national security policy and military doctrine, is the logical outcome of that necessity.

In this sequence of cause and effect, we see how modern high technology, especially that of informatics, interacts with Soviet history and doctrine to help forge new national security policies just as did the postwar nuclear and missile technologies. But the similarities are less impressive than the dissimilarities. Not only does the drive for informatics technology help to put glasnost' and perestroika in vogue, it dictates an opening to rather than a shutting out of the West.

Alexander Gerschenkron would be amused to see how the informatics technologies are standing Peter the Great and Stalin on their heads. No longer does it prove immensely effective for the Kremlin to combine "ancient measures of oppression with modern technology and organization." Indeed, all of the "advantages of industrialization in conditions of backwardness" seem to have been exhausted. The quest continues to adopt "the fruits of Western technological progress," but the means of doing so have become, we may dare to hope, both more civilized and more civilizing.

Notes

1. See the chapter by Steven Merritt Miner in this volume. Also see chapter 16 in Liashchenko (1956). The author wishes to thank the National Council for Soviet and East European Research for its financial support of the work upon which this chapter is based.

2. The cases discussed later illustrate how this point has worked out in the Soviet case. In fact, the United States also responds asymmetrically to Soviet leaps ahead in various heats of the military technology race. Reflect, for example upon the American response to the surprise of *Sputnik* and to the various "missile gaps."

3. A crisp account of the Soviet effort to develop the technologies of nuclear weapons and delivery systems is to be found in "Military Technology" in Amann et al. (1977), pp. 446–89. See also Josephson (1987).

4. In translation, this book appeared as Sokolovskii (1963).

5. Informatics, *informatika* in Russian, is used by the Soviets to mean the entire panoply of computer and communications technologies and their applications. The word is used here with that same meaning.

6. The letters ES are from *edinaia sistema*, or "unified system."

7. The letters SM are from *sistema malaia*, or "small system."

8. See, for example, Glushkov and Kanygin (1980), p. 11. Academician Glushkov, now deceased, was one of the intellectual fathers of Soviet computer science and founder of the research institute that now bears his name in the Ukrainian Academy of Sciences. In this article, the authors point up the fragmented nature of the "machine informatics" industry in the USSR. They fault the State Committee for Science and Technology with failing to provide unified leadership for developing and applying computer technology.

9. The entity was established in 1983.

10. These difficulties certainly attend the civilian sectors. They are present also in the military sphere, though probably to a lesser degree.

11. The word *industrial* is used generically to include manufacturing, extraction, construction, and transportation, though industries such as machine building, energy, and electronics are clearly in the top spot. The definition excludes trade and services.

12. ASUTP is the Soviet acronym for automated process control system.

13. This report used the words "Politbiuro obsudilo i *v osnovom* odobrilo obshche-gosudarstvennuiu programmu" (emphasis added).

14. Glasnost' has produced abundant confirmation of the bureaucratic straitjacket that binds Soviet efforts to develop the informatics industries. See, for example, A. Tarasov's (1988) sorry tale of how the Soviets have failed to produce and deploy fiber optics communications networks.

15. For an exposition of an emerging new view of the Soviet information society, see Ershov (1988), pp. 82–92.

16. For evidence of the failure of various MNTKs to cope, see Giglavyi and Gutkin (1988), p. 1; Tarasov (1988), and Kotel'nikov (1988).

References

Amann, R., J. M. Cooper, and R. W. Davies (1977). *The Technological Level of Soviet Industry.* New Haven, CT: Yale University Press.

Emelanov, V. S. (1979). *S chego nachinalos.* Moscow.

Ershov, A. (1988). "Informatizatsiia: Ot komp'iuternoi gramotnosti uchashchikhsiia k informatsionnoi kul'ture obshchestva." *Kommunist*, 2.

Gerschenkron, Alexander (1962). "Patterns and Problems of Russian Economic Development, 1861–1958." In C. Black, ed., *The Transformation of Russian Society*. Cambridge: Harvard University Press, 1960. Reprinted in A. Gerschenkron, ed., *Economic Backwardness in Historical Perspective*. New York: Praeger.

Giglavyi, A., and M. Gutkin (1988, March 6). "Tormoza komp'iuterizatsii." *Uchitel'skaia gazeta*, p. 1.

Glushkov, V., and Iu. Kanygin (1980). "Stanovlenie otrasli." *Ekonomicheskaia gazeta*, 52, p. 11.

Graham, L. (1984, March 11). "The Soviet Union is Missing Out on the Computer Revolution." *Washington Post*, pp. C1–C2.

Hershey, J. E. (1986). "The U.S. and the Soviets Use Different Approaches to the Cutting Edge of Defense Computing." *Defense Science and Electronics*, 5(11), 21–28.

Josephson, Paul T. (1987). "Early Years of Soviet Nuclear Physics." *Bulletin of the Atomic Scientists*, 43(11), 36–39.

Judy, Richard W. (1987). "The Soviet Information Revolution: Some Prospects and Comparisons." In Joint Economic Committee, United States Congress, *Gorbachev's Economic Plans*. Washington, DC: U.S. Government Printing Office.

Kotel'nikov, V. A. (1988). "O prioritetnykh napravlenniakh razvitiia nauki." *Vestnik Akademii Nauk SSSR*, 7, 64–74.

Liashchenko, I. I. (1956). *Istoriia narodnogo khoziastva SSSR*, Vol. 1, 4th ed. Moscow.

Pravda (1985a, January 4). "V Politbiuro Tsk KPSS." P. 1.

——— (1985b, June 12). "Korennoi vopros ekonomicheskoi politiki partii, doklad tovarishcha M. S. Gorbacheva." Pp. 1–2.

Sokolovskii, V. D. (1963). *Soviet Military Strategy*. Englewood Cliffs, NJ: Prentice-Hall.

Tarasov, A. (1988, February 26). "Paradoksy 'Svetovoda.'" *Pravda*, p. 2.

Time (1985, April 15). "Playing Computer Catch-Up." Pp. 84–85.

Velikhov, E. P. (1984). "Personal'nye EVM—segodniashchiaia praktika i perspektivy." *Vestnik Akademii Nauk SSSR*, no. 8.

——— (1987). "O zadachakh Akademii Nauk SSSR v svete reshenii iiun'skogo (1987 g.) plenuma TsK KPSS." *Vestnik Akademii Nauk SSSR*, 12, 14–26.

Vinokurov, V., and K. Zuev (1985). "Aktual'nye problemy razvitiia vychislitel'noi tekhniki." *Kommunist*, 5, 18–25.

Voinov, Iu. (1986). "Technical State of the Soviet Army and Navy." *Soviet Military Review*, 3.

• CHAPTER SEVEN •

Domestic Politics and Gorbachev's Security Policy

William J. Bishop
Denison University

November 7, 1987 was the seventieth anniversary of Lenin's October Revolution. Not only is the anniversary perceived to be a turning point in Soviet history by the current Soviet leadership, it is very likely to be seen as such by subsequent generations. At stake, and perceived to be so by the Soviet leadership, is the continuing status of the USSR as a superpower into the twenty-first century. Gorbachev and other Soviet leaders are publicly articulating the fear that unless something major is done soon, the Soviet Union can expect to follow a path of gradual but sure decline. The USSR must find ways to solve problems of poor – quality production and low worker productivity. A debate over what to do and how swiftly to do it is now engaging the energies of a new generation of Soviet leaders.

The discussion among Soviet leaders over what to do about the economy is in fact a debate over national security policy. At risk in the long run for the Soviet Union is loss of status and power in world politics as countries with more effective and efficient productive technologies surpass the USSR first in the economic realm and eventually in the military realm as well. Though falling behind as an economic power must be unpleasant for all Soviet leaders, efforts to reform their own system and make it more productive involve risks. Foremost among them is the possibility that reform may bring unwelcome changes in the realities of political power. This chapter addresses the relationship between the dynamics of leadership change and emerging Soviet foreign and security policy. In so doing it examines the nature of Soviet coalition politics, the players in Soviet foreign and security policy, the military since 1985, and Gorbachev's strategy and the future.

Soviet Coalition Politics

The prospect of decline for the USSR is a question that has become the focus of conflict within the Soviet political elite. The Soviet political class has rejected the Brezhnev regime and its policies as a failure. The Gorbachev regime is under construction, well along but not yet completely built. The USSR is now between the decay and disintegration of the Brezhnev regime and the completion of a successor regime. Gorbachev has secured the key position of the Soviet hierarchy, the general secretaryship of the Communist party, and has become chair of the Presidium of the Supreme Soviet, an office with newly defined roles to make it a much more powerful player in the day-to-day activities of the state. He has, as we have seen in the preceding chapters, defined the restructuring of Soviet society and economy, the Soviet spirit, and Soviet foreign policy as essential tasks.

But Gorbachev has not yet been able to galvanize his coalition of leaders and constituencies into enthusiastic action. Although there has been much frank talk and exposure of past error (*glasnost'*), as well as a "new thinking" encouraged from on high, there still appears to be a lack of zeal for comprehensive reform among the general population. Within the ruling *nomenklatura* class as well as within the top leadership there has yet to appear great enthusiasm for change.

The difficulty of the task and the absence of a clear and painless solution to it are dividing the leadership. The Soviet economy continues to suffer declining rates of economic growth while producing commodities that are for the most part well below international standards. A campaign against the abuse of alcohol has predictably accelerated the production of home brew. A posture of openness has led to public leadership bickering over the truth about past achievements and the extent of current social and political problems.

Soviet leadership is a coalition of leaders, interests, constituencies, and institutions which can agree that there is no alternative to restructuring, *perestroika*. There is thus leadership unity in principle. But at the same time, the coalition seems to find it difficult to take decisive, coherent action. Despite a politically secure general secretary who has been able to eliminate his rivals, there continues to exist division and inertia that prevent action. On January 1, 1988, a restructuring of the Soviet economy formally began. While it is too early to pass final judgment upon the reform package as it emerged at the January and June Central Committee plenums of 1987, and subsequent enactments, it does appear that the reform is riddled with compromises and contradictions that raise questions about how effective it can be. The emerging Soviet leadership thus appears to have agreed upon the necessity to restructure but is fearful of the consequences of deep restructuring, and thus it is coming forward with programs for change that are flawed from the outset.

The divisions within the coalition seem to be, first, disagreement over how deep the restructuring need be and how much of the past must be jettisoned in order to address the problem of decline. At risk in particular are the privileges and authority of the nomenklatura stratum, the roughly 3 million-strong class of bosses who run the USSR (Voslensky 1984: 95). Restructuring, if it is to be serious and to address the problems that a leadership consensus defines as critical, necessarily entails loss of power and privilege for this class. Decisions, especially economic ones, need to be made much more than they now are, on the basis of economic criteria. The arbitrary and predatory power of the Soviet political class and the corruption it generates and protects in the economic sphere need to be greatly reduced, if not entirely eliminated.

A second major division within the Soviet leadership runs along an ethnic or national line. The constituencies and bases of power of the previous Brezhnev coalition were largely at the periphery of the Soviet Union. Although himself an ethnic Russian, Leonid Brezhnev had a long political career (Stalin's purges elevated him to a very high position at a relatively young age) which enabled him to build networks of clients in the Ukraine, Moldavia, and Kazakhstan as he served as a lieutenant and ally of Khrushchev. In addition, in the early years of his general secretaryship he was able to manage the Russian half of the Soviet Union by tactics of divide and rule.

By contrast, the coalition currently in power has a Russian center of gravity. Within this coalition is a strain of Russian chauvinism that has already reflected itself in policy. At the end of 1986 the collective leadership coalition replaced the native Kazakh party leader of Kazakhstan, D. A. Kunaev, with a new man, a Russian, who was sent to Alma Ata by Moscow to clean up the native corruption. The consequence was an uprising that was put down with force. Such nationality questions and economic restructuring questions are directly related in the Soviet context.

Restructuring means, among other things, new investment in plant and equipment. The Russian and other Slavic regions of the USSR have labor shortages. In the regions of Islamic heritage on the southern periphery of the USSR, however, there is a demographic explosion and a labor surplus. Finally, the rich resources, the development of which must be a key component of any restructuring, are in Siberia east of the Russian/Slavic center of industry and population and well to the north of the major concentrations of Islamic peoples. Conflicting regional and ethnic interests will necessarily be a component of the politics of restructuring.

A third cleavage within the current coalition is a division over foreign and security policy. Gorbachev, who is to be identified with the more impatient (but not the most impatient) of the restructurers and also with the less Russian chauvinist part of the leadership, is vigorously pursuing a foreign policy of relaxation of tensions with the outside, especially with the United States and the West. This foreign policy is perceived by Gorbachev and others to be a necessary part of restructuring for at least two reasons. First, as Richard W. Judy points out in the previous chapter, regular and large-scale access to Western markets and technologies is seen to be an important part of restructuring. Second, the burden of military production on the USSR is considerable and has been so for decades. Relaxed relations with the West could help to free resources now allocated to defense purposes for much-needed investment in the machine-building industries. Beyond the heavy baseline defense burden of the past, a new element has substantially added to Soviet concern.

The new concern is the U.S. strategic defense initiative (SDI). SDI presents to the new Soviet decision makers the prospect of an accelerated technological race with the United States for new generations of military equipment. The very powerful military-industrial centers of the USSR and the Soviet military—especially those sectors responsible for ballistic missiles and air/space defense—are particularly concerned. Also concerned are those who, for whatever reason, are more suspicious of the motives of "imperialists" and the sinister driving forces of capitalism. They are reluctant to permit a redefinition of Soviet security policy that involves greater contact with the outside world, a flow of new ideas and aspirations, and the consequent contamination of the USSR.

The three major dimensions of conflict within the Soviet political establishment concern the pace and dangers of internal restructuring, the proper place of the Russian nation in Soviet society, and the threat from the outside world. Although there is clearly conflict and division within the Soviet establishment, there is also a consensus that the situation is critical, that the Brezhnev way has been a failure, and that major changes must be made.

The Players in Soviet Foreign and Security Policy

Coalition politics in the USSR is not unidimensional. A simplified Soviet political spectrum, however, might place the military and the Russian chauvinists in the Soviet leadership to the right of Gorbachev. To the right should be placed all those fearful of the consequences of change and of an increase in foreign influence on the Soviet peoples. With views to the left of Gorbachev, there appears to be a part of the Soviet leadership —most conspicuously recently deposed Moscow city Party First Secretary Boris Yel'tsin as well as leaders in some of the union republics. Although all the evidence in the Yel'tsin case is not completely in, his demise undeniably represents a short-term defeat for bold restructuring. Those who do not yet see sufficient change occurring at the appropriate rapid pace must be disappointed and even apprehensive because of the fact and the abrupt manner in which Yel'tsin was discharged from the oligarchy.

Arguably all issues in domestic politics and hence all domestic players in politics are relevant to foreign and security policy. It is possible, however, to specify those players and institutions at the top of the Soviet hierarchy which are most relevant to a discussion of foreign and security policy. The top oligarchs or players in Soviet politics as of January 1, 1989 are listed in Table 7.1.

The list of players can be reduced to a subset of those who are known to be relevant to Soviet foreign policy. This identification is possible on the basis of two interrelated criteria: (1) the formal post or job of the individual and (2) observed activities (content of speeches, meetings attended, and obituaries signed). It is also possible to make observations and to draw inferences based on changes and continuities in the division of labor and the location of functions across the various centers of power of the Soviet system. Those centers of power relevant to foreign/security policy include the Secretariat of the Central Committee (CC) of the Party, the USSR Council of Ministers, the Ministry of Defense, the Ministry of Foreign Affairs, and the Committee for State Security (KGB). Some of the major political actors in Table 7.1 are located at regional centers of power and for that reason are of less significance for foreign policymaking.

All of the aforementioned institutions are bureaucratic hierarchies with large staffs. There is, however, another kind of institution in the Soviet scheme of things: the executive committee. In this context two are of special importance: the Politburo and the Defense Council (DC). Although the list of members and candidates of the Politburo is displayed in Table 7.1, the precise membership of the DC has not been publicly revealed. There are sound reasons to believe that the membership of the two groups overlaps. It can be reasonably assumed that the members of the

TABLE 7.1
Soviet Oligarchy as of January 1, 1989[a]

Status	Date in Buro	Year Birth	Year Party	Date (if any) Secretariat[b]	Job/date in[c]
Politburo					
M. S. Gorbachev	10/80	31	52	11/78	General Secretary 3/85; Chair Presidium USSR Supreme Soviet 10/88
V. I. Vorotnikov	12/83	26	47		Chair Presidium RSFSR Supreme Soviet 10/88
L. N. Zaikov	3/86	23	57	7/85	(defense and other industry); First Secretary Moscow Party 11/87
E. K. Ligachev	4/85	20	44	12/83	Chair CC Commission on Agriculture 9/88
V. A. Medvedev	9/88	29	52	3/86	Chair CC Ideological Commission 9/88
V. P. Nikonov	6/87	29	54	4/85	(agriculture)
N. I. Ryzhkov	4/85	29	56		Chairman USSR Council of Ministers 9/85
N. N. Sliun'kov	6/87	29	54	1/87	Chair CC Commission on Socio-Economic Policies 9/88
E. A. Shevardnadze	7/85	28	48		USSR Minister Foreign Affairs 7/85
V. M. Chebrikov	4/85	23	44	9/88	Chair CC Commission on Legal Policy 9/88
V. V. Shcherbitskii	4/71	18	41		First Secretary Communist Party of Ukraine 5/72
A. N. Iakovlev	6/87	23	43	3/86	Chair CC Commission on International Affairs 9/88

TABLE 7.1 (*continued*)
Soviet Oligarchy as of January 1, 1989[a]

Status	Date in Buro	Year Birth	Year Party	Date (if any) Secretariat[b]	Job/date in[c]
Politburo candidates					
A. P. Biriukova	9/88	29	56		Deputy Chair USSR Council of Ministers 10/88; Chair Council of Ministers Social Development Bureau 10/88
A. V. Vlasov	9/88	32	56		Chair RSFSR Council of Ministers 10/88
A. I. Luk'ianov	9/88	30	55		First Deputy Chair Presidium USSR Supreme Soviet
Iu. D. Masliukov	2/88	37	66		Chair, USSR State Planning Committee (Gosplan) 2/88
G. P. Razumovskii	2/88	36	61	3/86	Chair CC Commission on Party Work and Cadres Policy 9/88
Iu. F. Solov'ev	3/86	25	55		First Secretary Leningrad 7/85
N. V. Talyzin	10/85	29	60		Deputy Chair USSR Council of Ministers 10/88; USSR Rep. to Comecon 10/88
D. T. Iazov	6/87	23	44		USSR Minister of Defense 5/87
Other Central Committee Secretary					
O. D. Baklanov		32	53	2/88	(military industry)

[a] Members of oligarchy listed as they appear in Soviet press; Gorbachev first and others listed alphabetically in Cyrillic by rank.

[b] Dates provided when available.

[c] This column indicates full-time responsibilities. For some Central Committee secretaries presumed, apparent, or known functional responsibilities indicated in parentheses.

DC include relevant members and candidate members of the Politburo in addition to CC secretaries, some number of military officers including the chief of the General Staff of the Soviet armed forces, and some number of officials from the USSR Council of Ministers. The existence of the Defense Council is acknowledged by Soviet sources, but few details are provided (Akhromeev 1986: 684). Greater knowledge of the relationship between the Politburo and the DC could reveal valuable information about the linkage of domestic and foreign and security issues in Soviet decision making as well as information about the extent to which the General Staff serves as the staff base in the process of deciding military-political questions (and thereby has greater influence).

Of the twelve members of the Politburo listed in Table 7.1, five can be readily identified as especially relevant to foreign policy: Gorbachev, Iakovlev, Shevardnadze, Chebrikov, and Medvedev. Two others by implication are probably also quite significant: Ligachev and Ryzhkov. At the level of Politburo candidates Minister of Defense Iazov stands out; the chief economic planner Masliukov and the First Deputy Supreme Soviet Presidium Chair Luk'ianov may also be of some secondary significance. At the lowest level of status within the oligarchy, two names are particularly relevant for foreign/security policymaking: A. F. Dobrynin and V. M. Falin.

The Secretariat of the CC remains the locus of political conflict. Gorbachev does not yet firmly control it. The importance of the Secretariat in Soviet politics is clearly indicated by the fact that succession to the preeminent position in Soviet politics—first secretary in the cases of Khrushchev and Brezhnev and general secretary in the cases of Andropov, Chernenko, and Gorbachev—was achieved in each case from the steppingstone of senior secretary (defined as a secretary who is simultaneously a full member of the Politburo). If past precedent is upheld, Gorbachev's successor will come from the ranks of the current or future senior secretaries. As with Khrushchev and Brezhnev, an ally of today can become tomorrow's successor. The changes in the Secretariat in September 1988 may imply an overall weakening of Gorbachev's position. Although the scope of E. K. Ligachev's authority seems to have been limited by his demotion from "second secretary" to head of the CC agricultural commission, the promotion of V. A. Medvedev to head the ideology commission and the advancement of V. M. Chebrikov to the Secretariat as head of the legal policy commission suggest a dilution of Gorbachev's power within the Secretariat.

Of the senior secretaries relevant to foreign policy, the one closest to Gorbachev, and apparently his intellectual and political mentor, is A. N. Iakovlev. Iakovlev more than any other full member of the

Politburo seems to be dependent upon Gorbachev. Iakovlev was one of the early participants in the U.S.-Soviet academic exchange. As a high-level official within the Secretariat in the early 1970s he seems to have had his career derailed by being too critical of Russian nationalism. He was sent to Canada as ambassador from 1973 to 1983. From there his career was put back on track by Gorbachev, for whom he now serves as an adviser on foreign policy in his capacity of chair of the CC Commission on International Affairs and as a senior secretary (Politburo) colleague.

E. K. Ligachev was the informal second secretary; there is no formal post of second secretary. Ligachev has little apparent expertise in foreign affairs, and his responsibilities in the Secretariat do not include foreign policy questions in a major way. He has, however, since 1985 been chair of the Commission on Foreign Affairs of the Supreme Soviet Council of the Union. Ligachev, in his published speeches, frequently differs in emphasis, if not substance, from Gorbachev. It is not sufficient to say that Ligachev is simply subordinate to Gorbachev. Ligachev speaks with authority on his own. More than anything else, he seems to articulate the reservations and fears of the nomenklatura class. He insists that the past contributions of leaders be recognized and respected. He dismisses criticisms of the perquisites of cadres by those who do not understand past difficulties and sacrifices. Ligachev defends the privileges of his class as no less than just reward. Although he may become an alternative to Gorbachev, he does not appear to be that now. Ligachev seems to serve as a counterweight for the collective leadership to Gorbachev within the Secretariat.

Another full member of the Politburo, E. A. Shevardnadze, is the current minister of Foreign Affairs. A. A. Gromyko, who died in July 1989, was his immediate predecessor. Looking over seventy years of Soviet history, the role of the Ministry of Foreign Affairs was mostly secondary. This changed under Brezhnev. In 1973 Gromyko was advanced to full membership in the Politburo. The transfer of Gromyko in 1985 from his responsibilities as foreign minister to become head of state suggested the intent of putting forward a new face in foreign affairs, as well as relieving Gromyko from responsibility for the day-to-day conduct of foreign affairs while not removing him from the decision-making center.

The basis of Gromyko's influence was always his expertise, not his political base in the Party or even his management of the Foreign Ministry. Being moved to the post of head of state—the chair of the Presidium of the USSR Supreme Soviet—meant that he was not only a member of the Politburo but probably also a member of the Defense Council. He was presumably present for the critical debates and decisions on foreign policy. Because of his long experience and expertise and because he was at an age that presumably put him beyond ambition, Gromyko was well situated to hold Gorbachev accountable for Soviet foreign policy. Gromyko seemed to be another of those set up by a collective leadership to act as counterweight to Gorbachev. The retirement of Gromyko in September–October 1988 and the acquisition by Gorbachev of the post of head of state marked an important acknowledgment by the leadership of Gorbachev's success in foreign policy.

Shevardnadze has had a career in the Komsomol, Ministry of the Interior, and the Communist party in Soviet Georgia. His career runs parallel to that of Gorbachev in a number of ways. Both of their home regions, Stravropol (Gorbachev) and Georgia (Shevardnadze), are adjacent astride the Caucasus Mountains, the two leaders are close in age, and both began their political careers as Komsomol officials. Shevardnadze's choice as foreign minister is part of a general redesign of foreign policy machinery to concentrate the gathering of information and the formulation and execution of Soviet foreign policy in the hands of Gorbachev at the CC Secretariat. As an outsider at the Foreign Ministry, it is more likely that Shevardnadze will represent Gorbachev's views to the ministry rather than be a conveyer of the ministry's views to Gorbachev and the Politburo. The change to Shevardnadze as minister (as an outsider and nonspecialist but as a Gorbachev man) and the substantial changes in the capabilities of the CC Secretariat for foreign policy analysis all suggest a reduced role for the Foreign Ministry from the Brezhnev to the Gorbachev era.

Viktor Chebrikov, former head of the KGB, was a member of the Dnepropetrovsk circle—that is, a Brezhnev Party functionary. He was assigned to the KGB in 1967 presumably to keep an eye on Andropov. Once the Andropov coalition set itself in power, Chebrikov appeared to have been selected by the collective leadership as a counterweight to the new mainstream coalition. Chebrikov thus had been established as a guardian of Soviet state security independent of the particular political security needs of Gorbachev, his political coalition, and regime. As he was director of a huge data-gathering and operational organization, and as a man with long experience at the KGB, it must be assumed that the role of the KGB and its chief were, as in the past, of great importance. The relocation of Chebrikov to the CC Secretariat and his appointment as head of the Commission on Legal Policy in September 1988 would seem to give him authority from the Party side over all law and state security agencies.

Vadim Medvedev has had close career ties with Alexander Iakovlev, under whom he worked in the late 1960s and early 1970s in the apparatus of the Central Committee, and where he remained until 1978. His career was bolstered under Andropov when he was brought back to the Party apparatus, and he has now risen to be the new head of Party ideology, having been appointed chair of the new CC Ideological Commission in September 1988. Rather than having a position second in importance to the general secretary, as other chief ideologists have held in the past, Medvedev appears to share power with other important Politburo members such as Iakovlev and Chebrikov, who also hold Politburo and Secretariat positions (Yasmann 1988: 3). Nevertheless, his past experience as head of the CC Department for Liaison with Communist and Workers' Parties of Socialist Countries, and his expertise in the philosophical foundations of socialist economics, place him in a special position for assisting in the "new thinking" with respect to Eastern Europe and for helping to plot a new approach to thorny ideological issues, such as the coexistence of capitalist and socialist systems. His past speeches have demonstrated that he is an exponent of permitting diversity among Eastern European political systems and for abandoning the "class approach" in relations with capitalist nations. In other words, he addresses the analysis of international security from an angle that stresses flexibility and realism in dealing with friends and foes alike—a view compatible with Gorbachev's.

The chair of the Presidium of the USSR Council of Ministers, Nikolai Ryzhkov, is the general manager of the Soviet economy. He is the one who must actually implement an economic reform. As manager of the economy he must be concerned with foreign trade, acquiring foreign technology, and earning foreign exchange. More than anyone else, he knows the magnitude and nature of the burden of military spending on the Soviet economy. Despite all of the foregoing, Ryzhkov is probably little concerned with the day-to-day conduct of foreign policy and is occupied with it only as it has large-scale economic and financial implications.

An important theme touched upon earlier is the enhanced role of the CC Secretariat and the fundamental restructuring of the International Department (ID) of the Secretariat. Arguably the most accomplished Soviet specialist on the nature and dynamics of the United States is Anatoly Dobrynin, head of the ID from 1986 to 1988. Dobrynin served as ambassador to the United States from 1962 until 1986, when it was revealed to the world and to stunned Soviet specialists that he had been named a secretary of the Central Committee. With this move of the Soviets' most proven Americanist to work directly for the general secretary in Moscow and simultaneously restructuring and expanding the scope and domain of the Secretariat's concern with foreign policy, it became clear that Soviet foreign policy (especially with respect to the United States) would forthwith be run less through the Foreign Ministry (with the accompanying bureaucratic delays) and instead through Dobrynin almost directly to the general secretary. Such an organizational change eliminated many layers of bureaucracy, brought the top analyst to the side of the top decision maker, and thus enabled Gorbachev to conduct the high-intensity, high-priority, agile foreign policy with respect to the United States that has since dazzled the world.

Dobrynin's 1986 promotion indicated a special priority for U.S.-Soviet relations. The Foreign Ministry, as the primary instrument for gathering and analyzing information as well as for generating initiatives and proposals in relations with the West, was usurped. The reorganization of the ID for its new role also involved bringing expertise on military and arms control questions into the Secretariat. The loser in influence on Soviet political/military policy was the Ministry of Defense. That institution lost what hitherto had been a virtual monopoly on information and a near veto on the policy matters that concerned it most.

Dobrynin's status in the oligarchy was sharply reduced by his removal from the CC Secretariat in September 1988. He continued, however, as foreign policy adviser to Gorbachev and retained his post as chair of the Foreign Affairs Commission of the Soviet of Nationalities in the USSR Supreme Soviet. V. M. Falin replaced Dobrynin in the September Secretariat reorganization. The International Department was expanded to include what had been the Cadres Abroad Department and the Department for Liaison with Communist and Workers' Parties of Socialist Countries. Thus the ID's responsibilities—and presumably political power—were broadened even more.

The Military since 1985

During his tenure in office Gorbachev has been able to reduce greatly the place of the military in foreign policy decision making. Reducing the status of the minister of defense and removing a minister of defense in 1987 are part of this. In addition, Gorbachev has restructured the machinery for making political-military policy. One of the most important aspects of this has been to build centers of expertise outside the military, both in the Central Committee Secretariat and in the Foreign Ministry, which has the effect of greatly reducing the ability of the military to veto policies that affect it.

Beyond reducing the role of the military in the security policymaking arena, Gorbachev's restructuring depends on a very large increase in investment in the civilian economy, as Hans Heymann notes in his contribution to this volume. Although many military leaders understand that Soviet security and superpower status will depend on a large and sophisticated technological base, none of the branches of the Soviet military wants to see its resources reduced in the short run. Although this ambivalence within the military gives Gorbachev room to maneuver, it also sets up the potential for a backlash from the military should restructuring generally be seen to be failing.

The role of the military in Soviet succession politics in particular and in Soviet leadership politics in general continues to be a subject of interest and dispute. It has been suggested that during periods of leadership succession the military is in a position to make increased demands for resources (Sonnenfeldt 1978: 277–78). Presumably contenders for power in the Soviet Union will outbid one another for the support of the military and set in motion a spending cycle that will last for some years.

Appearances, however, now strongly suggest that the Soviet military as an institutional player has not done well in post-Brezhnev Soviet politics. Dmitri Ustinov, Minister of Defense from 1976 until his death in 1984, was replaced by his next in line, Marshal Sergei Sokolov. Sokolov, who was de facto minister in the months when Ustinov's health declined, may have been only an interim appointment from the start. His replacement in May 1987 was not in itself surprising. The use of the circumstances (the Rust flight to Moscow) was, however, startling. Not only did the Soviet leadership effect changes in the military hierarchy in the wake of the event, but it used the affair to underscore the principle that those at the very top of the military would be subject to public judgments of their performance, the same tenet as applied to those responsible for other sectors.

Both Sokolov and his successor, Dmitrii Iazov, were accorded only the status of candidate member of the Politburo, in contrast to Ustinov and his predecessor, Grechko, both of whom were accorded full membership status. In addition, Iazov's appointment to minister as well as his prior promotion to deputy minister of defense for cadres are widely viewed as indicating the personal choice of Gorbachev. The advancement of P. D. Lushev to be a first deputy minister of defense with responsibility for budget, administration, and procurement in 1986 is also seen as a choice of Gorbachev and not the military establishment (Weickhardt 1987: 1–11). The advancement of A. D. Lizichev in 1985 to head the Main Political Administration is also taken to be a choice made by Gorbachev. The politics surrounding the departure of N. V. Ogarkov as chief of the General Staff and first deputy minister of defense in 1984 and the advancement of S. F. Akhromeev to this post are still not clear, but Akhromeev has been conspicuously near Gorbachev at the Geneva, Reykjavik, and Washington summits. Akhromeev retired as chief of the General Staff in early December 1988 but continues as a personal adviser to Gorbachev. Although down, the military should not be counted out.

All these changes suggest that the political leadership, not the military, is in control of the top military personnel decisions. Four of the top five posts changed hands between 1984 and 1987. Furthermore, three changes at the next tier of Soviet military leadership (deputy ministers of defense) that date from 1983 not only suggest the primacy of political over military decision makers in military personnel questions but also reveal tensions and possibly conflict between the military and the political authorities. For the first time in the post-Stalin era the deputy minister of defense for armaments, V. M. Shabanov, was made a full member of the Central Committee in June 1983. The replacement in 1985 for Marshal Tolubko as commander-in-chief of the Strategic Rocket Forces, Iu. P. Maximov, was brought in from outside the rocket forces. Similarly when A. I. Koldunov, head of the VPVO (air/space defense), was replaced after the Rust incident, his replacement came from outside the service. These three changes suggest special treatment for the two most technical of the Soviet armed forces branches: rocket forces and air defense. These are the branches whose missions "require" the procurement of new generations of arms that are especially difficult, expensive, and burdensome for Soviet industry to produce.

Speculating further, it may be that increased investment in the Soviet machine-building sector, a hallmark of perestroika, is in direct conflict with the modernization of those two branches of the military. With the prospect of painful trade-offs, Gorbachev seems to be easing his political problems by placing officers without a career stake in charge of those two services and at the same time elevating the status of the deputy minister who has overall responsibility for armaments. The increase in the status of the armaments deputy minister raises him to the level of the heads of the two combat branches and makes possible nay-saying easier.

Gorbachev's Strategy and the Future

Beyond personnel changes, Gorbachev has allowed (or perhaps encouraged) expanded discussion of a reduction in forces. A military policy of "reasonable sufficiency" has entered the arena of public military discussion. At Reykjavik, the United Nations, and elsewhere Gorbachev has brought forth plans for comprehensive arms reductions. (See the chapters by Mary C. FitzGerald, Robert W. Clawson, and Robert L. Arnett for more discussion on these points.) What all this seems to suggest is that Gorbachev's strategy is being led by and may well be contingent on foreign policy success. He may not be able politically to make further systematic and sweeping changes in the military, which are very important for the success of perestroika, until his foreign policy efforts show success. The absence of the same kind of comprehensive change in the military evident in the Foreign Ministry and Secretariat seems to suggest that although military leaders can be and are removed for malfeasance and interservice rivals are exploited in critical top-level postings, final decisions about greatly reducing military spending and procurement must await a more complete demonstration by Gorbachev of success by political means against the main enemies.

The current Soviet leadership should be seen to be united by an in-principle consensus on the need for major change. In background, institutional base, generation, and some policy terms (beyond the basic consensus on perestroika), however, there are significant divisions among the top Soviet leaders. Because collective leadership collegiality rather than general secretary bossism is the current norm of Soviet politics, checking and balancing mechanisms (counterweights) have been established within the oligarchy to give force to the principle of collective leadership. For a lengthy discussion of Gorbachev's problems of regime construction from two somewhat different points of view, see the analyses of Gustafson and Mann (1987) and Hough (1986).

The situation that now exists in the USSR is complex. The problem for the new political coalition is how to make necessary systemic changes and still hold onto power. The Soviet system of today is the system Stalin built. Khrushchev's regime tried to reform it, and indeed succeeded in doing so to a point. The roles of terror, security organs, and concentration camps were radically altered. The dark side of Stalin's nature was partially exposed. In the 1950s Khrushchev succeeded, to some extent, in mobilizing the enthusiasm of a younger generation for change, an enthusiasm that was ultimately disappointed.

The Brezhnev regime reviewed the possibility of making changes in the Stalinist system in 1964–66 and did issue decrees, proclamations, and resolutions. When the time came to face up to the challenges of substantially reordering the power relationships that had been set in place by Stalin, however, Brezhnev and his colleagues retreated. The problems of the system, though understood by a number of top officials, were not aired publicly in the Brezhnev era. Brezhnev passed on to his successors the legacy of a systemic crisis.

Khrushchev and Brezhnev accepted or were forced to accept another important change in the Stalinist system. The unlimited powers over the Party and over the Party-state ruling class which Stalin enjoyed were not permitted to the top leaders of the succeeding regimes. Instead, norms of socialist legality and collective leadership were instituted to prevent the reemergence of a cult of personality. Khrushchev and Brezhnev were showered with contrived adoration and were granted titles, prizes, and medals, but they both managed the USSR with considerably less authority than Stalin wielded.

Collective leadership is the standard phrase the Soviet leadership offers to indicate that arbitrary, dictatorial rule by one person is unacceptable. This norm has been reiterated in prominent ways since Stalin's death. The expressed basis for removing Khrushchev in 1964 was his "subjectivism" and "volunteerism"—in effect his failure to take sufficient account of the views of his colleagues. The Stalin system without the unlimited powers that Stalin accumulated would seem to be one of the fundamental systemic contradictions pushing the Soviet Union into decline.

The honest response to the question, "Where are things going in the Soviet Union?" is to say we do not know and cannot know with certainty. However, it is possible to discuss five plausible outcomes based upon what is known.

1. In the first, Gorbachev attempts massive restructuring but is resisted, achieving only marginal success. A political coalition emphasizing collective leadership refuses to allow any of their number to have overwhelming power. Compromises are reached which basically retain the current Stalinist system of centralized directive planning as well as a Party structure that grants wide-ranging power for political leaders to intervene in economic decision making. The reform that e· .erges is minimal but is enough to create a basis for the leadership to declare it a success.

The betrayal of socialism becomes the slogan and rallying cry of opponents of perestroika as a way to justify and maintain their power. This stifles those innovators and innovations that could transform the system from within. The basic balance of power among institutions which existed at the end of the Brezhnev era is maintained. The changes that are allowed by the leadership are enough to bring about low but not disastrously low economic growth, say 1.5 percent per year. The long-term effect is slow but steady decline in the relative power of the USSR—the expressed fear of Gorbachev and others. In this scenario Gorbachev stays in power as spokesman for a collective leadership but is able to get only a small part of what he wants. Call it muddling along. This is the most likely outcome, as the obstacles to change in the USSR are formidable.

2. The second scenario can be called "Gorbachev persists." Unwilling to accept the limitations imposed by frightened and skeptical colleagues in the Politburo, and unable to push or to lead a passively resisting nomenklatura stratum entrenched at the middle and lower levels of the bureaucracy, Gorbachev attempts to force comprehensive change. The pace of his efforts leads to a backlash and a coup by a countercoalition. The countercoalition includes the military, which sees reductions in status and

military capability but does not see the promised results in an expanding technological base. Both the nomenklatura and the industrial working strata are eager to believe that the confusion, unemployment, inflation, and inequalities that inevitably must accompany comprehensive change can be reversed by restoring "true socialism." Further, they wish to believe that the familiar pattern of low standard of living with extensive paternalism, authoritarianism, and boss politics can be reestablished. Perhaps even foreign adventure in the gulf or elsewhere becomes a means by which a desperate leadership attempts to build internal cohesion through creating external conflict and tension. This scenario is a variant of the preceding possibility and is offered as less likely than the first. In the end Gorbachev may prefer the perquisites of power over getting everything his own way. The difference between 1 and 2 is that in 2 Gorbachev is removed.

3. A third and rather unlikely scenario is that Gorbachev achieves dramatic success under a banner that combines a revival of utopian Marxist ideals with modernization policies implemented by a new generation of engineers and specialists. Dramatic events crystallize youth, the idealistic among the technical intelligentsia, and the "more enlightened" part of the nomenklatura in a revival of utopian enthusiasm. The USSR opens to the world and achieves enormous benefit from growing participation in the international division of labor. Worldwide resource shortages as well as divisions within the Western world benefit Soviet reforms. Although some of the years of transition are difficult, the Soviet economy enters into a long period of sustained growth. The new Soviet educated middle class makes slow but continual gains against the obscurantist elements of the nomenklatura class. This scenario is too utopian for an educated and cynical Soviet population.

4. The fourth scenario, also rather remote, entails system breakdown, civil violence, and the emergence of a military dictatorship. Over a period of years increased corruption, rising national/ethnic tensions, and declining social and material conditions extend the current performance crisis of the USSR into a legitimacy crisis. The Communist party degenerates into a number of corrupt regional political machines that substitute national and regional particularism for Marxism-Leninism. The state security organs, too, become enmeshed in the corruption and ethnic conflict. In the end Russian nationalists in the military feel they have no choice but to intervene to end the corruption and redeem national honor. This scenario is unlikely unless the legitimacy of the system comes into question, which it has not so far.

5. More plausible than scenarios 3 or 4 but less so than 1 and 2, is slow, difficult, but steady incremental efforts that succeed in fundamentally transforming the USSR. In this scenario Gorbachev's coalition is able

simultaneously to stay in control without becoming corrupted and devitalized by power and is able to deliver modest but continuing increments of reform that satisfy enough constituencies to prevent the crystallization of an alternative to reform. The years through the 1991 Party Congress are critical. Over this period Gorbachev must accumulate authority and increase his power by having successes in foreign policy, in agricultural policy, and the revitalization of Soviet industry. He must be able continually to advance performers in his system and, more important, must find a way to replace those who do not perform. It is paramount that he find a way to replace his own allies of 1985–87 who turn out to be less interested in continuing sacrifices for modernization than in being comfortable in power.

For those who wish Gorbachev to succeed there is hope to be found in the fact that he is still the youngest of the full members of the Politburo. Within the wider leadership group of Table 7.1 Baklanov, Vlasov, Masliukov, and Razumovskii (his landsman from the North Caucasus) are younger. It is Razumovskii who is now identifying the talent that can be advanced to responsible positions in 1991 and thereafter. By 1991 a number of the key and critical elder statesmen could be retired from power. Particularly important in this respect is V. V. Shcherbitskii, first secretary of the Communist Party of the Unkraine, the largest subunit within the CPSU.

Critical for the outcome will be Gorbachev and his political coalition. Will it be able to deliver? Will it be able to stick together in the difficult periods? Can its members resist the corrupting effects of power? Will the coalition be able to renew itself in an orderly manner consistent with maintaining the élan of reform? It is important that the cynicism, careerism, and apathy that exist in all strata of Soviet society give way to a mood of hope and enthusiasm among a critical mass of people, especially within the Communist party. At this writing wariness and skepticism still seem to dominate the mood in the Soviet Union. People have not been able to decide if perestroika and glasnost' are real and have lasting power.

Foreign policy is perhaps the most important condition facilitating success for the current coalition and its policy thrust. It is here that Gorbachev is least dependent on the inert bureaucracy. It is here that words and style can have the greatest effect. It is here that Gorbachev seems to have concentrated his energies. An international situation fundamentally changed by a new Soviet leadership coalition will give his coalition a buffer of authority that can enable it to get over difficult times. Such a changed international situation can also provide tangible benefits. Those could include a declining military burden, as well as access to technology, capital, and markets.

Although these inputs to the Soviet reform efforts would likely generate social tensions and conflict as by-products, they could be managed with the existing apparatus of control and with a little good luck—such as a string of exceptionally successful harvests. These inputs would provide more margin for political maneuver and enable the USSR to modernize socially, economically, and even politically.

Such modernization might weaken those in the USSR who wish to maintain a superpowerful state at the expense of a chronically ill society. It might strengthen those forces that could build a society capable of imposing limits on an overbearing Party-state system. The USSR is not the same as South Korea, Spain, Greece, Brazil, or Argentina. Yet there is some hope to be derived from the pattern they present. As an educated, urbanized, and articulate "middle class" emerges, there is a sharp increase in demands on the political system. In the long run the need to respond to demands restrains and changes the system. M. S. Gorbachev is not only an intelligent and able leader, he is also a product of the changes in Soviet society that have come about because of the Stalin revolution and that may, in a dialectical fashion, be transforming that system.

Gorbachev seems to have mastered the dramatic potential in foreign relations and appears to believe that success in foreign policy may be employed to accelerate and facilitate domestic change. He also acts as if foreign policy achievements will provide currency that can be used in the domestic political environment. Structural changes in Soviet foreign policy decision-making machinery in 1985 and 1986 were among his earliest moves, preceding the efforts to redo the economy that were set in motion on January 1, 1988. Three summits in less than two years, an avalanche of arms control and other foreign policy initiatives, as well as sweeping personnel changes all testify to the priority that foreign policy has in Gorbachev's program. Foreign policy seems to be Gorbachev's engine for moving the Soviet train to future economic, political, and military security.

References

Akhromeev, S. F., ed. (1986). *Voennyi Entsiklopedicheskii Slovar'*. Moscow: Voenizdat.

Gustafson, Thane, and Dawn Mann (1987). "Gorbachev's Next Gamble." *Problems of Communism* 36 (July-August), 1–20.

Hough, Jerry (1986). "Gorbachev Consolidating Power." *Problems of Communism* 36 (July-August), 21–43.

Jones, Ellen (1984). "Committee Decision Making in the Soviet Union." *World Politics* 36(2), 165–88.

Sonnenfeldt, Helmut (1978). "Russia, America, and Détente." *Foreign Affairs* 56 (January), 275–94.
Voslensky, Michael (1984). *Nomenklatura: The Soviet Ruling Class* (trans. Eric Mosbacher). Garden City, NY: Doubleday.
Weickhardt, George G. (1987). "General P. G. Lushev: (The Very Model of a Modern [Soviet] General)." *Radio Liberty Research Bulletin*, RL 423/87, 1–11.
Yasmann, Victor (1988). "Vadim Medvedev: New Ideological Chief in the Kremlin." *Radio Liberty Research Bulletin*, RL 435/88, pp. 1–3.

• CHAPTER EIGHT •

Institutional Change and Soviet National Security Policy

Jan S. Adams
The Mershon Center

This chapter examines institutional change in the Soviet defense, foreign policy, and military-industrial establishments in the post-Brezhnev period. It assesses the probable impact of this change on Soviet national security policy and the policy process, estimates the present direction and rate of change, and considers some of the long-term institutional constraints on policymaking.

A transformational leader like Mikhail Gorbachev has hallowed precedents for his current institutional restructuring, for since the birth of the Bolshevik regime Soviet Party leaders have been profoundly convinced that organizational change can solve even the most difficult national problems. His instruments are familiar ones: legislative fiat, reshaping the administrative machinery, and control over the *nomenklatura* of key institutions. Although emphasis here is on the second instrument, structural reorganization, consideration is also given to staff changes that affect the balance of power among the institutional representatives who make national security policy.

Significant change affecting the Soviet national security policy process will be discussed in three contexts: the highest level of defense decision making (Politburo, Defense Council, and Central Committee Secretariat),

151

the defense and foreign policy establishments, and the economy, with emphasis on the military-industrial sector.

Change in the Politburo, Defense Council, and Central Committee Secretariat

Soviet national security policymaking at the highest level is the prerogative of the Defense Council (DC), a select group of some dozen Politburo and military leaders (Alexander 1978–79: 14–16; Jones 1985: 6–7; Nor-Mesek and Rieper 1984; Scott and Scott 1983: 45–48; Sejna and Douglass 1986: 30–45). Information about the DC's membership and activities is sparse, but it is clear that a major determinant of Defense Council decision making is the balance of power between the civilian and military members (Gelman 1984: 67). Currently Gorbachev chairs the DC.[1] By virtue of their government, Party, and military positions, other likely members are Prime Minister Ryzhkov (DC deputy chairman), Foreign Minister Shevardnadze, defense industries Central Committee Secretary Zaikov, Chief of Staff Moiseev (DC secretary), Minister of Defense Iazov (DC deputy chairman), two first deputy ministers of defense, Kulikov and Lushev, and Chief of the Main Political Directorate Lizichev. Central Committee Second Secretary Ligachev and KGB Chairman Chebrikov were likely members until September 30, 1988, when both were assigned to new posts. Richard Staar (1987: 111–12) lists five Politburo (full) members in 1987: Gorbachev, Ligachev, Ryzhkov, Shevardnadze, and Chebrikov, plus Masliukov, Sokolov, Akhromeev, Kulikov, and Lizichev.

Since the Brezhnev years within the organizational context of national security policymaking at the highest level, a marked diminution has occurred in the power of the military vis-à-vis the political decision makers. Gorbachev adroitly accelerated this power shift begun by his predecessors and, by using the supervisory powers of the Central Committee Secretariat, has further strengthened his own personal control over the entire defense establishment.

As the example of Khrushchev illustrated, military-political consensus on national security policy is never absolute. Maneuvering by both sides to influence policy is continuous; and in a period of restructuring by a reforming leader, because of the generally conservative outlook of the military on many issues disagreements between military and political leaders are especially likely to emerge.[2] Khrushchev's downgrading of the ground forces and other efforts to restructure the military were reversed by Brezhnev as early as 1967; thereafter military-political relations assumed a relationship "in which the military . . . enjoyed a significant amount of leverage to advance its interests in the policy-making process" (Gallagher and Spielmann 1972: 41–42; see also Wolfe 1969).

By 1977 organizational arrangements and the context of defense decision making placed the two most influential military representatives in a favored position to voice their preferences. Marshal Ustinov, the minister of defense, wielded great power as a full member of the Politburo and senior representative of the military establishment on the DC (with valuable political experience and contacts from his eleven years as Central Committee secretary for military-industrial affairs). And Marshal Ogarkov, as chief of the General Staff and secretary of the Defense Council, enjoyed a pivotal role (along with Brezhnev) in preparing the DC's agenda.[3]

Moreover, early in his regime Brezhnev, apparently mindful of the important division of labor and power between the select subset of Politburo members who sit as full members of the DC and those who do not, had restricted the number of Politburo members on the DC, giving himself a political advantage over his colleagues in the Politburo. This, however, gave the military members on the Defense Council a dominant voice in defense decision making, which Brezhnev subsequently sought to counter by enlarging the council's civilian membership. Shortly before his death, in addition to Brezhnev and Ustinov the DC included the following Politburo members: Tikhonov, Gromyko, Chernenko, and Andropov. Gelman notes, "the trend toward wider Politburo participation in the Defense Council appeared to be a function of the increasing political tension in the leadership as the succession to Brezhnev grew closer and as the economic costs of the growth of Soviet military spending mounted" (1984: 69). Brezhnev's efforts to control the military by bringing more of his Politburo colleagues into the decision-making process, however, seem only to have emboldened Ogarkov, who at this time was publicly seeking "to manipulate assessments of the likelihood of war to advance [the] claims [of the military] to a share of the resources" (Van Oudenaren 1986: 23).

As long as defense decision making was dominated by Ustinov and Ogarkov (or Ogarkov as minister of defense, should Ustinov retire),[4] the general secretary, whoever he might be, would find the military contingent hard to challenge. But evidence from the brief Andropov-Chernenko interregnum suggests that Brezhnev's successors had determined to control defense policies and budgets by placing in the critical military policy posts (minister of defense and chief of staff) military leaders amenable to Party control. Each of the post-Brezhnev Party leaders contributed to the implementation of this strategy, but Gorbachev brought the plan to fruition and reaped its benefits.

Ogarkov helped to undermine his own cause. In the early 1980s he became visibly embroiled in a dispute with Ustinov and the political leadership largely over the issue of economic resources for the military, and was slow to abandon his positions (Weickhardt 1985: 77–82). Thus it was no doubt with Ustinov's support that early in his regime Andropov began to groom other, less contentious candidates for advancement. On March 23, 1983, Sergei F. Akhromeev, Ogarkov's first deputy chief of the General Staff since 1979, was suddenly promoted to marshal, "such a promotion for a first deputy chief of the General Staff being without precedent in the history of that body" (Kruzhin 1984: 1). In retrospect this unusual promotion appears to have been intended to facilitate Akhromeev's later appointment as chief of staff when Chernenko suddenly transferred Ogarkov from that post in September 1984 to command the newly structured Western Theater of Operations. Thus the Ogarkov appointment was not only a significant implementation of Ogarkov's own military strategy; it was also an adroit political move by the Party leadership (with Ustinov's concurrence) to reduce military influence in policymaking in the DC. A new military leadership team was being shaped. And when Ustinov died in December 1984, instead of the outspoken and flamboyant Ogarkov, it was Marshal Sergei Sokolov (only eight months Ustinov's junior) who was named minister of defense and given a more modest, nonvoting seat on the Politburo.

When Gorbachev came to power, he increased the Party's control over the military leadership in the Politburo and the Defense Council even further. At the Twenty-Seventh Party Congress and at successive Central Committee plenums, Sokolov, the institutional representative of the military, failed to attain voting membership in the Politburo, and Marshal Ogarkov remained sidelined from the Moscow political arena, headquartered in a western provincial city. Then on May 30, 1987, two days after the unimpeded landing of a West German sport plane in Red Square had provided Gorbachev with a "heaven-sent" excuse, he replaced Sokolov with a relatively unknown army general, Dmitrii Iazov, whom Gorbachev had brought to Moscow as a deputy minister of defense for personnel just six months earlier. Military representation in national security policymaking at the highest level took a giant step backward.

In addition to strengthening the Party's ascendancy over the military in top-level decision making, Gorbachev has tightened his personal control over the entire military nomenklatura by putting his own man in charge of it. On January 28, 1987, he brought Anatolii I. Luk'ianov, chief of the Central Committee (CC) General Department, into the CC Secretariat and gave him a key defense task: to oversee the work of the CC Administrative Organs Department, which handles appointments and promotions in the Ministry of Defense, the KGB, and the Ministry of Internal Affairs.[5] According to past practice, control over the nomenklatura of the defense establishment should have been exercised by the "second" secretary, Egor Ligachev. But Ligachev's public disagreement with Gorbachev's rapid pace of restructuring made Ligachev a potential magnet for king-makers disillusioned with the general secretary and a likely target for attempted cooption by conservative military groups. With the Luk'ianov appointment, therefore, Gorbachev not only strengthened his own ability to control the military nomenklatura and the context of defense decision making but diminished the chances that a power base of conservative military forces could align itself with the second secretary to challenge the general secretary and drive a political wedge into his civilian leadership coalition.

The thorough restructuring of the CC apparat on September 30, 1988, consolidated Gorbachev's control even further. When Ligachev became the new Party commissioner for agriculture, with responsibilities limited to this field alone, he lost any real grounds for his claim to be second secretary. And although Luk'ianov left the Party Secretariat at this time to become first deputy chairman of the USSR Supreme Soviet Presidium, Party oversight of the nomenklatura of the defense establishment remained secure in the hands of another trusted Gorbachev lieutenant, Georgii Razumovskii, newly appointed as CC chairman for the Commission for Party Work and Cadres Policy.

Another staff change deprived the KGB as an institution of its official representation in the Politburo when Viktor Chebrikov was elevated from KGB chairman to CC secretary and CC chairman for the Commission on Legal Policy. Though his successor, Vladimir Kriuchkov, might regain the KGB's Politburo status sometime in the future, until that time the role of the KGB in Politburo decision making had been diminished. Meanwhile, the institution with overwhelming dominance in the Politburo, Gorbachev's CC Secretariat, had become even stronger, with eight of the ten CC secretaries sitting as full members and one as a candidate member. Six of these secretaries now head the new Party commissions, or superbureaus, created to guide the newly centralized and streamlined central Party apparatus.

These changes have given Gorbachev (and those colleagues on the Politburo and military leaders who support him) leverage to pursue policy goals favoring the restructuring of the civilian economy and giving less priority to defense expenditures.[6] This does not mean that Gorbachev has the full support of all his commissioners, especially Ligachev and Chebrikov, but so far he has been remarkably successful in positioning both his supporters and opponents so that he dominates the leadership team, remains in full control of defense decision making, and is able to move boldly in defense, foreign policy, and domestic decision making even to the point of reshaping the machinery and locus of much of the nation's decision making. Undoubtedly his best hope is to achieve positive economic results before political dissatisfaction, coalescing around another senior secretary, can challenge his power.

Change in the Defense and Foreign Policy Establishments

In the post-Brezhnev period the Soviet High Command and Armed Services experienced extensive restructuring and personnel turnover. Interestingly, these changes for the most part preceded those in other areas of the defense establishment and seem to have been triggered by the reorganization of commands (completed in late 1984) into strategic Theaters of Military Operation (*Teatr voennykh deistvii*, TVD). As Robert Clawson notes in this volume, Marshal Ogarkov's assignment to the Western TVD fitted neatly into this reorganization. The restructuring mirrored a war-fighting strategy using conventional weapons and swift and deep penetration of enemy territory which was being advocated by a number of Soviet military leaders (Gurkin 1984; Rudnev 1985: 12).[7] Ogarkov himself had strongly recommended the reorganization in an interview with *Krasnaia zvezda* on May 9, 1984, when he asserted that because of changes in the art of war, certain existing structures of the Soviet armed forces were obsolete. He had advised restructuring these military forces into main theater commands to provide greater combat readiness (FitzGerald 1986).

Staffing changes followed. In the thirteen months beginning in December 1984, more than twenty senior personnel changes took place; four of the five services received new commanders in chief (the fifth, the leader of the Air Defense Forces, was replaced in May 1987, two days after the Cessna affair). One first deputy defense minister, Marshal V. I. Petrov, newly appointed in February 1985, was replaced by P. G. Lushev in October 1986. And in July 1985 Army General Lizichev became chief of the Main Political Directorate of the Soviet Army and Navy, a sensitive post with respect to communicating changes in Party policy affecting the military.

One Western observer aptly summed up these changes as "a fundamental reorganisation of the Soviet High Command," in line with Ogarkov's theory of a Soviet nonnuclear strategic offensive and intended to "ensure optimum exploitation of advances in weapon capabilities" (Miller 1986: 5). In other words, as Mary C. FitzGerald so well documents in Chapter

Nine, the military restructuring under way in 1984 was apparently triggered by new weapons technology and a parallel revision of military doctrine.

However, wholesale generational change still awaits the defense establishment, for the new military commanders as a group, though younger than the men they replaced, are not as young as the new political leaders and managers in the civilian sector. The beginning of real generational change for the military may have been signaled in December 1988 when Marshal Akhromeev was replaced as chief of staff by the forty-nine-year-old Colonel-General Mikhail A. Moiseev.

Gorbachev's appointments of his close associates first—Luk'ianov and then Razumovskii—to oversee the nomenklatura of the armed forces indicated his intention to control the process of generational change when it comes. This control can be crucial to him in the years ahead because from a military perspective, his *perestroika* is likely to show negative before it shows positive economic results. Gorbachev needs military leaders who, if military projects begin to suffer visibly from underfunding, will continue to support his policies to revitalize the civilian economy.

Arms control is another sphere of national security activity which, in the post-Brezhnev period, has seen significant institutional change affecting the defense and foreign policy establishments. Although the early SALT negotiations were heavily influenced by the Soviet military (with the Ministry of Defense and General Staff apparently dominating Soviet arms control policy), the chief Soviet negotiators were senior members from the Ministry of Foreign Affairs (MFA). Through the 1970s and into the 1980s, the MFA played a growing role in these negotiations (Gottemoeller 1986: 94).

The ministry's preeminence through the Andropov and Chernenko years was personified in Gromyko, who wielded such enormous influence as both negotiator and overall foreign policymaker that he apparently came to resent the Party's role in shaping policy—especially the role of the Central Committee's International Department—complaining to his subordinates that "there should not be two centers for handling foreign policy" (Shevchenko 1985: 251). Gorbachev's replacement of Gromyko with Eduard Shevardnadze, a Party careerist with no professional background in foreign affairs, was an abrupt reassertion of Party control over policymaking and the MFA, which reduced the ministry's role in the making (though not the implementation) of policy.[8] Party control was further strengthened by the appointment, as Shevardnadze's deputy minister for personnel, of Valentin Nikoforov, former deputy head of the CC Organizational Party Work Department. These acts signaled Gorbachev's serious determination to pursue a new policy line, cutting defense expenditures, reducing dangers of U.S.-Soviet conflict, and (as

Robert L. Arnett indicates in this book) seeking ways to use arms control negotiations to achieve military objectives by political means.

In effect Gorbachev took foreign policymaking into his own hands and attempted to shape a unified policymaking center in his CC Secretariat.[9] He chose as his new secretary for international affairs Anatolii Dobrynin, an experienced diplomat thoroughly familiar with the MFA who possessed the substantive knowledge Gorbachev needed to formulate realistic policies, especially in dealing with the United States. In addition, Dobrynin was placed in charge of the nomenklatura of the MFA, a move clearly calculated to facilitate the MFA's achievement of Gorbachev's policy goals (Rahr 1986).

Three institutional changes made by Gorbachev were designed at least in part to bolster his efforts to dominate and bring greater cohesiveness to arms control policy. Two departments for arms control were formally established, one in the MFA—the Administration for Problems of Arms Reduction and Disarmament, headed by Ambassador-at-Large Viktor Karpov—and the other, an Arms Control Sector in the International Department (ID) of the CPSU Central Committee led by Lieutenant General Viktor Starodubov. And one Central Committee department was abolished, the International Information Department (IID), which appeared to have overstepped the bounds of its informational mission and had begun making arms control policy.

The establishment of the International Department's arms control unit formalized and strengthened the ID's role in arms control. Earlier, responsibility for arms control had been merely one of many duties of the ID's first deputy chairman, Vadim Zagladin; now it seemed incumbent upon Dobrynin as chief of the ID to make arms control a major focus of ID attention. And by coopting Starodubov, a former General Staff officer, the department acquired a valuable source of technical knowledge. Although arms control negotiations continued to be dominated as in the past by senior MFA and military personnel,[10] the establishment of the new state and Party arms control units had the effect of institutionalizing arms control as an enduring concern of state and Party, broadening civilian participation in the arms control decision-making process and providing an infrastructure designed to improve the coordination of policy formulation. In fact, Condoleeza Rice suggests this may be a step in creating an institution that would permit "civilian experts to devise options for Soviet strategy and force posture, and to debate those issues with the General Staff," a step toward making the ID a more active center for the study of national security issues (Rice 1987: 79).

Uprooting the International Information Department simplified arms control coordination. The IID was created in 1978 to clarify public understanding of Soviet foreign policy, but as Rose Gottemoeller notes, it soon became a "locus of planning and organization" for arms control activities, "laying the groundwork for Soviet arms control initiatives" and providing, along with the International Department, "an important political input to Soviet arms control policymaking" (1986: 89). Its chief, Leonid Zamiatin, and the ID's Zagladin were identified with the intransigent position the Soviets took regarding the U.S. deployment of Pershing II and cruise missiles (which precipitated the Soviet walkout at the INF talks in November 1983) and with the political campaign to build overwhelming Western European resistance to deployment. Failure of that campaign, coupled with the IID's policymaking proclivities, undoubtedly triggered the dismantling of Zamiatin's department and transfer of Zagladin's arms control duties to Starodubov.

The IID's formal mission "to make sure that the world understands Soviet foreign policy" (Gerasimov 1987b) went to the Ministry of Foreign Affairs. Its leadership was entrusted not to a diplomat, however, but to a professional journalist in line with a conscious ministry effort (confirmed by Shevardnadze in mid-1988) to combine these skills in the service of foreign affairs (Shevardnadze 1988: 20). The MFA Press Department now became the Administration for International Information, and its new chief, Gennadii Gerasimov, became the chief spokesman on international affairs for both Party and government. Dobrynin undoubtedly recommended Gerasimov after observing his work as Novosti representative in New York (1972–77) and with full confidence in his journalistic talents, American expertise, and ability to communicate the Soviet foreign policy line to the world. Interestingly, the new era of *glasnost'* has permitted Gerasimov particularly broad latitude in performing as Soviet spokesman. For example, in early 1987 Gerasimov surprised the radio editor of the Voice of Israel by accepting his unexpected call from Jerusalem and then immediately agreeing to a spontaneous interview, as the editor appropriately marveled, "without any need for consultations or approval from above" (Gerasimov 1987a).

Finally, institutional reorganization produced a major shakeup in the International Department itself, a move intended to have far-reaching implications not only for arms control but for Soviet foreign policy as a whole. The restructuring envisioned nothing less than a fundamental reorientation of the ID to curb its overly aggressive activities to extend Soviet ideology and influence, especially in the Third World. Wallace Spaulding, describing the 1985–86 changes in the ID, notes:

The ID will see to it that the CPSU's relations with the "Free World" political parties and its control of the international front organizations

—the two main ID functions—will more than ever be undertaken in the context of the USSR-US relationship (conceivably to the detriment of Third World concerns). (1986: 80)

The International Department inherited from its predecessor, the Comintern, responsibility for supporting Communist parties and pro-Soviet movements worldwide. Through the years this task often created problems for the Ministry of Foreign Affairs, interfering with the latter's diplomatic mission (Hammond 1976: 58), and frequently undermined major policy positions of the Politburo. In the 1970s, for example, the ID's aggressively anti-U.S. policies in the Third World had a devastating effect on Soviet-American détente. At the present time, when arms control negotiations have become a major mission for a restructured ID, its new leaders are expected to manage the political activism of the Soviet Party around the world in ways that will avoid any possible dysfunctional impact on U.S. relations and arms control negotiations.

The reshaping of the ID began with the removal of Boris Ponomarev, the Comintern official who had piloted the ID for over thirty years. It was significant that the two new leaders who replaced him—Dobrynin as chief and Georgii Kornienko as first deputy chief—were both Americanists with long careers in the MFA. The choice of Americanists indicated Gorbachev's desire to have experts sensitive to U.S. responses and intentions closely involved in overall foreign policy assessment. And selecting ministry experts to head the Central Committee department that prepares the Politburo agenda on international questions was clearly designed to bring greater coordination of ministry and Party views to the policymaking process at this top level.[11] Finally, creation of the new ID section for arms control and military affairs provided civilian leaders with a mandate (and the technical information) to prepare effective policy positions embracing both political and military aspects of national security policy.

Further restructuring of the ID and MFA continued through 1988 as the CC Department for Relations with the Socialist Countries was brought into the ID and some Party functions were consolidated. On September 30, 1988, the creation of the CC Commission for Foreign Affairs, headed by Gorbachev's close adviser, CC Secretary Aleksandr Iakovlev (and clearly reflecting Iakovlev's views),[12] marked a critical step in these efforts to integrate Party and state institutions while defining their separate functions more sharply, eliminating overlap, and streamlining the CC apparat. Together the commission, the ID, and the MFA emerged as an increasingly centralized Party-state agency for foreign affairs, a sleek superbureau designed to expedite Gorbachev's decisions. One countercurrent to this consolidation of the leader's control must be mentioned here, however, even though its impact cannot yet be assessed. This is the unprecedented and radical institutional restructuring of the political system proposed in October 1988 in amendments to the USSR Constitution, on "organizing a constitutionally empowered mechanism for discussing and adopting the most important foreign policy decisions" (Shevardnadze 1988: 9). This restructuring envisions shifting the locus of foreign policy decision making to a transformed Supreme Soviet, where public opinion would become a component of the policy process. The effect of these proposed changes lies in the future.

Change in the Defense Economy

By the end of the Brezhnev era, the decision-making machinery at the macro level in the defense economy was structurally very close to what it had been in the 1920s (Odom 1983: 11). And although Gorbachev has been "notably unadventurous in making [ministerial] changes in the military-industrial sector" (Gustafson and Mann 1987: 12), he moved quickly during his first year as general secretary to make three key appointments to secure his control over this sector. Beneath the supreme guidance of the Defense Council, the Party's control agency is the Central Committee Department for Defense Industries, headed by Oleg Semenovich Beliakov and overseen by the senior CC secretary for military-industrial affairs, Lev Zaikov, with the assistance, since 1988, of CC Secretary Oleg Baklanov.[13] On the government side, the Military-Industrial Commission (VPK), chaired by Deputy Prime Minister Iurii Masliukov, receives input from the ministry of defense and General Staff of the Armed Forces on military requirements and "provides a central focus and management for military requirements within the state economic bureaucracy" (Odom 1983: 11).

Significantly, all three of the decision makers just identified received these appointments under Gorbachev's aegis. Zaikov became CC secretary for military-industrial affairs in July 1985[14] and was catapulted into the Politburo as a full member on March 6, 1986; Beliakov was advanced from department deputy chief and Masliukov from first deputy chairman of the USSR State Planning Committee (Gosplan) in July and November 1985, respectively. Incumbents of these positions can "both impose the top leadership's will on the defense-industrial ministers and their subordinates and also speak up on the ministers' behalf on crucial policy matters" (Spielmann 1976: 61). Thus they can provide Gorbachev with reliable access to and control over decision making in the defense industries

sector at a time when the military industrialists are under great pressure
to contribute to the civilian economy.

Staff and structural changes in the military-industrial sector have
increased this pressure. Although the plethora of economic legislation
and reorganization that filled Gorbachev's first two years for the most
part was addressed to improving the civilian economy, some affected
defense industry directly or indirectly, especially measures specifically
designed to apply defense industrial expertise to the civilian sector.
For example, the new super-coordinating body in the USSR Council of
Ministers, the Bureau of Machine-Building, is intended to give the same
kind of oversight of machinery ministries in the civilian sector that the VPK
provides for the defense industries, and its chief, Ivan Silaev, is a former
defense minister and minister of aviation. Another target of legislation,
the State Committee for Science and Technology, was instructed to set
up various mechanisms to develop and diffuse new technology among
ministries. Since February 6, 1987, its chairman has been Boris Tolstykh,
an electrical engineer who, until this latest assignment, directed the
Elektronika factory, producer of aerospace and military equipment.
Tolstykh's appointment signified to one observer that "the 'restructuring'
of the cumbersome Soviet scientific bureaucracy" would be speeded up
and that "the new legislation affecting the State Committee for Science
and Technology that should have been completed by the end of last year
will now be pushed through" (Yasmann 1987).

The reshaping of Gosplan was similarly entrusted to defense industrialists. Its new head in 1985 was Nikolai Talyzin, an electrical engineer with
research experience in defense who was minister of communications from
1976 to 1980; he was replaced on February 6, 1988 by Iurii Masliukov,
chief of the Military-Industrial Commission. Talyzin was allowed to
restaff the leadership of Gosplan and was made one of four first deputy
chairmen of the Council of Ministers, as well as a candidate member
of the Politburo (the first time since the 1950s that a Gosplan chief
had achieved this status—Masliukov's subsequent elevation reaffirmed
the practice; see Teague 1986). In addition, Talyzin (and subsequently
Masliukov) headed the Commission to Improve Management, Planning,
and the Economic Mechanism, established in January 1986, to design an
extensive restructuring of the nation's economy.

If Talyzin's leadership was meant to reassure conservative political
and military forces that the economic model to emerge from perestroika
would not abandon centralized planning and control, and that economic
reform would mean improved performance within established parameters
of control, the economic reforms subsequently outined at the June 1987
Plenum of the CPSU Central Committee may have dispelled such notions.

John E. Tedstrom's chapter in this volume details these reforms, but it is worth repeating the main elements here. The institutional changes and prospective reforms of planning and prices discussed at the plenum called for a transformation of the control functions of Gosplan and of some civilian economic ministries, eventual elimination of much centralized management and planning, and reliance upon independent enterprise decision making. For some economic ministries this implied a radical curtailment of traditional ministry functions, staff cuts, amalgamation of certain ministries, and a reorientation of the attitudes of incumbent bureaucrats toward organizational objectives. Meanwhile, as Gorbachev noted in his report to the plenum, ways had not yet been worked out to coordinate the new ministry functions with those of the newly created super-coordinating agencies, though six of these agencies intended to manage national economic complexes were already in operation.[15] At the enterprise level the plenum asked regional and territorial soviets to organize production management boards to plan regional economic development, give guidance to enterprises within their jurisdictions, and encourage individual initiative. It was not made clear how these reforms would affect the traditional privileged status of the defense-industrial sector, but exceptions to decentralization in certain sectors were alluded to. Some orders and directives, it was indicated, would continue to be issued from the center to ensure the preservation of state interests.

The institutional changes proposed at the June plenum, though directed primarily toward the civilian economy, were so sweeping in intent and potentially destabilizing in the short run that they have broad implications for Soviet national security extending beyond the military-industrial complex. The reforms affecting the economic ministries place the Soviet economy in a vulnerable position for at least the next several years and put a premium upon Soviet avoidance of military conflict. Such vulnerability, in fact, lends a very practical basis and urgency to the appeals in the "new political thinking" for a relaxation of international tension.

Direction and Rate of Institutional Change

But how do we characterize these changes? Do they lend credence to Gorbachev's claims that he is changing institutional life dramatically? To answer these questions it is appropriate to return to the conceptual framework outlined in Chapter One. Do we find stability, significant change, or radical change?

Significant change has occurred at the apex of policymaking. Since the Brezhnev regime the military-political balance of power at the highest level of decision making in national security affairs has shifted sharply in favor of the political leadership. This shift has its roots in the late Brezhnev period; however, it is largely the result of Gorbachev's decisive actions to secure the consolidation of his own political power and to ensure his control of the Defense Council and the nomenklatura of the defense establishment. The relationship is reversible, of course, but currently, as compared with the Brezhnev period, the control by the political leadership of national security decision making appears firmly established.

Change in the defense establishment is significant. The fundamental reorganization of the Soviet High Command in late 1984 and the subsequent rash of personnel changes at the highest levels constitute significant change; moreover, given the fact that real generational change has not taken place in the military high command, further substantial quantitative change (which could well lead to radical change) can be anticipated before long. It would be quite in character for Gorbachev to activate the regulations that require the mandatory retirement of officers (ignored throughout the Brezhnev period; see Gallagher and Spielmann 1972: 42), although he would probably not use this device unless pushed to it by military efforts to make unilateral decisions he opposed. Meanwhile, Gorbachev's control of the nomenklatura of the Ministry of Defense through CC Commissioner Razumovskii has further strengthened his hand in dealing with the military.

Significant to radical change characterizes the institutional restructuring of the Soviet foreign policy establishment. Only the dissolution of the International Information Department qualifies as a minor change; IID duties were simply transferred elsewhere. The institutionalization of broader participation by the political leadership in arms control qualifies as significant change. The transformation of the Ministry of Foreign Affairs and the International Department of the Central Committee is close to radical in the sense that it attempts, by charting a new course for both institutions, to achieve greater overall coordination in Soviet foreign policy. In this regard the missions of both agencies have been sharply redrawn. In the case of the MFA, a generational turnover of ambassadors generally better educated and with more international experience than their predecessors is permitting the Soviet Union to project a new image and to implement Gorbachev's new political thinking, which reverses past dogma about the inevitability of global conflict and defines Soviet national security in terms of the mutual security of all nations in an interdependent world. In the case of the ID, new structures and functions call for new orientations and behavior to temper the aggressive pursuit of world communism that has guided the ID for over thirty years.

Incremental change appears in the military-industrial sector. Despite the rash of legislation, restructuring, and restaffing in the Soviet economy, the military-industrial sector appears only marginally affected at present. Admittedly, there is increasing pressure on defense industries to contribute in various ways to the greater abundance and quality of output of civilian goods, and unprecedented priority is being given to restructuring the civilian economy. Yet these efforts do not appear to challenge the privileged position of the military-industrial complex. As the reforms proceed this situation may change. And, indeed, instability resulting from reform may profoundly affect all sectors of the nation's economy. In the short term, however, the impact of change in the military-industrial sector seems incremental.

Institutional Constraints on Policymaking

Gorbachev's initial institutional reorganization has contributed positively to a stable regime and a national security policy consensus. Basing his power securely in his Central Committee Secretariat and providing himself with a network of loyal clients in key positions to control the national security policy process and the nomenklatura of the defense and foreign policy establishments, he has achieved an apparent consensus among decision makers in the Defense Council and Politburo supporting his policies. Given the nature of bureaucratic politics, however, the stability of such a consensus, and of the regime itself, is always problematic. In this final section I will look briefly at several factors in the institutional context of the defense decision-making process that may tend to reinforce or to impede the current policy consensus. Although I do not suggest that "purely abstract institutional and organizational interests motivate Soviet foreign policy actions" (Valenta 1984: 166), it is clear that the interests of the institution represented by a policymaker will shape his preference toward particular national security policy options. As a result, the institutional affiliation and specialized functions of Defense Council and Politburo members have the potential to encourage or block the crucial policy consensus Gorbachev must have to implement his preferred national security options.

It is beyond the scope of this chapter to identify fully the impact Gorbachev's perestroika is having on the long-standing interests of key national security institutions, on their achievement of organizational goals, or on their access to greater resources, power, and prestige. However, it would be useful here to consider some likely institutional responses toward Gorbachev's changes that could significantly influence future national security policies. The following survey of several organizational perspectives typical of three major groups—the military, the MFA, and the KGB—should suffice to suggest how these groups see their institutional interests being served by perestroika.

Of major importance is the military leadership, which acts in the Defense Council as a powerful pressure group with clear institutional interests and an overriding concern with budget issues (Valenta 1984: 167; Wolfe 1969). The dominant interests of the military, as noted by Kolkowicz, have been traditionally antireformist:

> The military does not normally seek change, nor does it evoke any camaraderie or trust from other groupings. If anything, it is looked upon as a consumer of badly needed resources . . . as a residue of orthodoxy and of blind adherence to Party dictates. The military is also seen as the institution which has most to gain from a deteriorating international environment, and possibly as the one which seeks to prevent the relaxation of international tensions. . . . In sum the military differs profoundly from those interest groups in Soviet society whose particularistic interests are also the larger objectives of people who seek long-postponed changes in the social, political and philosophical realities of an authoritarian system. (Kolkowicz 1971: 169)

Some aspects of Gorbachev's new policy orientation inject ambiguity into established military missions. For example, the task of the military to maintain a high degree of military preparedness is more onerous when Soviet policy in East/West relations proclaims a "defense orientation" for its military forces (Wettig 1987). As Rice comments, "It is difficult to believe that the General Staff agrees with Gorbachev's recent arms proposals" (1987: 75). In view of the weight of such traditional institutional military interests, Gorbachev's recent success in enlisting military support for his innovative programs, domestic and international and for a shift of resources from the defense to the civilian sector of the economy is an anomaly, a position seemingly maintained against a prevailing current of institutional forces.

A sharp contrast is presented by the case of the Ministry of Foreign Affairs, which, as an institution, seems to have gained most from Gorbachev's reform of the national security establishment. The new foreign policy posture of the USSR, which places great emphasis on the search for political (over military) solutions to international problems and tensions, has given the MFA a leading role to play. Moreover, it is a role well suited to the ministry's traditional missions, talents, and expertise and reinforces long-standing institutional values and objectives. In addition, the ministry has gained further institutional prestige as a result of the changes in its relationship with the International Department and its acquisition of the functions of the old International Information Department. MFA professionals must find particularly appealing the new instructions to the ID to manage its Party mission abroad—relations with Communist parties in the West and "progressive forces" in the Third World —so that these activities do not interfere with the MFA's diplomatic objectives. (From the ID's institutional viewpoint, however, it would not be surprising if the response of the ID's old-line Party professionals to these changes affecting their thirty-year-old mandate was less than enthusiastic.)

Finally, the institutional bias of the KGB tends to be ambivalent depending on how separate national security issues affect its internal or external interests. Détente, for example, is a policy that generates a more or less continual internal controversy and tension in the policy process and one which directly affects the domestic mission of the KGB, permitting an influx of Western "ideological sabotage" that makes the KGB's job more difficult (Chebrikov 1987). The question of whether to use military or nonmilitary forces abroad elicits a competitive response from the KGB. Thus institutional bias is a possible reason that the KGB may have opposed Soviet military action in Poland and Afghanistan, on the grounds that nonmilitary initiatives would enhance the KGB's role over that of the military. In short, from an institutional perspective the KGB is troubled by Gorbachev's encouragement of peaceful exchanges with the West, which increase the danger of Western ideological inroads, but it benefits from his expanded use of nonmilitary solutions, diplomacy, propaganda, and active measures, which serve to enlarge the international role and power of the KGB (Knight 1987).

These examples illustrate the kinds of institutional interests that can motivate Soviet national security decision makers and influence policymaking. Institutional factors are only one component in the shaping of policy, but they inevitably figure prominently in the complexities of the national security policy process. Given the dynamics of bureaucratic politics, they will be a constant potential challenge to Gorbachev's national security policy consensus and are likely to place conservative constraints on the future policy process.

Notes

1. A legal basis for civilian leadership of the DC appears in Article 121 of the Draft Law on Constitutional Amendments (*Pravda*, October 21, 1988), which designates as head of the USSR Defense Council the chairman of the USSR Supreme Soviet, the post to which Gorbachev was elected on May 25, 1989.

2. "The forecaster cannot be reminded too often that the Soviet military's outlook, whatever its relation to changing circumstances, is on most substantive issues fundamentally and perhaps irrevocably conservative. Only the need to respond to change beyond the army's boundaries can make it a force for political innovation, let alone transformation. On most basic questions facing Soviet society soldiers are firmly wedded to the status quo" (Colton 1979: 288).

3. "The key figures in preparing the [DC] agenda [in Soviet Communist systems] are the Secretary of the Defense Council [normally chief of the General Staff] and the head of the Administration Department, with the General Secretary making the final decisions" (Sejna and Douglass 1986: 36).

4. Ustinov was seventy-five years old when Brezhnev died; Ogarkov, as first deputy minister of defense and chief of staff, seemed certain to succeed Ustinov.

5. Luk'ianov headed the General Department from 1985 until May 1987, when Gorbachev's aide for domestic affairs, Valery Boldin, was given this new assignment. It is important to note, as Gustafson and Mann (1987: 6) point out, that both Luk'ianov and Georgii Razumovskii, Gorbachev's secretary for cadres, have close ties with the general secretary and were hand-picked by him for these positions.

6. E. Primakov reiterated this position in *Pravda* on July 10, 1987: "Given the sharp acceleration in the economic and social development of the Soviet Union, the need for optimizing the ratio between productive and military expenditures necessary for reliable security has become manifest as never before" (p. 4).

7. Ogarkov's plan probably stirred opposition from some military leaders opposed in principle to experimentation and from the commander of the Warsaw Pact Forces, Kulikov, over uncertainty about how the new Western Theater Command would relate to his command. See also McConnell (1983: 23 ff.).

8. Shevardnadze's only international experience before becoming minister of foreign affairs was membership in the Presidium of the Soviet Committee for Solidarity with Asian and African Countries (1958–?) and trips to Tunisia (1960), Austria and Bulgaria (1974), Hungary (1975–81), Portugal (1979 and 1983), Brazil (1980), Czechoslovakia (1981), India (1982), and Algeria (1984).

9. Increasing the Party's formal role in the arms control process strengthens Gorbachev's political power, which, as Peter Reddaway (1986) stresses, is rooted in the Secretariat even more than in the Politburo.

10. In arms control talks at Reykjavik (1986) and Washington, D.C. (1987), American officials say that Marshal Akhromeev, not the MFA officials, took charge and made key decisions (*New York Times*, December 8, 1987, p. 9).

11. According to David Albright, "What is beyond doubt is his [Dobrynin's] intention not only to play a major role in shaping Soviet foreign policy but also to make the International Department the central institution for coordinating the implementation of the USSR's foreign policy" (1987: 52).

12. Both the departure of the two Americanists, Dobrynin and Kornienko, from the helm of the ID and their replacement by diplomat-journalist and Western Europeanist Valentin Falin reflect Iakovlev's policy preferences.

13. Luk'ianov, Gorbachev's "surrogate watchdog over the secret police and the military" until September 30, 1988, was also nominally supervised by Zaikov (Hough 1987: 35). Stressing the importance of the CC secretary for military-industrial affairs, Rice says (1987: 71), "If a change in priorities is indicated, this is the key position for the General Secretary to control." In November 1987, when Zaikov succeeded Boris El'tsin as Moscow Party chief, he apparently retained responsibility for military-industrial affairs; since February 18, 1988, however, he has shared this responsibility with Oleg

Baklanov (USSR minister of General Machine-Building since 1983) who was also named CC secretary for the military-industrial complex.

14. In 1983, when Zaikov, "who was only sixth in the regional Party hierarchy and who had no previous experience of Party work," succeeded Romanov as Leningrad obkom secretary, Gorbachev was the Politburo member in charge of appointments (Medvedev 1986: 128–29).

15. These are the State Agro-Industrial Committee (Gosagroprom), State Committee for Construction (Gosstroi), Bureau for Machine-Building, Bureau for the Fuel and Power Complex, Foreign Economic Commission, and Bureau for Social Development.

References

Albright, David E. (1987). *Soviet Policy toward Africa Revisited*. Washington, D.C.: Center for Strategic and International Studies.

Alexander, Arthur J. (1978–79, Winter). *Decision-Making in Soviet Weapons Procurement*, Adelphi Paper no. 147–48. London: International Institute for Strategic Studies.

Chebrikov, Viktor (1987, September 11). "A Great Example of Service to Revolutionary Ideals." *Pravda*, p. 3.

Colton, Timothy J. (1979). *Commissars, Commanders, and Civilian Authority: The Structure of Soviet Military Politics*. Cambridge: Harvard University Press.

FitzGerald, Mary C. (1986). "Marshal Ogarkov on the Modern Theater Operation." *Naval War College Review*. 39, 6–25.

Gallagher, Matthew P., and Karl F. Spielmann, Jr. (1972). *Soviet Decision-Making for Defense*. New York: Praeger.

Gelman, Harry (1984). *The Brezhnev Politburo and the Decline of Détente*. Ithaca, NY: Cornell University Press.

Gerasimov, Gennadii (1987a). "Voice of Israel Interview." FBIS, *Daily Report: Soviet Union*, III(40), March 2, H/4.

——— (1987b,). "Interview in Prague, May 23, 1987." FBIS, *Daily Report: Soviet Union*, June 2, AA/3.

Gottemoeller, Rose E. (1986). "Soviet Arms Control Decision Making since Brezhnev." In Roman Kolkowicz and Ellen Mickiewicz, eds., *The Soviet Calculus of Nuclear War*. Lexington: MA: D. C. Heath.

Gurkin, Major General V. (1984). "Certain Questions Arising from Experience of the Formation and Activity of Main Commands of Theaters of Operations during the Initial Period of the Great Patriotic War." *Voenno-istoricheskii zhurnal*, 7.

Gustafson, Thane, and Dawn Mann (1987). "Gorbachev's Next Gamble." *Problems of Communism*, 36(4), 1–20.

Hammond, Thomas T. (1976). "Moscow and Communist Takeovers." *Problems of Communism*, 25(1), 48–67.

Hough, Jerry F. (1987). "Gorbachev Consolidating Power." *Problems of Communism*, 36(4), 21–43.

Jones, Ellen (1985). *The Red Army and Society*. Boston: Unwin Hyman.

Knight, Amy (1987, November 5). "The Party, the KGB and Soviet Policymaking." Presented at the 19th Annual American Association for the Advancement of Slavic Studies Convention, Boston.

Kolkowicz, Roman (1971). "The Military." In H. Gordon Skilling and Franklyn Griffiths, eds., *Interest Groups in Soviet Politics*. Princeton, NJ: Princeton University Press.

Kruzhin, Peter (1984, October 26). "The Riddle of Marshal Ogarkov." *Radio Liberty Research Report*, 415/84.

McConnell, James M. (1983). *The Soviet Shift in Emphasis from Nuclear to Conventional*. Alexandria, VA: Center for Naval Analyses (CRC 490), 2.

Medvedev, Zhores (1986). *Gorbachev*. New York: W.W. Norton.

Miller, George (1986, January 22). "Ogarkov: Clue to Military Changes." *Soviet Analyst*, 15(2), 4–6.

Nor-Mesek, Nikolaij, and Wolfgang Rieper (1984). *The Defense Council of the USSR*. Frankfurt am Main: Institut fuer Sowjet-Studien.

Odom, William E. (1983). "Choice and Change in Soviet Politics." *Problems of Communism*, 32(3), 1–21.

Primakov, E. (1987, July 10). "The New Philosophy of Foreign Policy." *Pravda*, p. 4.

Rahr, Alexander (1986, July 16). "Winds of Change Hit Foreign Ministry." *Radio Liberty Research Report* 274/86.

Reddaway, Peter (1986). "Meeting Report, September 3." Washington, DC: Kennan Institute for Advanced Russian Studies.

Rice, Condoleeza (1987). "The Party, the Military, and Decision Authority in the Soviet Union." *World Politics*, 40(1), 55–81.

Rudnev, I. (1985). "The Aggressiveness of U.S. Military Doctrine Is Growing." *Zarubezhnoe voennoe obozrenie*, 6.

Scott, Harriet Fast, and Wm. F. Scott (1983). *The Soviet Control Structure*. New York: Crane, Russak.

Sejna, Jan, and Joseph D. Douglass, Jr. (1986). *Decision-Making in Communist Countries: An Inside View*. Washington, DC: Pergamon-Brassey's.

Shevardnadze, E. A. (1988). "Abridged Version of Report to July 25th Conference of the Ministry of Foreign Affairs." *Vestnik Ministerstva Inostrannykh Del SSSR*, No. 15, August. Federal Broadcast Information Service, *Daily Report: Soviet Union, Annex, 88–184*, September 22, pp. 1–24.

Shevchenko, Arkady N. (1985). *Breaking with Moscow*. New York: Ballantine.

Spaulding, Wallace (1986). "Shifts in CPSU ID." *Problems of Communism*, 35(4), 80–86.

Spielmann, Karl F. (1976). "Defense Industrialists in the USSR." *Problems of Communism*, 25(5), 52–69.

Staar, Richard (1987). *USSR Foreign Politics after Détente*. Stanford, CA: Hoover Institution Press.

Teague, Elizabeth (1986, July 8). "Turnover in the Soviet Elite under Gorbachev: Implications for Soviet Politics." *Radio Liberty Supplement*.

U.S. Department of Defense (1986). *Soviet Military Power, 1986*. Washington, DC: U.S. Government Printing Office.

Valenta, Jiri (1979). *Soviet Intervention in Czechoslovakia: Anatomy of a Decision*. Baltimore, MD: Johns Hopkins University Press.

—— (1984). "Decisionmaking in Czechoslovakia, 1968." In Jiri Valenta and William Potter, eds., *Soviet Decisionmaking for National Security*. Boston: Unwin Hyman.

Van Oudenaren, John (1986, Summer). *Deterrence, War-Fighting and Soviet Military Doctrine*. Adelphi Paper No. 210. London: International Institute for Strategic Studies.

Weickhardt, George G. (1985). "Ustinov versus Ogarkov." *Problems of Communism*, 34(1), 77–82.

Wettig, Gerhard (1987, November 20). "Has Soviet Military Doctrine Changed?" *Radio Liberty Research Report* 465/87.

Wolfe, Thomas W. (1969). "Are the Generals Taking Over?" *Problems of Communism*, 18(4–5), 106–10.

Yasmann, Viktor (1987, February 11). "Boris Tolstykh: The New Chairman of the USSR State Committee for Science and Technology." *Radio Liberty Research Report* 59/87.

• PART FOUR •

Change in the Elements
of Soviet National Security

As the arguments in this section make clear, it is difficult to chart an obvious, cumulative path of change in the elements of Soviet national security policy. Nevertheless, there are changes, some of them bordering on radical.

Mary C. FitzGerald argues in Chapter Nine, for instance, that the course of Soviet military doctrine holds great potential for producing radical change in the composition and deployment of Soviet military forces. The emphasis in doctrine today is on the downgrading of nuclear weapons as possible weapons for future wars and the examination of the potentialities of sophisticated conventional weapons, arguments begun under the Brezhnev administration. In this sense current doctrine represents only incremental change. Yet the notion of reasonable sufficiency manifests itself in a greater emphasis on the defense, a possible radical doctrinal change. Nevertheless, given the newness of the doctrinal shifts and the slowness of transferring them to behavioral change, scholars and policymakers must be careful about assessing future Soviet intentions.

Western Europe is the arena where new views of national security may be put into operation first. Robert W. Clawson in Chapter Ten documents the incremental to significant changes he sees occurring in the Soviet Union's Western European policy. It is in the political sphere that Gorbachev evinces the greatest change. Clawson contends that Gorbachev's ideas about new thinking and reasonable sufficiency demonstrate that far more than Brezhnev, the new Soviet leader is willing to engage the West in meaningful political-military concessions in order to create the conditions for economic reforms at home. The implications of these activities are multifaceted and could lead to a number of scenarios that Clawson discusses.

No less important to Soviet policy is Eastern Europe. In Chapter Eleven Robin Alison Remington, who examines Soviet policy toward Eastern Europe and the Warsaw Pact, sees the basic stability of Soviet policy in maintaining its strong commitment to preserving the infrastructure for alliance relations. Yet political relations may be making a turn toward the USSR's recognition that decision making in the alliance necessitates the more equal participation of Eastern European nations. Remington notes that the internal struggle in the USSR will be of major importance in bringing significant change to Soviet Eastern European policy, but changes in the leadership of Eastern European nations and Western attitudes about the USSR will also have inputs into the process. She sees the current pattern of politics within the Warsaw Pact as exhibiting stability to incremental change and suggests scenarios of change at the end of her chapter.

Roger E. Kanet, however, sees a slightly greater level of alteration— possibly significant change—in Gorbachev's Third World policy, as discussed in Chapter Twelve. The USSR recognizes that to be a true world power today, it must compete with the West economically and diplomatically—not just militarily—in the Third World. One of the results of this realization is increased activism and flexibility in the Third World. In spite of the new flexibility of Soviet policy, an important dilemma presents itself: whether to expand Soviet contact with nonsocialist Third World nations and risk losing Soviet gains in other (poorer) Third World nations, or to continue past commitments and alienate new or potential allies in the Third World. In part this depends on the progress of restructuring the Soviet economy, from which vitalized Soviet trade with Third World nations might profit, and on reactions of the United States.

An area of great change is Soviet arms control policy, discussed in Chapter Thirteen. Even here, however, there are substantial elements of stability from the past, as Robert L. Arnett points out. Soviet leaders still perceive arms control as having propaganda, military, and economic value and as reducing the likelihood of war. The concepts of new political thinking, reasonable sufficiency, asymmetric reductions, and on-site inspection have all lent new language to Soviet arms control policy under Gorbachev. But have they led to new policy? Arnett chronicles the emergence of significant change. Arms control appears to be playing a greater role in overall Soviet national security policy under Gorbachev. Changes over the last several years are seen as flowing from domestic economic and military imperatives and are supported by changes in military doctrine. Yet how far Gorbachev can go in applying his new concepts to arms control remains uncertain and depends in part on his political fortunes at home.

CHAPTER NINE

Gorbachev's Concept of Reasonable Sufficiency in National Defense[1]

Mary C. FitzGerald
Georgetown University

As a consequence of parity in nuclear retaliatory capabilities, the Soviet politico-military leadership has long viewed deterrence as the optimal role for nuclear forces. Top Soviet military figures now argue that the nuclear impasse has convinced the West to concentrate on fighting wars with only advanced conventional munitions (ACMs). Indeed *Discriminate Deterrence*, published by a blue-ribbon panel of U.S. defense experts (Iklé and Wohlstetter 1988), lends substantial credibility to this view with its call for the development of ACMs as a high-tech complement to, if not replacement for, nuclear forces. Marshal N. V. Ogarkov, chief architect of Soviet military strategy in the 1980s, has acknowledged that Soviet military science has not only incorporated this shift into the training and equipping of Soviet troops but has also adapted the forms and methods of combat action accordingly.

Both the deterrent role for nuclear forces and the new thinking on conventional warfare are reflected in General Secretary Gorbachev's concept of "reasonable sufficiency" in military potentials. This concept envisions the reduction of nuclear and conventional forces to the limits "sufficient for defense," a level that would eliminate their use as offensive potentials. A critical feature of reasonable sufficiency is the new defensive doctrine in Soviet conventional strategy. In May 1987 the Warsaw Pact called for reductions in conventional armed forces and armaments to a level that would preclude surprise attacks and "offensive operations in general." In his UN speech of December 7, 1988, Gorbachev went so far as to announce that unilateral cuts of one-half million Soviet troops —including six divisions based in Eastern Europe—would occur over the next two years. If these ground-breaking Soviet proposals are genuine and can be implemented, such restructuring could portend one of the most radical shifts in the politico-military landscape of the postwar world.

The present chapter will examine Gorbachev's new thinking on national defense by reviewing relevant Soviet politico-military writings since 1977. In examining the state of change in Soviet military doctrine under Gorbachev, I conclude that a significant to radical change has indeed occurred, though doctrine has yet to be fully implemented.

Since the late 1960s a shift away from nuclear and toward conventional war-waging has been occurring in Soviet military policy. But the implications of this shift have emerged most tangibly since former General Secretary L. I. Brezhnev's 1977 address in the city of Tula. Since that time, two currents of Soviet military policy have paved the way for Gorbachev's concept of reasonable sufficiency in national defense: the declining military utility of nuclear weapons and the enhanced combat capabilities of ACMs. If the concept of reasonable sufficiency is more than smoke and mirrors, the West must understand its causes and consequences on both the nuclear and conventional levels.

Reasonable Sufficiency on the Nuclear Level

On the nuclear level, Gorbachev's concept of reasonable sufficiency proceeds from at least two decades of changing Soviet doctrine on nuclear war. Soviet military leaders have themselves traced the current disutility of nuclear war to evolving technological developments in nuclear weaponry.

With the advent of parity in the late 1960s to early 1970s, the Soviet politico-military leadership began to acknowledge that each side possessed an assured capability to deliver an annihilating retaliatory strike on the other—even after subjection to a first strike (FitzGerald 1989). In signing the 1972 ABM Treaty, the Soviet leadership may have concluded that preserving this deterrent balance was more feasible than trying to limit damage through active measures.

In 1977 Brezhnev affirmed at Tula that the Soviet Union was not striving for superiority in armaments with the aim of delivering a first strike (*Pravda* 1977: 2). "First strike" was understood in the Western sense: a unilateral damage-limiting capacity in all-out nuclear war achieved through some combination of offensive means and active and passive defensive means (ABM, counterforce against land and sea, civil defense).[2] Soviet military thought had now concluded that neither side could achieve a unilateral damage-limiting capability; defense of the population against the inevitable retaliatory strike was unattainable (Igolkin 1983: 117).

Soviet acknowledgment that a first-strike capability was both unattainable and irrelevant led logically to Soviet acceptance of the reality of "mutual assured destruction" (MAD) in present-day conditions. G. Gerasimov explicitly confirmed the Soviet acceptance of MAD in 1983: "Then, as now, both sides in the nuclear confrontation possessed an assured capability to inflict an annihilating retaliatory strike on the aggressor (*the Soviet formula*), or to inflict 'unacceptable damage' on the attacking party as long as the situation for 'mutual assured destruction' exists (*the American formula*)." He then stressed that "this capability is determined, apart from everything else, by very restricted limitations on developing missile defense in the Soviet Union and the United States" (Gerasimov 1983: 99, emphasis added; see also Ogarkov 1984: 3; Trofimenko 1985: 15).

Soviet acceptance of the reality of MAD in present-day conditions led logically to another consensus: Nuclear war is so unpromising and dangerous that it remains an instrument of policy only in theory, an instrument of policy that cannot be used (see Chernenko 1985: 15–16; FitzGerald 1989; Ogarkov 1985: 88; Ponomarev 1980: 2; Rybkin, Tyulin, and Kortunov 1982: 141; Trofimenko 1980: 57; Velikov 1982: 5). Since Tula numerous Soviet commentators have explained the disutility of nuclear war as an instrument of policy in terms of the law of passage from quantitative to qualitative change. Writing in the *Military-Historical Journal* in 1985, Colonel-General M. A. Gareev, deputy chief of the General Staff, referred to a qualitative "turning point" in the development of military affairs that was connected with quantitative developments in nuclear weapons (Gareev 1985b: 28). According to Colonel L. Semeiko, the postwar quantitative changes in nuclear weapons soon led to an unprecedented phenomenon: "the potential for the repeated destruction of each of the sides" (Semeiko 1986: 3). Above all, he stressed, this development proved that "nuclear war cannot be a means of resolving international disputes. The inevitability of mutual destruction has made the unleashing of nuclear war suicide for an aggressor himself" (p. 3).

In his 1984 *Red Star* interview and again in his posttransfer article
in *Communist of the Armed Forces*, Marshal Ogarkov wrote that one
need not be in the military to understand that the further expansion
of nuclear arsenals is senseless (Ogarkov 1984: 3). In his 1985 book
he reiterated that the nuclear weapons stockpiled in the world today
"are indeed absurd from a military point of view" (1985: 88). And he
asserted that in the 1970s and 1980s, "the rapid quantitative growth of
nuclear weapons . . . led . . . to a break from previous views on their
role and importance in war, . . . *and even on the possibility of waging
war at all with the use of nuclear weapons*" (1985: 51, emphasis added).

Throughout the 1980s the Soviet politico-military leadership has thus
viewed *deterrence* as the optimal role for nuclear forces. (Here it should
be noted that Soviet writers often use "U.S./NATO doctrine" as a foil
for actual Soviet doctrine.) In his book Marshal Ogarkov described a
new role for U.S. strategic nuclear forces: the United States plans to
achieve its basic objectives in a European war by using its strategic
nuclear forces "*only as a potential threat*" (1985: 68, emphasis added).
Over the years *Foreign Military Review* has maintained that NATO plans
to achieve its military-strategic objectives in Europe without recourse to
nuclear weapons (FitzGerald 1987a). In addition, military theorists such
as Colonel V. Alekseev have explained that NATO plans to use only
conventional weapons "under the umbrellas" of both the Eurostrategic
and strategic nuclear forces (Alekseev 1987: 3).

In short, the essence of the Tula line was a downgrading of all
nuclear options. A growing body of evidence thus indicates that in
1977, coincidentally with Tula, Moscow accelerated its development
of an independent conventional option if war should come (FitzGerald
1989). Marshal Ogarkov and other hard-minded Soviet military figures
have themselves emerged as the architects of the Soviet shift away
from nuclear and toward conventional war-waging. At the same time,
Western analysts continue to present evidence of changes in Soviet
strategy, operational art, force structure, hardware, and exercises that
indicate a Soviet preference for conventional warfare (FitzGerald 1989).
The evidence for a Soviet shift to conventional warfare has become
so compelling, in fact, that Western analysts now speak of a new
"revolution" in Soviet military affairs (for example, see FitzGerald
1986a, 1986b, 1987a; Odom 1985). It was this ongoing phenomenon
that Mikhail Gorbachev confronted when he became general secretary
in March 1985.

Within a year of his accession to power, Gorbachev proposed, as
Philip D. Stewart and Margaret G. Hermann document earlier in this
volume, that a "new political thinking" should henceforth inform Soviet

national security policy. The concept of reasonable sufficiency is perhaps the most tangible element of the new thinking. Although many aspects of reasonable sufficiency can be traced to post-Tula military policy, Gorbachev's proposed agenda includes many elements that perhaps should be termed radical.

As already indicated, the Soviets have long acknowledged that the advent of parity made MAD an existential reality in present-day conditions. But Gorbachev argues the need to move beyond parity to mutual confidence and beyond national security to mutual security. At the Twenty-Seventh Party Congress in February 1986, he warned that the current level of nuclear arsenals is excessively high. Though it now ensures equal danger, a continuing race in nuclear arms will inevitably elevate this "equal danger," which could then reach levels at which "even parity ceases to be a factor of military-political deterrence." In our century, he continued, "genuine equal security is guaranteed not by the maximum, but by the minimum level of the strategic balance" (Gorbachev 1986a: 83–84).

Since Tula the Soviets have acknowledged that nuclear war has ceased to be an instrument of policy because it cannot produce political or military objectives. Gorbachev has further developed this post-Tula consensus. "The nature of modern weaponry," he declared at the 1986 Congress, "does not permit *any* state hope of defending itself by military-technical means alone, even by creating the most powerful defense. . . . Ensuring security is increasingly a political task, and can only be accomplished with *political* means" (Gorbachev 1986a: 81, emphasis added).

The Soviet shift away from military-technical and toward political means for ensuring national security may already be reflected in certain changes in the policymaking establishment. Western analysts have suggested that responsibility for threat definition, arms control, and defense analysis in general is being broadened to include nonmilitary Soviet experts. Certain institutes of the Academy of Sciences, for example, are apparently emerging as alternative centers of expertise on military-technical matters. Whereas Soviet military theorists once reigned over the formulation of military doctrine, civilians may now be assuming a larger role in such areas as defining the nature of a future war.

Throughout the 1980s the declining politico-military utility of nuclear weapons led the Soviet leadership to view the further expansion of nuclear arsenals as militarily senseless. In May 1987 Chief of the General Staff S. F. Akhromeev explicitly echoed Marshal Ogarkov's earlier views. "From a military standpoint," he wrote, "colossal quantities of nuclear weapons are becoming useless, since they cannot be used without catastrophic consequences for all of mankind. . . . The desire to further increase and improve nuclear weapons is both absurd and criminal" (1987: 2). Although Gorbachev's concept of reasonable sufficiency proceeds logically from the declining utility of nuclear weapons, he has developed an agenda that clearly surpasses the Tula heritage.

It should be noted that even before Gorbachev became general secretary, he was articulating the essence of reasonable sufficiency. In April 1983 he called for arms reductions "in which, as a first step, the overall balance would be preserved, but at the lowest possible levels" (Gorbachev 1983a: 2). One month later he asserted that "we are convinced of the erroneousness of the concept of equating the stockpiling of weapons with the strengthening of security" (Gorbachev 1983b: 4). Finally, at the Twenty-Seventh Party Congress Gorbachev announced that the Soviet Union was seeking to reduce its military potential to the limits of "reasonable sufficiency" (Gorbachev 1986a: 85).

Since the 1986 Congress Gorbachev and others have sought to clarify this ground-breaking concept. According to Gorbachev, reasonable sufficiency is that level of military potentials required to accomplish only "defensive tasks" (Gorbachev 1987b: 2). He has further stated that armed forces must be structured "to be sufficient to repel possible aggression, but not sufficient to conduct offensive operations" (1987c: 1). Writing in January 1987, Deputy Foreign Minister V. Petrovskii explained that limiting military potential to the level of reasonable sufficiency means "ruling out the possibility of using it as an offensive potential, as a potential for aggression."

It is important to note that Gorbachev advanced reasonable sufficiency as his criterion for military forces even when parity already prevails. In short, reasonable sufficiency envisions the most finite deterrence on both the nuclear and conventional levels: a parity in defensive potentials. As Robert L. Arnett documents later in this volume, Gorbachev has incarnated his concept in a revolutionary agenda for arms control.

In January 1986, even before he had introduced the concept, Gorbachev proposed a sweeping program for eliminating all nuclear weapons by the year 1999 (Gorbachev 1986b: 1). At least one element of his program—a 50 percent reduction in the strategic nuclear arsenals of the sides—continues to form the basis of U.S.-Soviet arms negotiations on the strategic level. In December 1987 Gorbachev signed the Intermediate-Range Nuclear Force (INF) Treaty, which constitutes a radical shift in Soviet arms control policy. For the first time in the history of that policy, the Soviets have not only accepted sharply asymmetrical reductions in missiles and warheads but have also relinquished certain weapons systems in which they held a clear advantage over the United States. In addition, the concept of reasonable sufficiency also envisions stunning reductions on the conventional level.

Reasonable Sufficiency on the Conventional Level

On the conventional level, Gorbachev's concept of reasonable sufficiency proceeds from at least a decade of changing Soviet doctrine on conventional war. Soviet military leaders have themselves traced the emerging preference for conventional warfare not only to the disutility of nuclear war, but also to evolving technological developments in conventional weaponry. Marshal Ogarkov wrote in 1984 that the ongoing development of ACMs is making them "almost as effective as weapons of mass destruction" (1984: 3). Especially in the context of the Air-Land Battle and the so-called Rogers Plan, numerous Soviet military spokespersons have equated the combat characteristics of ACMs with those of tactical, theater, and strategic nuclear weapons, focusing specifically on their tasks, target sets, and deep-strike ranges (FitzGerald 1987).

In short, the Soviet military views ACMs as strategic means capable of accomplishing strategic tasks even when nuclear weapons are not used (Makarevskii 1986a: 88). Among others, Marshal Petrov has noted that ACMs can accomplish tasks previously reserved for only nuclear weapons (Morozov 1983: 5). *Foreign Military Review* announced in late 1983 that ACMs can achieve the objectives of the first strategic operation in a general nuclear war: destroying the opponent's nuclear potential, defeating its armed forces, knocking out its command-and-control systems, and seizing its most important strategic targets and territories (Semin 1983: 16). Writing in the *Military-Historical Journal* in late 1985, General-Lieutenant A. I. Yevseev made a statement unprecedented in Soviet military thought. In contrast to past wars, he wrote, "the main content of the initial period in present-day conditions can be the delivery by the belligerents of nuclear strikes or strikes with conventional means of destruction . . . for achieving the war's main objectives" (Yevseev 1985: 14–15). Yevseev's statement is unique in that the initial period of a war has never been said to achieve the war's main objectives in the context of conventional weapons use. Soviet military thought could not have acknowledged more explicitly the potential of conventional weapons to accomplish nuclear tasks in a future war.

In addition, Soviet military writers have repeatedly stressed that ACMs offer certain advantages over other weapons when accomplishing these tasks. Military spokespersons such as General-Lieutenant Proskurin have asserted that precision-guided conventional means facilitate the delivery

of strikes to a significant depth without any need to increase the number
and staffing of troops or quantity of forces and means (Proskurin 1985:
3; see also Semin 1983). Writing in *Red Star* in early 1986, V. Kuznetsov
argued that using precision-guided conventional weapons will avoid the
political complications associated with nuclear weapons use and that
these conventional means can accomplish their tasks without radioactive
contamination of the ground and thus present no risk to one's own troops
at the front (1986: 3).

Numerous Soviet military spokespersons have also equated the target
sets of ACMs and nuclear weapons. Writing in *Red Star* in 1984,
General-Major Gontar' observed that NATO plans to use ACMs not
only against troop groupings, command-and-control points, airfields, and
communications networks of the Warsaw Pact countries but also against
the nuclear missile means of the Soviet Union (1984: 5). In his *Red
Star* article in late 1986, Colonel Alekseev focused on the opponent's
command-and-control systems and means of nuclear attack as targets of
the new conventional weapons (1986: 3). Using intermediate-range ballistic
missiles armed with conventional warheads, say the Soviets, NATO plans
to destroy Soviet intermediate-range nuclear missiles at their launch sites
(Khalosha 1986: 124).

In general Soviet military writers ascribe to ACMs the same ranges as
those of tactical and medium- and long-range nuclear weapons. Although
numerous spokespersons have asserted somewhat vaguely that the new
conventional weapons can strike targets "throughout the depth" of the
Warsaw Pact countries (Makarevskii 1966: 5), others have specified
those depths. Writing in *Red Star* in 1986, General-Major Makarevskii
noted that the Rogers Plan envisions the delivery of conventional strikes
throughout the entire depth of the Warsaw Pact's *operational-strategic* dispositions (1986: 3). Both General-Major Gontar' and General-Lieutenant
V. Aleksandrov have warned that the Air-Land Battle envisions the
delivery of conventional strikes throughout the entire *strategic* depth
of the Warsaw Pact (Aleksandrov 1986: 62). The Soviets also state
that ACMs can defeat the opponent's troop groupings "simultaneously
throughout the depth of a theater of military action (TVD)" even before
they are deployed (Khalosha 1986: 124).

Makarevskii became even more explicit in a 1986 *Red Star* article
when he wrote that medium-range missiles armed with conventional
warheads have ranges of up to 2,500 km, or the range of the U.S.
GLCM when armed with a nuclear warhead (1986: 3; see also Pretty
1984: 19). He and others have also referred to long-range cruise and
ballistic missiles armed with conventional warheads (Makarevskii 1986:
187). Finally, Ogarkov and others have written that rapid changes in the

development of conventional weapons are making many weapons "global" (1984: 3), or capable of covering the same distances as intercontinental nuclear weapons.

As noted earlier, a critical feature of reasonable sufficiency is the changing role of the defense in Soviet conventional strategy. But it should be emphasized that prior to Gorbachev's articulation of the concept, the Soviets had sound military reasons for reevaluating defensive operations in modern warfare. Leading military theorists had long been concerned that a preoccupation with the offense hindered a more balanced offensive-defensive mix of operations. A more integrated approach to military planning would also be better suited to overcoming the potential effects of attrition, especially on critical axes of advance. A switch to the defense on critical axes would permit troops on secondary axes to be utilized as reserves. Finally, throughout the 1980s the Soviet military has linked an enhanced role for the defense to the new combat capabilities of ACMs. For example, ACMs threaten critical targets located progressively deeper in the rear. According to the Soviets, it is precisely the potential of ACMs to deliver a simultaneous defeat throughout the opponent's depth that has predetermined the decisiveness of the objectives now assigned to defense (Sidorov 1986: 13). Although the Soviets had long noted that nuclear weapons significantly elevate defensive capabilities, the very similarity of ACMs to nuclear weapons has exerted the same impact on a defense conducted with conventional means alone.

The Soviets assert that the immediate consequences of reasonable sufficiency on the conventional level include "definite changes in the thinking of military professionals" (Kokoshin and Larionov 1987: 33). In particular the conviction that only a decisive offense leads to victory is already inapplicable to a nuclear war. The correlation of defense and offense, their advantages and disadvantages, is different in a nuclear age (Kokoshin and Larionov 1987: 33). These and other aspects of the new military thinking are reflected in Soviet perceptions of U.S./NATO strategy, reevaluations of defensive operations in World War II, changing formulas in Soviet military thought, and changing premises of Soviet operational art and tactics.

Throughout the 1980s Soviet military theorists have pointed to the enhanced role of the defense in U.S./NATO strategy. Edited by General-Lieutenant V. G. Reznichenko, the 1984 edition of *Taktika* used NATO exercises to demonstrate that the depth of the tactical zone of defense now exceeds by three to four times the tactical depth of the defense in World War II. As a consequence the defender now has extensive capabilities for countering a breakthrough (Reznichenko 1984: 91). In past wars, the authors continued, breaching a prepared enemy defense was the most complex and difficult stage of an offensive, the one that predetermined the success of the entire operation. The equipping of troops with extremely powerful combat means only complicates this task today. NATO exercises demonstrate the extent to which armored vehicles and mobile antitank weapons at the disposal of the defense have increased. According to the U.S. concept of the Air-Land Battle, argued the authors, the objectives of defensive action will now be achieved by delivering deep strikes on the first and second echelons and reserves of attacking troops, and by launching decisive counterattacks (Reznichenko 1984: 77–78).

Foreign Military Review announced in 1985 that NATO has assigned more decisive objectives to the defense recently than in the not-too-distant past. The defense is now responsible for not only halting the opponent's offensive but also defeating it decisively by mounting a counteroffensive. In this context, the journal continued, NATO focuses on deep strikes in organizing the defense: the ability to defeat the opponent simultaneously throughout its depth has increased the decisiveness of the objectives assigned to the defense (Sidorov 1986: 13).

Soviet reevaluations of defensive operations in World War II constitute another aspect of the new military thinking. Throughout the 1980s prominent military spokespersons such as Colonel-General M. A. Gareev have stressed that underestimating the role of the defense and neglecting the question of strategic defense led to severe consequences for the Red Army, as well as the loss of vast areas of the country (Gareev 1985c: 230–31). Burdened by the shortcomings of prewar military theory, they note, the Soviet Union was forced to organize and conduct strategic defense from the very outset of the war (1985c: 229). General-Major A. P. Maryshev has written that front troops, having had insufficient time to organize the defense, were compelled to conduct defensive operations in the face of an overwhelming enemy superiority in tanks and aviation, especially on axes of the main strikes (Maryshev 1986: 9). Military scientists and historians have thus been urged to reexamine certain defensive operations of World War II "from a military professional perspective" (Miranovich and Zhitarenko 1987: 2).

In 1985 a major historical work edited by then Defense Minister S. L. Sokolov observed that at the Battle of Kursk, the defense was intentionally organized and conducted on a large scale for the first time in history. Although they had the strategic initiative and general superiority in forces, Soviet troops assumed a defensive posture in order to utilize their advantages in a subsequent strategic offensive. A strong defense allowed them to quickly "grind down" the opponent's basic strike groupings, inflict severe damage on its tank troops, and mount a counteroffensive and later a general offensive (Sokolov 1985: 100). Writing in the *Military-Historical Journal* in 1986, General-Major Maryshev argued that the Soviet military should strive to create precisely such an intentional defense as the Battle of Kursk (1986: 16). A. Kokoshin and V. Larionov have written that in the history of wars and military art, the Battle of Kursk was the first instance of the stronger side assuming the defensive (Kokoshin and Larionov 1987: 36). Its outcome dispels all doubts as to whether a prepared positional defense can resist a powerful onslaught of offensive means. The Battle of Kursk, they note, demonstrated the possibility of withstanding an offensive when antitank defense is organized well and when there is a conscious and timely repudiation of the offense (1987: 39).

According to Colonel Yu. N. Sukhinin, the experience of World War II demonstrates that defensive engagements by tank armies typically compelled the opponent to either renounce its planned offensive or shift to the defensive. To a significant degree, he concludes, both the conduct of the defense and the organization of a counteroffensive by tank armies retain their importance in modern warfare (1987: 43).

One of the litmus tests for change in Soviet military thought is change in a standard Soviet formula. In at least three instances the new defensive strategy has stimulated changes in hitherto orthodox formulas. The first change indicates that Soviet attention has shifted from defense on tactical and operational levels to strategic defense in continental TVDs. According to the 1983 edition of the *Military Encyclopedic Dictionary*, strategic defense could be conducted "on an entire front or on a strategic axis" (Ogarkov 1983: 710). The 1986 edition, however, states that strategic defense can be conducted "in one or several TVDs (strategic axes)" (Akhromeev 1986: 710).

The second change suggests a growing role for the defense relative to the offense. Soviet military thought has perennially maintained that the offense is "the basic type of combat action" with decisive importance for achieving victory over the opponent (Skuibeda 1966: 259). As recently as 1986 the *Military Encyclopedic Dictionary* agreed that strategic offense is "the basic type of strategic action for achieving strategic objectives by the armed forces" (Akhromeev 1986: 711). Writing in the *Military-Historical Journal* in 1986, however, General-Major Maryshev used the foil of history to hint at a change in this sacred formula. In 1941 and 1942, he argued, strategic defense became "the basic type of military action" for the Soviet armed forces (Maryshev 1986: 9). One year later, speaking at a press conference on "the military-technical side of military doctrine," Colonel-General Gareev asserted that defensive operations and combat action will be "the basic method of action" of the Soviet armed forces for repelling aggression (*Krasnaia zvezda*, 1987b: 3).

Among others, Defense Minister D. T. Iazov has since echoed the new formulation. Soviet military doctrine, he wrote in 1987, views the defense as "the basic type of military action" for repelling aggression. The defense must halt the opponent's offensive, "bleed him dry," prevent the loss of territory, and defeat enemy groupings that have breached the defense (1987a: 32–33). It should be noted, however, that by consistently setting the new "basic type of military action" in the context of "repelling aggression," the Soviets could simply be presenting a bit of theoretical legerdemain.

Moreover, the Soviets continue to call for "counteroffensive" capabilities within the framework of the defense. Although he was discussing NATO's Autumn Forge-87 maneuvers, Colonel L. Levadov acknowledged that even under the guise of a "defensive" design, one can successfully accomplish *offensive* tasks such as counterattacks, counterstrikes, and mounting an offensive (Levadov 1987: 3). In fact, argued two colonels in late 1987, military hardware is used in exactly the same way in a counteroffensive as in offensive combat (Miranovich and Zhitarenko 1987: 2).

But Soviet military thought has long held that the defense is an engagement the objectives of which include "halting or rebuffing the offensive of a superior opponent, inflicting significant losses on him, and thereby creating favorable conditions for mounting a decisive offensive" (Reznichenko 1984: 45). As Defense Minister Iazov explained, it is impossible to defeat an aggressor by the defense alone. After rebuffing an attack, troops and naval forces must therefore be capable of conducting a decisive offense in the form of a counteroffensive against a well-armed opponent. This in no way contradicts the defensive nature of Moscow's conventional strategy, he insisted, because the offensive actions in question are directed against an aggressor who has attacked the Soviet bloc (Iazov 1987a: 33). Leading military officials such as General of the Army A. I. Gribkov have agreed that far from contradicting a defensive strategy, counteroffensive actions are not only possible but also necessary "*within the framework of defensive operations and engagements on individual axes*" (1987: 3).

The Soviets now believe that a defender armed with ACMs can take the initiative in battle by simultaneously delivering strikes throughout the attacker's strategic depth. In tampering with a third formula, however, Soviet military theorists have also gone so far as to suggest that the defense has an advantage over the offense. Evidence for this can be found in Soviet discussions of the law of unity and struggle of opposites, or the dialectic of arms development. In its 1978 *Kommunist* article, Marshal Ogarkov explained:

> The history of wars convincingly testifies . . . to the constant contradiction between the means of attack and defense. The appearance of new means of attack has always [inevitably] led to the creation of corresponding means of counter-action, and this in the final analysis has led to the development of new methods for conducting engagements, battles, and operations [and the war in general]. *This also applies fully to nuclear-missile weapons, whose rapid development stimulated military-scientific theory and practice to actively develop means and methods of counteraction. The appearance of means of defense against weapons of mass destruction in turn prompted the improvement of nuclear-missile means of attack.* (Ogarkov 1978: 117, emphasis added)

The foregoing passage was repeated verbatim in Ogarkov's 1982 book, with the addition of the words in brackets (p. 36). In a book published in 1985, however, Ogarkov made several significant changes in its standard discussion of this dialectical law. First, the italic sentences did not appear in 1985. Second, he added a discussion that had never appeared before. World War I, he said, had led to a situation in which the defense proved to be stronger than the offense. In the course of World War II, however, a new contradiction arose: the means of offense proved to be stronger than the means of defense. As a result, during the war and especially in the postwar period, defensive means such as antitank artillery, antitank mines, antitank guided missiles, various types of missile and antiair missile complexes, fighter aircraft, ASW ships, and so forth were developed at an accelerated rate, "whose skillful use at a certain stage balanced the means of offense and defense to some degree" (Ogarkov 1985: 49). By referring to a "balance" between the means of offense and defense, Ogarkov has moved away from the hitherto orthodox position that the historical competition between offense and defense would be tilted in favor of the offense.

Kokoshin and Larionov were even more explicit. In World War II, they observed, the development of armor-piercing, subcaliber, and hollow-charge shells and mines decided the outcome of the competition between mobile armor and antitank weapons in favor of the latter. Today "the same could be true of conventional means of offense and defense in a ground theater of military action" (Kokoshin and Larionov 1987: 40). It should be noted that Soviet views on the emerging primacy of defense relative to offense do not extend to antiballistic missile defense, which, according to the Soviet consensus, can be overcome by offensive means of counteraction (FitzGerald 1987b). Chief of the

General Staff Akhromeev thus announced in 1986 that the "eternal competition" between offensive and defensive means is being resolved today in not one but many directions. For every action reliable means of counteraction can be found (*Izvestiia* 1986b: 5).

Kokoshin and Larionov have further explained that the primacy of the defense is contingent upon implementation of the 1987 Warsaw Pact proposals. If conventional armed forces and armaments are significantly reduced, then conditions can be created in which "the defensive potentials of each side would obviously be superior to the potential for conducting offensive operations" (1987: 40).

Throughout the 1980s the defensive conventional strategy has also evolved in authoritative Soviet tomes on operational art and tactics. One indication of an expanding role for the defense has been its enhanced ability over time to thwart the accomplishment of tasks by the offense. In the 1966 edition of *Taktika* it is claimed that the attacker, possessing powerful means of destruction, could quickly inflict a decisive defeat on the opponent's groupings, destroy any fortified defensive structures, and rapidly change the correlation of forces (Reznichenko 1966: 245). Both the 1984 and 1987 editions, however, acknowledge that the increased power, accuracy, range, and rate of fire of ACMs, as well as the improved stability and aggressiveness of the defense, have significantly affected the accomplishment of tasks by the offense (Reznichenko 1984: 109).

The emergence of ACMs has also led the Soviets to see a growing convergence between offense and defense in modern warfare—particularly because a defender armed with ACMs can deliver strikes throughout the depth of the attacker's deployments. Colonel-General Gareev maintained that the convergence of offense and defense is becoming more and more apparent. In contrast to the successive nature of offensive operations in World War II, he noted in 1985, the modern offense constitutes a more decisive simultaneous defeat of the opponent throughout the depth of its combat dispositions. At the same time, the modern defense has powerful weapons that can defeat a superior opponent even at great distances (Gareev 1985c: 245).

According to a 1987 book edited by General-Major A. S. Milovidov, the correlation of offense and defense has become even more profound and complex. The defense delivers retaliatory strikes to an ever-greater degree and is often conducted with the same means used by attacking troops. Extensive changes are thus occurring in the convergence of the offensive and defensive potentials of troops. In addition, the transition from one type of military action to another is significantly more rapid and decisive today than in any past wars (Milovidov 1987: 252).

Soviet military theorists stress that it is precisely the deep-strike range of ACMs that enables a defender to take the strategic initiative and continuously inflict disproportionate losses on the attacker. In 1985 Colonel-General Gareev thus argued that because of the potential for attacking units to lose the initiative as a consequence of strikes by ACMs, greater attention must now be focused on training for defensive operations (1985a: 23).

The Impact of New Conventional Thinking

On the conventional level, as on the nuclear, the most radical consequence of reasonable sufficiency is Moscow's stunning agenda for arms control.

At the June 1986 meeting of its Political Consultative Committee, the Warsaw Pact formally incorporated Gorbachev's new concept into its military doctrine. This doctrine now envisions maintaining an equilibrium of military forces at the lowest possible level and reducing military potentials to the limits of "sufficiency" necessary for defense (*Izvestiia* 1986a: 2). The Warsaw Pact proposed decreasing the danger of a surprise attack by reducing the tactical strike aviation of both blocs and troops along the line of contact on the order of half a million men on each side. The member countries also proposed additional measures to increase the confidence of the Warsaw Pact, NATO, and all European countries that surprise offensive operations would not be mounted against them (*Izvestiia* 1986a: 1).

It should be noted that throughout the 1980s Soviet military theorists have stressed that ACMs will be used to deliver "surprise" or "preemptive" strikes against the opponent's most important state and military targets. Ogarkov asserted that the Air-Land Battle envisions simultaneous, surprise strikes by air, naval, and ground forces using ACMs (1985: 69). *Foreign Military Review* announced in 1986 that as long as the West continues to improve its ACMs, the threat of a surprise conventional attack against the Warsaw Pact will continually grow (Sidorov 1986: 9).

In May 1987 the Political Consultative Committee of the Warsaw Pact reiterated the 1986 general-purpose force reductions of half a million men on each side. It also proposed reducing conventional armed forces and armaments to the level at which neither side could launch a surprise attack or mount "offensive operations in general" (*Krasnaia zvezda* 1987a: 1). About two months later Soviet Defense Minister Iazov reiterated this ground-breaking proposal: "Proceeding from the principle of sufficiency, the Warsaw Pact member states propose to reduce, on a mutual basis of course, military potentials to the level at which neither side, while ensuring its defense, has the forces or means enabling it to mount offensive operations" (1987b: 2). As already indicated, the Soviet military had heretofore viewed the offense as the basic type of military action for the Soviet armed forces. But Iazov went so far as to urge that arms reductions be aimed at ultimately eliminating "the very military-technical capability for attacking each other" (Iazov 1987b: 2).

Since the Warsaw Pact meeting in May 1987 leading Soviet theorists have attempted to clarify the implications of a defensive conventional strategy. In July 1987 Rear-Admiral A. Astaf'ev explained that when the Warsaw Pact refers to the limits of sufficiency, it means "sufficiency for defense": "a sufficiency of military potentials that would rule out the victory of one side and the defeat of the other" (*Novoe vremiia* 1987: 18). But a major military work that went to the printer in 1986 still claimed that "the offense is the basic type of military action, and its objective is the opponent's complete defeat" (Milovidov 1987: 251). Not surprisingly, such veteran military spokespersons as Colonel Semeiko have announced that the Warsaw Pact doctrine is "truly revolutionary" because for the first time both sides would repudiate the offense, which traditionally has been considered basic (Semeiko 1987: 5).

The Soviet politico-military leadership has repeatedly explained that the new defensive strategy requires a radical restructuring of the Soviet armed forces. According to Gorbachev, the armed forces must be restructured to be "sufficient to repel possible aggression, but not sufficient to conduct offensive operations" (1987c: 1). Prominent military spokespersons such as General-Lieutenant M. A. Mil'shtein have stressed that the Warsaw Pact doctrine compels Soviet military science to elaborate the "military-technical aspects" of military doctrine. As a result Moscow envisions a restructuring of its armed forces in zones of contact that would preclude both the launching of a surprise attack and the conduct of offensive operations (*Novoe vremiia* 1987: 18). According to V. Avakov and V. Baranovskii, the objective is to reorganize the armed forces of the sides so that "defensive action would be guaranteed greater success than offensive operations" (1987: 30).

In June 1987 one of the participants in a Defense Ministry press conference went so far as to announce that the Soviet Union proposes reducing military potentials "so that the armed forces are structurally capable of conducting only defensive operations" (*Krasnaia zvezda* 1987b: 3). If the Warsaw Pact proposals are implemented, the Soviets say that every facet of their military establishment will be restructured to this end, including the size and structure of the armed forces, nature of armaments (Semeiko 1987: 5), military planning and training (Kokoshin and Larionov 1987: 33), and military doctrine itself (*Novoe vremiia* 1987: 19).

As early as February 1987 Gorbachev proposed a concrete measure to reduce the potential for a surprise attack: removal of the most dangerous offensive types of arms from the zone of contact (150 km on each side; see Gorbachev 1987a: 2). In May 1987 the Warsaw Pact incorporated its proposal into its military doctrine as a first step toward restructuring the armed forces for conducting only defensive operations (*Krasnaia zvezda* 1987a: 1). According to General-Major Makarevskii, offensive weapons include long-range tactical bombers, tactical missiles, long-range artillery, and large tank groupings (*Novoe vremiia* 1987: 20). If troops and such offensive weapons are withdrawn, General-Lieutenant Mil'shtein has explained, then a potential aggressor will have to regroup and concentrate before organizing an offensive. The other side will notice this and a surprise attack will be ruled out (*Novoe vremiia* 1987: 19).

In such a world an aggressor would reveal its intentions by the very posture it adopts. Moreover, if the defense actually has an advantage over the offense, states would have no incentive to procure offensive forces and could probably avoid an arms race altogether.

At the same time, however, there is ample reason for the West to exercise healthy skepticism concerning reasonable sufficiency on both the nuclear and conventional levels.[3] First, current Soviet force levels exceed by far the requirements for pure defense. Although one might dismiss this notion, arguing that current Soviet force levels reflect doctrinal decisions made ten to fifteen years ago, Western security must be predicated upon the adversary's capabilities rather than an uncertain interpretation of its intentions.

Second, though ACMs could enhance defensive strikes deep into the attacker's rear echelon by disrupting attack timetables and serving as a defensive force multiplier, traditional Soviet doctrine has long extolled the offensive. Today Soviet military figures stress the need for counteroffensive capabilities within the context of the defensive strategy. They thus acknowledge that an ambiguous distinction exists between offensive and defensive capabilities.

Third, it is true that if the Warsaw Pact proposals are implemented, the Soviets would necessarily give advance notice of aggressive intentions. But whether the West could achieve timely, sufficient reinforcement and resupply—an already difficult proposition—is hardly cause for optimism in Western capitals. Finally, with the Soviet economy in a shambles, a relaxation of East-West tensions could serve Soviet security interests by stimulating the needed influx of Western capital and technology.

Conversely , genuine Soviet interest in arms control has always included a desire to restrain the technological arms race. Matthew Evangelista has aptly described the historical pattern:

The United States typically originates technologically innovative arms systems; the Soviet Union first counters them, then imitates and produces them in large number. As a result, weapons that are initially touted as offering the United States a major advantage end up redounding to both sides' *dis*advantage when the Soviets adopt them as well. (1986: 580)

Gorbachev's concept of reasonable sufficiency could well reflect Moscow's recognition of the costliness of this pattern.

Furthermore, the conventional level is precisely the arena where a costly high-tech arms race in ACMs is occurring. Gorbachev's economic reforms are aimed at improving Soviet performance in the high-tech sector, but big investments in ACMs in the short run would undermine the needs and logic of its economic plans. Especially in light of the Soviet military's preoccupation with the threat from NATO's ACMs, halting such deployments might also be judged to yield significant security benefits. Dennis Gormley has noted that although the INF Treaty eliminates some of the dual-capable Soviet systems slated for the conventional high-tech option, it will have only a marginal effect on Soviet capabilities for fighting such a war (1988: 18).

Most important, Gorbachev has moved swiftly to actualize its proposals, including a shift from national to common security and the concept of reasonable sufficiency. Though proposing that common security be achieved through political rather than military means, for example, the general secretary withdrew Soviet forces from Afghanistan, reduced aid to Syria, and limited out-of-area naval activities. Though proposing reasonable sufficiency, he signed the INF Treaty, thereby agreeing to sharply asymmetrical cuts and the elimination of weapons systems in which the Soviets held an advantage over the West.

Finally, and doubtless in the face of intense opposition, Gorbachev has announced *uniliateral* reductions of conventional forces in Eastern Europe. This stunning development suggests a realization that its proposed reductions in strategic nuclear forces are unattainable without conventional force reductions. In signing the INF Treaty he stressed that the need for reductions in conventional forces and armaments is more crucial now than ever before, implying a necessary linkage between nuclear and conventional arms control (Gorbachev 1987d: 2–3). The political and military reasons for a defensive conventional strategy would thus coincide.

In summary, the increasing proliferation and lethality of the super-powers' nuclear arsenals has paved the way for Gorbachev's concept of reasonable sufficiency in national defense. Indeed, a careful review of Soviet doctrinal writings reveals that two decades of Soviet military thought have led logically to reasonable sufficiency on both the nuclear and conventional levels.

Notes

1. The views expressed in this chapter are those of the author and do not necessarily reflect the views of the United States government or any of its agencies.
2. For example, see Ustinov (1977), Simonian (1977: 4), and the discussion in McConnell (1985: 330–331).
3. I am indebted to Dr. John M. Weinstein for this discussion.

References

Akhromeev, MSU S. F., ed. (1986). "Strategic Defense." *Voennyi entsiklopedicheskii slovar'*. Moscow: Voenizdat.
—— (1987, May 9). "The Great Victory." *Krasnaia zvezda*, p. 2.
Aleksandrov, General-Lieutenant V. A. (1986). "The Evolution of American Views on the Possible Nature of Wars." *Voenno-istoricheskii zhurnal*, no. 6.
Alekseev, Colonel V. (1986, January 17). "Conventional Wars in the Plans of the Pentagon and NATO." *Krasnaia zvezda*. p. 3.
—— (1986, October 3). "Conventional Wars and Forms of Waging Them." *Krasnaia zvezda*. p. 3.
Avakov, V., and Baranovskii, V. (1987). "In the Interests of Preserving Civilization." *Mirovaia ekonomika i mezhdunarodnye otnosheniia*, no. 4.
Evangelista, Matthew (1986). "The New Soviet Approach to Security." *World Policy Journal*, 3(4).
FitzGerald, Mary C. (1986a). "Marshal Ogarkov on the Modern Theater Operation." *Naval War College Review*, 39(4), 6–25.
—— (1986b). "The Soviet Leadership on Nuclear War." *Soviet Union*, 13(3), 249–73.
—— (1987a). "Marshal Ogarkov and the New Revolution in Soviet Military Affairs." *Defense Analysis*, 3(1).
—— (1987b). *Soviet Views on SDI*. The Carl Beck Papers in Russian and East European Studies. Pittsburgh: University of Pittsburgh Center for Russian and East European Studies.
—— (1989). *Changing Soviet Doctrine on Nuclear War*. Center for Policy Studies, Dalhousie University.
Garthoff, Raymond L. (1979). "SALT I: An Evaluation." *World Politics*, 31(1), October 1978, in *Current News* (Special Edition), no. 409, April 19.
Gerasimov, G. (1983). "Current Problems of World Policy." *Mirovaia ekonomika i mezhdunarodnye otnosheniia*, no. 7.
Gareev, Colonel-General M. A. (1985a). "The Creative Nature of Soviet Military Science in the Great Patriotic War." *Voenno-istoricheskii zhurnal*, no. 7.
—— (1985b). "Soviet Military Science." *Voenno-istoricheskii zhurnal*, no. 7.
—— (1985c) *M. V. Frunze: Voennyi teoretik*. Moscow: Voenizdat.

Gontar' General-Major F. (1984, December 15). "With a View to Aggression." *Krasnaia zvezda*, p. 5.

Gorbachev, M. S. (1983a, April 23). Speech. *Pravda*, p. 2.

—— (1983b, May 19). Speech. *Pravda*, p. 4.

—— (1986a). *Politicheskii doklad Tsentral'nogo Komiteta KPSS XXVII S'ezdu Kommunisticheskoi Partii Sovetskogo Soiuza*. Moscow: Politizdat.

—— (1986b, January 16). Speech. *Pravda*, pp. 1–2.

—— (1987a, February 17). "For a Non-Nuclear World and Humanism in International Relations." *Pravda*, pp. 1–2.

—— (1987b, April 1). Speech. *Pravda*, p. 2.

—— (1987c, September 17). "The Reality and Guarantees of a Secure World." *Pravda*, p. 1.

—— (1987d, December 11). Speech. *Pravda*, pp. 2–3.

Gormley, Dennis M. (1988). "'Triple Zero' and Soviet Military Strategy." *Arms Control Today*, 18(1).

Gribkov, General of the Army A. I. (1987, September 25). "A Doctrine for Preserving Peace." *Krasnaia zvezda*, p. 3.

Iazov, General of the Army D. T. (1987a). *Na strazhe sotsializma i mira*. Moscow: Voenizdat.

—— (1987b, July 28). "The Military Doctrine of the Warsaw Pact Is the Doctrine of Defending Peace and Socialism." *Krasnaia zvezda*.

Igolkin, M. V. (1983). "History and Compromises." *Voprosy filosofii*, no. 8.

Iklé, Fred C., and Albert Wohlstetter, co-chairmen (1988). *Discriminate Deterrence: Report of the Commission on Integrated Long-Term Strategy*. Washington, D.C.: U.S. Government Printing Office.

Izvestiia (1986a, June 12). "The Warsaw Pact Appeal to NATO and All European Countries with a Program for Reducing Armed Forces and Conventional Arms in Europe."

—— (1986b, August 27). "Ending Nuclear Tests: Press Conference in Moscow."

Khalosha, B. M. (1986). "NATO—Generator of the Arms Race." In A. D. Nikonov, ed., *The Arms Race: Causes, Trends, Means of Halting*. Moscow: Mezhdunarodnye otnosheniia.

Kokoshin, A. and V. Larionov, (1987). "The Battle of Kursk in Light of the Modern Defensive Doctrine." *Mirovaia ekonomika i mezhdunarodnye otnosheniia* no. 8.

Krasnaia zvezda (1987a, May 30). "On the Military Doctrine of the Warsaw Pact States."

—— (1987b, June 23). "A Doctrine of Prevention."

Kuznetsov, V. (1986, January 31). "The Cart-Horse and the Race-Horse." *Krasnaia zvezda*, p. 3.

Levadov, Colonel L. (1987, November 19). "Yet Another Rehearsal." *Krasnaia zvezda*, p. 3.

Makarevskii, General-Major V. I. (1986a). "The Increase in Conventional Weapons and Problem of Limiting Them." In A. D. Nikonov, ed., *The Arms Race: Causes, Trends, Means of Halting*. Moscow: Mezhdunarodnye otnosheniia.

—— (1986b, February 18). "They Call Them Conventional . . . " *Krasnaia zvezda*, p. 5.

—— (1986c, February 21). "A Pressing Need." *Krasnaia zvezda*, p. 3.

Maryshev, General-Major (1986). "Some Problems of Strategic Defense in the Great Patriotic War." *Voenno-istoricheskii zhurnal*, no. 6.

McConnell, James M. (1985). "Shifts in Soviet Views on the Proper Focus of Military Development." *World Politics*, 27(3), 317–43.

Milovidov, General-Major A. S., ed. (1987). *Voenno-teoreticheskoe nasledie V. I. Lenina i problemy sovremennoi voiny*. Moscow: Voenizdat.

Miranovich, Colonel G. and Colonel V. Zhitarenko (1987, December 9). "What Makes Defense Strong?" *Krasnaia zvezda*, p. 2.
Morozov, V. (1983, December 1). Interview with MSU, V. I. Petrov, "Superiority . . . over Common Sense." *Sovetskaia Rossiia*, p. 5.
Novoe vremia (1987, July 13). Roundtable discussion "Of Reasonable Sufficiency, Precarious Parity, and International Security." No. 27.
Odom, William E. (1985). "Soviet Force Posture: Dilemmas and Directions." *Problems of Communism*, 34 (July-August) pp. 1–14.
Ogarkov, MSU N. V. (1978). "Military Science and Defense of the Socialist Fatherland." *Kommunist*, no. 7.
—— (1982). *Vsegda v gotovnosti k zashchite Otechestva*. Moscow: Voenizdat.
—— (1983). "Strategic Defense." In *Voennyi entsiklopedicheskii slovar'*. Moscow: Voenizdat.
—— (1984, May 9). "Defending Socialism: The Experience of History and the Present." *Krasnaia zvezda*, p. 3.
—— (1985). *Istoriia uchit bditel'nosti*. Moscow: Voenizdat.
Petrovskii, V. (1987). "Security through Disarmament." *Mirovaia ekonomika i mezhdunarodnye otnosheniia*, no. 1.
Ponomarev, B. N. (1980, September 25). "Preserve Mankind from the Horrors of War." *Pravda*, p. 2.
Pravda (1977, January 19). L. I. Brezhnev Speech.
Pretty, R. T., ed. (1984). *Jane's Weapons Systems: 1984–85*. New York: Jane's Publishing Co.
Proskurin, M. (1985, December 3). "What Lurks behind the Rogers Plan." *Krasnaia zvezda*, p. 3.
Reznichenko, General-Lieutenant, V. G. ed. (1966). *Taktika*. Moscow: Voenizdat.
—— (1984). *Taktika*. Moscow: Voenizdat.
Rybkin, Colonel Ye., I. Tyulin, and S. Kortunov (1982). "The Anatomy of One Bourgeois Myth." *Mirovaia ekonomika i mezhdunarodnye otnosheniia*, no. 8.
Semeiko, Colonel L. (1986, January 23). "A Dangerous Feature." *Krasnaia zvezda*.
—— (1987, August 13). "Instead of Mountains of Weapons. . . . On the Principle of Reasonable Sufficiency." *Izvestiia*, p. 5.
Semin, G. (1983). "NATO's Military Strategy." *Zarubezhnoe voennoe obozrenie*, no. 8.
Sidorov, Lieutenant Colonel V. (1986). "Conducting Operations with Conventional Means of Destruction." *Zarubezhnoe voennoe obozrenie*, no. 1.
Simonian, General-Major R. (1977, June 14). "On the Risk of Confrontation." *Pravda*, p. 4.
Skuibeda, Colonel P. I. (1966). *Tolkovyi slovar' voennykh terminov*. Moscow: Voenizdat.
Sokolov, MSU S. L., ed. (1985). *Vtoraia mirovaia voina: itogi i uroki*. Moscow: Voenizdat.
Sukhinin, Colonel Yu. N. (1987). "The Tank Army in the Defense." *Voenno-istoricheskii zhurnal*, no. 3.
Trofimenko, G. A. (1980). "Washington's Strategic Gambles." *SShA: Ekonomika, Politika, Ideologiia*, no. 12.
—— (1985). "U.S. Military Strategy—Instrument of an Aggressive Policy." *SShA: Ekonomika, Politika, Ideologiia*, no. 1.
Ustinov, D. F. (1977). "Guardian of Peaceful Labor and Stronghold of Universal Peace." *Kommunist*, no. 3.
Velikov, Ye. P. (1982, November 28). "The Simple Truths of the Century." *Sovetskaia Rossiia*, p. 5.
Yevseev, A. I. (1985). "On Several Trends in the Changing Content and Character of the War's Initial Period." *Voenno-istoricheskii zhurnal*, no. 11.

• CHAPTER TEN •

Changes in Soviet National Security Policy toward Western Europe under Gorbachev

Robert W. Clawson
Lyman L. Lemnitzer Center for NATO Studies

During most of the Brezhnev years the main thrust of Soviet foreign policy in Western Europe was, in the absence of practical alternatives, to live with the continuation of the overall status quo while seeking to reduce U.S. influence and to augment the USSR's position at the margins through the pursuit of low-risk objectives. These include the following (Platt, 1986: V–X):

1. building and maintaining a substantial all-arms war-fighting military advantage in Europe, thereby ensuring comprehensive deterrence and Soviet security in the West;
2. loosening American political and military ties with the European allies, thus weakening the NATO threat;
3. creating a place for Soviet influence in key areas of Western European policy, particularly in questions of armaments and defense;
4. transforming Western European political policies ultimately by encouraging "progressive" political forces in allied NATO nations;

5. preserving as much of détente in Europe as possible and practical, especially international trade, ensuring continued access to important elements of Western technology;

6. augmenting and protecting the permanent legitimacy of their position in Eastern Europe; and

7. negotiating nuclear arms control agreements that enhanced Soviet national security by removing American weapons of mass destruction from Europe.

Under Brezhnev much of Soviet diplomacy was directed at European problems, as was a significant portion of its war-fighting military power and foreign trade. This has led one observer to consider Brezhnev's foreign policy to have been essentially Eurocentric (Van Oudenaren 1987). But Soviet Third World initiatives under Brezhnev were certainly substantial, including military and political intervention, massive arms sales and military assistance, as well as the recruitment and expensive support of new revolutionary movements and client states. The Third World during Brezhnev's regime was the only area where Soviet influence could be dramatically expanded without substantial risk to Soviet national security (Clawson 1986). However, that expansion did come at the cost of détente with the United States, a high price but one that the Soviets were willing to pay. "Eurocentric," then, is perhaps too strong a term for Brezhnev's foreign policy, although toward the end of his life the Soviet Union seemed to be suffering a decline in enthusiasm for Third World adventures.

The European portion of Soviet foreign policy that focused on major diplomatic efforts, such as those that eventually resulted in the European security conference and the Helsinki accords of the mid-1970s, were designed to help attain important policy objectives including diminishing American influence in Western Europe, reinforcing the USSR's position in Eastern Europe, and eventually denuclearizing the entire continent. These efforts as well as others, such as those aimed at preventing the American neutron bomb and intermediate nuclear forces (INF) deployments, required major commitments of conventional diplomacy and international political action as well as supporting propaganda and disinformation. Trade between Western Europe and the USSR continued to be important long after the United States had largely withdrawn from the Soviet market. In addition, maintenance of the Soviet military instrument in Europe continued to act as an effective deterrent against any NATO or American attempt to use military power for political leverage in the region. Western Europe did indeed attract its fair share of Soviet attention under Brezhnev (Shenaev, Melnikov, and Maier 1981).

Brezhnev's death came at about the same time that the Soviets appear to have decided that the results of their foreign policy in Western Europe amounted to something less than that for which they had hoped. The Helsinki agreements were mainly being used to embarrass the USSR, and although they had twice been able to block U.S. consideration of positioning the neutron bomb in Europe, they had been completely defeated in their campaign against the INF deployments of cruise and upgraded Pershing missiles. Their immediate response was to begin to dismantle the framework for détente in Europe, as they had threatened to do if European members of NATO allowed emplacement of the INF missiles on their soil. But the continuity of Soviet foreign policy toward Western Europe during this period suffered first from the rapidly deteriorating health of Leonid Brezhnev and then the quick demise of his two immediate successors, Yuri Andropov and Konstantin Chernenko. In the event the USSR stopped short of discarding European détente; instead they deployed the new highly accurate short-range, dual-capable SS-21 and SS-23 rockets in Eastern Europe as a direct response to the NATO INF missiles. They then seem to have put Western Europe on hold (Van Oudenaren 1987).

Foreign Policy Changes under Gorbachev

Following his selection as Soviet Communist Party General Secretary in March 1985, Mikhail Gorbachev moved surprisingly quickly to reinvigorate Soviet foreign policy. He almost immediately began a program of reglobalization in which the USSR would build on its strengths in the Third World (e.g., India, not Angola) while seeking to defuse hostile situations such as relations with China and the United States. Soviet diplomatic and political efforts that had been focused primarily on Western Europe under Brezhnev were broadened and refocused to do regularized and vigorous business with the established governments of virtually all of the major industrial and political powers of the world, especially with China, Japan, and the ASEAN countries (Van Oudenaren 1987).

At the same time that Gorbachev was reglobalizing Soviet foreign policy he was intent on a settlement in Western Europe. He paid an early visit to France before his meeting with former President Reagan in Geneva in an attempt to convince President François Mitterrand to agree to negotiate the elimination of French nuclear missiles. The various minor agreements he took back to Moscow were only small successes in the light of Mitterrand's blunt "non" to missile negotiations of any kind. The general secretary's subsequent meeting with the American president focused on preliminaries to future arms control talks. Some negotiations had been resumed under Chernenko, canceling earlier Soviet declared policy of not negotiating until the U.S. weapons were withdrawn. Following his meeting with Reagan, Gorbachev gave Soviet representatives in Geneva instructions to step up the pace of the talks on the INF missiles.

At Reykjavik in November 1986 Gorbachev accepted virtually the whole American INF reduction package and more but linked it all to the United States' abandoning the Strategic Defense Initiative (SDI). Reagan's refusal to negotiate away SDI resulted in only a momentary pause in Gorbachev's efforts to seek a settlement in Europe. He subsequently bombarded the Americans and Europeans with a series of proposals for the reduction of intermediate and short-range missiles. When that startled European and American generals into the realization that their troops might be faced with conventional combat against heavy odds, he reenergized his earlier proposal, made in Budapest in June 1986, for the creation of a new, all-European format to negotiate the reduction of conventional armed forces to the point where neither side could mount a successful surprise attack (Lebedev and Podberyozkin 1987). He also suggested negotiations for the removal of battlefield nuclear weapons from European territory.

By the spring of 1987, Gorbachev was peppering the allies with these various initiatives free of any linkage to the American SDI program, the British nuclear force, or French missiles. In Prague on April 10, 1987 he amplified his Budapest appeal, offering the Western Europeans a denu-clearized as well as conventionally reduced "common European home" (Gorbachev 1987a). In May 1987 Polish General Wojciech Jaruzelski proposed essentially an evolved version of the Rapacki plan of 1957. He was suggesting the elimination of all nuclear weapons and the reduction of conventional troop levels in five NATO and four Warsaw Pact member states (Fouquet 1987a: 5). Later in May the Warsaw Pact party general secretaries meeting in Berlin endorsed a six-point plan for the elimination of nuclear and chemical weapons, conventional force reductions in Europe, the creation of a workable system of verification for each, the establishment of meaningful confidence-building measures, and, finally, an end both to NATO and the Warsaw Pact in order to terminate the "abnormal" division of Europe into two opposing blocs. The plan, labeled the Warsaw Pact Doctrine, was published in *Krasnaia zvezda* on May 30, 1987.

Washington and the NATO capitals reeled under the assault. The United States, with its own proposals being forcefully argued by the Soviet general secretary, assumed something must be wrong. The Western European leaderships, faced at last with the real prospect of Europe being made once again safe for conventional war, seemed to be clinging to their nuclear security blankets hardly daring to imagine that Gorbachev might be serious about negotiating real conventional force reductions throughout the European area. Despite some important European and American reservations, by late summer 1987 most Western objections had been overcome and the ground was well prepared for major agreements to be concluded for the elimination of intermediate and short-range U.S. and Soviet missiles; a mutually acceptable verification scheme was also in hand. The INF Treaty was signed in December 1987 at the Washington summit.

A year of caution followed in the West, a waiting period to see whether or not the Soviets would do anything substantive to reduce their ability to launch a surprise attack against NATO. Then in December 1988 Gorbachev once more took the initiative. In a wide-ranging speech before the U.N. General Assembly in New York, he declared that the Soviet Union would unilaterally withdraw and disband six armored divisions from Eastern Europe and begin to reduce the number of assault landing troops and assault crossing units located there; it was the beginning of the reconfiguration for which Western decision makers had been waiting. In addition, Gorbachev promised to cut the total number of Soviet armed forces by 500,000 men over two years and to take a series of associated weapons reduction measures. These various steps would not, of course, lower Warsaw Pact numerical superiority to the satisfaction of most NATO leaders. But it would be another substantial step toward reducing the military confrontation in Europe. Meaningful negotiations for conventional troop reductions as well as for the elimination of all classes of battlefield nuclear weapons would help complete Gorbachev's program for the denuclearization of the continent and a settlement of the European security question. Details of Soviet European-focused arms control initiatives can be found in Robert L. Arnett's chapter in this volume.

Although Gorbachev seeks to reduce reliance on the military instrument to achieve policy objectives, and though he promises to reconfigure Soviet armed forces into a truly defensive deployment, it is important to examine the nature of the development of Soviet military doctrine, strategy, operations, and tactics in the European context. Although the Soviet leadership has declared its intentions to shift to an essentially new way of thinking about international security, were a war to start in Europe today, the Soviets and the Warsaw Pact would go into battle prepared to fight in a manner evolved from traditional Soviet military thinking. The core of this chapter will examine the modern development of that thought and changes in the still essentially pre-Gorbachev employment guidelines that continue to characterize Soviet military policy.

The Military Dimension: Pre-Gorbachev

Soviet national security policy toward Europe during and immediately after the Brezhnev years was more fully developed than toward any other major portion of the world. The economic and political instruments, as well as a host of minor means, were important elements in the Soviet effort to maintain security in the European theater. However, as in virtually all other contexts, the military instrument remained the most important one available to the leadership of the USSR. The deployment of the Soviet armed forces, especially in the German Democratic Republic, Poland, Czechoslovakia, and the western USSR, constituted in most cases the precondition for the attainment of virtually all Soviet foreign policy objectives and played the principal role in promoting the USSR's national security in Europe.

Fundamentally the USSR tried to convey two essentially passive and political messages through the instrument of its armed forces in the European theater. The first was that Soviet military capability was enormous and, if employed against NATO Europe, would be irresistible. Implicit in this message was that the armed forces of the United States in Europe could not and would not help much; reliance on friendship with the USSR would be a better alternative. The second message was that Soviet forces posed no threat to Western Europe but were simply a legitimate response to an aggressive U.S.-inspired anti-Soviet policy and reflected the traditional experience of Russia and the Soviet Union with invasion and devastation from its neighbors. Although there was a certain mutually contradictory nature to these two messages, it was also clear from attitude surveys that many Western Europeans accepted both as a fair representation of reality in the European context. Both of these messages were intended to help Soviet efforts to attain critical foreign policy and national security objectives.

In support of Soviet policy toward Western Europe, the military instrument was also used for intimidation purposes. Although intimidation might act to contradict the second message of Soviet peaceful intent, it could help to validate the first message of Soviet military power. Much intimidation appears to have been aimed at the extreme flanks of the NATO alliance, particularly at the north. Submarine violations of territorial waters, aircraft overflights, and military deployments near the borders, particularly of Norway and Denmark, were a steady part of Soviet military activity in the north aimed at continually reminding Norway and Denmark of how vulnerable they were and implying that nonaligned alternatives would buy their safety.

Another form of intimidation was the military exercise. On numerous occasions Soviet and Warsaw Pact military exercises, though primarily for training purposes, served to remind NATO allies of the power of Soviet military forces in Europe or to make specific points about NATO conduct of which the Soviets disapproved. Finally, the USSR used the nuclear card. The most obvious case was the standing offer that any NATO country that refused to play host to U.S. nuclear weapons (aside from Britain and France with their own nuclear capabilities) could rest assured that the Soviet armed forces would never employ nuclear weapons against them (Van Oudenaren 1986a: 44–50).

The Soviet Military Buildup in Europe

The principal motivation for the sustained and systematic Soviet force buildup in the central region was consistently to maintain or enhance military deterrence, not to make war or to convey political messages. In order to present what they felt was a measure of superiority safe enough to ensure deterrence as well as to fight a successful battle for Europe should deterrence fail, the Soviets concentrated on building a convincing war-fighting capability. Simple deterrence of a defensive victory-denying nature can be termed "minimalist," and deterrence based on a convincing war-fighting offense can be characterized as a "maximalist" solution (Van Oudenaren 1987: 40–41). NATO has from its very beginnings inevitably opted for a minimalist posture in Europe, whereas the Soviets under Brezhnev and his immediate successors seemed to prefer a maximalist position.

The reason for the Soviet choice was a matter of continued debate in the West. Many NATO armed forces commanders assumed that the USSR's maximalist effort was just what it looked like on the surface, a continuous Soviet buildup in preparation for an overwhelming "bolt from the blue" surprise attack on Western Europe. Other analysts cited past Russian and Soviet military misfortune as underlying a basic commitment to have adequate forces to guarantee that they would fight the next war on foreign soil. Yet another explanation rested on more basic assumptions about Soviet thought. Benjamin S. Lambeth has argued that Brezhnev's national security doctrine combined a Hobbesian world outlook with Clausewitzian military theory. Thus the world was viewed as an inevitably hostile place where the likelihood of war, though diminished to some extent by the presence of nuclear weapons on both sides, nonetheless could not be ignored as a real possibility. Against this possibility the Soviet leadership felt obligated to maintain a military capability to seize the initiative in the event of war, and to ensure that the outcome would be more favorable to the USSR than to its enemies. One of the principal problems posed by this ultra-Hobbesian view of the external international environment was that it provided for no natural end point to their force accumulation, especially with regard to weaponry (Lambeth 1983).

The Soviets seemed to have been committed to seeking absolute maximalist national security no matter what the cost to East-West relations. This persistent approach to the problem continued to undercut the Soviet Union's other efforts to reach a range of policy objectives in Europe through nonmilitary means (Van Oudenaren 1986a).

By the early l980s the Soviets, along with their Warsaw Pact allies, had built up a comprehensive maximalist military capability in the central theater and to a lesser extent on NATO's flanks. They had modernized both conventional and nuclear forces with technologically advanced weapons in significantly superior numbers. Valid or not, Soviet national security policy had never looked more threatening to the core NATO leadership, especially to the Americans

In order better to understand the impact of the Soviet military buildup in Europe under Brezhnev and his two immediate successors, it is important to consider the development of Soviet theater military policy. The first great postwar revolution in Soviet military thought and practice modernized the armed forces to fight in a nuclear environment. The second era, becoming visible to the West only in the late l970s, has been characterized by recognition of the disutility of nuclear weapons for theater warfare and the development of conventionally armed highly accurate missiles and unique employment doctrines to fight and win a war without nuclear weapons. The Soviet national security leadership is currently developing a whole new generation of conventional weapons based on emerging technologies further to enhance their ability to wage successful conventional theater war. The next section will consider these stages in more detail, starting from the immediate postwar years and leading up to the present. The theoretical aspects of these developments have been covered in the previous chapter.

The Era of Nuclear War Planning for Europe

Both the United States and the Soviet Union ended World War II with millions of soldiers in their respective armed forces. The Americans demobilized at an exceptionally rapid rate; the Soviets more slowly. Complicating the picture, Soviet demobilization seems to have bottomed out by 1948, leaving several million men in uniform. About 1951 the

Soviet armed forces embarked on a modernization program that resulted in the introduction of a new generation of weapons and equipment producing considerably enhanced conventional combat capabilities (Park 1986: 22–23).

In October 1953 the American government declared that it would be prepared to use tactical nuclear weapons in a future European war. This was to lead eventually to the stationing of more than 7000 nuclear devices in Western Europe (Park 1986: 30). NATO's early deployment of theater nuclear weapons there is usually explained as the Western reaction to its perception of massive Soviet conventional superiority and the complete impossibility of matching that capability. The actual motives appear to be considerably more complicated than that. In the first place tactical nuclear weapons were seen, especially by the U.S. Army, as having basic military utility; for many American army generals it made good sense to consider employing low-yield nuclear explosives in the event of a war in Europe. In addition, once these weapons went into production, a kind of procurement push took over producing much larger numbers than made military sense. Finally, the Eisenhower administration, which had taken office in January 1953, saw tactical nuclear weapons as a cheaper alternative to conventional forces in the defense of Europe. The British very quickly agreed; the other allies were brought along subsequently (Park 1986: 31).

The Soviets, while still in the early days of developing a force of intercontinental ballistic missiles, had succeeded in creating several effective intermediate-range missiles suitable for nuclear warheads. They could be fired from Soviet territory and hit targets in most of European NATO territory. They were not very accurate but could carry high-yield warheads capable of great destruction. The Soviets may have had a few tactical missiles available for use in Europe as early as 1954; the more widely accepted period is the late 1950s through the early 1960s. The latter is certainly more correct for their deployment of the intermediate-range SS-4 and SS-5 (Park 1986: 68).

However, despite acquisition of this inventory of nuclear weapons, the Soviet armed forces, especially the army, remained essentially a reequipped version of the Red Army that had won World War II. They trained to fight in deep battle zones and were heavy in tanks combined with conventional artillery and accompanying masses of infantry.

By the late 1950s Soviet leaders, especially Party First Secretary Nikita Khrushchev, raised questions about their ability to fight a modern nuclear war. Under his direction a substantial demobilization of the conventional army accompanied Soviet development of strategic rocket forces. A prolonged debate ensued which, in fact, outlasted Khrushchev. The culmination resulted in a return to prominence by the modernized Soviet ground forces.These ground forces were trained to think offensively and to attack with the advantage of numerical superiority and surprise. When hostilities were inevitable, they were to strike first and to do so in massive two- or three-echelon waves. The first wave was to continue attacking until it ceased to be an effective force; the second and subsequent echelons were to pick up and maintain the momentum of attack. They were taught three principal offensive actions. First, Soviet ground forces would train for the "meeting engagement" or attack from the line of march, seizing and maintaining the initiative. Second, they were to learn to take advantage of the breakthrough. Breaches in the enemy's defenses were to be exploited immediately and with overwhelming force. Finally, they were trained to destroy the enemy completely through pursuit (Binder and Clawson 1982).

From the beginning of Soviet nuclear weapons deployment a substantial degree of ambiguity characterized the Soviet military attitude toward the use of tactical (or short-, intermediate-, medium-range or theater) nuclear weapons in what was or could be a combat environment. Some Soviet authorities emphasized the potential of the attacking conventional forces (Sidorenko 1970). Others were convinced of the inevitability of nuclear war-fighting on the battlefield and argued for the development of winning strategies, operations, and tactics (Sokolovskii 1968). Perhaps the most striking characteristic of much Soviet military attention devoted to the use of tactical nuclear weapons during the period up to the early 1970s was the generally common assumption that they would, in fact, be used. Soviet authors argued that tank and motorized rifle units, although they would have to take special mechanical and tactical measures in the nuclear blast "environment," nevertheless would push through. A widely read book on armored warfare by Soviet Marshal A. Kh. Babadzhanian (1970) contained sketches illustrating dozens of Soviet tanks charging around and between tiny mushroom clouds.

Dennis M. Gormley (1985) has noted the eventual emergence of a set of Soviet assumptions about the most likely characteristics of a future European war. He argues that three basic scenarios developed over the years. The first covered massive use of USSR-based nuclear missiles and aircraft-delivered bombs against European targets followed by occupation by Soviet and other Warsaw Pact troops. The second possibility seen by Soviet commentators was that of escalating combat whereby a relatively short period of conventional war would be followed by widening use of nuclear weapons, either proceeding fairly directly to a strategic exchange against the two superpower homelands, or remaining at the theater level for some time before becoming global. The third scenario was that of a conventional war kept at that level. This became a realistic possibility only after the Americans and then NATO adopted "flexible response" as part of their assumptions about the nature of a possible war in Europe.

At some point, argue Western specialists, the Soviet national security leadership decided to adopt a program to develop a realistic conventional war-winning option based on new tactics, operations, and strategies and employing high technology to deliver conventional weapons with pinpoint accuracy and enhanced destructiveness. Mary FitzGerald and James McConnell believe that new Soviet programs emerged most tangibly following Brezhnev's speech at the ancient arms manufacturing city of Tula in January 1977 (FitzGerald 1986, 1987; McConnell 1985). Others have argued for a much earlier turning point in the late 1960s (MccGwire 1987: 32–35). At any rate, by the late 1970s the Soviets were concentrating on designing the ways and means to fight winnable conventional war in Europe.

An Emerging Option in Europe: Conventional Victory over NATO

Following decisions by the Soviet national security leadership to develop a capability to fight successful conventional war, the European theater received the highest-priority attention. It was there that the superpowers and their allies faced each other with hundreds of thousands of troops and enough nuclear weapons to destroy the continent many times over.

Since the beginning of this process, it has been possible to identify three general stages of development, the last of which is only now getting started. The first stage was the development of the necessary new tactics, operations, and strategies to implement the most basic or elementary version of modernized conventional war against NATO. To carry out these tactics, operations, and strategies it was also necessary to create new formations; deploy a new generation of modernized aircraft, tanks, artillery, and other basic weapons; upgrade the system of command, control, communications, and intelligence; and reorganize the command structure to fit a much larger scale of warfare than had earlier been anticipated.

The second stage in the development of plans for a modernized conventional war option was characterized by raising the level of theater combat technology in a fundamental way. This was accomplished through the development and deployment of the new, precisely accurate missiles capable of carrying highly effective conventional warheads to within a few dozen meters of the target.

The third stage is to develop and deploy advanced conventional weapons and sensors incorporating emerging technologies in the fields of microelectronics, directed energy, and genetic engineering. This would not only match NATO goal capabilities but, when combined with already deployed missiles of extremely high accuracy, provide the Soviet armed forces with a considerable advantage.

Stage One: Development of New Tactics, Operations, and Strategies

Western specialists in Soviet military history agree that high-mobility "blitzkrieg" deep operations were developed by Soviet theorists in the very early days of Soviet power (Turner 1986). However, until the latter part of World War II the USSR had neither the means nor the opportunity to implement that kind of warfare. And deep-penetration attack was certainly the exception rather than the rule in the Soviet defeat of Nazi Germany. The definitive Soviet World War II deep-strike offensive at the operational level was the last-minute attack on Japanese-held Manchuria.

Following World War II the Soviets elaborated on ground forces doctrine based upon their more common experience with multiple-echelon assault designed to overwhelm prepared enemy defenses through unceasing pounding by massed artillery followed by continuous waves of armor and motorized infantry (Erickson, Hansen, and Schneider 1986: 20–49). But the Soviets eventually decided that a seemingly overwhelming multiple-echelon approach alone would most likely provoke a NATO nuclear strike at least at the theater level and despite continued Soviet theoretical and practical dedication to maintaining the option of fighting a ground war in a nuclear environment, an alternative to the old pattern of attack would have to be found (Vigor 1983). The Soviet preference would be for a war against NATO that would be won quickly in which NATO would be deprived of its nuclear options through the modern adaptation of their deep-strike successes of World War II (Dick 1983).

The first key to waging quick, nonnuclear war against NATO was surprise. Were war to be deemed unavoidable by the USSR, an attack against the NATO central area would best be started at a time when NATO forces were not mobilized and in their forward defense positions; this would not likely be a particularly difficult problem given the NATO allies' deep reluctance to risk the provocation of mobilization or of deployment of forces from their geographically dispersed home bases. The Soviet attack would be launched, as much as possible, from a standing start (Dick 1986).

Hostilities would open with a critically heavy set of blows designed to crush the NATO military infrastructure including command, control, and communications capabilities, nuclear and chemical delivery systems, any deploying and follow-on forces, as well as supply systems. These would be attacked initially by air strikes, special forces, and sabotage groups (Hansen 1986a, 1986b).

In order to be effective, the Soviet and Warsaw Pact forces would have to attack to the operational depths of major NATO positions. This could be truly successful only if it were carried out by ground forces supported by close air support and deep air strikes. The key to keeping the battle for Europe non-nuclear would be not only to destroy on the ground as many theater nuclear weapons as possible but also to mix and mingle attacking forces so thoroughly with NATO defenders that use of tactical nuclear weapons would be made impossible (Donnelly 1984).

To exercise this conventional option Soviet and Warsaw Pact forces would have to rely on superior tactics, operations, and strategies rather than on ultra-high-technology weapons and systems that they did not as yet have. Superior tactics include greatly increased attention devoted to the problem of battlefield logistics (Baxter 1986: 28–31).

Enhanced operations would include the use of the Operational Maneuvre Group as an alternative or an addition to a second echelon. Based on similar formations used in the latter part of World War II (Mobile Groups), these high-mobility units are designed to insert major combat forces deep into the operational depths of NATO defenses preventing the formation of a front line and depriving NATO of its resort to tactical nuclear weapons. These Groups would have as their major targets the same set of critical NATO capabilities first attacked from the air and by special forces and sabotage groups, as well as the general destruction of NATO cohesion. They would be of various sizes, depending upon the tasks, but the most usual group would be at least of division size. Their job would not be to break through significant opposition but to exploit weaknesses or take advantage of areas already softened up. Air superiority over the axes of attack of the Operational Maneuver Groups would be essential given the groups' vulnerability. In addition, mobile heavy artillery would constitute critical support (Donnelly 1984). Although the Soviets have been experimenting with these groups in major field exercises since Zapad 81, the problems of coordination are such that this cannot even yet be considered an entirely reliable operation from the Soviet viewpoint ("New Generation" 1986).

Improved operations also include raising the level of control to the Theatre of Military Operations (TVD), a command headquarters designed for use in wartime to coordinate, in the European context, the groups of Soviet forces and the military districts that would be turned into *fronts* upon or just before the outbreak of hostilities. The TVD is characterized by an emphasis on the combined-arms ground forces concept of battle, as well as air attack, and air defense operations commanded by the TVD group forces commander while coastal naval operations are also controlled by the TVD. Allied armed forces would be "corseted" into the battle by the TVD commander (Hines and Peterson 1986).

The modern shape of the conventional option is a significant departure from the pre-1980s Soviet way of doing battle and presents a number of difficult problems for Soviet forces. First, this kind of warfare makes extremely heavy demands on command, control, and communications in a manner unique for Soviet experience. Second, the intended speed of operations puts a difficult strain on logistical support. In addition, the centralization of command and control to the higher TVD level, while at the same time demanding increased independent initiative from Operational Maneuvre Groups and other deep-penetration commanders, could appear on the surface to contain inherent contradictions (Donnelly 1984). But if surprise and speed are not attained, the Soviets are prepared to fight a prolonged conventional war in Europe and collateral areas.

Stage Two: Deployment of New Missiles

For many years Soviet ground forces had short-range missiles available for their support. These missiles (named Frogs, Scuds, and Scaleboards by NATO) were upgraded in range and payload over the years between 1965 and 1977 but still remained inaccurate enough to require the use of nuclear warheads to ensure target destruction. Improved airpower and new self-propelled artillery were no substitute for highly accurate short-range ballistic missiles in support of the conventional war option (Gormley 1985).

By the late 1970s the Soviets were prepared to begin deployment of fully developed, superaccurate replacements for their upgraded but obsolete short-range missiles. The SS-21 with a 120-kilometer range replaced the old 70-kilometer range Frog-7. The SS-23 with a range of 500 kilometers was replacing the 200-kilometer-range Scud. The SS-22 with its long 900-kilometer range was to replace the Scaleboard of the same range. All of these missiles were deployed in Eastern Europe with Soviet ground forces. It also appeared that the Soviets had increased the number of launchers deployed with each Soviet army group and military district (Gormley 1985).

The Soviet armed forces had the means at hand to launch the kinds of strikes necessary to provide the environment for a winnable conventional attack. Before any ground forces make contact with NATO forces, the Soviets would have launched pinpoint missile attacks on the NATO command, control, and intelligence infrastructure, nuclear and chemical delivery systems, deploying and follow-on forces, logistics systems, and antiaircraft SAM belts. Of course a certain number of the new battlefield missiles would have to be reserved for nuclear warheads in case NATO immediately responded with a nuclear strike using whatever missiles were left or available from other sources. However, these Soviet missiles were deemed by Gormley (1985) to have been responsible for "turning the possibility of a conventional-only contingency into a probability." This conclusion is supported by Mary C. FitzGerald's chapter.

In short, the Soviets had taken two very long strides toward achieving the ability to impose a conventional war on NATO. The final step, the acquisition of weapons and systems incorporating emerging technologies, constitutes stage three.

Stage Three: Emerging Technologies

For some time now authoritative Soviet military writers have been arguing for the swift incorporation of emerging, advanced, nonnuclear technologies into the Soviet Union's military capabilities. In response partly to their own military research and development and partly to the NATO alliance's development of a follow-on forces attack doctrine based on the use of precision-guided munitions and other emerging technologies, the Soviets have recognized the need to add another set of capabilities to their strategy for nonnuclear war in Europe. It would require not only innovative nonnuclear war-winning formations and operations as well as superaccurate missiles but also the timely development and deployment of Soviet precision-guided munitions and submunitions and other systems based on the possibilities inherent in microcircuitry, directed energy, and genetic engineering (Bodansky 1985; FitzGerald 1986; Odom 1985; Weiss 1985).

As FitzGerald has documented in this book, the most prominent advocate of high-tech nonnuclear solutions to Soviet war-fighting problems has been Marshal Nikolai Vasilevich Ogarkov, chief of the General Staff between 1977 and 1984. If that high-tech, nonnuclear, war-fighting doctrine constitutes a "third revolution" in Soviet military affairs, as General William Odom argues, then Marshal Ogarkov has been its most prominent and persistent leader. Marshal Ogarkov was also probably the principal force behind the transformation of the Soviet system of command to concentrate at the TVD level, reflecting his argument that the new technologies had widened the zones of possible combat action. His apparent appointment to the command of the Western (European)

TVD may be the natural result of his arguments, as Jan S. Adams argues in her chapter of this book.

In sum, major changes have been and continue to be made in the military dimension of Soviet national security toward Western Europe. They have continued, with some important caveats, under the leadership of Mikhail Gorbachev. They consist of the development and perfection of tactics, operations, and strategies as well as the advanced technologies to fight and win a conventional war in Europe should one become inevitable. By preventing the NATO allies from employing their nuclear weapons and by occupying the critical portions of Western Europe rapidly and effectively, the Soviets evidently had hoped at that point to decouple the United States from Europe. Forcing a U.S. "Dunkirk" withdrawal from Europe without resort to its strategic nuclear arsenal would be the optimum goal of this Soviet strategy.

That there are many difficulties standing between this strategy and its successful employment goes without saying; some have already been noted. Here it is important only to note that even for the Western allies, the emerging technologies are taking an inordinate amount of time to emerge. Even the most elementary of these systems, advanced precision-guided munitions and submunitions, are not likely to appear in the combat inventories of the NATO forces in Europe within the near-term future. This is largely because of what is turning out to be a remarkably long R&D cycle for these systems. If only because Soviet deployment of similar weapons and systems depends at least partly on the impetus generated from the challenge of these technologies being deployed by Western forces and partly on technology leakage or theft, this slowdown in the development of these weapons by the United States will have a retarding effect on Soviet acquisitions of similar systems.

The Gorbachev Security Changes: Growth of the Political Dimension

Mikhail S. Gorbachev is the first Soviet leader since Lenin not to have taken an active part in a war. He never performed national service in the Soviet armed forces. He clearly views the conduct of international affairs as requiring more than the use of the military instrument. Of course he has not stopped the elaboration of the new military tactics, operations, or strategies, nor has he stopped the development or deployment of weapons incorporating emerging technologies. But he has undertaken policies that are bound to affect Soviet national security policy in profound and startling ways. This is especially true in the Western European context.

The general overhaul of Soviet security policy under Gorbachev is dealt with in detail by other authors in this volume. Philip D. Stewart and Margaret G. Hermann have presented an analysis of Gorbachev's "new thinking" in terms of his attempt to shift the weight of Soviet national security policy from reliance on military means toward political measures. This includes an effort to reduce the perceived "Soviet threat" through significant and meaningful arms reduction as well as the strengthening of political and other nonmilitary instruments of national security policy including diplomacy, propaganda, and disinformation as well as espionage (Davis 1987). As Stewart and Hermann point out, he also emphasizes "mutual security" as an essential foundation upon which to build Soviet national security. "Reasonable sufficiency" is a principal slogan with reference to conventional forces, especially in the European context; one implication of this would be the adoption of a less maximalist and more defensive military posture in the central theater, a matter FitzGerald discusses in Chapter Nine.

Glasnost' and Perestroika in Soviet Military Affairs

A crucial element in Gorbachev's new thinking about the role of the armed forces in Soviet national security policy has been the application of the policies of *glasnost'* and *perestroika* to the military. He started even before the Twenty-Seventh Party Congress in February-March 1986 by attempting to convince senior officers that the military could no longer expect to get everything it wanted. And he sought to force them to recognize that they were going to have to accept the fact that they were an integral part of the Soviet economy, not an autonomous group within it (Meynell 1987: 3–7).

Following the congress there was a steady flow of articles in the military and civilian press about the need for glasnost' and perestroika in military affairs. But those exhortations to raise discipline and operational standards had a rhetorical and somewhat perfunctory character. The Soviet armed forces had long cultivated the assumption that they constituted the most efficient component of the Soviet system (Meynell 1987: 3).

However, in the months immediately after the Party Central Committee Plenum in January 1987, a stream of authentic glasnost' began to appear in the Soviet military press, especially in the official newspaper of the Ministry of Defense, *Krasnaia zvezda*. Exposés of bureaucratic bungling, nepotism, cover-ups, cruelty to recruits, and undiluted corruption began to appear on a regular basis. Colonels and even generals were reported to have been deprived of their Party memberships and relieved of their commands for unfair, arbitrary, or corrupt behavior. The untouchable status of the Soviet armed forces was beginning to crumble (IRCCS 1987a).

When young Mr. Rust flew his Cessna 172 into the center of Moscow in late May 1987, Gorbachev took that remarkable opportunity to fire not only the minister of defense, Marshal Sergei Sokolov, but also the commander-in-chief of Soviet air defense forces, Marshal Aleksandr Koldunov, as noted in the chapters by Bishop and Adams. This was followed by the dismissal of much of the top leadership of the air defense forces as well as a host of other senior commanders. The Moscow Air Defense District and the Moscow Military District were subsequently the subject of special exposés of their incompetence, lack of preparation, and falsification of reports to cover up the whole dismal situation. The staffs of a number of districts were subject to close investigation; many were deprived of their Party memberships and expelled from the armed forces ("Gorbachev Tightens" 1987). The inescapable conclusion was that all that money spent on the armed forces had bought less security than anyone had realized.

Following May 1987 the Soviet military and civilian mass-circulation press featured wide-ranging stories on fundamental questions about the utility of the military instrument in Soviet national security policy. Even before Mr. Rust's landing, the May 10, 1987 edition of *Literaturnaia gazeta* featured a story questioning the wisdom of universal conscription. *Pravda* and *Izvestiia* both printed articles critical of Soviet military academy training and both called for a comprehensive review of current Soviet military doctrine (IRCCS 1987b).

Although the tone of articles critical of the military was subsequently moderated, Gorbachev's principal goals of forcing the military into an integral rather than autonomous role within the national economy, accepting the reimposition of complete Communist party control over the armed forces, thoroughly revising political-military training, as well as promoting a "restructured" military doctrine, appear to be well in hand. An effective neutralization of military opposition would appear to have been a prerequisite to the implementation of these authentic programs of perestroika in the military (IRCCS 1987b; Meynell 1987).

Arms Reduction

Gorbachev's various arms control initiatives constitute a substantial change in Soviet national security policy. He has worked indefatigably to denuclearize Europe, but in concert with proposals to reduce the conventional military confrontation as well (Gorbachev 1987b: 142). Similar proposals concerning the elimination of chemical weapons form an important supplement to the more central issues. His further initiatives in the more complex areas of strategic weapons reductions and strategic defense will undoubtedly form the subject of long negotiations in the 1990s.

The crucial point about the nature of Gorbachev's arms control policies is that they do seem to constitute an important change in the Soviet approach to the questions. His emphasis on the idea of mutual security, that the Western allies do not have to lose in order for the Soviets to win, is a timely development. And it is also important to underscore the fact that the Gorbachev leadership, in changing its arms control policy so dramatically, has indeed had to make concessions to the West.

Motivations for the Gorbachev Security Changes toward Western Europe

First, it should be reemphasized that many of the changes in the general nature of Soviet national security doctrine were already well advanced before Mikhail Gorbachev was appointed to the post of Party general secretary in March 1985. The change to an emphasis on conventional war, the changes resulting from the anticipation of the addition of high-tech weapons based on emerging technologies as well as important innovations in operations and organization of the armed forces, all predate Gorbachev. The important changes made by the new leader—including the shift to threat reduction, the emphasis on mutual security, the acceptance of reasonable sufficiency, the implementation of glasnost' and perestroika in Soviet military affairs, and the serious negotiation of major arms control agreements—have reinforced and at the same time undercut the direction of change established before his ascendancy to the top leadership position. Those innovations primarily devised by Gorbachev potentially undercut the older changes in doctrine because his drift is to move away from such heavy reliance on the military instrument in national security policy.

Gorbachev's other motives for undertaking these dramatic changes are, of course, manifold. It seems clear that he and many of his colleagues agree with the military leadership that nuclear and other weapons of mass destruction have very little real utility and can be reduced through mutual agreement without posing a danger to the homeland. Where he may differ significantly from some of his principal military leaders is in his apparent assumption that masses of conventional troops permanently positioned on various borders and armed with enormous quantities of weapons, ammunition, emerging technology, and supporting resources may not yield the most effective and rational return on the huge investment required to maintain them. At any rate, one of his motives is clearly to reduce the nonproductive drain on the Soviet economy which has characterized the Soviet armed forces' privileged position in the process of resource allocation.

It is also evident that by changing the relative mix of the basic ingredients of Soviet national security policy, he can continue to reassert more comprehensive Party control over the Soviet military. Most Western analysts were unaware just how far Party control had slipped until glasnost' was turned full blast on the military. At the same time that control is regained, Gorbachev is freer to make even more basic changes in the weight given to the military viewpoint in the formulation of Soviet national security policy, as argued in Jan S. Adams's chapter.

Gorbachev's motivations for changes in Soviet national security policy, specifically toward Western Europe, reflect a number of the foreign policy goals characteristic of the Brezhnev period. At the same time, Gorbachev's changes represent new priorities and opportunities. His goals include the following:

1. *Loosening and even possibly dissolving American political and military ties with the European allies, thus weakening or even eliminating the NATO challenge.* His proposals and policy initiatives have been couched in terms of a general settlement in Europe based on mutual security and including the dissolution of both NATO and the Warsaw Pact. He has tried to make this more realistic and attractive to the European and American allies by proposing meaningful conventional arms reductions in the central theater. This is more than Brezhnev could have ever hoped for because he was never willing to make the concessions necessary for this to be even a faintly possible outcome.

2. *Reviving and expanding détente (while relegating the term to history) not only with Western Europe but with the United States as well.* It is clear that this time, unlike détente in the 1970s, the Soviets under Gorbachev's leadership are willing to undertake meaningful political and military détente first, thus providing a firmer basis for economic détente. The domestic economic reforms as well as major changes in the Soviet system of foreign trade and the evolution of joint venture policy provide an innovative base for more permanent access to the world economy and Western technology.

3. *Negotiating nuclear arms control agreements that enhance mutual security by removing all nuclear weapons from Europe: the denuclearization of the continent.* Gorbachev has pledged to make this more attractive than it was under Brezhnev by offering to conclude

conventional arms reductions designed to ensure only "reasonable sufficiency" on both sides.

It is manifest that Gorbachev and his foreign policy leadership have much less interest in pursuing a number of Brezhnev's other goals. For example, they seem to have abandoned the effort to secure a place of influence in key areas of Western European policy other than through conventional diplomatic activity. They no longer seem to think that they can some day achieve veto power over European armament and defense policy by dangling the carrot of increased trade and wielding the stick of armed forces buildup. This has reflected a somewhat startling Soviet realization that there are limits to power beyond which it is useless to aspire.

In this same spirit the Soviets appear to be very much less interested in encouraging "progressive" political forces in Western Europe in order to transform political policies. This too reflects a realistic assessment of Soviet capabilities, including Gorbachev's evident confidence that he can deal effectively with the leaders of Western Europe, be they British or Bavarian conservatives or French socialists.

Through all of this the Soviets hope that they can insulate their position in Eastern Europe from Western European or American disruption or interference. On this score they seem relatively optimistic.

Consequences and Implications of the Gorbachev Security Changes

One immediate result of the conclusion of large-scale nuclear arms reductions in Europe, and even of conventional force reduction in the central theater, could be the accelerated development of smart conventional weapons based on emerging technologies. These would probably have to be devised and deployed through the loopholes of the various agreements, but it would be folly to assume that the defense establishments of both sides would not try. Gorbachev might find the effort more expensive than he likes, but he might have to trade that off in order to get his military leadership to support his other programs. And as long as the Western nations continue to develop these technologies, the Soviets will feel forced to do so themselves. A logical next step might be to negotiate restrictions on this field of weapons development. The conclusion of this kind of agreement would surely rest on the success of the verification procedures built into the nuclear and conventional force treaties.

Another immediate response has to do with allied perceptions. The bulk of the military and some of the political leadership of the NATO alliance do not view the Gorbachev initiatives as a comprehensive program designed to result in a settlement based on mutual security in Europe. Worst-case analysis requires that they regard each Soviet initiative separately; but it is inevitable that each will be viewed as part of a yet-to-be-revealed scheme to strip NATO of effective deterrent power. This has been one response to the INF Treaty. American and European force commanders have hustled to fill what they see as a hole left by the U.S. agreement to eliminate the cruise and Pershing missiles from Europe. Their anguished responses have ranged from proposals to base B-52 SAC bombers on European airfields, to the possible deployment of new battlefield nuclear missiles in Turkey. This kind of response will characterize much of the NATO leadership in the short run. It would be unreasonable to assume that a similar mirror-image reaction does not have proponents among the Soviet establishment. This behavior is the inevitable legacy of the distrust built up between East and West over the last several decades; it will not be easily dissipated without a lot of confidence-building experience for both sides.

The precise long-term consequences for NATO are difficult to predict. Given past experience even with limited détente, however, it is reasonable to consider at least one middle-range scenario. A very likely and understandable response of many member states to the achievement of the principal Gorbachev arms control objectives would be to reduce participation through a shift in their investment priorities away from defense. The organization's many weaknesses, papered over when the Soviets and their allies posed a relatively unambiguous security challenge to Western Europe, would probably then become increasingly evident. The centrifugal forces would become more powerful and the long-term existence of the alliance would be in doubt. The Soviet Union could, if it were very careful, significantly augment its influence in Western European affairs while at the same time watch the American influence wane.

Conversely, with a great deal of luck and an unusual, even unprecedented, amount of good intentions on the part of all concerned, the Gorbachev national security changes could lead to a denuclearized Europe, a conventionally disengaged continent, and a European theater free of chemical and biological weapons of all kinds. This would not necessarily be a Europe without an American military presence, but it would most likely be. It would also mean a much different Soviet force configuration from anything the Soviets have in mind at present. Much depends on the success of the first several new arms agreements that result from the current impetus. At this point it is too early to take any odds on the chances of this scenario actually occurring; suffice to say that they are not very likely.

Finally, a development that is not too far-fetched would be the removal of Gorbachev from his position of general secretary by a coalition of the Soviet military-industrial complex and other dissatisfied elements in the top Soviet leadership. A repeat of Khrushchev's dismissal by his friends is not beyond the realm of the possible. No leader in the post-Stalin era has done quite so much to irritate the lately almost untouchable military establishment. Gorbachev's changes in Soviet national security policy are at some distance from the mainstream of traditional orthodox Soviet theory and practice. This, along with the other unpopular departures that he has sponsored, could be enough to see him removed by his associates for the good of the homeland.

References

Babadzhanian, A. Kh., ed. (1970). *Tank i tankovye voiska*, Moskva: Voenizdat.

Baxter, William (1986). *Soviet AirLand Battle Tactics*. Novato, CA: Presido Press.

Binder, John J., and Robert W. Clawson (1982). "Warsaw Pact Ground Forces, Formations, Combat Doctrine and Capabilities." In Robert W. Clawson and Lawrence S. Kaplan, eds., *The Warsaw Pact: Political Purpose and Military Means*. Wilmington, DE: Scholarly Resources.

Bodansky, Yossef (1985). "1985—A Turning Point in Soviet Defence." *Jane's Defence Weekly*, 3(6), 212–13.

Clawson, Robert W., ed. (1986). *East-West Rivalry in the Third World*. Wilmington, DE: Scholarly Resources.

Davis, Christopher (1987). "*Perestroika* in the Soviet Defense Sector, 1985–87." Presented at the Conference on Elites and Political Power in the USSR, Birmingham, England, July 1–3.

Dick, C. J. (1983). "Soviet Doctrine, Equipment Design and Organization: An Integrated Approach to War." *International Defense Review*, 16(12), 1715–22.

—— (1986). "Catching NATO Unawares: The Soviet Army Surprise and Deception Techniques." *International Defense Review*, 19(1), 21–26.

Donnelly, Christopher (1984). "Soviet Fighting Doctrine." *NATO's Sixteen Nations*, 29(3), 64–67.

Erickson, John, Lynn Hansen, and William Schneider (1986). *Soviet Ground Forces: An Operational Assessment*. Boulder, CO: Westview Press.

FitzGerald, Mary C. (1986). "Marshal Ogarkov on the Modern Theater Operation." *Naval War College Review*, 39(4), 6–25.

—— (1987). "Marshal Ogarkov and the New Revolution in Soviet Military Affairs." *Defense Analysis*, 3(1), 3–19.

Fouquet, David (1987a). "U.S. House Support of Troop Level, Polish Plan Highlight Conventional." *The NATO Report*, 21(31).

—— (1987b). "Western Experts Examine Soviet Military Planning." *The NATO Report*, 21(42).

Gareev, Makhmut (1987). "The Military Doctrine of the Warsaw Pact Countries: For Lasting Peace." *Soviet Military Review*, 12, 3–5.

Goldberg, Andrew (1986). "Soviet Nuclear War Strategy." *KIARS Meeting Report*, November 5.

Gorbachev, Mikhail (1987a). *Za "obshcheevropeiskii dom," za novoe myshlenie*. Moscow: Novosti.

—— (1987b). *Perestroika*. New York: Harper & Row.

"Gorbachev Tightens Grip on Soviet High Command" (1987). *Jane's Defence Weekly*, 7(23), 1192–94.

Gormley, Dennis M. (1985). "A New Dimension to Soviet Theater Strategy." *Orbis*, 29(3), 537–69.

Hansen, James (1986a). "Soviet Vanguard Forces—Spetsnaz." *National Defense*, 70(416), 26–27.

—— (1986b). "Soviet Vanguard Forces—Airborne." *National Defense*, 70(417), 25–44.

Hines, John G., and Philip A. Peterson (1986). "Changing the Soviet System of Control —Focus on Theater Warfare." *International Defense Review*, 19(3), 281–89.

IRCCS (Jerusalem) (1987a). "Military Developments." *USSR Overview*, 3(3).

—— (1987b). "Military Developments." *USSR Overview*, 3(6).

Lambeth, Benjamin S. (1983). "Trends in Soviet Military Policy." In Herbert J. Ellison, ed., *Soviet Policy toward Western Europe*. Seattle: University of Washington Press.

Lebedev, Yuri, and Aleksey Podberyozkin (1987). "A Historic Change for Europe." *International Affairs*, 6, 3–11.

MccGwire, Michael (1987). *Military Objectives in Soviet Foreign Policy*. Washington, DC: The Brookings Institution.

McConnell, James M. (1985). "Shifts in Soviet Views on the Proper Focus of Military Development." *World Politics*, 37(3), 317–43.

Meynell, Charles, ed. (1987). "The Military Factor." *East European Newsletter*, 1(1).

"New Generation Weapons and the Doctrine of Tactics" (1986). *Jane's Defence Weekly*, 5(23), 1102–4.

Odom, William E. (1985). "Soviet Force Posture: Dilemmas and Directions." *Problems of Communism*, 34(4), 1–14.

Park, William (1986). *Defending the West: A History of NATO*. Boulder, CO: Westview Press.

Platt, Allen (1986). "Soviet-West European Relations." RAND Report no. R-3316-AF. Santa Monica, CA: RAND Corporation.

Shenaev, V. N., D. Y. Melnikov, and L. Maier (1981). *Zapadnaia Evropa v sovremennom mire: Ekonomika, politika, klassovaia bor'ba, mezhdunarodnye otnosheniia*. Moscow: Izdatel'stvo Mysl'.

Sidorenko, A. A. (1970). *Nastuplenie*. Moscow: Voenizdat.

Sokolovskii, V. D. (1968). *Voennaia strategiia*. Moscow: Voenizdat.

Turner, Frederick C. (1986). "Forward." In John Erickson, Lynn Hansen, and William Schneider, *Soviet Ground Forces: An Operational Assessment*. Boulder, CO: Westview Press.

Van Oudenaren, John (1986a). "Soviet Policy toward Western Europe: Objectives, Instruments, Results." RAND Report no. E3310-AF. Santa Monica, CA: RAND Corporation.

—— (1986b). "Deterrence, War-Fighting and Soviet Military Doctrine." *Adephi Papers*, 210.

—— (1987). "Gorbachev and Western Europe." *KIARS Meeting Report*, January 21.

Vigor, Peter H. (1983). *Soviet Blitzkrieg Theory*. New York: St. Martin's.

Weiss, Peter (1985). "Room at the Top for Ogarkov Again." *International Defense Review*, 18(10), 1559–60.

• CHAPTER ELEVEN •

Changes in Soviet Security Policy toward Eastern Europe and the Warsaw Pact

Robin Alison Remington
University of Missouri

In thinking about changes in Soviet security policy toward Eastern Europe one immediately becomes entangled in the conceptual debate that divides Western scholars and policymakers over the more fundamental nature of Soviet–Eastern European relations. There are imperial and hierarchical system models, theories of dependency and interdependence, disagreements over whether that relationship is or is not "organic," with different under-standings of what that means. Conflicting perceptions reflect differences of approach and emphasis. Those who consider the Soviet Union and Eastern Europe as a multinational colonial empire understandably see a different order of Soviet security policy than do scholars who approach the Warsaw Treaty Organization as an arena of Communist coalition politics in which the systemic homogeneity of member states is one of a package of variables influencing alliance dynamics.

This is a genuine problem because whereas we can say that Soviet–Western European security issues are a matter of Soviet foreign policy, with respect to Eastern Europe that is not so clear. If Korbonski is correct that "in substance Moscow treats Eastern Europe as an 'internal problem' and as an extension of the Soviet state" (1983: 293), then the line between foreign policy and domestic politics has been substantially blurred and what constitutes security is harder to come to grips with.

Clearly 1980s national security planners in Moscow do not plan to defend the Kremlin against an attack from Eastern European armed forces or anticipate a repeat of the Russian–Polish war of 1920. Indeed, whether or not one conceives the Soviet–Eastern European relationship as "organic," notwithstanding differences as to what that means, the Warsaw Treaty signed in 1955 is a collective defense arrangement. According to Articles 4 and 5:

Article 4

In the event of armed attack in Europe on one or more of the Parties to the Treaty by any state or group of states, each of the Parties to the Treaty, in the exercise of its right to individual or collective self-defense in accordance with Article 51 of the Charter of the United Nations Organization, shall immediately, either individually or in agreement with other Parties to the Treaty, come to the assistance of the state or states attacked with all such means as it deems necessary, including armed force. The Parties to the Treaty shall immediately consult concerning the necessary measures to be taken by them jointly in order to restore and maintain international peace and security.

Article 5

The Contracting Parties have agreed to establish a Joint Command of the armed forces that by agreement among the Parties shall be assigned to the Command, which shall function on the basis of jointly established principles. They shall likewise adopt other agreed measures necessary to strengthen their defensive power, in order to protect the peaceful labour of their peoples, guarantee the inviolability of their frontiers and territories, and provide defense against possible aggression. (Remington 1971: 201)

Article 4 is generally assumed to commit Moscow to respond militarily in the event of an attack on an Eastern European member of the Warsaw Pact. In that sense it is fair to say that Soviet national security includes the military security of Eastern Europe. Unlike NATO, it also requires a common denominator of political and ideological agreement with respect to "protecting the peaceful labour of their peoples" (assumed to be a euphemism for the socialist political systems) referred to in Article 5.

At the same time, Article 5 of the Warsaw Treaty introduces ambiguity concerning the extent of Moscow's obligation vis-à-vis Eastern European security as a component of Soviet national security. Establishing just what that common denominator of political and ideological agreement should be is a matter of political struggle among Soviet–Eastern European decision makers. Conflicting Western interpretations of the outcomes result in part from the contradictory analytical approaches of the scholars involved.

This analysis assumes that Soviet security concerns in Eastern Europe are a mixture of ideological, political, economic, and military worries flowing from the interaction of Soviet domestic imperatives with perceived obstacles and opportunities within two arenas: East–West and intra-Communist politics. It is to be expected that the nature of such concerns reflects changes in each of these political environments; that the weight given ideological, political, economic, and military aspects of security has and will vary. It assumes that Soviet security planners do not have a formula so much as a body of precedent and past experience. Therefore, to understand change in Soviet security policy toward Eastern Europe, a ten- to twelve-year time frame is too limiting. Conceptualizing change is a matter of understanding initial assumptions; the impact of transformations of the Kremlin's domestic, East–West, and intra-Communist political arenas; and restraints/options inherent in previous Soviet responses to perceived security threats in Eastern Europe.

The Starting Point: Military/Political/Ideological Considerations

Soviet security planners did not start with a blank page where Eastern Europe is concerned. Long before there was a Soviet Union, Russian tsars considered Eastern Europe a natural sphere of influence to be consolidated. That geopolitical objective was reinforced by the tsarist sense of messianic mission; rationalized by theology and pan-Slavism. In 1917 the Russian Revolution substituted ideological millenarianism and the obligation to "save" fraternal socialist countries, yet the underlying military goal remained much the same.

Eastern Europe was historically a highway for attacking armies marching toward Moscow. As World War II drew to a close, Churchill and Roosevelt viewed Stalin's insistence on "friendly" governments in Eastern Europe as an expression of legitimate Soviet security concerns. The concessions at Yalta reflected Western as well as Soviet political priorities and military realities (Clemens 1970).

From the beginning the Red Army played a powerful political role in Eastern Europe. For the most part Eastern European Communists returned home in the wake of Soviet liberation. Soviet military presence assured their ability to join postwar coalition governments. As Truman reluctantly acknowledged, Stalin called the shots in Eastern Europe because the Soviet military had defeated the German army. Churchill was unrealistic to think he could push the Soviets out of the Balkans politically when they won the real estate militarily. Nonetheless, as long as there was hope of Western reconstruction aid, Eastern Europe as a springboard for socialist revolution took a back seat.

According to the theory of "people's democracy," the Red Army is given credit for facilitating the "fundamental revolutionary transformation" of Eastern Europe[1] not onto the road to socialism, but in the form of "national democratic revolution." In short, as World War II wound down the Soviets perceived the role of force in Eastern Europe to be that of defeating the Germans, giving indigenous Communists access to the political game, and neutralizing their opponents. In the shadow of the Red Army, Eastern European revolutions could avoid the trauma of civil war that had wracked the young Soviet state from 1918 to 1921. Ideologically, Eastern European Communists could afford the luxury of Marx's two-stage revolution rather than follow Lenin's accelerated great leap into the dictatorship of the proletariat. Economically, Eastern Europe remained part of the world capitalist economy while its political system was being "creatively reshaped," a transitional situation.

As Brzezinski points out, there was no intrinsic reason why that transition was so brief (1971: 50). Subsequent Soviet redefinition of the people's democracies as dictatorships of the proletariat came about because of the collapse of Europe into "two camps"; Stalin's dissatisfaction with the unseemly way in which Eastern European Communists took him at his word about "national roads to socialism" and the imperatives of the Soviet–Yugoslav break in 1948. Stalin's confrontation with Tito established Soviet willingness to use limited military means when faced with Eastern European resistance to Moscow's control. The Yugoslav *White Book* (1951) documents that Soviet tactics included military maneuvers and the threat of force along with economic blockade, show trials of Titoists in other Eastern European countries, and efforts to convince Tito's party and army to throw him out.

Thus by 1948 we could say that Soviet security policy toward Eastern Europe had changed from facilitating national democratic revolutions "friendly" to USSR military needs, to assuring Eastern European political and economic systems built on the Soviet model. The countries were led by mini-Stalins who understood that their political survival and, indeed, their lives depended on Stalin's whim. Formal trappings of sovereignty aside, a feudal, personalistic control characterized the Stalinist interstate system in Eastern Europe. This system was based on the dominant-subordinate relationship flowing from Soviet hegemony in the intra-Communist political environment, where Stalin was the godfather and Moscow, the Mecca of the Communist world. Soviet cadres penetrated Eastern European parties, security services, and armies.

A Soviet empire was established in Eastern Europe. The Red Army became a crucial part of the infrastructure making that empire possible. Soviet security policy focused on crushing potential opposition, integrating Eastern European armies into the Soviet military establishment, and facilitating political consolidation of Communist parties dedicated to Soviet national interests. Although East–West aspects surfaced in the Soviet–Yugoslav split and even more in the Berlin crisis of 1948, on balance Stalin treated security in Eastern Europe as a domestic problem.

Domestic Transformation and Alliance Politics

As it turned out, the Stalinist interstate system required Stalin. But even with his death in 1953, Soviet troops were used in putting down an uprising in East Germany to repress domestic opposition—a task identical to that they would have performed under Stalin himself. Yet the domestic transformation that accompanied the power struggle among Stalin's would-be successors, Malenkov's New Course, and de-Stalinization changed not only internal Soviet politics but, unintentionally, Soviet-Eastern European dynamics as well. Within this context Khrushchev moved to substitute institutional infrastructure for the Stalin myth. That move led to the creation of the Warsaw Treaty Organization (WTO) to coordinate Soviet-Eastern European political and military security issues in Europe.

There is good reason to think that Khrushchev wanted this alliance primarily as a potential throwaway card in his game of summit diplomacy with Eisenhower and secondarily as an instrument of Soviet security policy vis-à-vis Western Europe (*Pravda* 1956). From the beginning the Warsaw Pact faced East as well as West. According to the Soviet military newspaper *Krasnaia zvezda* (1956), the Red Army saw the alliance as a vehicle of military integration to ensure that no power on earth could tear one country from the road to socialism. For Molotov the Warsaw Pact was an instrument of socialist consolidation, military preparedness, and defense. And from the military press accounts that ignored Khrushchev's contribution to European security, highlighted in *Pravda* coverage of the 1956 Prague meeting of the WTO Political Consultative Committee, it would seem that Molotov had influential supporters within the Soviet military. Although Molotov lost politically, both his and Khrushchev's views were reflected in WTO institutional development. Hence the Warsaw Pact became a component of Soviet strategic doctrine (East–West function) and acquired an unanticipated role during a string of Eastern European crises (intrabloc function).

Crisis Management and Security Policy

Notwithstanding Brezhnev's emphasis on the Warsaw Treaty Organization as the "main center" for coordinating the foreign policies of European Communist states, echoed in Gorbachev's calls for alliance "unity and cohesion," during the three decades since 1955 there have been open challenges to Soviet hegemony by every Eastern European member of the pact except Bulgaria (*Pravda* 1971, 1985a). If we consider these events roughly chronologically we have (1) the Polish October and Hungarian uprising of 1956; (2) Romanian maneuvering dating from 1957 with respect to Sino–Soviet differences (Fischer-Galati 1967); (3) open defiance from Albania at the November 1960 Moscow meeting culminating in Tirana's unilateral withdrawal from the Warsaw Pact in 1968; (4) Dubcek's effort during the Prague Spring to return to Czechoslovakia's tradition of democratic socialism; (5) Soviet–East German differences over the pace of détente 1969–71; (6) the fall of Gomulka in 1970; (7) Solidarity's challenge to the leading role of the Polish United Workers' Party, 1980–81; and (8) Honecker's attempt to protect East-West German relations from the fallout of NATO deployment of Pershing II and cruise missiles in Europe, 1983–84.

Soviet security behavior in these situations resulted in the following:

1. Polish October: threat of force, Soviet troops start moving toward Warsaw; reportedly stop when the Poles inform visiting Soviet Politburo members that if the Soviets advanced another ten kilometers, Polish forces would fight
2. Hungarian uprising: unilateral Soviet intervention
3. Romania: Soviet forces withdrawn in 1958, conflict containment within the Warsaw Pact and the Council for Mutual Economic Assistance (CMEA)
4. Czechoslovakia 1968: months of negotiations in a context of military maneuvers and implied use of force dating from Yepishev May 5, *Le Monde* interview, culminating in allied socialist intervention
5. Poland 1970: economic bailout
6. GDR 1969–71: does not appear to have involved use or threat of force
7. Poland 1980–81: threat of force indicated in both December 1980 Warsaw Pact meeting and maneuvers on Polish borders
8. GDR 1983–84: differences over strategic dialogue, open polemics, and conflict containment

These responses tell us that for thirty years an underlying common denominator of Soviet security policy toward Eastern Europe has been a resort to force or the threat of force when faced with unacceptable domestic change on the part of an Eastern European member of the "family of socialist nations."

This list also tells us that other variables such as the cohesion of the local Communist party, the prospect of popular resistance, the intrabloc and East–West context, and timing influenced the outcome in terms of the instruments with which Moscow attempted to achieve ideological and political security in Eastern Europe. It is fair to say that Soviet behavior when faced with Eastern European challenges has rather consistently reflected a rough cost/benefit/risk calculation not substantially different from security policy in Washington toward Central America when faced with unacceptable ideological and political challenge.

Military Doctrine and Cost-Benefit Analysis in Moscow

What may have changed, however, is Soviet assessment of the long-range cost of military solutions in Eastern Europe. In the early 1960s Soviet strategic doctrine shifted to the idea of "coalition warfare" that redefined and expanded the role of Eastern European armies in Soviet military planning (Mackintosh 1969). This was undoubtedly based on the assumption that despite the renationalization of Eastern European armed forces following 1956, their professionalism and Soviet training of Eastern European officers made these military establishments a reliable extension of the Red Army capable of assuming increased military responsibility within the Warsaw Pact. Western analyses increasingly focused on the reliability of non Soviet Warsaw Pact forces because, although figures varied when they were counted, they made up a substantial part of the troops that NATO security planners worried about in attack scenarios (Nelson 1984; Volgyes 1982). This view portrayed Eastern Europe as an instrument in Soviet security policy vis-à-vis NATO.

Yet coalition warfare proved a mixed blessing. On the one hand, the Czechoslovak desire for a more independent military doctrine, presumably one that would avoid destroying 60 percent of Czechoslovak armed forces within the first three days of a limited nuclear war, exacerbated Soviet-Czechoslovak tensions in the Prague Spring of 1968. On the other hand, the invasion and occupation of Czechoslovakia essentially wiped out the Czechoslovak officer corps despite the lack of organized military resistance. Reportedly as many as 58 percent of Czechoslovak officers under thirty years old left the army at their own request after

1968; literally thousands of others were purged for political unreliability (Johnson, Dean, and Alexiev 1982: 116, 134). Despite some progress at rebuilding the officer corps, reports of low educational level and lack of morale continue. The Hungarian military also has not fully recovered from the trauma of 1956. Romanian–Soviet differences, furthermore, have visibly reduced Romanian willingness to participate in the military aspects of the Warsaw Pact or to accept defense burden sharing as defined in Moscow (Alexiev 1979; Nelson 1986).

Nor did martial law in Poland come without cost to Warsaw Pact military capabilities. Undoubtedly the effort to spare the professional army the job of policing the Polish population was made somewhat successfully. But notwithstanding the official lifting of martial law in 1983, the extent to which Polish officers have been reassigned to political and economic roles while General Wojciech Jaruzelski struggles to rebuild the Polish United Workers' Party continues to make it more difficult for the Poles to focus on their military mission as the second largest army in the Warsaw Pact. Equally if not more worrisome from Moscow's point of view, Poland has a conscript army riddled with Solidarity supporters (Johnson and Kliszewski 1982). In these circumstances it is not surprising that Eastern European military modernization lags behind that of Moscow's more favored Third World clients. As Ross Johnson has pointed out, the writings of Ogarkov ignore coalition warfare. The evidence, however, is not yet sufficient to conclude that this is incremental abandonment of Soviet strategic doctrine vis-à-vis the Eastern European role in Soviet military planning for war in Europe. It is a potential trend that should be tracked.

More cautiously we can say that in the intrabloc arena, dating from Soviet response to Polish food riots that brought down the Gomulka government in 1970, there has been a preference for nonmilitary solutions ranging from bailing out Gierek with a reported $100 million in hard currency in lieu of sending in the Red Army (*Zycie Warszawy* 1971), to the sustained pressure on Polish Party and army leaders to confront Solidarity without the promised assistance of their Warsaw Pact allies.

Perestroika and the Warsaw Pact: The Gorbachev Chapter

In institutional terms there has been no "restructuring" of the Warsaw Pact or campaign for a *perestroika* of the alliance parallel to Mikhail Gorbachev's exhortation for "radical" reform of the Soviet economy and society. When it came to preserving the existing infrastructure of Soviet–Eastern European relations, Gorbachev opted for continuity. In April 1985, barely a month after the Soviet leader took over as general secretary, the members of the Warsaw Pact signed on for another twenty years. Gorbachev has praised the value of the alliance as a political actor in Europe, briefed his allies on his efforts at summit diplomacy, and emphasized their support for Soviet disarmament proposals (*Pravda* 1985b). In short, the East–West diplomatic mission of the pact continues as an active part of Soviet security policy. At the same time, Gorbachev has stressed the value of the alliance as a channel for the exchange of socialist experience and, like Brezhnev before him, has alluded to the need for new mechanisms of cooperation (TASS 1985). From this perspective, chapter 1 of the Gorbachev era must be chalked up to stability of security ideas and assumptions, policy, and behavior.

Yet if we shift from commitment to the Warsaw Pact itself to the political substance of Soviet relations with the Eastern European members of that alliance, the situation is much less stable. Karen Dawisha and Jonathan Valdez have documented the internal Soviet debate on the nature of "socialist internationalism" between those such as O. Vladimirov, who stoutly defends proletarian internationalism from those unnamed "anti-Communist theoreticians and opportunists"[2] who consider it out of date, and their opponents, who reject "domineering methods," hegemonic pretentions, and efforts to define "socialist internationalism as subordination of national sovereignty" (Dawisha and Valdez 1987: 2–3).

That there have been differences of opinion within the Soviet policy establishment over the rules of the game for intra-Communist relations is not new. If such differences had not existed, it is highly unlikely that the 1976 Berlin Conference of European Communist and Workers' Parties would have been held at all. What is new is that these differences have surfaced in a public debate involving official newspapers and academic journals. That is *glasnost'* creeping into Soviet decision making regarding the political and ideological components of security policy toward Eastern Europe. It might signal a change in the manner in which that policy is formed. I would call this an incremental change with potential to become a significant change. The change agent is Gorbachev's commitment to glasnost' as a prerequisite for perestroika.

Related to but separate from the polemics swirling around "socialist internationalism" are divisions among Soviet leaders themselves as to what extent perestroika is appropriate in Eastern Europe. There is no little irony in Yegor Ligachev's warning to Hungarians that "slavish imitation" of the Soviet reform efforts could cause "serious political, economic and moral damage."[3] Given Gorbachev's own Eastern European travel schedule and his increasingly open pressure on Eastern European political leaders to join the ranks of reformers, there is little doubt about policy differences within the Politburo concerning the wisdom of Eastern Europeans attempting to follow the zig-zag of Soviet reforms.

The related maneuvering within the Soviet leadership and among Eastern European political factions reminds one of Malenkov's New Course and Khrushchev's de-Stalinization campaign. Tactically this is not change. However, the consequence of success might well produce significant change in the degree of political conformity demanded from Moscow's Eastern European allies in the name of Soviet security. The potential for change, then, is tied not to tactical innovation so much as to the as yet unforeseen consequences of country-specific Eastern European reforms potentially legitimized by such innovation.

When one tries to identify change agents, there are no end of difficulties created by the fact that we are faced with tactical continuity—that is, a Soviet leader who tells his Eastern European comrades that what is good for Moscow is good for Prague, Warsaw, Sofia, Bucharest, and so on while at the same time sanctioning potentially non-Soviet solutions. For the logical consequence of glasnost' in Eastern Europe is that Moscow's form of perestroika may or may not be appropriate elsewhere.

But it is something of a cop-out to conclude that Gorbachev is simply an unwitting change agent. There is a genuine question as to why the Soviet leader took his show on the road; why Eastern Europe became a necessary component of his attempt to prepare the Soviet Union for the twenty-first century. David Mason (1987) has argued cogently in favor of an economic change agent, underlining the extent to which the restructured Soviet economy that Gorbachev has in mind requires Eastern European economies geared to increased productivity and substantially higher-quality production than those economies currently yield.

I would not dispute the significance of economics. Yet the political momentum of the reform debate within the Soviet Union between policymakers, their allies within academic communities, and unofficial refformers striving to participate in the process is also a factor (Theen 1986). The domestic and foreign policy lines blur as Soviet scholars tilt toward Hungarian, East German, or even Bulgarian reform varieties, while Eastern European reformers cite selectively from Soviet sources to defend their preferred strategies at home. This is intellectual ferment within the policy establishment and outside it. It is not "upheaval" in the Soviet Union or Eastern Europe. Not yet.

For the moment I would argue that Gorbachev expanded the struggle for perestroika to Eastern Europe as much to counter his domestic opposition as to create healthy Eastern European partners for a restructured Soviet economy. Ligachev's warning in Hungary echoed in Moscow. Thus, Gorbachev was pushed by political imperatives to commit

Eastern European regimes to the reform process, thereby increasing the unpredictability of perestroika and the potential cost in terms of the stability of his Eastern European allies. In absolute terms the stakes for Soviet national security are higher than before; yet the political and ideological components of security are harder to calculate.

It is a gamble that could backfire. Gorbachev, however, is aware of the lessons of 1956. It appears that he has accounted for the possibility of Eastern European social and political unrest that could follow in the wake of perestroika. There are two aspects of his approach to the dynamics of Eastern European reforms that fall into this category.

First, with respect to the substance of Gorbachev's efforts to become the godfather of Eastern European as well as Soviet perestroika, he has gone beyond Khrushchev's pledge of national roads to socialism to stress the possibility that the exchange of socialist experience is not a one-way street. Indeed, the Soviet Union might have something to learn from Eastern Europe in the search for new directions. For example, as early as June 1986 Gorbachev not only praised the accomplishments of the Hungarians in Budapest's efforts to solve complex economic and social problems but referred to the willingness of the CPSU "to make use of anything that is advantageous or appropriate for our own country" (*Pravda* 1986). This is new. It recognized the possibility that Moscow can follow as well as lead in the task of socialist construction. Second, such recognition was the logical sequence of Gorbachev's positions as spelled out at the Twenty-Seventh CPSU Congress. It is worth recalling his assessment of the international Communist movement:

> The communist movement's immense diversity and the tasks that it encounters are likewise a reality. In some cases this leads to disagreements and divergencies. . . . There generally cannot be an identity of views on all issues. . . . We do not see the diversity of our movement as a synonym for disunity, much as unity has nothing in common with uniformity, hierarchy, interference by some parties in the affairs of others or the striving of *any party* to have a *monopoly over what is right*.[4]

Though Gorbachev has not put the Soviet model on the "rubbish heap" of socialist experiments, he has come down squarely on the side of legitimate socialist pluralism within the intra-Communist arena. Thus increased Eastern European autonomy on the road to reform has been legitimized by Soviet acknowledgment of changing inter-Party relations. This is not the same as the Malenkov/Khrushchev insistence that the Soviet road to socialism had turned a corner with the New Course and all fraternal ruling parties should get in line. Rather, Gorbachev has insisted that in the sphere of ideology "the CPSU stands for pooling the efforts of the fraternal parties aimed at studying and using experience in building socialism" (*New Times* 1986: 42).

Dawisha and Valdez describe how after the Twenty-Seventh Congress some well-known conservative Soviet authors began to revise their opinions, citing the case of Yegor Bugaev's change of heart on the nature of Poland's ongoing economic and ideological crises. These authors conclude that Moscow has become more interested in performance than in insistence on the Soviet model; that under Gorbachev Eastern European reform is supported but not demanded. Although less confident about the line between support and demands, I would agree that increasingly an efficient end result is more important to the Soviets than how it is achieved.

There are, however, still more significant implications in Bugaev's uncharacteristic conclusion when, after summarizing conflicting Polish views on the Polish United Workers' Party's resolution for agricultural reform, he states "it is not for me to judge which side is right in this argument."[5] Whether tactical or sincere, this signals a change in the dominant/subordinate attitude that has permeated Soviet scholarship and policy vis-à-vis Eastern Europe. Here the change agent is undoubtedly Gorbachev's commitment to a new style of intra-Communist relations, reinforced by the author's need to get on Gorbachev's bandwagon as he appeared to be consolidating his position. If it is not for the Soviets to pass judgments on Eastern European public policy alternatives in such key arenas as agricultural reform, that is tantamount to a hands-off policy vis-à-vis internal reform dynamics. Such a policy implies willingness to accept declining Soviet control over Eastern European domestic politics. It is directly related to ten years of eroding Soviet hegemony within the intra-Communist arena that has spilled over into alliance politics.

Ever since the 1976 Pan-European Communist Conference substituted voluntary cooperation for proletarian internationalism as the fundamental guideline for relations among Communist parties and countries on the road to socialism (*New Times* 1976: 17–32), Soviet efforts to coordinate Warsaw Pact policy have had to contend with "creative interpretations" of how best to facilitate European détente. As long as Brezhnev considered himself the architect of East-West détente, such Eastern European initiatives were acceptable, even welcomed.

But when Moscow walked out of U.S.–Soviet arms negotiations over the issue of NATO deployment of Pershing II and cruise missiles in Europe, alliance policy coordination became visibly less successful. East German leader Erich Honecker emphasized the need to continue dialogue with the West and to limit the damage. The Hungarians stressed the importance of efforts by small and medium-sized European socialist states to get détente back on track. Undoubtedly Soviet security planners were somewhat taken aback when the April 1984 Warsaw Pact communiqué on these matters came substantially closer to the GDR–Hungarian statements than to Gromyko's hard-line positions (Asmus 1984; TASS 1984).

This is an often ignored aspect of what had emerged as an open debate on the role of national initiatives versus international obligations. Before the Budapest meeting Czechoslovakia had characteristically championed internationalism against national "deviations" of unnamed Warsaw Pact allies. Not surprisingly, the Hungarians defended the constructive, peace-loving efforts of small and medium-sized states devoted to European security. The Soviet media predictably reprinted the attack from Prague.

That exchange stopped being business as usual when the East Germans came down on the side of national initiatives. The GDR position signaled an unexpected break in the ranks of "real socialism" as defined in Moscow. Notwithstanding the successful Soviet pressure on Honecker to postpone his September 1984 visit to Bonn, the East Germans have pursued an increasingly independent policy vis-à-vis the "other" Germany. It is equally important to note that Gromyko resumed the Soviet-U.S. disarmament dialogue in New York in September 1984—that is, when Honecker would have been in Bonn.

In short, Soviet control over Warsaw Pact security policy had slipped before Gorbachev took over as head of the Soviet Party in March 1985. Notwithstanding the new Soviet leader's pledge to make the improvement of intrabloc relations his "first commandment" (*Pravda* 1985a), his commitment to cohesion and unity, the issue of national initiative versus international obligation remained unresolved. Esoteric exchanges surrounded the October 1985 Warsaw Pact meeting. In December of that year disagreement reportedly surfaced on issues of defense burden sharing. By anyone's definition, differences on détente strategy and who pays the bills for alliance response to NATO missiles and Reagan's strategic defense initiative are matters of security policy.

Within the larger context of the political component of Soviet security issues in Eastern Europe, these problems of coordinating Warsaw Pact security policy are likely to remain difficult to manage. Gorbachev did not preside over the shift from proletarian internationalism, as defined in Moscow, to "voluntary cooperation" and "creative indig-enous interpretation" in the struggle for world socialism. He inherited the running debate on matters of national initiatives and international obligations. One could not say that he has changed the dynamics of the debate; however, he has contained its consequences by accepting diversity (contradictions) as a normal, unavoidable condition of the international

Communist movement. His report to the Twenty-Seventh CPSU Congress stressed

> the importance of coordination of actions in matters of principle, comradely interest in each other's success, strict carrying out of commitments, and a profound undertaking of both national interests and common international interests in their organic interconnection. (*New Times* 1986: 42)

Gorbachev's handling of Moscow's differences with East Germany represent a change in style and substance from the Chernenko period when Soviet pressure appeared to be polarizing relations with the Honecker leadership. In April 1986 the general secretary attended the Eleventh Congress of the East German Socialist Unity Party (SED). He was the first head of the CPSU to appear at an East German congress since 1971. He praised the GDR's impressive economic performance and generally seemed to have accepted East Germany's official lack of enthusiasm for glasnost' and perestroika—or at least he resolved not to make an issue of it. As for relations between East and West Germany, most analysis agrees that Erich Honecker's postponed visit to Bonn took place in September 1987 with Gorbachev's approval, if not his enthusiastic blessing.

One can tentatively say that Gorbachev appears to have adopted a less abrasive response to pressure from his Warsaw Pact Eastern European allies for recognition of their role in Alliance policy. In the GDR's case this included continued improvement of relations with the "other Germany." But it is too soon to talk of patterns. Certainly his blunt criticism of Romania (*Pravda* 1987a) made clear that in Gorbachev's view, some of his allies are much more in need of perestroika than others.

Whether or not we are seeing the tip of an iceberg of significant change, I think it is useful to identify the pressures for such a change. One such pressure flows from the Soviet need for Eastern European support of Soviet policy initiatives vis-à-vis European security and arms control issues. In the intra-Communist arena, China is less of a problem for Gorbachev than his predecessors. However, in the East–West arena a phalanx of support for his disarmament platforms remains important. Second, Moscow's procedural and ideological concessions dating from the Berlin 1976 conference with respect to proper principles for relations among Communist parties and states make it ever more difficult for the Soviets to pull rank when it comes to differences of views or exchange of experience. Finally, Eastern European regimes are pushed by their own internal economic, political, and ideological crises increasingly to respond to domestic pressures that emphasize socialist patriotism and national interests. Thus one might say that over time conflicting Soviet policy priorities have combined with external conditions to act as change agents in Soviet-Eastern European relations. The question is not whether there are change agents so much as whether or not there is policy and behavioral change as opposed to statements of Soviet good intentions.

The Ideological Dimension of Security: The Brezhnev Doctrine Revisited

Ideology is an inadequate explanation for the totality of Soviet foreign policy. Yet when it comes to what has sent Soviet troops into the territory of an Eastern European ally, ideology has been a factor. Political and ideological considerations in 1956 were weighted more toward the political than the ideological; in 1968 they were somewhat more ideological than political. But both instances led to a military solution.

This is not the place to rehash Soviet security perceptions in the Hungarian crisis of 1956 or what turned the Prague Spring into that long, hot summer of 1968. Nonetheless, the Brezhnev Doctrine put forward as the rationale for sending "allied socialist" soldiers in to "save Czechoslovak socialism" is relevant to coming to terms with what circumstances might precipitate the use of force during future instances of Eastern European crisis. That doctrine presumed that Moscow had a responsibility to intervene—militarily if necessary—if developments within any given socialist country inflicted damage on socialism with that country or the basic interests of other socialist countries. The bottom line was a doctrine of limited sovereignty within the socialist commonwealth, a principle unrestricted in theory but in practice presumed to be something of a Monroe Doctrine for Eastern Europe. Yet the basis of what in the West we call the Brezhnev Doctrine was not simply the socialist version of might makes right. Consider the following excerpt:

> Those who speak of the illegality of the allied socialist countries' actions in Czechoslovakia forget that in a class society there is and can be no such thing as nonclass law. Laws and norms of law are subordinated to the laws of class struggle and the laws of socialist development. These laws are clearly formulated in the documents jointly adopted by the Communist and Workers' Parties.[6]

It is not only that this justification became considerably less plausible in light of the 1976 Berlin conference affirmation of voluntary cooperation and creative indigenous interpretation of how best to apply

Marxism-Leninism on the road to socialism. The Brezhnev Doctrine presumed agreement on the "laws of class struggle" and "laws of socialist development." In order to mobilize "allied socialist" politicians to send fraternal armies into "save socialism" there has to be a substantial perceived threat to shared norms, a common understanding of what "socialist laws" are being violated, and a consensus on the substance of "real socialism."

This is where Gorbachev's rhetorical commitment to radical reform introduces considerable confusion. After 1968 Eastern European policymakers had a relatively clear idea of "real socialism" as understood in Moscow, although Brezhnev's tolerance for Hungarian reform implied that there might be more latitude in practice than in principle. Under Gorbachev there is a remarkably open debate on the substance of Soviet economic and political reform involving officials, academics, and even dissidents. As yet there is no consensus about direction.

In what we might call a socialist marketplace of ideas, scholars have their official patrons. Policymakers support academic clients while Soviet-Eastern European reformers quote from each other's works in a war of words about where to go to bring the Soviet and Eastern European economies into the year 2000.

There are distinct differences between the Hungarian and Bulgarian models, for example. Both have highly placed advocates in Moscow. In June 1986 Gorbachev himself openly praised the search for solutions to complex social and economic problems in Hungary and complained about the pace of implementation of reforms called for at the February Twenty-Seventh Party Congress. His public support for Kadar and decision to stay home from the Bulgarian and Czechoslovak Party Congresses appeared as a somewhat open signal of the Soviet leader's effort to transform the substance of "real socialism" in the Soviet Union itself.

To quote Gorbachev's own statement on the implications of perestroika for relations among "fraternal" countries:

> The entire range of political, economic, and humanitarian relations with socialist countries is being cast anew. This is dedicated by the objective needs of each country's development and by the international situation as a whole, rather than by emotions. (Gorbachev 1987: 164)

The relationships to which the general secretary referred clearly still are in the process of becoming. Official willingness to reassess the star-crossed Czechoslovak reform of 1968 expressed during the seventieth anniversary of the October Revolution will accelerate the rate—perhaps even the nature—of change.[7] I would not go so far as the oft-quoted, perhaps apocryphal statement of the Soviet foreign ministry spokesman who reportedly answered the question concerning differences between Soviet reforms and the Prague Spring of 1968 in two words: "Nineteen years."[8] Nonetheless, as the debate continues differences on the relationship of economic to political reform along the Czechoslovak spectrum of progressive, centrist, and dogmatic are almost inevitable.

The Future of Soviet Policy

It is the outcome of that internal Soviet struggle that will determine whether or not one can realistically speak of a significant change with respect to Soviet security policy toward Eastern Europe. There are too many unknowns these days to make a prediction about the outcome. Gorbachev has not fully consolidated power despite his impressive strides in that direction. There are at least three possible Soviet domestic scenarios that could affect Soviet–Eastern European policy. First, Gorbachev successfully eliminates lurking rivals and bureaucratic resisters and presses forward with his revolution from above. If so, we do not know how the "real" Gorbachev will come down on a range of issues once he no longer needs the allies he is cultivating today. One never knows how someone will behave as a leader until he is *the* leader. It is instructive to note that Tito badly misjudged Khrushchev's intentions. Khrushchev, restrained by the Anti-Party Group, had a very different order of priorities than the Khrushchev at the 1957 Moscow meeting. The substance of the Gorbachev revolution depends on the nature of his successes and failures along the way.

Second, Gorbachev fails to consolidate, and his political career shatters over unacceptable reform policies. In that case prediction depends on the unity or lack of unity of those waiting in the wings. It is likely that whether or not Ligachev became the pointman of a successful conservative backlash, the emphasis would be to slow down reform within the Soviet Union and Eastern Europe alike. Gorbachev could become the Dubcek of a Moscow Spring, sitting on the political sidelines to be rediscovered by the next generation of Soviet reformers twenty years later. Or he might represent the first abortive attempt at "real" reform, politically dead-ended by rivals who kept the substance of his program as Khrushchev did with Malenkov's New Course.

Third, notwithstanding substantial opposition, Gorbachev continues to survive by maneuvering between his conservative detractors and his more radical supporters, putting in place piecemeal perestroika. The general secretary's handling of the political fall of Boris Yelt'sin indicates that he has no intention of being trapped into what in the Soviet context would be politically suicidal "adventurism." Yet his long-run survivability depends on establishing some visible domestic economic successes and achieving foreign policy payoffs from his disarmament initiatives.

Undoubtedly Eastern European reformers across the board would suffer a setback if Gorbachev's revolution was to be redefined as a "counterrevolution" in Moscow. Yet the timing of whatever happens to Soviet perestroika will be as important to Eastern European repercussions as the fate of Gorbachev's reforms.

For the age structure of top Party leaders of the Eastern European Communist regimes comes into play. The non-Soviet members of the Warsaw Pact are predominantly aged politicians set in their ways. For many of them the pressure to reform requires self-criticism of their own past. Gorbachev can talk about radical transformation of the Brezhnev legacy. His Eastern European colleagues for the most part can only reform against themselves. When Gorbachev took office these men were Todor Zhivkov (Bulgaria), born September 7, 1911, first secretary of the BCP since 1954; Gustav Husak (Czechoslovakia), born January 10, 1913, head of the KSC since 1968; Erich Honecker (GDR), born August 25, 1912, first secretary of the SED since 1971; Janos Kadar (Hungary), born May 22, 1912, first secretary of the Hungarian Socialist Workers' Party since 1956; Wojciech Jaruzelski (Poland), born July 6, 1923, first secretary of the Polish United Workers' Party since 1981; and Nicolae Ceausescu (Romania), born January 26, 1918, head of the RCP since 1965.

Kadar was an exception in that the Hungarian New Economic Mechanism can be seen as a predecessor of Soviet perestroika. General Jaruzelski embraced the language of perestroika in an attempt to legitimize his efforts to put the Humpty-Dumpty of the Polish economy together in post-Solidarity Poland.

On a country-specific basis the consequences of any of the foregoing scenarios depend on when genuine generational change takes place in Eastern European Communist parties. The first to go was the head of the Czechoslovak Communist party, Gustav Husak. It is too soon to tell whether Milos Jakes (age 65), who replaced him in mid-December 1987, will represent an effort to hold the line with a transitional figure more acceptable in Moscow or will be "the first step in a slow turnaround" (Newman 1987).[9]

Nor are the repercussions of the replacement of Hungarian leader Kadar a simple liberal-conservative split. Kadar followed Husak into retirement in May 1988. Prime Minister Karoly Grosz (age 57) took over as head of the Hungarian Party. Grosz is clearly of the Gorbachev generation. He has a reputation of being on the side of democratization of the one-party system as essential for economic efficiency. Notwithstanding his initial tough line on dissent and non-Party opposition, Grosz either led or acquiesced in the Hungarian Central Committee's official endorsement of a multiparty system.

This is more than a matter of political personalities and elites. No matter who rules in the countries of Eastern Europe, these Communist regimes are beset with a range of systemic, ideological, economic, and political dilemmas. The position of Eastern European leaders today is not as fragile as that of those pressed to follow Malenkov's New Course and the zigzags of de-Stalinization thirty years ago. Still, whether Eastern European policymakers resist or join the perestroika bandwagon, the process will increase demands for expanded domestic access to the political game. Therefore, Eastern European leaders will be more rather than less likely to tilt toward "socialist patriotism" at the expense of their "international obligations" (Soviet defined). That likelihood is reinforced by the fact that as the ideological and political substance of such obligations has become more ambiguous, Soviet economic incentives are less available.

This makes it all the more plausible that in either the first or third scenario the WTO will operate less as an instrument of Soviet policy toward Eastern Europe than as an arena of bargaining and conflict containment reflecting an admittedly asymmetrical form of mutual advantage.

The most likely spillover in Warsaw Pact politics would be that Moscow's Eastern European allies may become substantially more resistive to Soviet desired levels of defense burden-sharing. This is not so much a change as a more general applicability of what in the 1960s would have been considered the Romanian pattern of interaction. Politically by the 1980s that pattern expanded to include the Hungarians and the East Germans, the most recent—once unthinkable—defenders of "national initiatives" and "creative application" of indigenous experience on the road to socialism.

When, and if, change in the USSR affects alliance economics depends on to what degree lower military budgets become a priority of Gorbachev's perestroika and European reaction to the agreed-upon elimination of intermediate-range nuclear missiles in Europe. For example, if Western European defense budgets increase to compensate for perceived increased strategic vulnerability, that will not allow the Soviets to devote Warsaw Pact cost savings to the domestic economy unless the Eastern European allies pay a larger share of joint military expenses. Logically those Eastern European leaders most closely identified as advocates of indigenous perestroika and whose legitimacy depends on domestic economic and political reform might be the most reluctant to do so.

The logic of perestroika entails economic/military trade-offs for Soviet and Eastern European reformists alike. Gorbachev's December 7, 1988, announcement to the U.N. General Assembly of unilateral troop reductions in Eastern Europe was most likely related to this dilemma. The resulting restraints will influence Warsaw Pact attitudes toward the Vienna negotiations on conventional armed forces in Europe that began in March 1989 and will be reflected in intra-alliance politics of the 1990s.

In the meantime, to sum up what we might consider chapter 1 of the Gorbachev administration, the Soviet leader has continued the Khrushchev and Brezhnev emphasis on the importance of the alliance, attempted to use it to validate his summit diplomacy, and referred to the need for "new mechanisms" of cooperation. Institutionally this is continuity, not change. In addition, if we look at past Soviet security policy toward Eastern Europe, the intrabloc aspect of that policy was highly country-specific. I would expect that pattern to continue.

Although there are much more powerful domestic-foreign policy linkages when it comes to Eastern Europe than in other arenas of Soviet security policy, since the collapse of the Stalinist interstate system that policy has moved beyond a mere reflection of Moscow's domestic policies. Here my analysis disagrees with Korbonski's that Soviet national security policy toward the GDR "is not much different than toward the Ukraine" (1983: 293). The Ukraine does not have its own armed forces or the West Germans to complicate matters.

This incremental but important change, however, was under way long before Gorbachev became directly responsible for Soviet security policy vis-à-vis Eastern Europe. Brezhnev opened the Pandora's box in the 1970s when he accepted the principle of national Eastern European initiatives on the road to détente. Soviet pressure on the East German leadership to normalize relations with West Germany, including the signing of the Basic Treaty between the two German states in 1972, ended the GDR's international isolation. Although the consequence of the changed East German status was not immediately clear, it subtly affected Soviet–East German relations and allowed the GDR more flexibility in its own Warsaw Pact politics. The decision to opt for martial law in Poland as the least worst choice in 1981 upgraded Jaruzelski within the alliance even as it made the Polish military less available to perform its East–West mission within the Warsaw Pact.

Overall Soviet–Eastern European coalition politics as a part of Soviet security policy have been largely a matter of continuity under Gorbachev, not change. His options have been restrained by past Soviet policy choices and conflicting priorities vis-à-vis the diplomatic and military role played by the Eastern European members of the Pact.

This has not been strictly an East–West dynamic. It also has been reinforced by Soviet efforts under Brezhnev to enlist Eastern European support for Moscow's global objectives in the Third World, dealt with in Roger E. Kanet's chapter. The resulting boundary disintegration between Eastern Europe and non-Communist political arenas has weakened Soviet mechanisms for control.

Such disintegration was not "against" Soviet policies; rather, it was a unintended consequence of shifting Soviet policy priorities. Nor is Gorbachev free from the temptation to make trade-offs between Soviet regional and global objectives. Therefore, though he seems to have abandoned "benign neglect" of Eastern Europe, I predict that he will continue what some scholars see as Moscow's "dynamic ambiguity" (Barrows 1974: 210), whether or not that would be his first choice.

Although military fears concerning the need for Eastern European buffers to protect the Soviet heartland have become increasingly atavistic in light of strategic weapons technology, they are complicated by the perceived symbiotic political and ideological relationship of Soviet–Eastern European Communist systems. To the extent that Gorbachev's commitment to diversity and threshold for socialist pluralism, put forward in his message to the Twenty-Seventh CPSU Congress, alters the Soviet perception of an organic bond with Eastern Europe, there would be less need to "save" future Eastern European reform Communists from themselves even if Eastern European reforms went faster or in directions as yet untried by Moscow. Certainly in these days of glasnost' and perestroika, Czechoslovak socialism with a human face would not have been a "nationalist deviation" or dangerous brand of "counterrevolution." Gorbachev's willingness to legitimize a higher level of socialist pluralism than his predecessors may have decreased the salience of ideological and political considerations in the minds of Soviet security planners. As with their Western debts, Eastern European domestic politics may be increasingly seen as their own problem for which Moscow will not assume responsibility. If so, that *is* significant change.

Certainly Soviet reaction to the Polish government's efforts to get striking workers back to work and to parry the demands to legalize Solidarity cannot be considered business as usual. Who would have expected *Sovetskaia Rossiia* to argue that recent Polish strikes and the call for replacing the government were not counterrevolution but a "healthy sign of democracy" (Runov 1988) or that *Izvestiia* would advise Jaruzelski to compromise with the opposition in an "anti-crisis pact" (Toporkov 1988)?

There are a range of possible interpretations of the Soviet media response: impatience that Jaruzelski could not hold the line, reluctant willingness to accept Solidarity as a major player in Polish politics, a warning to the Polish government to cut its losses before the cost-risk ratio became even worse, a need to reaffirm that strikes and negotiations with strikers are legitimate aspects of socialist pluralism in light of the ongoing Armenian protests over Nagorno-Karabakh, or perhaps all of these. But for the perspective of this chapter, the Soviet response to date signals that Moscow would not consider Polish socialism in danger if General Jaruzelski stepped down or compromised with Solidarity. There is no implication that the Red Army or "allied socialist" forces should be preparing to "save" Polish socialism from "counterrevolutionary" forces.

This brings us back to the second scenario; to the darker side of what scholars call the Moscow Spring. What if the momentum of perestroika grinds to a halt in the bowels of Soviet bureaucracy? What if the gamble of pushing for Eastern European reform strategies backfires unacceptably or, as Charles Gati puts it, the effort to combine Communism and glasnost' "unravels in Warsaw, Budapest or Prague" (Gati 1987: 975)? Given the history of efforts to raise prices in Poland, the angry alienation of the younger, more militant Solidarity supporters, and their suspicion of Lech Walesa's willingness to compromise (Diehl 1988), that is not a strictly hypothetical question. Soviet response to the Hungarian Party's public acknowledgment that a multiparty system would provide a "better safeguard" against abuse of power than retaining the Communist party's monopoly of political power, will provide some tangible evidence for or against this scenario (*Times* of India, February 4, 1989; see also Reisch 1989: 5).

It could happen. Yet Western scholars who see Gorbachev's task as most impossible tend to discount the fact that the inertia of the Soviet system can work in his favor as well as against him. Notwithstanding the disasters of the Hungarian uprising and the loss of control symbolized by the 1956 Polish October, Khrushchev outmaneuvered the "antiparty" group. He survived the Cuban missile crisis. In April 1987 Ligachev appeared to be echoing Molotov's cautions vis-à-vis spreading perestroika through Eastern Europe. In retrospect we might remember that being right about political consequences did not advance Molotov's career any more than Trotsky was able to effectively use Stalin's failures in China to get rid of him.

With respect to Eastern Europe, there will continue to be a delicate balancing act, what might be called a succession choreography, as contenders to replace Gorbachev's aging allies attempt to keep their options open in the event that Gorbachev is not the Soviet leader they need to relate to when the changing of the guard takes place on their own political turf. The outcome of those Eastern European successions is a significant variable in the calculations of Soviet security planners. The weight given that variable undoubtedly reflects the state of East–West progress as well as of Soviet-Eastern European relations and Moscow's hopes or fears for Eastern European perestroika.

In short, radical changes in Soviet strategic security policy toward Eastern Europe require change not only within Eastern Europe but in the Soviet/Western European/U.S. security policy axis as well. Only if détente moves back into the mainstream of foreign policy in Washington, London, Bonn, and Paris will the military component of Soviet security policy toward Eastern Europe make dramatic shifts.

Notes

1. Explicitly recognized by the Polish leader W. Gomulka (1947). For Soviet discussion of this concept, see Trainin (1947).
2. *Pravda* (June 21, 1985). Vladimirov is assumed to be a pseudonym of Oleg Rakhmanin, first deputy head of the CPSU Department for Liaison with Ruling Workers and Communist Parties.
3. Budapest TV Service, April 26, 1987; EE-FBIS, April 27, 1987, and *Pravda*, April 26, 1987. Ligachev's warning can be seen as an extension of his reservations about domestic glasnost' (*New York Times*, September 24, 1987).
4. *New Times* (1986: 39, emphasis added). This was also reinforced with the general secretary's statement to those celebrating the seventieth anniversary of the Russian Revolution that "socialism does not, and cannot have, a model against which all are compared" (*Pravda* 1987b).
5. See Bugaev, "A Strange Position," *Kommunist*, no. 14, (1984), quoted in Dawisha and Valdez (1987: 13).
6. *Pravda* (September 26, 1968). Quoted by Remington, (1969), p. 415.
7. Director of the Institute of Marxism-Leninism Georgi L. Smirnov let it be understood in Moscow that the events of 1968 were being reexamined (Taubman 1987).
8. Quoted by Gati (1987), p. 972. See also Bovin on perestroika and the fate of socialism (*Izvestiia*, 1987). For foreign policy implications, see Primakov (*Pravda* 1987).
9. That the Czechoslovak media retranslated Gorbachev's telegram to Jakes of best wishes for "renewal of socialism" into "strengthening of socialism" (*Rude pravo*, December 18, 1987) signaled ongoing resistance to perestroika Soviet-style. For analysis, see Kusin (1987).

References

Alexiev, Alexander (1979). *Romania and the Warsaw Pact: The Defense Policy of a Reluctant Ally*. Santa Monica, CA: RAND Corporation.
Asmus, Ronald D. (1984). "East Berlin and Moscow: The Documentation of a Dispute." *Radio Free Europe Research Bulletin*, August 25.
Barrows, Walter L. (1974). "Speculations on a Multipolar 1984." In Louis J. Mensonides and James A. Kuhlman, ed., *The Future of Inter-Bloc Relations in Europe*. New York: Praeger.

Bourne, Eric. (1987, December 14). "Pluralism in Soviet Bloc Stands Better Chance— This Time Around." *Christian Science Monitor*, pp. 9–10.

Bovin, A. (1987, July 11). "*Perestroika* and the Fate of Socialism." *Izvestiia*.

Brzezinski, Z. K. (1971). *The Soviet Bloc: Unity and Conflict.* Cambridge: Harvard University Press.

Clemens, Diane Shaver (1970). *Yalta.* Oxford: Oxford University Press.

Dawisha, Karen, and Jonathan Valdez (1987). "Socialist Internationalism in Eastern Europe." *Problems of Communism.* 36, 1–14.

Diehl, Jackson (1988, September 19–25). *Washington Post National Weekly Edition.*

Fischer-Galati, Stephen (1967). *The New Rumania: From a People's Democracy to a Socialist Republic.* Cambridge: MIT Press.

Gati, Charles (1987). "Gorbachev and Eastern Europe." *Foreign Affairs*, 65(5), 958–75.

Gomulka, W. (1947). *W Walce o Demokracje Ludowa.* Warsaw.

Gorbachev, Mikhail (1987). *Perestroika: New Thinking for Our Country and the World.* New York: Harper & Row.

Johnson, A. Ross, Robert W. Dean, and Alexander Alexiev (1982). *East European Military Establishments.* New York: Crane, Russak.

Johnson, A. Ross, and Barbara Kliszewski (1982, October 14). *The Polish Military after Martial Law: Report of a RAND Conference.* Santa Monica, CA: RAND Corporation.

Korbonski, Andrzej (1983). "Eastern Europe." In Robert F. Byrnes, ed., *After Brezhnev: Sources of Soviet Conduct in the 1980s.* Bloomington: Indiana University Press.

Krasnaia zvezda (1956, January 29). "Deklaratsiia goludaret—uchastnikov Varshavskogo Dogovora o druzhbe, sotrunichestve i vzaimnoi pomoshchi." P. 1.

Kusin, V. V. (1987). "*Rude Pravo* Mistranslates Crucial Word in Gorbachev's Telegram to Jakes." *Radio Free Europe Research Bulletin.* RAD Background Report/244, December 23.

Mackintosh, J. M. (1969). "The Evolution of the Warsaw Pact." *Adelphi Papers* 58. London: International Institute for Strategic Studies.

Mason, Davis S. (1987, August 21). "Glasnost and Eastern Europe." Presented at the Hudson Institute, Indianapolis, Indiana.

Nelson, Daniel N., ed. (1984.) *Soviet Allies: The Warsaw Pact and the Issue of Reliability.* Boulder, CO: Westview Press.

——— (1986). *Alliance Behavior in the Warsaw Pact.* Boulder, CO: Westview Press.

Newman, Barry (1987, December 18). "Husak Resigns Czechoslovakia Party Position; His Successor Is Also Likely to Resist Wide Reforms Pressed by Gorbachev." *Wall Street Journal*, p. 18.

New Times (1976, July). "Conference of the Communist and Workers' Parties of Europe." Speech by L. I. Brezhnev, Head of the CPSU Delegation, pp. 17–23; and "For Peace, Security Cooperation, and Social Progress in Europe, Conference of the Communist and Workers' Parties of Europe," pp. 24–32.

——— (1986, March). Moscow.

Pravda. (1956, January 28).

——— (1971, March 31).

——— (1985a, March 12).

——— (1985b, November 15).

——— (1986, June 10).

——— (1987a, May 27).

——— (1987b, November 3).

Primakov, E. (1987, July 10). *Pravda.*

Reisch, Alfred (1989, March 23). "HSWP CC Compromised on 1956 and Endorses Multiparty System." *Radio Free Europe Research* 14, no. 12, pp. 3–5.

Remington, Robin Alison, ed. (1969). *Winter in Prague: Documents on Czechoslovak Communism in Crisis*. Cambridge: MIT Press.

——— (1971). *The Warsaw Pact: Case Studies in Communist Conflict Resolution*. Cambridge: MIT Press.

Runov, V. (1988, September 15). "Poland: Barrier of Mistakes on the Path to Reform. In Connection with the Upcoming Convocation of an Extraordinary Session of the Polish Sejm." *Sovetskaia Rossiia*, p. 5. As translated in Foreign Broadcast Information Service (FBIS), *Daily Report: Soviet Union*, September 19, 1988, pp. 35–36.

TASS (1984, April 20).

——— (1985, November 7).

Taubman, Philip (1987, November 5). "Soviets Won't Push Policy on Allies, Gorbachev Says." *New York Times*, pp. A1, A14.

Theen, Rolf H. W. (1986). "Current Reform Thinking in the Soviet Union." Presented to the Annual Conference of the Central Slavic Association, Kansas City, Missouri, October 10–11.

Toporkov, L. (1988, September 15). "Anti-Crisis Pact. Such, in the Opinion of the Poles, Is the Basis for a National Accord." *Izvestiia*, p. 5. As translated in *FBIS*, September 19, 1988, pp. 33–34.

Trainin, I. P. (1947). "Democracy of a Special Type." *Sovetskoie Gosudarstvo i Pravo*, nos. 1, 3.

Volgyes, Ivan (1982). *The Political Reliability of the Warsaw Pact Armies: The Southern Tier*. Durham, NC: Duke University Press.

White Book on Aggressive Activities by the Governments of the USSR, Poland, Czechoslovakia, Hungary, Rumania, Bulgaria, and Albania towards Yugoslavia. (1951). Belgrade: Ministry of Foreign Affairs.

Zycie Warszawy (1971, April 16). Warsaw.

• CHAPTER TWELVE •

Changing Soviet National Security Policy in Relations with the Third World

Roger E. Kanet
University of Illinois

Little more than a decade ago Soviet leaders and analysts were enthusiastically optimistic about the direction and pace of international developments and about Soviet prospects for the future. They wrote and spoke incessantly of the "changing international correlation of forces," by which they meant the global shift in relative political, economic, and, especially, military strength in favor of the Soviet Union, its allies, and the "forces of peace" and against the forces of Western imperialism (Deane 1976; Sanakoyev 1974; Shakhnazarov 1974). Developments of the prior decade or so tended to support this viewpoint.

In the area of strategic nuclear capabilities the Soviet Union had closed the gap with the United States and achieved strategic parity. This strategic equality—and by extension Soviet equality as a global power—had been recognized in a series of agreements negotiated at Vladivostok, Moscow, and Helsinki. The Soviets' conventional forces in Europe, as well as their expanded ability to project military power beyond their immediate borders, had been enhanced by the modernization of Warsaw Pact forces and by the creation of a "blue water" navy and long-distance air transport capability (Kanet 1987c; Menon 1986).

The West's acceptance at Helsinki of the postwar status quo in Europe, the defeat of the United States in Vietnam, as well as the coming to power of self-proclaimed Marxist-Leninist "national liberation" movements throughout the Third World (often with direct Soviet support) gave further evidence of the enhanced role of the Soviet Union in world affairs. In the international economic realm the Soviets envisaged the establishment of a socialist international division of labor that would first counter and eventually replace the dominant capitalist world market.

Domestically economic growth rates, though they had slowed since the immediate postwar period, still enabled the Soviet leadership to fulfill its promises to meet growing domestic consumer demand and simultaneously to maintain the expanding military and economic commitments necessitated by the USSR's new role as a global power.

However, in the wake of the defeat in Vietnam and of the Watergate scandal, the U.S. leadership seemed incapable of responding to Soviet initiatives. The détente relationship of the 1970s was, from the Soviet perspective, merely tacit recognition on the part of the United States that it could no longer ignore Soviet interests and was forced by the new realities of world affairs to accept and recognize as legitimate the interests of the USSR and of those "progressive" forces and movements it supported.

Despite this optimism of the 1970s and the apparent reality that underlay it, by the beginning of the present decade the USSR found itself increasingly on the defensive. The détente with the West (especially the United States) had collapsed into a new cold war complete with an economic embargo, revitalized U.S. military spending, and a new U.S. assertiveness in foreign policy. Soviet blustering did not prevent Western European NATO states from agreeing to the deployment of intermediate-range nuclear weapons, or the Reagan administration from proceeding with the development of the Strategic Defense Initiative. In short, a new round in the postwar arms race had begun.

In the Third World the USSR had been effectively frozen out of participation in key developments in the Middle East. Several of its new allies/clients had failed to create stable political-economic systems and were increasingly challenged by domestic insurgencies supported by the United States and others. The result was a growing demand for Soviet military and economic support, including the direct takeover by Soviet troops of responsibility for the security of the Marxist-Leninist regime in Afghanistan. Along with this came criticism of Soviet intervention by a wide range of developing countries themselves.

In yet another area the Soviets found that the political attractiveness of their socioeconomic-political model had weakened dramatically and thus reduced their global influence. The unity of the Soviet-led world Communist movement had long since shattered. In Western Europe Communist parties had either lost domestic support or asserted their independence from Moscow—or both. In the Third World a growing number of Marxist regimes were in the process of modifying their commitment to socialism and reestablishing or strengthening economic and political ties with the West.

These problems arose at the very time when the weaknesses of the Soviet economy were becoming most apparent. By the beginning of the 1980s economic growth rates had, in the words of General Secretary Mikhail Gorbachev, "fallen to a level close to economic stagnation" (Gorbachev 1987a: 19). The technological gap between the Soviet economy and those of its major competitors, including a number of developing countries, was expanding (Gorbachev 1987a: 19; Poznanski 1987). After decades devoted to "catching up" with the West in a wide range of fields and establishing themselves as a global power, the Soviets faced the prospect of stagnation and decline.

Briefly, the situation inherited by Brezhnev's successors was one filled with contradictions. Although the Soviet Union had emerged as a global superpower with wide-ranging interests and capabilities, this position was based largely on military power. The nuclear stalemate with the United States, the renewed activism of U.S. policy, and the expanding role of other countries in global affairs, however, precluded turning this enhanced military position into effective political gains. The weaknesses of the Soviet economy raised questions about possible overextension of Soviet international commitments and limited the relevance of the USSR for many of the most pressing international problems: economic development, trade, and debt servicing.

Since assuming the leadership of the CPSU in 1985, Mikhail Gorbachev has spoken repeatedly of the domestic and foreign policy problems facing the USSR. As the previous chapters in this volume note, he has committed himself to a major reform, or *perestroika*, of the entire Soviet system as a means of resolving these problems. One of the primary objectives of Gorbachev's campaign of perestroika—though by no means the sole one—is his recognition that the position of the USSR in the world is dependent on a dramatic improvement in the functioning of the Soviet economy. In his report to the Twenty-Seventh Party Congress in early 1986 he expressed this point most forcefully: "In a word, comrades, acceleration of the country's economic development is the key to all our problems; immediate and long term, economic and social, political and ideological, domestic and foreign" (Gorbachev 1986a: 29).[1] Perestroika is his call for major reform with the goal of revitalizing the economy, closing the technology gap, and turning the USSR into a fully competitive global superpower—not the "incomplete superpower" of today that lacks virtually all but military power as an instrument to influence world developments (Dibb 1986; Hough 1988).

Moreover, as Gorbachev has also noted, a period of stability in Soviet foreign policy is essential to the overall success of his reform policies. Without a reduction in the tensions that have characterized relations with the United States during much of the present decade and those with China for a quarter of a century, the Soviet leadership will be unable to devote either the attention or the resources required to implement domestic reform. Thus the domestic and foreign policies of the USSR are intertwined in two distinct but overlapping ways. Maintaining and improving the global role of the USSR is a prime determinant of the domestic politics of reform; simultaneously a shift in foreign policy aimed at reducing tensions and, in particular, the economic and political costs of a renewed arms race is a necessary condition for the successful implementation of reform.

Gorbachev's "New Political Thinking" in Foreign and Security Policy

Although Gorbachev has dramatized the problems that face the new Soviet leadership in both the domestic and the international realms, he is neither the first nor the only important Soviet figure to point to the need to turn the USSR around. Yet given his position as general secretary, Gorbachev's assessments carry special weight. Obviously the essential question, from the perspective of the analyst, concerns the degree to which Gorbachev's reevaluation of Soviet foreign and security policy is more than mere rhetorical updating of Soviet policy and thus likely to influence actual behavior. Although it is not possible to provide a conclusive answer to this question, a growing body of evidence indicates that Gorbachev's call for "new thinking" is more than mere rhetoric meant for propaganda purposes, as we shall see later.

In his report to the Twenty-Seventh Party Congress (1986) Gorbachev gave some indication of the content of the new political thinking when he raised issues seldom, if ever, discussed publicly by Soviet political leaders in the past.[2] The major points that he mentioned included the following.

1. Recognition of the existence of "global problems affecting all humanity," the resolution of which requires "cooperation on a worldwide scale . . . close and constructive joint action by the majority of countries" (1986a: 18–19).

2. Explicit stress on the interdependence of states, for the "dialectics of present-day development consists in a combination of competition and confrontation between thetwo systems and in a growing tendency towards interdependence of the countries of the world community. This is precisely the way, through the struggle of opposites, through arduous effort, groping in the dark as it were, that the contradictory but interdependent and in many ways integral world is taking shape" (1986a: 19).

3. The argument that "it is no longer possible to win an arms race, or nuclear war for that matter" and that "the striving for military superiority can, objectively speaking, bring no political dividends to anybody." A continuation of the arms race will increase the mutual threat to a point "where even parity will cease to be a factor of military-political deterrence" (1986a: 55).

4. Strong criticism of the "'infallibility' complex" and the "inertness and conservatism" that characterized previous Soviet policy (1986a: 64).

Not all of the specific elements of the new political thinking on foreign policy outlined by Gorbachev at the 1986 Party Congress were incorporated into the resolutions approved at the conclusion of the congress, nor are all included in the Party Program approved at the congress (CPSU 1986a, 1986b). This would appear to indicate that not all of these points are agreed to by the full leadership of the Party. However, since the congress the call for "new thinking" has been a dominant theme in the Party press.[3] Probably the two most authoritative recent speeches on the topic have been given by Eduard Shevardnadze in July 1988 and Gorbachev himself at the United Nations in December 1988. These addresses repeat the elements of "new thinking" noted earlier and specify how they are to be applied to specific issues in Soviet foreign policy.

The new political thinking, as presented in these and other authoritative Soviet sources, contains three basic components. The first is a revitalization of Soviet foreign policy by rejecting aspects of Brezhnev's foreign policy and by appealing for greater flexibility in the implementation of policy. The second is the introduction of at least two new concepts or issues on the agenda of the top leadership: global problems and interdependence. The third is a reevaluation of the sources of national security which leads to the following conclusions: (1) parity will soon cease to be a factor of political-military restraint; (2) national and international security have become indivisible; and (3) a multifaceted approach to problems of international security must be employed.

Gorbachev's views draw heavily on those of academic analysts who a number of years ago began discussing most of the issues that have now been placed on the agenda of the top political leadership. For example, since the mid-1970s a number of academic writers as well as some Party officials have developed the arguments concerning growing interdependence in the contemporary world, especially in the area of security, and the importance of "global problems" the solution of which requires increased cooperation.[4]

Also relevant to understanding the background of Gorbachev's new political thinking has been what William Odom (1985) has called "the third revolution" in Soviet military affairs. This revolution has involved a major reassessment of the relevance of nuclear weapons in maintaining security or accomplishing policy objectives. Chief among those who have pointed to the catastrophic consequences of nuclear war and, therefore, the need to overcome the "inertia of thought and a stubborn, mechanical, unthinking attachment to the old ways" has been Marshal N. V. Ogarkov (1983: 2), former chief of the Soviet General Staff. Ogarkov and others have presented this argument in order to buttress their call for the resources needed to take advantage of recent technological developments to modernize the conventional military capabilities of the USSR.[5] However, their depiction of the limited military and political utility of nuclear weapons is directly relevant to aspects of the new political thinking advocated by Gorbachev, who has argued that an arms race cannot be won and will likely increase mutual threats to the point that nuclear parity will no longer guarantee deterrence.

New thinking also characterizes Soviet assessments of its policy in the Third World. Whereas the 1961 Party Program (CPSU 1961: 2, 3) had spoken with great optimism about prospects for liberation and the role of the USSR in supporting the liberation struggle, the new program (CPSU 1986a: 43) emphasizes the revitalized role of neocolonialism and imperialism in the Third World and notes only that the "CPSU supports the just struggle waged by the countries of Asia, Africa and Latin America against imperialism" and that the "Soviet Union is on the side of the states and peoples repulsing the attacks of the aggressive forces of imperialism and upholding their freedom, independence and national dignity." Progressive states are informed that the tasks of building a new society are primarily their own responsibility, though the "Soviet Union has been doing and will continue to do all it can to render the peoples following that [socialist-oriented] road assistance in economic and cultural development, in training national personnel, in strengthening their defences and in other fields." The three major concerns that appear in Soviet writing and statements on current developments in the Third World relate to the escalating costs borne by the Soviet Union in supporting its clients, the poor record of these clients after independence in creating stable political systems and functioning economies, and the negative impact that involvement in the Third World has had on other Soviet foreign policy concerns—particularly in relations with the United States.

Building on arguments that had already been developed quite extensively in Soviet academic publications,[6] Brezhnev's first successor as general secretary, Iurii Andropov (1983: 14–15), argued that the primary source of economic development had to come from Third World socialist countries themselves.[7] This theme dominated Soviet pronouncements during 1984 and 1985. For example, writing on "Real Socialism and the Liberated Countries," Boris Ponomarev (1984), then head of the International Department of the Central Committee, noted the importance of past Soviet economic aid but concluded that

> the Soviet Union fundamentally rejects the demands [of the developing countries] that, on a par with the imperialist countries, it allocate for aid to the developing countries a fixed part of its gross national product. . . . One cannot agree with the point of view that it is only an influx of resources from without that can guarantee the resolution of the burning problems of the developing countries.

Thus by the time of the Twenty-Seventh Party Congress the official Soviet position was quite clear: although the Soviets have provided assistance in the past and will continue to do so, primary responsibility for economic growth rests with developing countries themselves. The most important task to be carried out by the USSR is to set the example, as a developed socialist society, that will provide the model for developing countries following the socialist path (Kapitonov 1983: 8; Novopashin 1982). The Soviets will continue to provide assistance but will not expand commitments.

In addition to raising the issue of the cost of supporting Third World clients, the Soviets have also questioned the long-term viability of some of their client states. During the 1970s, while continuing efforts to expand contacts with key non-Marxist developing states the Soviets gave special attention to the promotion of Marxist-Leninist vanguard parties. As S. Neil MacFarlane (1985: 140) has argued, "in the early and mid-1970s, the USSR faced an environment in the Third World in which important constraints limiting its activities had been removed or weakened, important stimuli for such activity had emerged or re-emerged, and its capabilities to undertake such activities had increased." The end result was an optimism about the prospects for revolutionary change in the Third World that went far beyond Soviet expectations of the 1960s. The Soviets now envisioned the growth of vanguard parties and socialist states in the Third World as part of the "changing international correlation of forces" and the establishment of a "socialist international division of labor" that would eventually replace Western economic dominance. This view had been expressed officially by Premier Alexei Kosygin (1971: 6) at the Twenty-Fourth Congress of the CPSU in 1971, when he claimed that Soviet economic relations with developing countries were "acquiring the nature of a stable division of labor, counterposed in the sphere of international economic relations to the system of imperialist exploitation." Other Soviet writers noted that the creation of "revolutionary democratic" regimes enhanced "cooperation with the socialist countries to a new level and deliberately promote the expansion of such cooperation" (Ul'ianovskii 1984: 16).

In the 1980s the Soviets have been far less sanguine about the prospects for Marxist-Leninist vanguard parties and states and have been critical of the policies of some of these parties. Among the more important of those who have voiced second thoughts has been Rostislav Ul'ianovskii, long-time (but retired) deputy director of the International Department of the CPSU and originally one of the strongest proponents of the model of "revolutionary democracy."[8] Whereas Ul'ianovskii now emphasizes the long and tortuous path that the building of socialism will entail, another deputy director of the International Department, Karen Brutents (1982: 4; 1984b: 108), seems to emphasize the greater long-term value for the Soviet Union of the establishment and strengthening of relations with capitalist countries in the Third World. He notes the positive aspects of their foreign policies and emphasizes the growing importance of their relations with the Soviet Union. This point is made by Aleksandr Iakovlev as well (1987: 9), who emphasizes the growing contradictions between the interests of the newly industrializing states and the established capitalist states.

Although the Soviets do not openly admit that many of their Third World clients face domestic insurgencies, prominent in their writings and statements in recent years has been commentary about the rejuvenated role of imperialism in the Third World and the challenge to newly liberated countries presented both by capitalist economic domination and U.S. military intervention (Kanet 1987b: 228–42). When added to the questiiiiiiiions posed about the seriousness of the commitment to Marxism-Leninism of some of their allies and the errors in their policies, Soviet comments about U.S. intervention provide evidence of growing concern about the appropriateness of the past emphasis on vanguard Marxist-Leninist parties. In fact the program approved at the Party Congress in 1986 (CPSU 1986a: 43), following the line advocated by Iakovlev and Brutents, points to the existence of "a realistic basis for cooperation of those young states that are following the capitalist road of development" resulting from "a sharpening contradiction between the interests of the[ir] peoples and the imperialist policy of diktat and expansion."

Concern about the negative implications of greater Soviet activism in the Third World for the core area of Soviet foreign policy—relations with the United States—has been evident not only in the writings of Soviet academics but also in the statements of Soviet leaders. For example, speaking to a plenary session of the Central Committee in 1983, General Secretary Andropov (1983: 15) referred to the implications of the risk of conflict with the United States for the entire Communist movement:

> The preservation of peace on earth is both today and in the foreseeable future the pivotal problem of the foreign policy of our party. And not only of our party. The threat of nuclear war hanging over the world induces one to reevaluate the basic concept of the activities of the entire Communist movement.

Responding to the more activist policy pursued by the United States in the Third World since the late 1970s, Soviet commentators have emphasized the threat to "progressive" forces emanating from Washington and the fact that the resolution of regional conflicts everywhere is difficult because, in the words of prominent Soviet analyst Dmitrii Volskii (1983: 5–7) of "the unwillingness of the imperialist quarters to recognize the principle of the equality of states and peoples, the striving of some countries to dominate others, to exploit their natural resources and to use their territory for their own strategic purposes." The increased "bellicosity" of the United States in the Third World has meant a heightened danger of the possible escalation of local wars into regional and even global conflicts, especially in the Middle East. Moreover, highly placed Soviet analysts have argued that the Soviet ability to support national liberation movements is at least partially contingent on the state of U.S.-Soviet relations. In periods of heightened global confrontation the Soviets are less able to provide economic and other support to developing countries that are suffering from Western economic domination (Bovin 1984: 5; Brutents 1984a: 33; Ponomarev 1984).

One direct result of this reassessment of relations with the Third World has been a rather dramatic reinterpretation of the role of military power in the resolution of regional conflicts in the Third World. As Francis Fukuyama (1987b) has demonstrated, the optimistic views of the Soviet ability to project military power in the Third World to support allies and clients that characterized writings of the 1970s has dropped off dramatically in the 1980s. Moreover, the naval construction programs that were to provide this power projection capability have not been brought to fruition.

At least at the level of public pronouncement Soviet academic analysts and highly placed officials have presented a much less optimistic and more complex interpretation of the Third World in recent years than that which characterized the expectations expressed a decade ago. Yet the question remains whether this reassessment represents mere tactical modification in Soviet doctrine or whether it is the external manifestation of a learning process in which the Soviet leadership is increasingly aware of its basic inability to mold the international environment to meet its own objectives.

This review of recent Soviet writing concerning the new political thinking in foreign policy demonstrates that the political leadership in Moscow (at least the general secretary and his key supporters) is committed to a new approach to foreign policy. This new approach is based on a more complex view of the international system and appears to take into account the fact that in the contemporary world no country, including the USSR, is able to impose its view of world order on the international system. At least at the rhetorical level the Soviet leadership appears to understand the realities of the international system in which it is operating.

By no means does this imply that Gorbachev faces no opposition or that his views on foreign policy—or domestic policy, for that matter—will necessarily win out in the long run. However, assuming Gorbachev's basic success in implementing his own policy preferences, the crucial question that remains to be answered concerns the impact that his new thinking has had, or is likely to have, on actual Soviet foreign policy behavior. This is the issue that will be addressed in the remainder of this chapter.

Implementation of the "New Political Thinking"

To this point it should be clear that, at least at the level of rhetoric, change has been occurring in Soviet foreign policy. For Gorbachev and other key foreign policy decision makers and advisers in Moscow, the shift is necessitated by the demands of the domestic economic and political reform that is essential to the long-term viability of the USSR as a global power, as well as by the mixed record of success in Soviet foreign policy. Before examining the relationship of this new thinking to actual Soviet foreign policy behavior, it is first necessary to discuss briefly the major elements of Gorbachev's reassessment of Soviet foreign policy, which include (1) greater flexibility in making and implementing policy, (2) the introduction of several innovative ideas into the agenda for consideration by the top leadership, and (3) a reexamination of the sources and requirements for Soviet national security in the nuclear age.

Flexibility in making and implementing policy requires a decision-making process that permits a rapid and effective response to change in both the internal and external environments. Gorbachev has explicitly criticized the Brezhnev leadership for lethargy and stagnation in foreign policy. Moreover, since assuming the leadership role in 1985, he has taken major steps to streamline and reinvigorate the Soviet foreign policy establishment, as William J. Bishop and Jan S. Adams discuss in their chapters. Substantial reorganization has occurred within the Ministry of Foreign Affairs, the Central Committee International Department, and the foreign trade sector; the International Information Department of the Central Committee has been disbanded and its international propaganda activities brought under the control of Politburo member Iakovlev. It appears that the primary purpose of these staffing and organizational changes within the ministry has been to reassert Party control over decision making and thus to ensure the introduction of the new policy line advocated by Gorbachev and his supporters. Change has also occurred in the mechanisms under which foreign trade is conducted, discussed in John E. Tedstrom's chapter.

Although these and other administrative and personnel changes introduced since 1985 do not guarantee changes in actual Soviet policy, they do represent a first step toward streamlining the policymaking process and thus facilitating a more flexible approach to policymaking.

Opposition to Gorbachev's stated policy objectives in the international arena has been muted and is not nearly so evident as that concerning domestic economic and political reform (Hanson 1987a; Rahr 1987b; Teague 1986, 1987a, 1987b). Those within the Soviet political elite likely to have questioned openly new political thinking have, for the most part, been retired. The major source of criticism of Gorbachev's proposals appears in the military area. First of all, implementation of his domestic investment policies will likely have adverse budgetary implications for the military. Moreover, the ongoing discussion of "reasonable sufficiency" in the security realm, with proposals for possible unilateral and asymmetrical reductions in the conventional military capabilities, illustrates quite different perspectives between civilian and military analysts (Akhromeev 1987; Legvold 1988; Lobov 1988; Schroder 1987; Zhurkin, Karaganov, and Kortunov 1987a, 1987b, 1988). For example, in response to questions raised by a prominent Soviet political analyst (Bovin 1987: 3) and supporter of restructuring about both the cost and wisdom of having built and deployed the SS-20 missiles, Major-General Iurii Lebedev asserted that the fact that the Soviet Union was willing "to eliminate medium-range missiles from Europe does not mean at all that this country created a problem and is now seeking a way out of it" (1987: 3).

In addition to the need for flexibility and the personnel to carry out a new policy, innovative ideas are also essential to any changes in Soviet behavior. Important here is the modification of the concept of national security in the recent pronouncements of the Party leadership. Soviet security, as conceived by Gorbachev, depends increasingly on political, economic, and military factors and cannot be guaranteed unilaterally by a mere increase in Soviet military capabilities.[9] Recent shifts in the Soviet position on arms control negotiations—especially concerning intrusive on-site verification—and the creation of sections responsible for arms control within the Ministry of Foreign Affairs and the International Department seem to indicate a new commitment to negotiation that coincides with this broadened view of security. It is possible that in line with his plans for revitalizing the economy, Gorbachev will begin to transfer resources from the military to the civilian sector. To date the only evidence to support such an assertion is circumstantial and based on remarks made by Gorbachev that indicate that he is not about to increase military spending, so that he can accomplish political and economic gains which, over the long run, would enhance Soviet security.[10] Most important is the need to rebuild and modernize the economic base of the Soviet Union.

Although none of these developments yet provides conclusive evidence that the Soviets under Gorbachev are about to restructure their foreign and security policies, they indicate an understanding of the failures of past policy and the need for change if the USSR is to establish a more effective policy in the future. Since 1985 growing evidence suggests that actual Soviet behavior has been undergoing change as well—and change of a sort consistent with the new political thinking. In virtually all areas of their relations with the outside world the Soviets have attempted to revitalize their role, and that "revitalization" has not merely been based on pursuing the standard policies of the late Brezhnev era.

The importance of Gorbachev's new thinking about Soviet foreign and security policy results partly from the recognition that the U.S. position in the world is not based exclusively on military capabilities, as important as they are for the U.S. role as a superpower. If the Soviet Union is to become a full-fledged global power, it must be able to compete with the United States economically and diplomatically, as well as in the military sphere. However, only by very basic, long-term changes can it keep up in the scientific and technological race and thereby retain the hope of becoming an economic superpower. Thus the major efforts to restructure the Soviet domestic economic and political systems are meant, in part, to strengthen the economic base from which the USSR can operate in the future. The strategy of interdependence is meant to move the Soviet economy toward joining the world market for the dual purposes of gaining greater benefits for the USSR and of expanding Soviet influence in international economic affairs (Hardt 1988; Hough 1988). Moreover, unless the Soviets are able to keep pace with technological developments in the West, the military capabilities of the USSR will likely fall behind those of the United States by the end of the century.

The success of Gorbachev's efforts to restructure the Soviet economy and to close the existing (and growing) technological gap requires a relaxation in the arms race and a reduction in policies likely to result in confrontation and tension with the West.[11]

New Political Thinking and Recent Soviet Behavior in the Third World

One of the most visible characteristics of Soviet international behavior since Gorbachev assumed the leadership of the CPSU has in fact been its renewed activism. In virtually all areas of importance to the Soviet Union —from relations with the United States and China to developments in the Middle East—the new Soviet leadership has demonstrated, in the words of Dimitri Simes (1987: 491), "a new sense of purpose, a new realism and a new creativity." Gorbachev's primary objective has been to reverse the decline in both the effectiveness and the credibility of Soviet policy that had set in during the final years of the Brezhnev leadership and to regain the initiative in international affairs.[12]

Of primary concern has been the state of Soviet-U.S. relations, which had deteriorated dramatically since the mid-1970s. More important, however, than the mere fact of the increased hostility in relations with the United States was the renewed vigor with which the United States was pursuing its international interests. In the military realm the Reagan administration had initiated a major program aimed at modernizing and expanding U.S. military capabilities. In the Third World former President Reagan had in effect declared war on a number of Soviet clients and made clear that the Soviets would not be permitted to make additional gains comparable to those of the mid-1970s. In other words, despite strategic parity in the military area, the Soviets were not accepted by the United States as an equal in the international political system. Moreover, the revitalized U.S. arms build-up, symbolized most dramatically in the Strategic Defense Initiative, threatened to vitiate past Soviet efforts to gain strategic parity with the United States.

When we turn to an examination of recent Soviet policy in the Third World, the evidence indicates revitalized efforts, including a number of innovative initiatives, to reestablish or consolidate the Soviet role as a major world actor. As Simes (1987: 489) has noted,

> [those] who saw Gorbachev's realistic assessment as a sign that Soviet involvement in the Third World would be scaled down to save resources and improve relations with the United States have been disabused of such hopes. A sense of overextension may have limited Moscow's willingness to accept costly new responsibilities, but it has not led Moscow to reduce its support for friends and clients, particularly those directly or indirectly challenged by the United States.[13]

Since Gorbachev took over as head of the CPSU in March 1985 the Soviets have attempted to reestablish their position in the Middle East —the Third World region of primary importance for their long-term security interests. For example, in line with prior policy, they have made new commitments of military aid to both Syria and Libya (Brown 1987) and have continued to support Iraq in its war against Iran while simultaneously working to normalize relations with the latter. However, they have also expanded their efforts to reach out to more moderate Arab states—such as Egypt, Jordan, and Kuwait—and even to open discussions with Israel. Since 1986, for example, they have mediated a reconciliation of competing factions of the Palestine Liberation Organization, initiated talks with Egypt concerning a possible Middle East peace conference, responded to Kuwaiti requests for protection of their oil tankers against Iran by leasing to Kuwait three Soviet tankers that now carry Kuwaiti oil, held various informal discussions with Israel, and signed economic agreements with Iran (Abele 1987; Harsch 1987; Keller 1987; Kifner 1987; van England 1987).

In Afghanistan the Soviets under Gorbachev have now withdrawn all their troops and have engaged in widespread reassessments of their past policy there. The motivation for the decision was to reduce the political costs to the Soviet Union in areas considered of far greater importance —for instance, relations with the United States and China.

Relations with India, the single most important non-Communist developing country for the USSR, have been reinvigorated by mutual visits of Rajiv Gandhi and Mikhail Gorbachev and by new Soviet credits for military and civilian purchases. The Soviets are well aware of the fact that unless they can continue to remain "relevant" for the primary Indian concerns—security against Pakistan (and China) and economic development—relations are likely to stagnate (Banerjee 1987; Mukerjee 1987).

In Africa the Soviets have expanded support for their embattled clients in Angola and Ethiopia. In fact the increase in U.S. assistance to UNITA in Angola has resulted in expanded Soviet military aid and even greater Angolan dependence on the Soviets and their Cuban allies. However, there is evidence that they have lost their enthusiasm for extending armed struggle to South Africa, a development that would likely undercut most of their recent efforts to improve relations with the West (Albright, 1987: 42–43; Clough 1986; Joliffe 1987; Nahaylo 1986; Press 1987). Finally, Foreign Minister Shevardnadze's official visits to Latin America in early fall 1987 gave evidence of the Soviets' desire to expand diplomatic relations with major Latin American countries. Economic concerns and a wide range of other international issues were on the agenda during the discussions with leaders in Brazil, Argentina, and Uruguay. Most important, however, was Shevardnadze's effort to project the image of a Soviet Union concerned about the problems of the region and willing to assist in resolving them (Foreign and Commonwealth Office 1987; Michaels 1987).

Thus Soviet policy in the Third World has not undergone any dramatic change in recent years despite the reassessments of the role of the Third World in Soviet policy that were described earlier. What is evident is a greater degree of flexibility in Soviet initiatives, as in the Middle East, but not an abandonment of past commitments. There is an enhanced interest in normalizing and expanding relations with the larger and regionally more significant states, even though they are capitalist. Moreover, the Soviets appear to be distinguishing between those Third World clients to whom they have made firm commitments—such as Afghanistan, Angola, and Ethiopia—and others, such as Nicaragua and Mozambique, where their past commitments have been more limited and where long-term prospects for stable, pro-Soviet regimes are less promising (Ford 1987; Fukuyama 1987a; Levy 1985; Nahaylo 1986).

The Soviet Union and the Asian-Pacific Region

In East Asia the Gorbachev leadership has engaged in a wide range of activities aimed at increasing the political and economic role of the USSR in an area where, despite greatly enhanced military capabilities, the Soviet Union remains largely a marginal actor. Gorbachev's speech (1986b) on Asian affairs made in Vladivostok in late July 1986 was by far the most comprehensive statement concerning Asia ever presented by a Soviet leader and set the tone for a new Soviet approach. In fact, more than a year earlier he (1985) had broached some of the issues when he referred to the possibility of an all-Asian forum that would bring together all Asian countries, including China, in order to improve relations and to deal with issues of common concern. The purpose of Gorbachev's Vladivostok speech was to emphasize the fact that the USSR is indeed an Asian power and to apply specifically to the Asian-Pacific region the elements of new thinking in Soviet policy. At least half of the general secretary's remarks were devoted to domestic economic concerns and bluntly describe the gravity of the problems in Soviet Asia and the need for dramatic reform. The remainder discussed foreign policy considerations, with special attention to the objective of normalization of relations with China as well as other countries in the region, and the possibilities for economic cooperation.

The major focus of Soviet efforts has occurred in policy toward China, and for good reason. The military-oriented, hard-line policies of the past had proved to be counterproductive. In fact they had gone far toward driving China into a de facto alliance with the United States, Japan, and Western Europe. The Soviet leadership has made major initiatives in an attempt to normalize relations with China—initiatives that promise to reduce Soviet military pressure on China and assist China in its economic modernization program.

In an interview dated December 29, 1987 with the Chinese weekly *Liaowang*, Gorbachev (1988a) called for a Sino-Soviet summit as the logical continuation of the steady improvements in relations between the two countries; Foreign Minister Shevardnadze has visited Beijing, and the summit occurred in mid-May 1989. Since the beginning of the decade relations between the two Communist states have warmed considerably. Bilateral trade turnover has expanded significantly in the past few years to reach more than 1.8 billion rubles in 1986 compared with less than 500 million three years earlier (SSSR 1983, 1986). The polemics that earlier dominated Sino-Soviet relations have been toned down dramatically. The Soviets no longer denounce the domestic reforms introduced by Deng Xiaoping, and the Chinese have largely stopped calling for a "united front against hegemonism" (Heinzig 1987).[14]

Important as well has been progress on all of the "three obstacles" to normalization of relations referred to by the Chinese: the Soviet occupation of Afghanistan, the huge numbers of Soviet troops massed along the Sino-Soviet border, and the Vietnamese occupation of Cambodia. As mentioned earlier, the Soviets have withdrawn their forces from Afghanistan. They have also indicated their willingness to negotiate a mutual draw-down of forces along the Sino-Soviet border. Gorbachev's December 1988 commitment (Gorbachev 1988b: 18) unilaterally to withdraw "a considerable part" of Soviet troops from Mongolia should help to ease tensions and stimulate further force reductions. Moreover, the INF agreement reached with the United States calls for the dismantling of Soviet intermediate-range missiles in Asia as well as in Europe. The Vietnamese have committed themselves to withdrawing their troops from Cambodia by 1990 and, as of this writing, have extracted about 40 percent of their 120,000 occupying forces. The Soviets seem to be increasingly unhappy with the nature of their relationship with Vietnam and with Vietnamese use of Soviet assistance (Kimura 1987: 5; Manning 1987–88: 69–71).

Even though the three obstacles have not been eliminated, relations between the Soviet Union and China have moved toward normalization in all but name. As Thomas Hart has argued, "the spectacular improvement already made in Sino-Soviet relations bears witness to another fact that simply cannot be ignored—namely that considerable progress can be made *despite* the differences remaining on a wide range of fundamental questions" (1987: 110). From Moscow's perspective the primary objective is to reduce tensions in Asia by eliminating a prime cause for China's allying itself with the West. As we have seen, the reduction of tension as a prerequisite for successful economic restructuring is a core element of Gorbachev's program.

The tone of Soviet relations with Japan has improved as well, though there is little evidence that the Soviets are yet willing to consider the essential problem in bilateral relations: the territorial dispute concerning the southern Kuril Islands, occupied by the USSR since World War II. Soviet policies of the Brezhnev years, which included the dramatic expansion of military capabilities in the Asian-Pacific region and the deployment of Soviet forces in the Kurils, raised the level of Japanese concern about its military security. The result was a substantial increase in Japanese military capabilities, a strengthening of the alliance with the United States, and the expansion of economic and political ties with China (Kimura 1986, 1987: 7–10; Scalapino 1987: 63–64; Stephan 1987).

In attempting to improve relations with Japan the Soviets find themselves in a very difficult position. Although access to Japanese capital and technological know-how are important for the Soviet economy, there is little that the Soviets have to offer the Japanese, short of returning the Kuril Islands. As Hiroshi Kimura has put it, "the Soviet Union needs Japan technologically, economically, and hence diplomatically, but Japan can get along without the Soviet Union as long as its security is assured" (1987: 10).

In Southeast Asia the Soviets have mounted increasing efforts to expand both diplomatic and economic contacts with the members of ASEAN—largely without success to date (Abele 1986; Heinzig 1987: 33–38). Yet their close ties with Vietnam, which most ASEAN members see as a potential security threat to the region, and their basic irrelevance to the economies of the region make prospects for any dramatic breakthrough in relations most unlikely in the foreseeable future. For example, total Soviet trade with ASEAN in 1986 was valued at $487 million, compared with ASEAN trade with Japan of $29 billion and with the United States of $24 billion (Manning 1987–88: 68).

The Soviets have also been active in establishing relations with the new microstates of the South Pacific which give them access to fishing rights and port facilities.[15] These activities have raised concerns in the United States and Japan about the possible long-term political-military objectives of the Soviet Union in the region. One result has been the decision of Japan, at U.S. urging, to commit expanded economic assistance to these countries.

Although Soviet policy throughout the region in the recent past has emphasized the need to reduce tension and establish improved relations and cooperation, its policy toward North Korea has followed an apparently quite different tack. The transfer of substantial amounts of modern military equipment to Korea has increased concerns about the possibility of a new outbreak of fighting on the Korean Peninsula. Yet despite the dramatic expansion of political contacts and military cooperation, the regime of Kim Il Sung continues to court Chinese support (Ha and Jensen 1986: 148–54; Heinzig 1987: 30–33).

Gorbachev's new policy in Asia is based on a recognition that the policies of the past have largely failed. The expansion of Soviet military power in the region did not bring with it comparable political gains and, in fact, was important in pushing the Chinese toward Japan and the United States, in strengthening the security ties between Japan and the United States, and in preventing a meaningful expansion of relations with the countries of ASEAN. The new approach, which combines efforts at a new economic relationship with indications of some movement in the military area (for example, the commitment to withdraw SS-20s from Asia as well as Europe and the indication of a willingness to reduce military manpower along the Chinese border), coincides with the new thinking in Moscow.

New Political Thinking and the Future of Soviet Policy

We return now to the questions posed earlier concerning the meaning and implications of the debate on new political thinking for the future of Soviet foreign and security policy. Does the debate portend a substantive shift in Soviet policy, or does it merely concern the tactics to be employed to pursue more effectively policies long in place?

In responding to this question it is important, first, to outline the guidelines for Soviet policy that emerge from the discussions in Moscow. The first essential point is Gorbachev's recognition that significant improvement in the Soviet economy is the indispensable basis for future Soviet power in the world. He and his associates recognize that the positive assessment (from a Soviet perspective) of the "international correlation of forces" that dominated Soviet thinking in the 1970s was premature at best. It overestimated the role of military power in the ability of the Soviet Union to accomplish its foreign policy objectives and greatly underestimated the ability of the United States effectively to renew its military, political, and economic challenge to the USSR. What is required, if the Soviet Union is to become a full-fledged superpower in the twenty-first century, is a vital and vibrant Soviet society with an economic base from which to challenge continued U.S. predominance. Thus for the foreseeable future the Soviets will give priority to domestic economic reform and to the political and social "restructuring" necessary to accomplish this goal.

In order to accomplish these objectives, however, the Soviets require a period of respite from the global conflict that has characterized much of the past decade. An upsurge in international tension and an increase in military expenditures would exacerbate the difficulties of economic reform and dim the prospects for significant improvement in Soviet economic performance. Thus in the future the Soviets will pursue policies aimed at reducing international crisis and improving relations with the West—in other words, a policy that will permit the Soviets to devote their resources and attention to domestic concerns.

Yet this policy will not result in renewed isolationism or in a withdrawal from the international gains of the past. Rather, competition with the United States will continue, as we have witnessed since Gorbachev's appointment as general secretary, but with different emphases. One of the major objectives of what can only be viewed as a reinvigorated Soviet diplomacy is to refurbish the image and credibility of the Soviet Union as a global power and, concomitantly, to undermine those of the United States. Soviet initiatives in the arms control area have already tended to force the United States on the defensive, as have the broadened Soviet diplomatic initiatives in the Middle East and the Persian Gulf region. Essential to current Soviet policy as well is a "normalization" of U.S.-Soviet relations, which would bring numerous benefits for the Soviet leadership. Most important would be the reduction of external pressure on the Soviet leaders at a time when they are concerned primarily with overcoming the long-neglected problems that challenge their domestic social and economic system. In addition, although Gorbachev has made quite clear that he will not pursue foreign economic policies that would result in dependence on the West, he does expect that the Soviet economy will benefit from increased trade, investment in the form of joint ventures, and technical know-how from the West.

A policy of retrenchment does not mean either abandonment of gains already made in the Third World or of the use of force when threats arise to valued clients or national interests. The Soviets will attempt to retain the gains of the past when the political costs are not exorbitant, even if this involves new commitments of support. Pressures on the West can also be maintained through indirect means, principally by taking advantage of conflicts between the industrial states and the developing world. Expansion of political and diplomatic contacts with key non-Communist developing states might bring far greater long-term benefits for the Soviets than their past emphasis on radical Marxist-Leninist regimes, such as those in Angola and South Yemen.

A restructured Soviet policy of this type implies the creation of alignment structures tilted against the United States that would incorporate a growing range of developing countries; meantime direct military competition with Washington is reduced. These alignments could build on the cleavages within the Western alliance and on the inherent anti-Americanism wide-spread in the developing world, including that in countries currently closely tied to the United States (Rubinstein and Smith 1985), and would aim at shifting the burden of "containing" the United States to Soviet clients and to states opposed to U.S. policies, even though they might be capitalist and firmly within the Western sphere of influence. A Soviet Union that saw itself as an integral part of the existing international system rather than as the besieged center of a competing alternate system would likely be even more pragmatic in its search for allies and friends and in the policies that it pursued than the USSR has been to date. Moreover, it would probably be more successful in establishing the type of global role that so far has eluded the Soviet leadership.

The lines of future policy that emerge from the recent Soviet discussions of new thinking, as well as from Soviet behavior, appear to go beyond mere tactical modifications in past policy. Agreement on a reduction of the Soviet nuclear arsenal and expanded efforts to establish contacts with non-Marxist regimes in the Third World that are not based primarily on military relations are more than mere tactical modifications of past policy. However, even if these changes are meant only as tactical modifications of existing strategy, they can have longer term implications for the evolution of Soviet policy. Given that the motivation for the new thinking in Moscow is based on the desire to rebuild Soviet economic capabilities and to refurbish the USSR's international image and claims to superpower status, this process is likely to be an extended one, as Gorbachev himself has admitted. Yet a long-term policy of the type outlined earlier may bring the seeds of more fundamental change in Soviet domestic and foreign policy.[16] One result might be the lessening over time of the overt military threat posed by the Soviet Union and the emergence of Soviet international behavior more in line with that of a traditional great power.

By no means does this imply that U.S.-Soviet competition will lessen or that the Soviets will cease to challenge U.S. interests. In fact a revitalized Soviet Union armed with economic and political capabilities to match its military strength would in many ways be a more formidable competitor than it has been in the past. It would be more capable of benefiting from the conflicts among Western states and those between the West and the developing world, were it not viewed as a potential security threat by the leaders of so many countries and were it able to provide economic alternatives to the West.

The Soviets would present a more variegated and more complex challenge to U.S. interests—one that continued, though on a reduced basis, to employ its military might to accomplish important goals but also that could count on stable alignments with non-Marxist governments. Yet that challenge would be less fraught with the dangers of military confrontation between the two superpowers. Moreover, new thinking is likely to survive only if it produces success in terms of the Soviet ability to accomplish its international interests more effectively than have the policies of the past. It will require success in the reform programs currently being put in place that enable the USSR to play a more effective international economic role. Its continuation will also depend on the U.S. response to Soviet initiatives. Were the U.S. to continue to pursue a policy based on maximizing military capabilities, new thinking would likely be adversely affected.

The requirements of the policy discussed here also imply profound dilemmas. There is the long-standing issue of choosing between ideological clients and bourgeois elements whose revolutionary credentials are intrinsically flawed. Support for the latter may arrest or defeat promising movements (as in South Africa) and undermine what has been achieved (such as in Nicaragua). The choice is more complex than simply choosing between interparty and state-to-state priorities. The choice confronting the Soviets is whether to remain isolated within their own socialist system or to draw on the greater resources and stimulus of the nonsocialist world to spur internal techno-economic growth. The latter requires accommodating themselves to a world in which the Soviet model of socialism is less attractive and also reconciling central Party control with the demands of a more competitive market.

In the process of accommodation and adaptation, the Soviet Union runs the risk of losing its revolutionary soul and the confidence of its allies in the developing world. Worse, it may set adrift the European provinces of its empire, the anchor of its external power. As Gorbachev's visit to Romania in summer 1987 revealed, Moscow may be in competition with its own clients for favor from the West. For different reasons its own internal reforms may also incite greater destabilizing forces within the Eastern bloc. A conservative counterreaction to reform in Eastern Europe and heightened worker dissatisfaction, arising from expectations of harder work with no immediate prospect for material gain or greater freedom, may produce a coalition of the right and the left in Eastern Europe, with adverse repercussions on the stability of the Gorbachev regime itself. Although the logic of perestroika and "new political thinking" is strong and no doubt attractive, resistance to it remains strong as well.

Notes

1. Even prior to assuming the position of general secretary Gorbachev emphasized the interrelatedness of Soviet domestic and foreign capabilities. In December 1984, for example, he stated (1984: 1):

> The course of intensification is dictated by objective conditions, by the entire course of development of the country. There are no alternatives. Only an intensive economy, developing on a state-of-the-art scientific-technical base, can serve as a reliable material base for increasing the welfare of workers, guaranteeing the strengthening of the position of the country in the international arena, ensuring that it will deservingly enter the new century as a great and prospering power.

2. The present discussion of the meaning and importance of Gorbachev's political report has benefited greatly from the studies of Glickham (1986), Timmermann (1986), and Wettig (1987b). For a commentary by a noted Soviet analyst, see Sanakoyev (1986).

3. Gorbachev himself repeated and expanded upon many of these points in a major article (1987b: 1, 2). This was followed by an interview with Evgenii Primakov (1987b) in which he referred to Gorbachev's article as "the quintessence of ideas that enable one to understand the new Soviet approaches to world problems, how we regard the world today, and what it will be like in the near future."

4. See, for example, the works by Gromyko and Lomeiko (1984; 1986), Shakhnazarov (1984), Smirnov (1983), Maksimova (1979), and Men'shikov (1983). It is important to point out that these writings of the early 1980s concerning global problems and interdependence represented a minority, but expanding, view among Soviet analysts. The dominant position remained that of virtually total hostility and conflict between the USSR and the United States. For a discussion of the early Soviet "debate" on these issues, see Clemens (1978).

5. For a comprehensive examination of the views of Marshal Ogarkov and of other Soviet military analysts who argue for a renewed emphasis on conventional military capabilities, see FitzGerald (1986).

6. See, for example, Novopashin (1982). The present discussion has benefited from a

number of important treatments of changing Soviet interpretations of the Third World. These include, especially, works by Breslauer (1987), Fukuyama (1986a, 1986b, 1987a), Hough (1986), Papp (1985), Valkenier (1983, 1986), and Zamostny (1984).

7. See also Andropov's earlier article (1979: 2). The Party Program approved in 1986 (CPSU 1986a: 43) used virtually the same wording as that of Andropov when it noted that "every people creates, mostly by its own efforts, the material and technical base necessary for the building of a new society, and seeks to improve the well-being and cultural standards of the masses." On the costs of Soviet empire see Wolf, Brunner, Gurwitz, and Lawrence (1983), Wolf, Crane, Yeh, Anderson, and Brunner (1986), and, for a different interpretation, Spechler and Spechler (1988).

8. Cautioning his readers against overoptimism concerning developments in the Third World Ul'ianovskii (1984: 16) notes that the transition to socialism will be lengthy and "the fact that one party or another proclaims itself to be Marxist-Leninist and its revolution socialist does not change the essence of the matter." For a comprehensive examination of the evolution of Ul'ianovskii's thinking, see Stoecker (1986).

9. For a perceptive analysis of Gorbachev's views on security that relates them to actual policy initiatives, see Evangelista (1986). For assessments of the recent Soviet discussion on "reasonable sufficiency" in defense, see Wettig (1987a, 1987d).

10. On verification see Gorbachev (1986a: 56); on military spending see Gorbachev (1986a: 52), where he states: "Today we can declare with all responsibility that the defense capability of the U.S.S.R. is maintained on a level that reliably protects the peaceful life and labors of the Soviet people." Compare this with comments by former General Secretary Brezhnev (1982: 1) made shortly before his death: "We should tirelessly strengthen the defenses of our country and be vigilant. . . . The level of combat readiness of the army and navy should be even higher." The replacing of Defense Minister Marshal Sergei Sokolov by the relatively unknown and politically unconnected General Dmitrii Iazov in June 1987 (supposedly because of inadequacies in the Soviet air defense system exposed by the flight of a small private plane from Finland to Moscow) is part of a house-cleaning in the military, comparable to those that have already occurred in the Party leadership, which has already enhanced Gorbachev's decision-making flexibility. See Rahr (1987c) and Schroder (1987: 7–11).

11. However, virtually no Western analyst believes that even with the best of luck, the Soviets will be able to accomplish the stated goal of closing the technology gap with the West by the end of the century. The policies being advocated by Gorbachev are based on a strategy that includes mobilizing production reserves in the labor pool through greater discipline and efficiency, modernization of the capital stock of the Soviet economy, and reform and restructuring of the economy in order to facilitate implementation of the first two aspects of the strategy. Essential to the success of the entire program is an increase in the amount of investment funds available. Given already high levels of investment in the Soviet economy, it is very doubtful that they can be increased without at least a short-term reduction in military expenditures. For excellent overviews of current Soviet economic strategy, see the chapter by John E. Tedstrom in this volume and Losch (1986). For other discussions of the Soviet domestic economic reform, see Hewett (1988) Hohmann (1986), Amann (1986), and Goldman (1987).

12. The entire review of recent Soviet foreign policy has benefited from the substantive chapters in Kolodziej and Kanet (1989).

13. Similar conclusions are reached in Rubinstein (1986: 363), Gelman (1986: 245–46), and Herrmann (1987).

14. An example of the changed tone of Soviet writing about China can be found in Matyayev (1987). The author presents a basically accurate and at times even sympathetic

picture of Chinese economic reform. For excellent treatment of the change in mutual perceptions, see the studies by Rozman (1985, 1987); also see Hart (1987).

15. Recently the Soviets signed a fishing agreement with Vanuatu. An earlier agreement with Kiribati, signed in 1985, was not renewed. By late 1987 the Soviets maintained diplomatic relations with eight of the twenty-two states of the South Pacific. See Heinzig (1987: 36–37) and Herr (1987).

16. For an innovative and provocative discussion of the possibility of change and learning in Soviet ideology as the framework within which Soviet policy is formulated, including both the stimuli and the impediments to change, see Breslauer (1987).

References

Abele, Daniel (1986). "The Soviet Diplomatic and Trade Offensive among the ASEAN Countries." *Radio Liberty Research Bulletin*, RL 333/86, August 12.
—— (1987). "Recent Soviet Moves in the Persian Gulf Region." *Radio Liberty Research Bulletin*, RL 307/87, August 10.
Adams, Jan S. (1987). "Institutional Change and Soviet National Security Policy." Presented at "A Third Revolution in Soviet National Security Policy?" seminar sponsored by the Mershon Center, The Ohio State University, Columbus, Ohio, October 29–30.
Akhromeev, Sergei F. (1987). "Doktrina predotvrashcheniia voiny, zashchity mira i sotsializma." *Problemy mira i sotsializma*, 12, 24–26.
Albright, David E. (1987). *Soviet Policy toward Africa Revisited*. Significant Issues Series, 9(6). Washington, DC: Center for Strategic and International Studies.
Amann, Ronald (1986). "The Political and Social Implications of Economic Reform in the USSR." In Hans-Hermann Hohmann, Alec Nove, and Heinrich Vogel, eds., *Economics and Politics in the USSR: Problems of Interdependence*. Boulder, CO: Westview Press.
Andropov, Iurii V. (1979, February 23). "Pod znamenem Lenina, pod voditel'stvom Partii." *Izvestiia*, p. 2.
—— (1983) "Rech' General'nogo Sekretaria TSK KPSS Tovarishcha Iu. V. Andropova." *Kommunist*, 9, 4–16.
Banerjee, Jyotmirnoy (1987). "Moscow's Indian Alliance." *Problems of Communism*, 36(1), 1–12.
Bialer, Seweryn, and Joan Afferica (1986). "The Genesis of Gorbachev's World." *Foreign Affairs*, 64(3), 605–44.
Bovin, Aleksandr (1984, November 12). "Difficult Roads of Freedom." *Izvestiia*, p. 5. Translated in *Current Digest of the Soviet Press*, 36(48), December 26, p. 3.
—— (1987). "Breakthrough." *Moscow News*, 10, 3.
Boysen, Sigurd (1987). "Gorbatschows Abrustungsvorschlage: Politische und militarische Bewertung der sowjetischen Abrustungsinitiativen 1985/86." *Berichte des Bundesinstituts for ostwissenschaftliche und internationale Studien*, 1, 1–70.
Breslauer, George W. (1987). "Ideology and Learning in Soviet Third World Policy Today." *World Politics*, 39(3), 429–48.
Brezhnev, Leonid (1982, October 28). "Soveshchanie voenachal'nikov v Kremle." *Pravda*, p. 1.
Brown, W. (1987). "Soviet Union Promises Syria and Libya More Military Aid." *Radio Liberty Research Bulletin*, RL 212/86, May 30.
Brutents, Karen (1982, February 2). "Sovetskii Soiuz i osvobodivshiesia strany." *Pravda*, p. 4.

—— (1984a). "Dvizhenie neprisoedineniia v sovremennon mire." *Mirovaia ekonomika i mezhdunarodnye otnosheniia*, 5.

—— (1984b). "Osvobodivshiesia strany v nachale 80kh godov." *Kommunist*, 3, 102–13.

Clemens, Walter C., Jr. (1978). *The U.S.S.R. and Global Interdependence:' Alternative Futures*. Washington, DC: American Enterprise Institute for Public Policy Research.

Clough, Michael, ed. (1986). *Reassessing the Soviet Challenge in Africa*. Berkeley: University of California, Berkeley, Institute of International Studies.

CPSU (1961, November 2). "Programma Kommunisticheskoi Partii Sovetskogo Soiuza." *Pravda*, pp. 3–8.

—— (1986a). "The Programme of the Communist Party of the Soviet Union. A New Edition." *New Times*, 12, 20–48.

—— (1986b). "Rezoliutsii XXVII s"ezda Kommunisticheskoi Partii Sovetskogo Soiuza po politicheskomu dokladu Tsentral'nogo Komiteta KPSS." *Kommunist*, 4, 81–98.

Deane, Michael J. (1976). "The Correlation of World Forces." *Orbis*, 20(3), 625–37.

Dibb, Paul (1986). *The Soviet Union: The Incomplete Superpower*. Urbana-Chicago: University of Illinois Press.

Dobrynin, Anatolii (1986). "Za beziadernyi mir, navstrechu XXI veku." *Kommunist*, 9, 18–31.

Evangelista, Matthew (1986). "The New Soviet Approach to Security." *World Policy Journal*, 3(4), 561–99.

FitzGerald, Mary C. (1986). "Marshal Ogarkov on the Modern Theater Operation." *Naval War College Review*, 39(4), 6–25.

Ford, Peter (1987, June 8). "Nicaragua Looks to Latin America as Soviets Appear to Limit Aid." *Christian Science Monitor*, pp.1, 11.

Foreign and Commonwealth Office (1987). "Soviet Interest in Latin America." *Background Brief*. London: Author.

Fukuyama, Francis (1986a). "Gorbachev and the Third World." *Foreign Affairs*, 44(4), 715–31.

—— (1986b). *Moscow's Post-Brezhnev Reassessment of the Third World*. RAND Report no. R-3337-USDP. Santa Monica, CA: RAND Corporation.

—— (1987a). "Patterns of Soviet Third World Policy." *Problems of Communism*, 36(5), 1–13.

—— (1987b). *Soviet Civil-Military Relations and the Power Projection Mission*. Santa Monica, CA: RAND Corporation.

Gelman, Harry (1986). "Gorbachev's Dilemmas and His Conflicting Foreign-Policy Goals." *Orbis*, 30(2), 245–46.

Glickham, Charles (1986). "New Directions for Soviet Foreign Policy." *Radio Liberty Research Bulletin*, Supplement 2/86, September 6, pp. 1–26.

Goldman, Marshall I. (1987). *Gorbachev's Challenge: Economic Reform in the Age of High Technology*. New York: Norton.

Gorbachev, Mikhail S. (1984, December 11). "Zhivoe tvorchestvo naroda. Doklad tovarishcha M.S. Gorbacheva." *Pravda*, p. 1.

—— (1985, May 22). "Rech' Tovarishcha M. S. Gorbacheva." Presented during a state visit of Prime Minister Rajiv Gandhi of India. *Pravda*, p. 2.

—— (1986a). "Politicheskii doklad Tsentral'nogo Komiteta KPSS XXVII S"ezdu Kommunisticheskoi Partii Sovetskogo Soiuza. Doklad General'nogo Sekretaria TsK KPSS Tovarishcha Gorbacheva M. S. 25 Feveralia 1986 goda." *Kommunist*, 4, 5–80.

—— (1986b, July 29). "Rech' Tovarishcha Gorbacheva M.S. na Torzhestvennom

Sobranii posviashchennom Vnycheniiu Vladivostoku Ordena Lenina."*Pravda*, pp. 1–3.

—— (1987a). *Perestroika: New Thinking for Our Country and the World.* New York: Harper & Row.

—— (1987b, September 17) "Real'nost' i Garantii Bezopasnogo Mira." *Pravda*, pp. 1, 2.

—— (1988a, January 11). "Otvety M. S. Gorbacheva na Voprosy Redaktsii Zhurnala 'Liaovan.'" *Pravda*, p. 1.

—— (1988b, December 8). "M. S. Gorbachev's Speech at the U.N. Organization." *Pravda*, pp. 1–2. Translated in Foreign Broadcast Information Service (FBIS), *Daily Report: Soviet Union*, December 8, pp. 11–19.

Gromyko, Anatolii, and Vladimir Lomeiko (1984). *Novoe myshlenie v iadernyi vek.* Moscow: Mezhdunarodnye otnosheniia.

—— (1986). "New Way of Thinking; New Globalism." *International Affairs*, 5, 15–27.

Ha, Joseph M., and Linda Beth Jensen (1986). "Soviet Policy Toward North Korea." In Jae Kyu Park, Byung Chul Koh, and Tae-Hwan Kwak, eds., *The Foreign Relations of North Korea: New Perspectives.* Boulder, CO: Westview Press; Seoul: Kyungnam University Press.

Haass, Richard N. (1987). "The 'Europeanization' of Moscow's Asia Policy." *SAIS Review*, 7(2), 127–41.

Hanson, Philip (1987a). "The Reform Debate: What Are the Limits." *Radio Liberty Research Bulletin*, RL 237/87, June 23.

—— (1987b). "Reforming the Foreign-Trade System." *Radio Liberty Research Bulletin*, RL 104/87, March 19.

Hardt, John P. (1988). "Changing Perspectives toward the Normalization of East-West Commerce." In Gary K. Bertsch, ed., *Controlling East-West Trade and Technology Transfer: Power, Politics, and Policies.* Durham, NC: Duke University Press.

Harsch, Joseph C. (1987, June 2). "Kuwait, the U.S. and Moscow." *Christian Science Monitor*, p. 15.

Hart, Thomas G. (1987). *Sino-Soviet Relations: Re-examining the Prospects for Normalization.* Aldershot-Brookfield: Gower Publishing.

Heinzig, Dieter (1987). "Sowjetische Asian- und Pazifikpolitik unter Gorbatschow: Dynamik in Richtung Osten" *Berichte des Bundesinstituts fr ostwissenschaftliche und internationale Studien*, 26.

Herr, Richard A. (1987). "The Soviet Union in the South Pacific." In Ramesh Thakur and Carlyle A. Thayer, eds., *The Soviet Union as an Asian Pacific Power: Implications of Gorbachev's 1986 Vladivostok Initiative.* Boulder, CO: Westview Press; Melbourne: Macmillan Australia.

Herrmann, Richard (1987). "Regional Conflicts and Soviet Security: 'New Thinking,' Changing Policies, or Old Patterns?" Presented at "A Third Revolution in Soviet National Security Policy?" seminar sponsored by the Mershon Center, The Ohio State University, Columbus, Ohio, October 29–30.

Hewett, Ed A. (1988). *Reforming the Soviet Economy: Equality versus Efficiency.* Washington, D.C.: The Brookings Institution.

Hohmann, Hans-Hermann (1986). "The Place of Economic Policy Objectives on the List of Soviet Political Priorities." In Hans-Hermann Hohmann, Alec Nove, and Heinrich Vogel, eds., *Economics and Politics in the USSR: Problems of Interdependence.* Boulder, CO: Westview Press.

Hough, Jerry F. (1986). *The Struggle for the Third World: Soviet Debates and American Options.* Washington, DC: The Brookings Institution.

—— (1988). *Opening Up the Soviet Economy*. Washington, DC: The Brookings Institution.

Iakovlev, Aleksandr N. (1986). "Mezhimperialisticheskie protivorechiia — sovremennyi kontekst." *Kommunist*, 17, 3–17.

—— (1987). "Dostizehnie kachestvenno novogo sostoianiia sovetskogo obshchestva i obshchestvennye nauki." *Vestnik Akademii Nauk SSSR*, 6, 51–80.

Joliffe, Jill (1987, May 4). "Rising Tension in Angola Heightens Nation's Reliance on Soviets." *Christian Science Monitor*, pp. 18, 19.

Kanet, Roger E. (1987a). "Commentary (on Soviet Foreign Economic Relations)." In John P. Hardt and Richard F. Kaufman, eds., *Gorbachev's Economic Plans. Study Papers Submitted to the Joint Economic Committee, Congress of the United States*, vol. 2. Washington, DC: U.S. Government Printing Office.

—— (1987b). "Soviet Propaganda and the Process of National Liberation." In U.S. Department of State, *Contemporary Soviet Propaganda and Disinformation*, no. 9536, edited by Albert L. Salter with the assistance of William J. Colligan. Washington, DC: U.S. Government Printing Office.

—— (1987c). "The Soviet Union and the Third World from Khrushchev to Gorbachev: The Place of the Third World in Evolving Soviet Global Strategy." In Roger E. Kanet, ed., *The Soviet Union, Eastern Europe, and the Developing States*. Cambridge: Cambridge University Press.

Kapitonov, Ivan (1983). "A Working Class Party, the Whole People's Party: 80th Anniversary of the Second Congress of the RSDLP." *World Marxist Review*, 36(7).

Kautsky, E. (1988). "Bonn and Moscow: At the Threshold of a New Era?" *Radio Free Europe Research Report*, BR/1, January 8.

Keller, Bill (1987, May 25). "USSR Expands Contacts with Third World." *New York Times*, pp. 1, 4.

Kifner, John (1987, May 11). "Soviet Acts to Win Back Influence in Mideast." *New York Times*, pp. 1, 6.

Kimura, Hiroshi (1986). "The Soviet Military Buildup: Its Impact on Japan and Its Aims." In Richard H. Solomon and Masataka Kosaka, eds., *The Soviet Far East Military Buildup: Nuclear Dilemmas and Asian Security*. Dover, MA: Auburn House.

—— (1987). "Soviet Focus on the Pacific." *Problems of Communism*, 36(3), 1–16.

Kolodziej, Edward E., and Roger E. Kanet, eds. (1989). *The Limits of Soviet Power in the Third World: Thermidor in the Revolutionary Process*. London: Macmillan; Baltimore: Johns Hopkins University Press.

Kosygin, Alexei (1971, April 7). "Direktivy XXIV S'ezda KPSS po piatiletnemu planu razvitiia narodnogo khoziaistva SSSR na 1971–1975 godu." *Pravda*, p. 6.

Lebedev, Yuri (1987). "Why SS-20 Missiles Have Appeared." *Moscow News*, 11, 3.

Legvold, Robert (1988). "Gorbachev's New Approach to Conventional Arms Control." *The Harriman Institute Forum*, 1(1).

Levy, Sam (1985, August 6). "Though Marxist, Mozambique Is Shifting toward the West." *Christian Science Monitor*, p. 14.

Lobov, Vladimir (1988). "The Armed Forces and the New Thinking." *New Times*, 8, 12–13.

Losch, Dieter (1986). "The USSR's Economic Strategy up to the Year 2000: Aims, Methods and Chances of Success." *Intereconomics: Review of International Trade and Development*, 21(4), 203–9.

MacFarlane, S. N. (1985). *Superpower Rivalry and Third World Radicalism: The Idea of National Liberation*. Baltimore, MD: Johns Hopkins University Press.

Maksimova, M. (1979). "Vsemirno khoziaistvo, nauchno-tekhnicheskaia revoliutsiia i mezhdunarodnye otnosheniia (chast' vtoraia)." *Mirovaia ekonomika i mezhdunarodnye otnosheniia*, 5, 21–33.

Manning, Robert A. (1987–88). "Moscow's Pacific Future." *World Policy Journal*, 5(1), 55–78.

Matyayev, Vitali (1987). "Some Aspects of China's Socio-Economic Development." *International Affairs*, 11, 86–95.

Menon, Rajan (1986). *Soviet Power and the Third World*. New Haven, CT: Yale University Press.

Men'shikov, S. M. (1983). "Global'nye problemy i budushchee mirovoi ekonomiki." *Voprosy filosofii*, 4, 102–15.

Michaels, Julia (1987, October 1). "Shevardnadze's Visit to Brazil Brings Talk of Apples Oranges — and Increased Trade," *Christian Science Monitor*, pp. 7, 8.

Mukerjee, Dilip (1987). "Indo-Soviet Economic Ties." *Problems of Communism*, 36(1), 13–25.

Nahaylo, Bogdan (1986). "Recent Soviet Policy towards Southern Africa." *Radio Liberty Research Bulletin*, RL 196/86, May 20, esp. 2–5.

Novopashin, Iurii (1982). "Vozdeistvie real'nogo sotsializma na mirovoi revoliutsionnyi protesess: methodologicheskie aspekty." *Voprosy Filosofii*, 8, 3–16.

Odom, William E. (1985). "Soviet Force Posture: Dilemmas and Directions." *Problems of Communism*, 34(4), 6–14.

Ogarkov, N. V. (1983, May 9), "Pobeda i sovremennost.'" *Izvestiia*, p. 2.

Papp, Daniel (1985). *Soviet Perceptions of the Developing World in the 1980s: The Ideological Basis*. Lexington, MA: Lexington Books.

Plimak, E. G. (1986, November 14). "Marksizm-leninizm i revoliutsionnost' konca XX veka." *Pravda*, pp. 2, 3.

—— (1987). "Novoe myshlenie i perspektivy sotsial'nogo obnovleniia mira." *Voprosy filosofii*, 6, 73–89.

Polkowski, Andreas (1987). "The Soviet Union in Search of a New Economic Model." *Intereconomics: Review of International Trade and Development*, 22(6), 307–8.

Pond, Elizabeth (1988, January 15). "Kohl Hails Thaw in West German, Soviet Relations." *Christian Science Monitor*, p. 10.

Ponomarev, Boris (1984). "Real Socialism and the Liberated Countries." *Slovo Lektora* 3. Translated in FBIS, *Daily Report: Soviet Union*, annex, 3, June 14, pp. 2–6.

Poznanski, Kazimierz (1987). *Technology, Competition, and the Soviet Bloc in the World Market*. Berkeley: University of California, Berkeley, Institute of International Studies.

Press, Robert M. (1987, April 7). "Soviets Lead Angola Buildup." *Christian Science Monitor*, pp. 1, 8.

Primakov, Evgenyi (1987a, July 16). Excerpts of an interview with Primakov in Paul Quinn-Judge, "Soviet Shift in World Policy." *Christian Science Monitor*, pp. 1, 10.

—— (1987b). "In the Same Boat" *New Times*, 42, pp. 14–15.

—— (1987c, July 10). "Novaia filosofiia vneshnei politiki." *Pravda*, p. 4.

Rahr, Alexander (1986). "Winds of Change Hit Foreign Ministry." *Radio Liberty Research Bulletin*, RL 274/86, July 16.

—— (1987a). "The Apparatus of the Central Committee of the CPSU." *Radio Liberty Research Bulletin*, RL 136/87, April 10.

—— (1987b). "The Ouster of Boris El'tsin—The Kremlin's 'Avant-Gardist.'" *Radio Liberty Research Bulletin*, RL 506/87, December 18.

—— (1987c). "Red Square Landing Shakes up Top Military." In Vojtech Mastny, ed., *Soviet-East European Survey, 1986–1987: Selected Research and Analysis from Radio Free Europe/Radio Liberty*. Boulder, CO: Westview Press, 135–38.

Rozman, Gilbert (1985). *A Mirror for Socialism: Soviet Criticisms of China*. Princeton: Princeton University Press.

—— (1987). *The Chinese Debate about Soviet Socialism, 1978–1985*. Princeton: Princeton University Press.

Rubinstein, Alvin Z. (1986). "A Third World Policy Waits for Gorbachev." *Orbis*, 30(2), 355–64.

Rubinstein, Alvin Z., and Donald E. Smith, eds. (1985). *Anti-Americanism in the Third World: Implications for U.S. Foreign Policy*. New York: Praeger.

Sanakoyev, Shalva (1974). "The World Today: Problem of the Correlation of Forces." *International Affairs*, 11, 40–50.

—— (1986). "27th Congress on Soviet Foreign Policy Main Directions." *International Affairs*, 19, 9–20.

Scalapino, Robert A. (1987). *Major Power Relations in Northern Asia*. Latham, IL: University Press of America.

Schroder, Hans-Henning (1987). "Gorbatschow and die Generale: Militrdoktrin, Rostungs-politik und offentliche Meinung in der 'Perestrojka.'" *Berichte des Bundesinstituts für ostwissenschaftliche und internationale Studien*, 45.

Shakhnazarov, G. Kh. (1974). "K probleme sootnosheniia sil v mire." *Kommunist*, 3, 77–89.

—— (1984). "Logika politicheskogo myshleniia v iadernuiu eru." *Voprosy filosofii*, 5, 63–74.

Shevardnadze, E. A. (1988). "Shevardnadze Speech to July Conference Noted." *Vestnik Ministerstva Innostrannykh Del SSSR*, August 12. Translated in FBIS, *Daily Report: Soviet Union*, Annex, September 22, pp. 1–24.

Simes, Dimitri K. (1987). "Gorbachev: A New Foreign Policy?" *Foreign Affairs*, 65(3), 477–500.

Smirnov, G. L. (1983). "Za reshitel'nyi povorot filosofkhikh issledovanii k sotsial'noi praktike." *Voprosy filosofii*, 9, 3–19.

Sobell, Vladimir (1986). "The USSR and the Western Economic Order: Time for Cooperation?" *Radio Free Europe Research*, BR/128 (East-West Relations), September 15.

Spechler, Dina R., and Martin C. Spechler (1988). "The Economic Burden of Soviet Empire: Estimates and Reestimates." In Rajan Menon and Daniel N. Nelson, eds., *The Limits of Power*. Lexington, MA: Lexington Books.

SSSR, Ministerstvo Vneshnei Torgovli (1983, 1986). *Vneshniaia Torgovlia SSSR*. Moscow: Finansy i Statistika.

Stephan, John J. (1987). "Japanese-Soviet Relations: Patterns and Prospects." In Herbert J. Ellison, ed., *Japan and the Pacific Quadrille: The Major Powers in East Asia*. Boulder, CO: Westview Press.

Stoecker, S. W. (1986). *R. A. Ulianovsky's Writings on Soviet Third World Policies, 1960–1985*. RAND Report no. P-7177. Santa Monica, CA: RAND Corporation.

Teague, Elizabeth (1986). "How Widespread Is Popular Dissatisfaction with Gorbachev's Policies." *Radio Liberty Research Bulletin*, RL 472/86, December 17.

—— (1987a) "Gorbachev Answers His Critics." *Radio Liberty Research Bulletin*, RL 280/87, July 15.

—— (1987b). "Signs of a Conservative Backlash." *Radio Liberty Research Bulletin*, RL 474/87, November 18.

Timmermann, Heinz (1986) "Gorbatchows aussenpolitische Leitlinien: Die internationale

Beziehungen Moskaus auf dem 27. Parteitag der KPdSU." *Berichte des Bundesinstituts für ostwissenschaftliche und internationale Studien*, 13.

——— (1987). "Die sowjetische Westeuropapolitik unter Gorbatschow." *Berichte des Bundesinstituts für ostwissenschaftliche und internationale Studien*, 15.

Ul'ianovskii, Rostislav (1984). "O natsional'noi i revol'iutsionnoi demokratii: puty evol'iutsii." *Narody Azii i Afriki*, 2.

Valkenier, Elizabeth Kridl (1983). *The Soviet Union and the Third World: An Economic Bind*. New York: Praeger.

——— (1986). "Revolutionary Change in the Third World: Recent Soviet Reassessments." *World Politics*, 38(3), 415–34.

van England, Claude (1987, August 12). "Iran Set to Pipe Oil through Soviet Union." *Christian Science Monitor*, p. 1.

Volskii, Dmitrii (1983). "Local Conflicts and International Security." *New Times*, 5, 5–7.

Weeks, Albert L., compiler (1987). *Soviet Nomenklatura: A Comprehensive Roster of Soviet Civilian and Military Officials*. Washington, DC: Washington Institute Press.

Wettig, Gerhard (1987a). "Has Soviet Military Doctrine Changed?" *Radio Liberty Research Bulletin*, RL 465/87, November 20.

——— (1987b). "Das 'neue Denken' in der UdSSR—ein Abrocken von alter Klassenpolitik?" *Berichte des Bundesinstituts für ostwissenschaftliche und internationale Studien*, no. 12.

——— (1987c). "A New Soviet Approach to Negotiating on Arms Control." *Berichte des Bundesinstituts für ostwissenschaftliche und internationale Studien*, no. 2.

——— (1987d). "Sufficiency in Defense—A New Guideline for the Soviet Military Posture?" *Radio Liberty Research Bulletin*, RL 372/87, September 23.

Wolf, Charles, Jr., Keith Crane, K. C. Yeh, Susan Anderson, and Edmund Brunner (1986). *The Costs and Benefits of the Soviet Empire, 1981–1983*. RAND Report no. R-3419-NA. Santa Monica, CA: RAND Corporation.

Wolf, Charles, Jr., K. C. Yeh, Edmund Brunner, Jr., Aaron Gurwitz, and Marilee Lawrence (1983). *The Costs of the Soviet Empire*. RAND Report no. R-3073/1-NA. Santa Monica, CA: RAND Corporation.

Zamostny, Thomas J. (1984). "Moscow and the Third World: Recent Trends in Soviet Thinking." *Soviet Studies*, 36, 223–35.

Zhurkin, Vitalii, Sergei Karaganov, and Adrei Kortunov (1987a). "O razumnoi dostatochnosti." *SShA: Ekonomika, Politika, Ideologiia*, 12, 11–21.

——— (1987b). "Reasonable Sufficiency—or How to Break the Vicious Circle." *New Times*, 40, 13–15.

——— (1988). "Vyzovy bezopasnosti—starye i novye." *Kommunist*, 1, 42–50.

• CHAPTER THIRTEEN •

Arms Control in Soviet National Security Policy under Gorbachev

Robert L. Arnett
U.S. Department of the Army

In March 1985 Mikhail Gorbachev became general secretary of the Communist party of the Soviet Union. Since then the Soviet Union has signed the INF Treaty, agreed in principle to major reductions in strategic nuclear weapons and conventional forces in Europe, and called for a complete ban on chemical weapons. Western officials have been given access to Soviet military installations at Shikhany, Krasnoyarsk, and Gomel. In addition, Gorbachev has publicly advocated a "new political thinking" that includes such concepts as "mutual security," "reasonable sufficiency," and "asymmetric reductions." Do these intitiatives represent a major change in Soviet national security policy? More specifically, has there been a change in Soviet thinking regarding arms control and the role it plays in supporting Soviet national security policy? Furthermore, if there has been a major change, what factors have led to the alteration of arms control policy? To analyze possible recent changes in policy it is useful to begin by briefly examining the history of arms control in Soviet national security policy.

Soviet Arms Control Policy before Gorbachev

Soviet interest in arms control and disarmament dates from at least 1921
(Petrovskii 1984: 6). Since that time Soviet officials have made countless
proposals calling for the banning, limitation, or elimination of almost every
type of means of warfare (Vigor 1986).

During the period from the early 1920s to 1959, Soviet leaders realistically expected little from their arms control and disarmament proposals
except for the propaganda value. During most of the 1930s, as the
threat of war increased until the end of World War II, Soviet interest
in arms control and disarmament understandably disappeared. After the
war Stalin's main interest in arms control was for its propaganda value—
especially in inhibiting or blocking the U.S. buildup of nuclear weapons.

During Khrushchev's early years as first secretary the main objective and
role of arms control in Soviet national security policy continued to echo
the past. Thus, Soviet arms control policy during this period (1921–59) was
basically limited to supplementing Soviet diplomatic efforts to influence
foreign public and leadership opinion.[1]

Between 1959 and March 1985 arms control began to play an expanded
role in Soviet national security policy.[2] Soviet leaders signed eighteen
arms control treaties, agreements, and protocols. For the first time Soviet
leaders realistically saw potential for arms control measures—beyond
merely propaganda value—which had military and economic value and
which could reduce the likelihood of nuclear war. In their view the USSR
was very forthcoming in its approach to verification, a key issue in arms
control.

Gaining military value from arms control did not become a reality for
Soviet leaders until the early 1970s, when the SALT I agreements were
signed. According to a former Soviet official,[3] Soviet leaders feared an
unrestrained arms race at that time because of U.S. economic, technological, and military advantages.[4] According to the official,

> There was . . . serious interest in getting an agreement on SALT. The Soviet
> leadership craved parity with the United States. Additionally, the Politburo's
> anxiety about the uncertain outcome of a spiraling competition for strategic
> advantage was paralleled by increasing concern about the costs entailed in
> its military program. . . . Moreover, America's unquestionable lead in vital
> computer technology had aroused Soviet fears that the United States might
> emerge the winner in the arms rivalry. (Shevchenko 1985: 201–2)

Soviet leaders also pointed to the military value of the ABM Treaty
(as part of SALT I). Marshal Viktor Kulikov, then chief of the General

Staff, stated, "The [ABM] Treaty signed on May 26 of this year halts the further buildup of ABM defense systems in the USSR and the United States, which prevents the emergence of a chain reaction of competition between offensive and defensive arms" (quoted in Barsukov 1972: 2).

Soviet participation in the SALT I agreements, therefore, is one example of their recognition of the military value achievable through arms control. The Soviets were able to avoid widespread ABM deployments at a time when it was not to their advantage, and were able to limit offensive system deployments to levels more in line with their military plans.

Although for many years Soviet leaders have made it clear that defense of the country is the top priority, they have also been painfully aware of the cost of such a decision. In his memoirs, Khrushchev revealed,

> When I was the leader of the Party and the Government, I decided that we had to economize drastically in the building of homes, the construction of commercial services, and even in the development of agriculture in order to build up our defenses. (Talbott 1970: 516)

Soviet officials have long been aware that arms control can result in both direct and indirect economic benefits. The SALT I agreements in 1972, however, probably afforded the Soviets their first realistic expectation of such advantages. The direct benefit of the agreement was addressed by V. Kuznetsov, then first deputy foreign minister when he noted that large expenditures could be saved by avoiding an ABM race as well as the large buildup of offensive weapons which would likely result from the defensive system deployments (*Pravda* 1972: 2). He wrote:

> The mutual renunciation of the development of ABM systems on a nationwide scale provided for by the treaty places both sides in the same position from the viewpoint of security and makes it possible to avoid the large expenditures in which the sides would have been involved in developing ABM systems. Moreover, a race in the field of ABM defense would inevitably cause both sides to suffer additional expenditures on offensive strategic forces with a view to increasing their ability to overcome the other side's ABM defense. (*Pravda* 1972: 2)

A former Soviet official also has described Soviet expectations of direct economic benefits of the SALT II agreement. According to Arkady Shevchenko, Georgii Arbatov was asked at a private party of Soviet officials in 1976 why there was a need to speed up the SALT negotiations. Arbatov "reiterated arguments about the connection between arms-spending and the failing health of the Soviet economy" (Shevchenko 1985: 47).

The potential direct economic benefits of SALT II were also mentioned by another Soviet, who noted,

> But at the same time it is an incontestable fact that, but for the new treaty, there would inevitably be a further escalation of the strategic offensive arms race and a new twist in the spiral with all the ensuing unfavorable consequences for the stability of the strategic situation and a steep rise in military spending. (Platonov 1979: 22)

Potential indirect economic benefits of arms control come about because such agreements can contribute to the creation of better relations between nations, which in turn creates the possibility for greater access to trade and technology.

Soviet leaders, like their U.S. counterparts, have long been concerned about the possibility that a nuclear war might be triggered by accident or as the result of a misunderstanding. The Cuban missile crisis in October 1962 almost made that fear a reality. As a result, the Soviet Union joined the United States in June 1963 in signing the "Hot Line" Agreement, which established a means for rapid communications between the leaders of both countries.[5]

In 1971 the Soviet Union also signed the bilateral agreement on "Measures to Reduce the Risk of Outbreak of Nuclear War." The agreement provided for several risk reduction measures including "advance notification of any planned missile launches beyond the territory of the launching party and in the direction of the other party" (U.S. Arms Control and Disarmament Agency 1982: 110).

Soviet interest in arms control as a means to reduce the likelihood of war is evident in their signing the Non-Proliferation Treaty in July 1968. The treaty sets forth measures to prevent the further spread of nuclear weapons to other nations. V. Yemelanov spoke of the importance of the treaty to the USSR:

> It is easy to imagine how greatly the danger of a nuclear conflict would increase and how the achievement of international agreements of arms limitation and disarmament would be made more difficult if the present so-called 'nuclear club' was joined by new members. . . . The threat is quite real.
>
> Special danger may come from the acquisition of A-bombs by countries situated in the so-called 'hot spots' of the globe. . . . A nuclear conflict in any of these areas may spark off a general nuclear war. (Yemelanov 1982: 5–6)

In looking at the pre-Gorbachev history of arms control, it is clear that arms control has had propaganda value. Historically Soviet propaganda efforts have been directed toward achieving a variety of objectives. The immediate purpose, of course, is to influence foreign public and leadership opinion for both general and specific objectives. At the general level, propaganda efforts are intended to portray the Soviet Union in a favorable light while attaching negative connotations to its opponents. Soviet proposals for general and complete disarmament or for nuclear disarmament, for example, are aimed at presenting the Soviet Union as a peace-loving nation while casting those who do not accept the proposals as opponents of peace. Beyond this general objective, Soviet proposals can have specific objectives. The long-held proposal to eliminate all foreign military bases, for example, is not only intended to reflect favorably upon the Soviet Union but also would have been advantageous if carried out. Two main specific objectives of Soviet propaganda efforts before Gorbachev have included disrupting relations between the United States and its allies and undermining Western domestic support for military programs and actions. Thus propaganda, if successful, can have military value in addition to its usefulness in supplementing Soviet diplomatic efforts.

Soviet awareness of the propaganda value of arms control is clearly evident in the timing and manner of Soviet proposals. V. Petrovskii, for example, in discussing Soviet disarmament proposals of the 1920s and early 1930s, notes that "though Soviet efforts failed to bring tangible results they nonetheless had a tremendous political effect in promoting sympathies toward the USSR in the remotest parts of the globe" (Petrovskii 1984: 29). Discussing Soviet disarmament proposals in the late 1940s and early 1950s, when the United States had a nuclear monopoly, he noted that "the struggle for banning the new weapons of mass destruction was not waged in vain. It mobilized democratic public opinion, with which the U.S. government had to reckon" (Petrovskii 1984: 29). The propaganda value of arms control proposals was clearly evident during the Khrushchev era. In his memoirs Khrushchev admitted that his proposal to dismantle both the NATO and Warsaw Pact alliances "was intended to serve a propagandistic, rather than a realistic purpose" (Talbott 1974: 410). In addition, a former Soviet official from the Ministry of Foreign Affairs disclosed that Khrushchev had lectured him about the propaganda value of arms control, saying:

Never forget the appeal that the idea of disarmament has in the outside world. . . . A seductive slogan is the most powerful political instrument. The

Americans don't understand that. They only hurt themselves in struggling against the idea of general and complete disarmament. (Shevchenko 1985: 101–2)

Petrovskii, in discussing the Soviet concept of disarmament, admitted,

It is very important to make use of all the factors of peace, according to the Soviet concept of disarmament, and the public has a special role to play here. The idea of disarmament, once it has taken hold of the mass of people, can become an important material force in world politics. (1984: 6)

From 1959 to 1985, a period in which arms control agreements were signed which affected both U.S. and Soviet military capabilities, the issue of verification became extremely significant. The perception in the West was that the Soviets were resisting adequate verification. The Soviet view was quite different.

Soviet officials have argued that the Soviet Union has always been an advocate of reliable verification (Timerbaev 1984). Prior to the Gorbachev era, the basic Soviet view was that satellite photography or other nonintrusive collection efforts, called national technical means (NTM), were adequate for verification and that the United States was trying to use other means of verification to spy on the USSR. Soviet fears of foreign knowledge of Soviet military "secrets" are well known. In his memoirs Khrushchev wrote about why the Soviet Union opposed a U.S. proposal for on-site inspection made in the 1960s:

We couldn't allow the U.S. and its allies to send their inspectors criss-crossing around the Soviet Union. They would have discovered that we were in a relatively weak position, and that realization might have encouraged them to attack us. (Talbott 1974: 536)

Other Soviet officials have also accused the United States of proposing verification for improper reasons: "In the West the substance of the question is in fact often reduced to gaining an opportunity for spying on the structure and activity of the Soviet Armed Forces. It is obvious the Soviet Union cannot agree to such control" (Mozgovoi 1986: 5).

Before Gorbachev was selected as general secretary, Soviet officials also argued that NTM was more than adequate for the arms control agreements in effect and under consideration. For example, "both sides have among their national technical facilities, space, radiometric and other apparatus capable of obtaining the necessary data to verify the other side's observance of its commitments" (Platonov 1979: 21).[6] In

1984 R. Timerbaev wrote a book that provided a detailed examination of the verification means used in various arms control agreements. He concluded that the verification means used—national technical means, exchange of information, consultations, and international procedures —were adequate. As far as on-site inspection (OSI) was concerned, Timerbaev concluded that "this method of verification is advisable only for exceptional instances, e.g., when all the other techniques cannot yield the desired result and ensure confidence that the obligations assumed by the Parties are fully honored" (Timerbaev 1984: 90).

In May 1984 a top official on the Soviet General Staff, General-Major Y. Lebedev, wrote a major article in *Pravda* on the Soviet view of verification. He argued that in monitoring the fulfillment of agreements, "indisputable priority" must be given to NTM "which are most in accordance with the state's interests" (1984: 4). OSI is conspicuously absent in his discussion:

> Additional measures can be adopted to help enhance the effectiveness of verification by national technical means. This means, first and foremost, notification of various kinds, the exchange of quantitative data about armaments, and assigning appropriate distinguishing marks to certain categories of arms. Other measures of this kind could also be elaborated. But in any event they must not serve as an instrument for interference in internal affairs or be detrimental to any side. The USSR is categorically against "inspectors" like those which the United States has put forward at various times—the notorious "Baruch plan," the "open sky" concept, and others frankly of an intelligence nature. (Lebedev 1984: 4)

This view would change markedly under Gorbachev.

Arms Control under Gorbachev

It is clear that after Gorbachev became general secretary in March 1985, he ordered a reexamination of Soviet national security policy. That reexamination led to what the Soviets call "new political thinking" based on current realities. The new thinking has led to new concepts and new initiatives in Soviet national security policy and arms control policy.

Gorbachev has advocated four concepts that have potentially significant implications for arms control: mutual security, reasonable sufficiency, asymmetric reductions, and on-site inspections. At the broadest level, Gorbachev has called his new approach to international relations one of mutual security as opposed to the concept of unilateral security. Under the old concept each nation builds its military forces and conducts foreign policy to increase its security unilaterally. Gorbachev argues, however, that this policy has led to a continuing increase in the levels of parity of nuclear weapons. The result, he claims, is a decrease in the security of all nations involved, and therefore he maintains that new approaches must be undertaken to deal with national security problems.

The second major concept deriving from the new political thinking is reasonable sufficiency. Semeiko explained the difference between previous and current thinking on what military forces are needed to ensure Soviet national security:

> The old thinking proceeds in principle from the idea of "the more, the better," the idea that gaining military supremacy over an opponent can almost automatically guarantee a victorious outcome in a potential war.
>
> The new thinking denies this confrontationist approach. It favors a minimum and not a maximum of military might for both and favors excluding the idea of seeking a military solution to disputed international problems. (Semeiko 1987: 5)

The concept was first publicly proclaimed in late 1985 and was reiterated in Gorbachev's political report to the Twenty-Seventh Party Congress in February 1986. Public leadership support for the concept was slow in coming. It was not until mid-1987 that widespread public leadership support was evident. Since that time the concept has been widely discussed.[7]

In July 1987 the minister of defense defined the concept as it related to both nuclear and conventional forces:

> When we speak of maintaining the armed forces and our military potential at a level of reasonable sufficiency, we have in mind that at the present stage the essence of sufficiency regarding the Soviet strategic nuclear forces is determined by the need to prevent anyone getting away with impunity with a nuclear attack in any, even the most unfavorable, circumstances. As for conventional means, sufficiency amounts to a quantity and quality of armed forces and armaments capable of reliably ensuring the collective defense of the socialist community. (Iazov 1987: 5)

The following month, Dr. Semeiko discussed the political, military, and economic aspects of the concept (1987: AA2–AA5). The political aspect is the emphasis on political solutions to international disputes, the stress on reducing the level of military confrontation, and strengthening strategic stabilty through arms limitations and reductions to reasonable limits. The military aspect involves the reduction and restructuring of military forces so other nations do not feel threatened, but to levels that are sufficient to rebuff any surprise attack. The economic aspect, discussed in part in the chapters by John E. Tedstrom, Hans Heymann, Jr., and Richard W. Judy, involves recognition of the diminishing returns acquired from further increasing the levels of military spending and the saving of resources that can result from the concept.

A third new concept raised by Gorbachev—asymmetic reductions— also has important potential implications for arms control. The concept involves the recognition that for a variety of reasons, an asymmetry has developed in the armed forces of the Warsaw Pact and NATO. The Warsaw Pact has the lead in certain elements, such as tanks, while NATO has a lead in other categories, such as anti-tank weapons. Soviet officials suggest that it is possible to negotiate an agreement that would eliminate the asymmetries that cause the most concern to Warsaw Pact and NATO leaders. The Soviets make it clear, however, that resolving the asymmetries must be accomplished by reducing the forces of the side with the advantage, not by increasing the forces of the other side (Gorbachev 1987: AA23). The concept was apparently first mentioned in public by Gorbachev in February 1987, a year after he put forth the concept of reasonable sufficiency. This new idea next surfaced in May 1987.

A fourth concept of significance to arms control that Gorbachev advanced was that of on-site inspections. The notion was not new to the Soviets; it had been acknowledged and discussed for many years by Soviet spokespersons. The basic Soviet position before Gorbachev, however, was that NTM was sufficient and that OSI might be required only in exceptional circumstances. As a result Soviet reluctance on verification (especially OSI) had long been an important impediment in the negotiations on START, INF, MBFR, LTBT, and the chemical arms talks.

The public Soviet view on this issue changed significantly under Gorbachev. In January 1986 in a major speech on arms control, Gorbachev suggested that the Soviet position on OSI had changed. He offered OSI as a means to verify (1) the reduction and elimination of nuclear weapons, (2) a ban on nuclear testing, (3) the destruction of chemical weapons, (4) a ban on space weapons, and (5) the reduction of troops in Europe ("Statement" 1986: AA1–AA9).

Gorbachev's proposal received the support, at least in public writings, of Soviet military officials. General-Major Yuri Lebedev, noted earlier as resistant to OSI in his 1984 article in *Pravda*, apparently changed his view:

The Soviet Union continues to advocate verification by national technical means. . . . However, in applying definite agreements, the Soviet Union

is ready to expand verification measures to include on-site inspections.
(Lebedev 1986: 6)

Other Soviet military officials have espoused the new policy. In March 1986
General of the Army and Deputy Minister of Defense for Armaments V.
Shabanov, wrote that "other measures [for verification] may be adopted
up to and including on-site inspection" (1986: 5).

New concepts, however, do not necessarily mean a change in policy.
It is necessary to examine whether Soviet actions have echoed the new
pronouncements.

INF. When Gorbachev became general secretary (March 11, 1985), the
Soviet Union was not even involved in formal negotiations in Geneva
with the United States on INF. Soviet officials had walked out of the
negotiations almost sixteen months earlier, in November 1983. Even when
negotiations resumed in Geneva (March 12, 1985), the United States and
the Soviet Union were far apart in their proposals. Over time, however,
the Soviet position changed. The Soviets dropped their demands that
an INF agreement be contingent on progress in other negotiations, all
medium-range nuclear forces be included (as opposed to just missiles),
British and French nuclear forces be included, and the reductions apply
only to Europe. In addition, they broke with their earlier position and
agreed to intrusive verification measures. The result was an agreement
signed in December 1987 whereby both sides agreed to the elimination
and future ban on all medium-range and shorter-range INF missiles.

The change in the Soviet position was significant in several respects.
First, the Soviets agreed to major reductions in INF missiles. This was
a U.S. objective in the negotiations. Second, the Soviets agreed to
asymmetric reductions in forces. The Soviet Union will be required to
destroy systems capable of carrying more than 1500 nuclear warheads
whereas the United States will destroy systems that could carry only about
400. In addition, the Soviet Union will destroy about 100 shorter-range
missiles; NATO has no missiles in that range to destroy. Third, the Soviet
Union has agreed to unprecedented verification measures. Detailed data
on forces were exchanged. Both sides will be allowed on-site inspection
to verify the destruction of the INF missiles and associated equipment and
will be able thereafter to visit "declared facilities" on short notice if there
is any suspicion of illegal activity. In addition, the United States will be
allowed inspectors at the SS-20 plant at Votkinsk.

START. In December 1983, at the end of the fifth round of START
negotiations in Geneva, the Soviet Union refused to agree on a date for
the next round of talks. Thus when Gorbachev became general secretary,
there had been no formal negotiations on strategic arms for over a year.

Negotiations began the day after he was selected in a new forum in Geneva —the nuclear and space talks (NST).

Initially under Gorbachev there was no indication that the Soviet position on START would change. The Soviets called for modest reductions from the SALT II levels and did "not acknowledge sufficiently the need to go beyond national technical means to guarantee effective verification of an agreement" (U.S. Department of State 1984: 2).

The first indication of change under Gorbachev regarding START became evident in the fall of 1985. The Soviet proposal presented in Geneva, though containing serious drawbacks from the U.S. perspective, for the first time accepted the principle of deep reductions which the United States had long advocated. Setbacks have occurred since that time. Serious differences remain in the negotiations, but overall there has been movement toward resolving differences. From the U.S. perspective, the major impediments include Soviet insistence on linking the agreement to what amounts to a ban on SDI, as well as refusal to accept certain sublimits, reductions on throwweight, and a ban on mobile missiles.

Although these serious problems remain, progress has been made under Gorbachev. In addition to the acceptance of 50 percent reductions, the Soviet Union has agreed to reduce its heavy ICBMs by half (an issue of great importance to the United States), and advances have been made for counting bombers. According to the United States, the unusually specific Soviet draft proposal of July 31, 1987 "was a necessary step in the process of negotiating a START agreement" (U.S. Department of State 1987c: 1). In addition, the Soviet Union has agreed in principle on important verification procedures, although agreement on acceptable procedures still remains to be reached.

Conventional Arms Talks

The United States and the Soviet Union have been negotiating since 1973 to reduce conventional forces in Central Europe. The fourteen years of negotiations, known as the Mutual and Balanced Force Reduction (MBFR) Talks, have made little progress. Major impediments include serious disagreement over verification measures required, the types of reductions (proportional or asymmetric), and the basic data base (that is, agreement on the actual number of Warsaw Pact troops in the area).

Since Gorbachev became general secretary, Soviet officials have publicly indicated greater flexibility on the verification issues, called for

major reductions in forces, urged the expansion of the geographic area
covered by the talks, and claimed that asymmetries should be corrected.
Gorbachev's December 7, 1988 announcement of a unilateral reduction of 500,000 men and 10,000 tanks suggests that over time there
is the potential for significant progress in conventional arms control
talks.

Confidence building measures for Europe. Modest progress has been
made at the Conference on Confidence- and Security-Building Measures
and Disarmament in Europe (CDE). In September 1986 the Soviets
agreed for the first time to allow on-site inspection on Soviet territory.
The agreement was part of a set of measures designed to increase openness
and predictability of military activities in Europe. In August 1987, as a
result of the agreement, U.S. officials conducted the first on-site inspection
of a Soviet military exercise.

Nuclear testing. Before Gorbachev assumed leadership no progress was
being made on the issue of nuclear testing. The 1974 Threshold Test
Ban Treaty (TTBT) and the 1976 Peaceful Nuclear Explosions Treaty
(PNE) had yet to be ratified by the United States. Moreover, no formal
negotiations had been held since November 1980. Discussions were at an
impasse over the issue of verification and the immediate objective of the
negotiations. The United States wanted stricter verification measures and
to focus negotiations on enabling verification of the 1974 and 1976 treaties.
The Soviets had a different view of what was required for verification
and wanted negotiations to focus immediately on a comprehensive test
ban.

Gorbachev's first initiative was an attempt to put political pressure on
the United States to halt nuclear tests at least while negotiations were
under way. In July 1985 Gorbachev announced a unilateral moratorium
to begin August 6 and to extend until December 31, 1985. He later
extended the moratorium several times. It finally ended in February
1987.

The moratorium certainly had a propaganda aspect—it began on the
fortieth anniversary of the U.S. bombing of Hiroshima. At the same
time, as the moratorium was extended Soviet military leaders expressed
concern about the decision.[8]

In addition to the moratorium, Gorbachev has undertaken practical steps
that have addressed some U.S. concerns. In November 1987 formal negotiations on nuclear testing began in Geneva after the seven-year-hiatus.
The Soviets accepted the immediate objective as being to work out verification measures for the 1974 and 1976 treaties. Progress has also been made
on the issue of verification. The Soviet Union has shown greater flexibility
on verification since Gorbachev's January 1986 speech on arms control.

The latest example is the agreement reached during the November 1987 negotiations to allow inspections of each country's nuclear test sites and to allow monitoring of several nuclear tests on each other's territory (Smith 1987: A23).

Chemical weapons talks. Under Gorbachev some progress has been made in negotiations to ban chemical weapons. During the summer of 1986 at the forty-nation Conference on Disarmament, the Soviets "agreed in principle to allow foreign inspectors to witness dismantling of chemical arms factories and broadly accepted United States approach on how to define a chemical weapon" (McCartney 1986: A28). Two major unresolved issues related to when countries should say publicly where their chemical weapons are located, and the U.S. insistence on mandatory on-site inspections if a nation is suspected of cheating. At the Conference on Disarmament in February 1987, however, the Soviets announced a willingness "to declare the location of all chemical weapon stockpiles shortly after a treaty is signed" and a willingness "to accept inspections on short notice of suspected chemical weapon facilities, except in cases where 'supreme' national interests would be jeopardized" (Smith 1987a: A6). In April Gorbachev announced that the Soviet Union had halted the production of chemical weapons and that a special plant was being constructed to destroy such weapons (TASS 1987: April 10). In December the Soviet Union announced that it had about 50,000 tons of chemical weapons in its arsenal (Nazarkin 1988: 6).[9] In October Western officials were invited to tour the Soviet chemical weapons production facility at Shikhany (Bohlen 1987: A17, A20). Progress is likely to be slow in this area, however, because controlling or eliminating chemical weapons is a complex matter and because many other nations will need to be involved in these negotiations.

Nuclear risk reduction. In September 1987 the United States and the Soviet Union signed an agreement to establish Nuclear Risk Reduction Centers in Washington, D.C., and Moscow. The centers will exchange information required under arms control and confidence-building agreements to help prevent the risk of conflict that might result from misinterpretation, accident, or miscalculation.

Defense and space talks. Under Gorbachev no progress has been made on defense and space issues. The United States has expressed concern about the long-term Soviet commitment to strategic defense and has stood firm in its commitment to evaluate the potential of the Strategic Defense Initiative. The Soviet Union, in turn, has made strict adherence to the ABM Treaty (and thus eventually undermining the SDI effort) a primary objective. As a result, the defense and space talks in Geneva remain at an impasse.

Strategy, Role, and Objectives of Arms Control under Gorbachev

There is evidence of both continuity and change in Soviet arms control strategy and objectives since Gorbachev took office. Like his predecessors, Gorbachev considers arms control proposals, negotiations, and sometimes agreements as playing a role in Soviet national security policy. Furthermore, like his predecessors (at least since 1959), Gorbachev perceives arms control as having potential propaganda, military, and economic value as well as helping to reduce the likelihood of war.

Under Gorbachev the timing and nature of certain arms control proposals and initiatives are clearly designed to influence foreign public opinion and foreign nations' actions. Arms control proposals continue to be made which are intended to divide the United States and its allies and to undermine support for Western military programs and actions.

The INF Treaty illustrates the continuing perception that arms control/reductions can have military value. Soviet leaders, as did U.S. leaders, evidently concluded that it was militarily beneficial to agree to eliminate and ban long-range and shorter-range INF missiles.

Soviet proposals regarding strategic nuclear weapons, conventional weapons and defensive systems suggest a continuing interest in the potential economic value of arms control. The perception that arms control contributes to improved relations and creates the possibility for greater access to trade and technology is currently evident. Finally, the Soviet signing of the agreement to set up risk reduction centers indicates a continuing belief that certain arms control measures can help to reduce the likelihood of war by accident.

In addition to continuity, however, changes in Soviet arms policy have occurred in Gorbachev's term. As discussed in Jan S. Adams's contribution to this volume, there is evidence that Gorbachev has altered the arms control decision-making process. The organizational scope of advice he receives has been expanded. Civilian institutes, for example, have a greater potential for influencing policy, especially in preventing decisions from being made on narrow military considerations.

Apparently the role of arms control policy has been elevated to play a greater role in Soviet national security policy. Gorbachev's words and actions indicate a belief that Soviet national security interests are not always best served by military solutions. The INF Treaty, the real possibility of major reductions in strategic nuclear weapons, and greater acceptance of intrusive verification measures suggest an interest in arms control as opposed to military solutions to resolve national security problems and concerns.

There has also been significant change in what is acceptable in arms control agreements. Two changes stand out: acceptance of major force reductions, and intrusive verification measures. In official negotiations Soviet leaders have long resisted agreements that called for major force reductions. The INF Treaty, however, as well as the agreement in principle in START for 50 percent reductions, clearly indicates a significant change in Soviet policy. Likewise, the verification measures agreed to in the INF Treaty, and accepted in principle in other ongoing negotiations, also reflect change in arms control policy that has occurred under Gorbachev. The concepts that Gorbachev has put forward—mutual security, reasonable sufficiency, and asymmetric reductions—also create the possibility for further significant arms control agreements.

Overall, both continuity and change in arms control policy have occurred under Gorbachev. The changes, however, are significant and have contributed to the signing of the INF Treaty and have made possible further arms control agreement breakthroughs.

Reasons for Change under Gorbachev

At this point it appears that Gorbachev has made changes in arms control policy for both military and economic reasons. First, he and other top officials have expressed concern that certain aspects of the military policy followed up to now may not be the best means to deal with the national security challenges facing the Soviet Union. One aspect of military policy that has been challenged is the notion that the greater the emphasis on military might, the greater the influence and security of the Soviet Union. Although recognizing that military strength is the basis of Soviet superpower status and has prevented any serious threat to the homeland, Soviet leaders have indicated a belief that after a certain point there are diminishing returns in the further buildup of weaponry. This belief has been most explicitly stated with regard to nuclear weapons. According to Gorbachev, "Continuation of the arms race will inevitably heighten this equal threat and may bring it to a point where even parity will cease to be a factor of military-political deterrence" (1986: 81). According to the Minister of Defense, Army General D. T. Iazov,

> Does this mean that as the level of military equilibrium rises, the strategic situation in the world will remain stable, security will remain reliable? No, it does not. On the contrary, experience indicates that a further rise in the level of parity does not result in greater security. The continuation of the arms race inevitably increases the threat of war and can increase it to such an extent where even parity stops being a factor of military-political deterrence. (1987: 5)

Primakov also discussed the long-held view that increasing combat capability was the only practical way to maintain security at the proper level:

> Today such assessments and interpretations are clearly inadequate and inaccurate. Even though the improvement of the Soviet Union's defense capability is as important as ever, political means of ensuring its security are now coming to the fore. We are dealing with a fundamentally new situation. (Primakov 1987: 4)

Gorbachev and other leaders suggest, therefore, in contrast to past policy, that Soviet national security can be maintained and possibly enhanced with lower levels of military force. Living with lower levels of force, of course, depends on reductions in NATO and U.S. forces. Gorbachev's arms control proposals are designed to explore this possibility.

Arms control initiatives suggested by Gorbachev seem intended to supplement his major domestic initiatives to accelerate the country's economic development. He is clearly alarmed at the current weakness of the economic system for both domestic and national security reasons.[10] The Soviet economy has generally been able to support the demands of the military in the past, but there are questions as to how well it will be able to do so in the future.[11] As several of the previous chapters have indicated, there is a question whether his economic reforms can succeed without removing some of the drain of resources by the military.[12] The general secretary believes that arms control can aid his economic reform plans in several possible ways. First, certain arms control agreements can result in direct economic benefits. Significant reductions in conventional forces, for example, could free both manpower and resources.[13] Furthermore, arms control agreements can contribute to improving East-West relations. Improved relations, in turn, can reduce the necessity of unplanned military programs and increase the possibility of trade and technology transfer. Reducing or stabilizing the drain of resources by the military and increasing trade and acquisition of critical technology cannot solve Soviet economic problems, but they can make the monumental task easier. In addition, this economic rationale for changes in arms control policy is made possible only by the fact that Gorbachev also perceives a military rationale for his new policy, a matter discussed in Mary C. FitzGerald's chapter.

Support for Gorbachev's Arms Control Policy

Whether Gorbachev succeeds will depend on a variety of factors including continued support by other Soviet leaders. Gorbachev undoubtedly has significant support thus far for his arms control initiatives, or he could not have carried out the measures he has already implemented. At the same time, there has been some evidence of reluctance and concern regarding his policy. During his nineteen-month unilateral moratorium on nuclear testing, for example, certain military officials indicated their uneasiness over the policy.[14] In addition, the fact that it took a year for his concept of reasonable sufficiency to get widespread leadership support in public suggests that the notion may not have been readily accepted.[15] Furthermore, there is recent evidence of leadership concern about opposition or skepticism regarding the INF Treaty. Numerous newspaper articles have attempted to explain why the Soviet Union gave up many more missiles and warheads than did the United States. Charges have apparently been made that the United States out-negotiated the Soviet Union and that Soviet national security may have been damaged. In answering such concerns a Soviet colonel wrote:

> The fears of people unversed in these matters that we might have been "outdone" by the United States must be dispelled. Let us state bluntly: No. It is, in the final analysis, not a question of arithmetic but of a balance of interests, a balance of security. (Morozov 1987:3)

A similar response was made by the chief of the General Staff in December 1987.[16]

While some high-level Soviet officers were defending the INF Treaty, other military officials were expressing concern about the direction and extent of Gorbachev's new policy. Lieutenant General of Aviation V. Serebriannikov, for example, warned about overreliance on political means and underestimating the necessity of military means. To make his point he cited the disastrous policy followed just before World War II: "The political measures that were taken to avoid war were not correctly linked with concern over maintaining the Armed Forces at a high state of vigilance and combat readiness" (1987: 12). He warned, "an underestimation of proper military means can do a great deal of harm to the matter of defending socialist achievements" (p. 12). Serebriannikov also warned about the dangers of negotiating with the West.[17]

General Secretary Gorbachev's changes in arms control policy thus far have received sufficient support for him to sign the INF Treaty and to allow Western officials to visit Soviet military installations. At the same time, as can be expected when long-time policies are changed, there are indications that serious concerns and skepticism exist regarding the policy he has pursued.

Gorbachev and the Future of Arms Control

The changes in arms control policy under Gorbachev create the opportunity for arms control treaties on a variety of issues. Major reductions in strategic nuclear weapons is now considered a near-term possibility. There is optimism that verification measures can be worked out that would enable U.S. ratification of the 1974 and 1976 nuclear testing agreements. There are greater prospects for further confidence-building measures from the negotiations at the Conference on Disarmament. Some progress is being made on a treaty banning chemical weapons. There are even renewed discussions about potential progress of the talks on conventional arms reduction in Europe.

Several points of caution should be noted, however, in assessing the future of arms control under Gorbachev. The first relates to the extent to which Gorbachev intends to go in achieving various arms control and disarmament agreements. His concepts of reasonable sufficiency and asymmetric reductions can provide the basis for serious arms control negotiations. Thus far, however, the concepts are ill-defined. For conventional reductions, for example, how much are Soviet leaders actually willing to cut back? What level is sufficient from their perspective? It is not clear that these issues have even been resolved in the Soviet Union. In addition, the appealing notion of asymmetric reductions—especially regarding conventional forces—is yet to be explored. The Soviets may be willing to make such reductions, but at what price to NATO?

The INF Treaty is evidence that Gorbachev is serious about implementing these concepts and allowing the types of verification which the United States believes are necessary. His December 1988 announcement of unilateral conventional force reductions is a further indication that he may intend to use reasonable sufficiency as a criterion for Soviet military force levels. It will be a greater test of Soviet intentions as the West finds out what Gorbachev has in mind in applying his concepts to the START and conventional force reduction talks. In addition, Soviet conduct in the implementation of the INF verification measures will be an important litmus test.

The future of arms control under Gorbachev, however, is not limited simply by how far he plans to go in his policy. It also depends upon how far he is *able* to go. As noted earlier, concern and skepticism have been expressed among Soviet officials about his arms control policy thus far. Allowing increasing numbers of U.S. inspectors to visit Soviet military installations and significantly reducing strategic nuclear and conventional forces are likely to be perceived by many Soviets as quite risky and undesirable actions. The general secretary will therefore face ongoing and probably increasing levels of opposition and concern if he tries to implement further arms control initiatives.

What, then, are his prospects? In view of Gorbachev's demonstrated ability to handle formidable opposition, the odds are that we will see further significant changes in Soviet national security policy which will have a major impact on the Soviet military and will increase the likelihood of negotiated arms control agreements.

Notes

1. During this period the Soviet Union agreed to only one arms control agreement—the Geneva Protocol prohibiting the use of poison gas and bacteriological weapons—signed in 1928. The views expressed in this chapter are those of the author and do not necessarily represent the views of the Department of the Army or United States government.

2. For a comprehensive review of U.S.-Soviet relations from 1969 to 1984, including Soviet perspectives on arms control, see Garthoff (1985).

3. Arkady N. Shevchenko served with the Soviet Ministry of Foreign Affairs from 1956 to 1978. During his service he had the opportunity to travel with Khrushchev and serve as personal adviser to former Foreign Minister Andrei Gromyko. Shevchenko defected to the United States in 1978. In 1985, he published *Breaking With Moscow*, a book about his experiences working in the Soviet government.

4. Shevchenko also stated: "General Nikolai Alekseyev, Ogarkov, and other sophisticated military officers approached SALT as a means to achieve by negotiations what the Soviets feared they could not attain through competition: a restraint on America's ability to translate its economic and technological strength into military advantage and a breathing space during which the USSR would work to narrow the gap" (1985: 204).

5. For a discussion of the crisis and its consequences, see Garthoff (1987).

6. Platonov is a pseudonym for retired deputy foreign minister and ex-SALT negotiator V. S. Semenov.

7. For example, in May 1987 Gennadii Gerasimov, chief spokesman of the Ministry of Foreign Affairs, made some interesting statements regarding reasonable sufficiency to the Soviet people. He noted that Secretary of Defense Robert McNamara had reasoned that "to deter another country from attack, there was no need to adhere to the principle of the more the better." Then Gerasimov made a rather startling admission: "We are returning to this not particularly complex idea for securing the possibility of a destructive retaliatory strike against an aggressor." The motives of such a statement would be suspect if made to a Western audience. The fact that it was made to a Russian audience suggests that this claim represents more than mere propaganda (Gerasimov 1987: AA10–AA11).

8. For example, see the interview with Army General Y. P. Maksimov, commander in chief of the Strategic Rocket Forces (Moscow Television Service in Russian, September 4, 1986; translated in Joint Publications Research Service (JPRS), TAC-86-077, September 25, 1986, p. 42).

9. Six months earlier, Nazarkin, head of the Soviet delegation at the Geneva CBW talks, had claimed he did not know the size of the Soviet CBW stockpile (Interview with Yuri Nazarkin, *Le Figaro*. [Paris], August 17, 1987, p. 5; translated in JPRS TAC-87-057, September 18, 1987, pp. 66–67). In the interim there had been an obvious change in Soviet policy regarding discussions of the size of the Soviet stockpile.

10. Gorbachev discussed the seriousness of the economic problem at the Twenty-Seventh Party Congress in February 1986. "Difficulties began to build up in the economy in the 1970s, with the rate of economic growth declining visibly" (1986: 27). The problems, he argued, were continuing and becoming more serious in the 1980s. He charged that past economic policy "had failed to apprehend the acute and urgent need for converting the economy to intensive methods of development," and that it failed to actively use "the achievements of scientific and technological progress in the national economy" (p. 28). He proposed a radical economic program to deal with the problem.

Gorbachev ascribed considerable importance to solving the economic problems. He maintained that "implementation of the policy of acceleration [of the economic and social programs] will have far-reaching consequences for the destiny of our Motherland" (p. 30). For Gorbachev accelerating the country's socioeconomic development is not simply a matter of raising the standard of living for Soviet citizens. It is much broader and more important.

> In short, comrades, acceleration of the country's socio-economic development is the key to all our problems: immediate and long-term, economic and social, political and ideological, domestic and foreign. That is the only way a new qualitative condition of Soviet society can and must be achieved. (Gorbachev 1986: 26–27)

An article in *Kommunist*, the Party's main theoretical journal, in January 1988 warned that Soviet economic weakness was undermining national security:

> The known discrepancy between our country's enormous foreign policy role and relative economic and scientific-technological power has recently become increasingly alarming because it began to increase during the years of stagnation. The accumulation of negative trends in the USSR's economic development in the seventies and the early eighties began to affect more noticeably and dangerously the dynamics of the correlation of forces between the two systems. (Zhurkin, Karaganov, and Kortunov 1988: 48)

11. According to Viktor Afanaseev, for example, "without accelerating [the nation's socioeconomic] development it would be impossible to ensure . . . the country's defense" (1986: 83).

12. Dr. L. Semeiko, for example, has warned about the economic dangers of "surplus military might." In arguing for the concept of "reasonable sufficiency," Semeiko stated: "Furthermore, the desire for a surplus military might has inevitably always led to the slowing down of socioeconomic and technological processes. For 400 years the Roman Empire directed its technological achievements above all to military requirements. The result was stagnation in all spheres" (1987: 5).

13. Semeiko, for one, believes direct economic benefits from arms control are possible. He noted that the implementation of the concept of reasonable sufficiency "means saving the huge means and resources which every state and all mankind need so badly to resolve constructive tasks" (Semeiko 1987: 5).

14. *Vremiia* newscast, interview with Army General Y. P. Maksimov (Moscow Television Service in Russian, September 4, 1986; translated in JPRS, TAC-86-077, September 26, 1986, pp. 42–43). Khrushchev faced similar pressure from military leaders when he declared a unilateral moratorium on nuclear testing, see Talbott (1974: 69).

15. Gorbachev put forth the concept in late 1985 but few officials reiterated the concept until 1987.

16. See the interview with Marshal of the Soviet Union Akhromeev, (*Pravda*, December 16, 1987, p. 4; translated in FBIS, *Daily Report: Soviet Union*, December 16, 1987, p. 1).

17. Serebriannikov stated, "History provides many other examples where aggressors used negotiations and even 'adjustments' to relationships to weaken the vigilance of future enemies" (Serebriannikov 1987: 13).

References

Afanaseev, Viktor (1986, March). "Strategy of Acceleration, Strategy of Peace: M. S. Gorbachev: 'Selected Speeches and Articles.'" *Problemy mira i sotsializma*, no. 3, 83–85.

Akhromeev, Marshal of the Soviet Union S. F. (1987, May 9). "The Great Victory." *Krasnaia zvezda*, pp. 1–2. Translated in Foreign Broadcast Information Service (FBIS), *Daily Report: Soviet Union*, May 15, pp. V4, V5.

Barsukov, Yu. (1972, August 24). In the Interests of Strengthening Peace." *Izvestiia*, pp. 1–2.

Bohlen, Celestine. (1987, October 5). "Soviets Allow Experts to Tour Chemical Weapons Facility." *New York Times*, pp. A17, A20.

Garthoff, Raymond L. (1985). *Détente and Confrontation: American-Soviet Relations from Nixon to Reagan*. Washington, DC: The Brookings Institution.

—— (1987). *Reflections on the Cuban Missile Crisis*. Washington, D.C.: The Brookings Institution.

Gerasimov, Gennadii (1987). Moscow television service in Russian. May 24, 1987. Translated in FBIS *Daily Report: Soviet Union*, June 25.

Gorbachev, Mikhail. (1986). *Political Report of the CPSU Central Committee to the 27th Party Congress*. Moscow: Novosti Press Agency Publishing House.

—— (1987). Statement at forum, "For a Nuclear-Free World, for the Survival of Mankind." Moscow Television Service in Russian, February 16, 1987. Translated in FBIS, *Daily Report: Soviet Union*, February 17.

Iazov, Army General D. T. (1987, July 27). "The Military Doctrine of the Warsaw Pact Is the Doctrine of the Defense of Peace and Socialism." *Pravda*, p. 5. Translated in FBIS, *Daily Report: Soviet Union*, July 27, pp. BB1–BB7.

Lebedev, General-Major Y. (1984). "Concerning Washington's Speculations over Questions of Monitoring." *Pravda*. Translated in FBIS, *Daily Report: Soviet Union*, May 3, pp. AA1–AA4.

—— (1986, August 12). *Die Welt*, p. 6. Translated in Joint Publications Research Service (JPRS) TAC-86-070, August 29, p. 57.

Morozov, Colonel V. (1987, December 11). "From the Military Viewpoint: Balance of Security." *Trud*, p. 3. Translated in FBIS, *Daily Report: Soviet Union*, December 14, p. 29.

Mozgovoi, A. (1986, January 29). "A Barrier Against Nuclear Death into the 21st Century — Without Weapons." *Sovetskaia Rossiia*, p. 5. Translated in FBIS, *Daily Report: Soviet Union*, January 30, pp. AA6–AA8.

McCartney, Robert J. (1986, August 30). "Chemical Arms Talks End, Gains Claimed." *Washington Post*, p. A28.

Nazarkin, Y. K. (1987, August 17). Untitled interview with Nazarkin. *Le Figaro* (Paris), p. 5. Translated in JPRS TAC-87-057, September 18, pp. 66–67.

—— (1988, January 18). "Ridding the World of Chemical Weapons." *Pravda*, p. 6. Translated in FBIS, *Daily Report: Soviet Union*, January 19, pp.1–2.

Petrovskii, V. (1984). *The Soviet Concept of Disarmament*. Moscow: Nauka Publishers.

Platonov, A. A. (1979). "Major Achievement in the Sphere of Arms Limitation." *SShA: Ekonomika, Politika, Ideologiia*, 9, 14–23.

Potiarkin, Ye., and S. Kortunov (1986). *The USSR Proposes Disarmament*. Moscow: Progress Publishers.

Pravda (1972, September 30). "An Important Contribution to the Strengthening of Peace and Security." Pp. 1–2.

Primakov, Ye. (1987, July 9). "New Philosophy of Foreign Policy." *Pravda*, p. 4. Translated in FBIS, *Daily Report: Soviet Union*, July 14, p. CC5.

Semeiko, L. (1987, August 13). "Instead of Mountains . . . On the Principle of Reasonable Sufficiency." *Izvestiia*, p. 5. Translated in FBIS, *Daily Report: Soviet Union*, August 21, pp. AA2–AA5.

Serebriannikov, Lieutenant General of Aviation V. (1987, September). "Correlating the Political and Military Methods in the Defense of Socialism." *Kommunist vooruzhennykh sil*, no. 18, 9–16.

Shabanov, Army General V. (1986, March 24). "A Most Important Element in the Disarmament Process." p. 5. Translated in FBIS, *Daily Report: Soviet Union*, April 1, p. AA9.

Shevchenko, Arkady N. (1985). *Breaking With Moscow*. New York: Knopf.

Smith, R. Jeffrey. (1987a, February 18). "Soviets Offer Arms Concession." *Washington Post*, p. A6.

—— (1987b, November 21). "U.S., Soviets Move toward Treaty Revisions." *Washington Post*, p. A23.

"Statement by M. S. Gorbachev, General Secretary of the CPSU Central Committee." (1986, January 16). *Pravda*, pp. 1–2. Translated in FBIS, *Daily Report: Soviet Union*, January 16, pp. AA1–AA9.

Talbott, Strobe, ed. and trans. (1970). *Khrushchev Remembers*. Boston: Little, Brown.

—— (1974). *Khrushchev Remembers: The Last Testament*. Boston: Little, Brown.

TASS Report (1985, October 4). "For the Peaceful, Free, and Prosperous Future of Europe and All Other Continents: Meeting with the French Parliament." *Pravda*, p. 1. Translated in JPRS TAC-85-042, October 21, p. 55.

—— (1987, April 10). Untitled. Translated in JPRS TAC-87-034, May 29, p. 92.

Timerbaev, R. (1984). *Problems of Verification*. Moscow: Nauka Publishers.

U.S. Arms Control and Disarmament Agency (1982). *Arms Control and Disarmament Agreements: Texts and Histories of Negotiations*. Washington, DC: Author.

U.S. Department of State (1984, April). "START Proposals." *GIST*.

—— (1987a, January). "U.S. Arms Control Initiatives." Special Report 160. Washington, DC: U.S. Government Printing Office.

—— (1987b, July). "Negotiations on Intermediate-Range Nuclear Forces," Special Report 167. Washington, DC: U.S. Government Printing Office.

—— (1987c, September). "Negotiations on Strategic Arms Reductions." Special Report 169. Washington, DC: U.S. Government Printing Office.

—— (1987d, November 19). "U.S. Arms Control Initiatives: A Status Report." Special Report 171. Washington, DC: U.S. Government Printing Office.

—— (1987e, December). "INF Treaty: A Success Story." *GIST*.

Vigor, Peter. (1986). *The Soviet View of Disarmament*. New York: St. Martin's Press.

Yemelanov, V. (1982). *Problems of Non-Proliferation of Nuclear Weapons*. Moscow: Nauka Publishers.

Zhurkin, Vitalii V., Sergei A. Karaganov, and Andrei V. Kortunov (1988, January). "Old and New Challenges to Security." *Kommunist*, 1, 42–50.

PART FIVE

Conclusions and Implications

CHAPTER FOURTEEN

Toward an Explanation of Change in Soviet National Security Policy and Implications for the United States

George E. Hudson
Wittenberg University and The Mershon Center

We were shooting a film about the Tsarist days and had developed a marvelous scenario for it . . . a glamorous train, people with fur coats and jewels. The day after, we were reviewing the film and discovered that an old Russian woman with a shopping bag had walked onto the film set during the shooting and had ruined the whole thing.

—Yevgeny Yevtushenko

How often Soviet leaders discover that the best efforts for change turn into fruitless endeavors undercut by the conservatizing elements of Soviet society. No leader since the end of World War II has faced this challenge as much as has Mikhail Gorbachev.

As we have seen in the previous chapters, Gorbachev feels he must make important alterations in the fields of both domestic and foreign policy and, within the latter area, in the sensitive area of Soviet national security policy. For the Soviet Union, he recognizes, is bound to the international environment. "I state with full responsibility," he notes, "that our international policy is more than ever determined by domestic policy, by our interest in concentrating on constructive endeavors to improve our country" (Gorbachev 1987a).

This book lends credence to the proposition that changes in the domestic economic and political environments are major driving forces behind changes in national security policy under Gorbachev. Although change in Soviet policy is the theme of the book, it is clear too that conservative elements of the Soviet Union, including Party officials, bureaucrats, and common citizens, combine with other factors producing powerful forces to prevent change. A "radical revolution" or "third revolution" in Soviet national security policy is no surety as we enter the 1990s.

Yet as the previous chapters document, changes have occurred in national security ideas, policies, and behaviors. This gives rise to four important questions to which this chapter addresses itself:

—What are the patterns of change and continuity?
—Do those patterns point to enough broad conclusions about the
    conditions and preconditions for change in Soviet national security
    policy—that is, to sufficient information to advance an explanation
    about change?
—Do changes point to different objectives in Soviet policy?
—What are the implications of change for U.S. policy toward the Soviet
    Union?

Change and Continuity in the Elements of Soviet Security

In the first chapter we undertook to identify and define three areas of change in the elements of Soviet national security: security assumptions and ideas, the system of views on which plans for enhancing Soviet security are founded; policy, the authoritative statements of leaders; and behavior, the actions designed to utilize the elements of policy. It is probably under the rubric of ideas and assumptions that one finds the greatest changes, verging on the category of radical change.

The current Soviet leadership has called into question at least two main assumptions that have underpinned the formulation and implementation of Soviet national security policy. First is the view that national security means military security only, a view popular under the Brezhnev and previous administrations and with strong roots in tsarist history. Policy reforms since 1985 demonstrate that the emerging definition of national security has come to encompass some of the principles of the new thinking, as discussed in Chapter Three. Domestic and international economic and political issues share a priority with military ones. Chapters Four through

Six document numerous areas of change, including the enactment of the Basic Provisions to establish a new incentive structure, the reorganization of the Soviet foreign trading apparatus, the recognition that the future of Soviet military power is dependent on domestic economic reform, and the push toward computerization and robotics to modernize the Soviet economy. If successful, these efforts could make the USSR more competitive with other economic powers and could thereby enhance Soviet national power and security.

Changes in the economic dimension are accompanied by efforts to shore up the diplomatic arm, analyzed in Chapters Seven through Thirteen. These include sweeping changes in personnel and the institutions of Soviet foreign policy to enable the enactment of policy reform and the generation of new ideas, a different stance toward Western Europe, the establishment of mechanisms of consultation within the Warsaw Pact, the beginnings of resolving important conflicts in the Third World, and the approval and implementation of an intermediate-range arms reduction agreement. A surge of remarks about the importance of international bodies to help maintain security through agreements on such matters as better security for and safeguards on the operation of nuclear power plants (Hall 1987: 13–22) buttress the new emphasis. Thus diplomacy helps to broaden the definition of what constitutes national security, to include economic and political security along with military security.

The second assumption involves a significant change in the focus of Soviet military security. At least until 1977 Soviet policy had concentrated on nuclear weapons as the "fundamental basis" of Soviet military strength, following the pronouncements of Khrushchev and codified in the writings of Marshal V. D. Sokolovskii. Beginning with Brezhnev, however, and elaborated on since his death, Soviet doctrine has come to emphasize the importance of new types of conventional weapons as the tools of choice for future wars and the irrationality of utilizing nuclear weapons for anything other than intrawar deterrence. To this, as Chapter Nine discusses, Gorbachev has added his notion of reasonable sufficiency, still a somewhat cloudy concept but one that denotes that even under the precepts of the new doctrine, the Soviet Union does not have to remain armed to the teeth to ensure its protection against potential enemies. It also signifies a possible change of Soviet doctrine from a fixation on the offense to an emphasis on the defense. Such a notion has strong connotations for future allotments to and programs for Soviet national defense and, if implemented, can be termed radical.

New assumptions have been accompanied by new policies and behaviors. The most dramatic from the U.S. perspective involve Soviet willingness to discuss new arms control measures, some of which could even include the asymmetrical reduction of conventional forces in Europe, to accept an extraordinarily intrusive verification regime in the new INF arms control agreement, and to agree to asymmetrical reductions of nuclear forces in Europe, also in the INF agreement. These are changes in policy and behavior that appear in part to flow from a reassessment of old Soviet assumptions and which border on a significant change, as noted in Chapter Thirteen. Another dramatic, behavioral manifestation of new thinking in Soviet security is the withdrawal of Soviet troops from Afghanistan. This could portend less use of the Soviet military to enforce Soviet will around its borders, which would be a significant change in policy. Current Soviet policy in the Third World indicates that the USSR will be more cautious and more selective in finding Third World allies than was the case under the Brezhnev administration.

Yet there are clearly a number of other key assumptions to which the leadership continues to cling in evaluating its security. One of these is the belief that the fundamental concern of Soviet international security at the global level is relations with the United States. This means, as in the past, that Soviet national security policy and behavior will be measured partly in terms of its impact on the United States' response to Soviet initiatives and formulated partly as a response to U.S. policy. Thus the Soviet decision to invade Afghanistan in 1979 was likely made with the knowledge that it would deal a blow to Soviet-American relations. Yet it was also conducted partly as a response to failed Soviet efforts to improve Soviet security by undermining the NATO decision to deploy Pershing II and ground-launched cruise missiles and to obtain a ratified SALT II treaty. Soviet policy continues to have a strong U.S. bias under Gorbachev, as evinced in well-publicized Soviet efforts for new arms control agreements and in the vast importance the USSR places on summit meetings with the United States.

Western and Eastern Europe remain another important emphasis of Soviet national security concerns and contain strong elements of policy stability, as the authors of Chapters Ten and Eleven remind us. To be sure, this is partly a result of the competition with the United States for influence in Western Europe and of Soviet concern that the United States does not gain undue influence in Eastern Europe. Yet there are matters independent of the United States that continue to loom large under Gorbachev. Of importance today, as in the past, are desires for the transfer of technology from Western Europe, particularly from West Germany. This was true in the famed pipeline purchase, when the USSR purchased pipeline from the Germans in exchange for natural gas, and it is true today as the Soviets continue their push for increased East-West trade. Eastern Europe—and the control thereof under the still uncertain conditions of *glasnost'* and leadership change—remains a security focus of the USSR. Politically unstable conditions there could cause Soviet insecurity, possibly demanding the use of Soviet troops. Hegemony is still a measure of Soviet power.

A third point of continuity is the assumption that the Third World is a proper place for the USSR to seek influence. The Soviets continue to view the Third World as an important area where competition with the United States may be played out and from which the USSR may be able to exact economic as well as political gains. This is evident from reading the discussion of Chapter Twelve. Thus the USSR has not withdrawn military aid from Angola; in fact, it has actually increased assistance (MacFarlane 1988: 5). Soviet relations with China continue their importance too, as Gorbachev has followed the Soviet lead since 1980 in attempting to defuse the tensions between the two large nations.

Finally, a strong element of continuity is that although the economic and diplomatic arms of Soviet policy are to be strengthened, the military will remain an important element of Soviet national security in the future. Military power holds important sway in Soviet self-perceptions and will continue to do so. The presence of large Soviet military budgets, troops in Eastern Europe, military aid to Angola, and Soviet arms transfers throughout the world, capped by continuing military competition with the United States, are manifestations of this attitude.

Thus an examination of the elements of Soviet national security demonstrate many variations of change under the Gorbachev administration. Not only do patterns of change vary among the elements, but within themselves the elements show a mix of different kinds of change. Alterations in ideas and assumptions (including the military doctrine discussed in Chapter Nine) appear to come first and sometimes evince significant to radical change, as portrayed in Table 14.1. They are followed by changes in policy and behavior—areas that are more difficult to transform and which demonstrate mostly incremental to significant change, as seen in the entries for the policy/behavior chapters (Chapters Ten through Thirteen) in Table 14.1. An important point to remember from the investigation of the elements of security is that the Soviet Union still views itself as a nation wanting to exercise power like any other large country; one could expect nothing less. But the factors that constitute the Soviet measure of power have expanded to include economic and political power in addition to military force. A summary of changes is presented in Tables 14.1 and 14.2, although one should keep in mind the complex, mixed nature of change that the authors present in their chapters. The tables present the results according to the rate of change

TABLE 14.1
Change in the Elements of Security

	Stability	Incremental	Significant	Radical
Military doctrine (Chapter 9)				---X---
Western Europe (Chapter 10)			---X---	
Eastern Europe (Chapter 11)		---X---		
Third World (Chapter 12)			---X---	
Arms control (Chapter 13)			X	

TABLE 14.2
Change in the Change Agents

	Stability	Incremental	Significant	Radical
Intellectual ferment (Chapter 3)				---X---
Economics (Chapters 4–6)		X		
Leadership (Chapter 7)			X	
Institutions (Chapter 8)				---X---

(stability, incremental, significant, radical) and the chapter in which it is discussed. Table 14.2 will be examined in the next section.

Toward an Explanation of Change in Soviet Policy

But why have the changes portrayed in Table 14.1 occurred at all in Soviet national security affairs? What, in other words, is at work within the Soviet political process that produces reasonable sufficiency, new arms control policies, or a withdrawal from Afghanistan?

A key here is to understand how the various change agents interact with the political system; to examine how their rates of change interplay with alterations in the elements of Soviet national security. In making these suggestions I will be working toward an explanation of change in Soviet national security policy. I will analyze each of the change agents roughly in the order of the immediacy of their impact, starting with leadership and referring back to the four sets of propositions originally raised about them in Chapter One.

Leadership and institutional change (hereafter referred to simply as leadership) is the change agent with probably the most immediate impact for change in the elements of Soviet national security. In fact leadership change appears to be a prerequisite for alterations in ideas, policy, and behavior when viewed from the perspectives of short-term and long-term change in the elements of Soviet national security. Furthermore, it also exercises considerable influence over the rate of change in the other agents: intellectual ferment and upheaval, external conditions, and economics.

The first proposition about change in Soviet national security policy, and in the other elements of national security, is that leadership is the most critical change agent for significant or radical change. Without significant or radical change in leadership, sharp departures from the past are unlikely. Steven Merritt Miner's examination in Chapter Two of change throughout Russian and Soviet history demonstrates well that in the past, leadership change from Peter the Great through Stalin has facilitated—along with other factors—changes in Russian and Soviet policy. The functions that leadership played then included changes in personnel, institutions, and economic policy and a strong thrust for changes in the basic concepts underlying policy discussions, from an encouragement of *glasnost'* under Catherine II and Alexander II to repression under Stalin. They also encompassed new views about the requirements for and threats to national security, reaching the heights of paranoia under Stalin, including a thorough and terrible purging of the national security apparatus in the 1930s. The relatively cadaverous policies of the Brezhnev administration in its last four years demonstrate the opposite: without a change in leadership, alterations of the elements of national security are difficult.

Gorbachev now has a chance to exercise the leadership functions above and change national security. He has moved decisively to do so. As portrayed in Table 14.2, we see significant changes in the composition of the top echelons of the CPSU and government accompanied by significant to radical organizational changes and the firing and hiring of personnel at lower levels of the Party and government. Alexander Iakovlev's appointment to head the newly created Central Committee Commission on International Policy and the reorganization of the Soviet trading apparatus are two examples of leadership changes over the last three years. They have, for example, helped to centralize control over national security affairs within the Party on the one hand and, on the other, have lent strong encouragement to the new thrust of international trade in Soviet foreign policy. We can conclude, then, in reviewing the first set of propositions in Chapter One that Gorbachev has been an important initiator of change, not merely a conduit of it or a captive of the system.

We shall see shortly how leadership change interacts with other change agents to make it the critical factor and precondition for change. Leadership finds itself in this position in the Soviet political process because the entire process is so centralized. Foreign policy and national security decision making is even more elitist than other policy areas, containing fewer domestic constituencies than, for example, policymaking on nationalities. Jan Triska and David Finley remind us of this fact in their analysis of Soviet foreign policy making (1967: 88–89). Leadership change, then, has the opportunity to influence national security ideas, policies, and behaviors quickly because the communication of information from level to level in the political process is relatively easy compared with other policy domains.

The flux for change is glasnost', strongly encouraged by the Gorbachev administration. This is the basis of the second proposition about change in Soviet national security. Not only are Soviet-American relations discussed openly—even involving public television broadcasts of the treaty ratification process for the INF agreement in the Supreme Soviet—but the most sensitive issues of Soviet national security are now being discussed and evaluated, including the new political thinking and reasonable sufficiency. Debates over the wisdom of invading Afghanistan occur in Party circles, the outlines of which are leaked to the Western press (Keller 1988), and in public discussion in the open Soviet press (Bogomolov 1988; Prokhanov 1988). Shevardnadze (1988: 9) has criticized the decision-making process that brought about the invasion. Such intellectual ferment is unprecedented as a part of the Soviet national security policy process since Lenin's death and strongly fuels the fires for change in Soviet security affairs.

Intellectual ferment can produce change in the very assumptions under which national security operates, including very specific areas such as the use or nonuse of nuclear weapons during war or much broader notions as reasonable sufficiency. (It is interesting to note the similar rates of change between ferment and military doctrine in Tables 14.1 and 14.2.) They even appear to be changing the very definition of what constitutes national security to the broader economic/political/military approach noted in the previous section. The ideas generated from this intellectual ferment reflect nearly a radical change, even surpassing leadership change, though dependent on it. Ferment helps the leadership by laying out options for change, sometimes to extremes. Then the leadership may make assessments of them to help generate what is permissible. Gorbachev and his advisers appear to be using glasnost' to help themselves to develop a measuring stick for change in Soviet national security affairs. Intellectual ferment can be a very useful tool in the hands of a clever leader. In looking back to the fourth set of propositions in Chapter One, we can conclude that intellectual ferment is an important part of the change process and is taken seriously as such by key elites.

Even the most rational leadership cadre cannot easily manipulate the external conditions with which it must deal. That they are often less maleable than domestic conditions deserves special mention here. The international environment imposes important constraints on Soviet national security policy over which Gorbachev has little control but with which he must interact. First, the actions other nations initiate or do not initiate impose constraints and force the Soviet Union to behave in certain ways. Japan's long-standing view that the return of part of the Kuril Island chain, which the USSR gained after World War II, is the *sine qua non* for the improvement of Soviet-Japanese relations stands as an instance of policy the Soviets cannot change. They must therefore live with the reality of considerable hostility from the Japanese and try to deal with it even while attempting to engage the Japanese in the trade of high-technology items. Or the Soviets could accede to Japanese policy by returning the four disputed islands—something no longer inconceivable —and reap the likely considerable economic and political gains. The list of these kinds of constraints that nation-states impose on the USSR is virtually endless.

A second limitation on Soviet power is what Edward A. Kolodziej reminds us is the "incipient anarchy of the world society" and the accompanying global diffusion of military, political, and economic power (Kolodziej 1989). Such international phenomena limit, for example, Soviet arms transfers, which have been an important element for Soviet attempts to exert influence in the Third World and have also been a productive source of hard currency. Nations such as China and Israel now produce quantities of older Soviet-designed weapons and spare parts for those weapons which directly compete with Soviet efforts to sell the same items. A third limitation is the force of geography. It means, for instance, that the USSR has to contend with staffing four different fleets that have a very difficult time joining forces and which divide the Soviet naval budgetary pie so that the USSR is unable to maintain a strong seaborne power projection force.

In spite of these factors, the Soviets still have control over and can change the impact of some external conditions. This leads to the third main proposition in the explanation of change: that the Gorbachev administration is influencing the international environment to attempt to affect *perestroika* at home. The mechanism portrayed here involves the self-reinforcing process pictured in Figure 1.5 of Chapter One whereby changes in leadership lead to Soviet policies that through their external consequences and implications play into efforts at home to restructure Soviet society. (External conditions were not dealt with as a single chapter but were discussed in many; they were not therefore included in Table 14.2. It is clear, however, that Gorbachev is working toward at least significant change in them.)

The focus of the proposition is to point out that Gorbachev is actively attempting to alter the international environment in order, in George Breslauer's (1982) words, to "build his authority" at home so he may portray himself as an effective problem solver and politician. Success in the international environment, in other words, tends to breed support and policy success at home. The signing of the INF treaty and the superpower summit in Moscow in May 1988 occurred immediately prior to the June 1988 CPSU Party conference, where Gorbachev actively sought—and apparently gained—significant support for his restructuring program and some basic changes in the Soviet political process. It would stretch credulity to believe that the timing of these events suggests a simple coincidence.

Gorbachev has engaged in numerous international conferences—with Margaret Thatcher in 1984, even as he was garnering support for the general secretaryship of the CPSU, a trip to France as his first "official" international visit, four summit meetings with Ronald Reagan—a bevy of arms control proposals, and activity on human rights that has resulted in large-scale emigration from the Soviet Union. All of these represent welcome changes from the immobilism of the three previous Soviet administrations and have been well greeted by Western governments and populations. Gorbachev as the vigorous, smiling, worldwide peacemaker fashions a stark contrast to the wan trio of Brezhnev, Andropov, and Chernenko, and augments his authority at home. The sum of the aforementioned constraints and Gorbachev's manipulation of the international arena reflect on the third set of propositions from Chapter One. External conditions interact strongly to help redefine Soviet national security policy.

Each of the three change agents examined thus far—leadership, intellectual ferment, and external conditions—has demonstrated change and an impact on the elements of Soviet national security. Although each contains conservatizing elements that help to prevent change in Soviet policy, they nevertheless contain enough significant and radical change to assist the overall process of altering Soviet security outlooks, policies, and behaviors. The interaction of these with one another and with the policy and behavioral outcomes in national security is complex and probably not entirely knowable. Yet it is clear that the effect can be documented, and it appears that leadership change holds sway as the most important factor for change.

Economics as a change agent occupies a special place in this analysis. It was the necessity for economic reform that prompted Gorbachev and his supporters to embark on their plans to examine Soviet foreign and domestic policies and the process of decision making in the first place. As such, economics is a "prior cause" for change in Soviet national security policy. Yet as shown in the examination of leadership, intellectual ferment, and external conditions, economics is not the sole factor manifesting alterations of Soviet policy. When one examines the *permanence* of change in Soviet policy, however, the force of economics and the important related implications of economic change must be felt.

For the fourth and final major proposition in this explanation of change states: significant or radical economic change is essential for fundamental alterations in the elements of Soviet national security over the long term. This proposition is underlaid by an important corollary: economics is the most difficult area to change of all the change agents discussed so far and necessarily must take place over a long period. If these two assertions are correct, then they point to the tenuousness of the changes mapped out in Soviet national security up to the present. New assumptions, policies, and behaviors may not suggest long-term trends unless economic change takes place as well. This view supports the portion of the second set of propositions in Chapter One which contends that economic conditions and changes in the entire economy—including the civilian sector—are important in generating policy change.

If the economists contributing to this volume appear tentative or even pessimistic in their projections for change in the future, arguing mostly, as shown in Table 14.2, that incremental change is possible, it is probably because their arguments are based on a recognition of the foregoing corollary. If the political scientists in the book appear somewhat more optimistic in their views, it is likely because they have addressed their analyses to the impact of the other change agents. One's view of change in the national security "elephant" (or bear) is strongly affected by the sorts of questions one asks.

Focusing on the corollary for a moment, why is economic change more difficult to manage, and why does it take more time to accomplish than the other factors? Primarily it is because change in economics involves changes in the fundamental Stalinist systems of management and incentives and the corresponding difficulties dealing with the ideology that helped to produce it and which emanated from it. The heritage of in-bred conservatism about economic change that traces its roots back to the tsarist days is also a complicating factor. This is not the place to trace the details of what needs changing, as the matter is discussed well in Chapters Four to Six and is the subject of a book by Ed A. Hewett (1988) which discusses the problems of economic reform in the Soviet economy. Dismantling the Stalinist economic system is an enormous task, to put it mildly, and contains important political implications, to be discussed shortly, which add to the amount of time that change will take.

Permanent change in Soviet national security policy demands a restructuring of the old economic apparatus. Mikhail Gorbachev has not only called for such a perestroika, but has pushed to enact important legislation dealing with it, such as the new enterprise law that took effect January 1, 1988. These efforts to change the old system have strong implications for Soviet national security policy, some of which include (1) a change in the economic underpinnings of defense involving a shift of priorities in military construction to modern conventional weapons; (2) a shift from investments in defense to investments in basic civilian industries, such as machine building and computer technology; and (3) a restructuring of Soviet industry to allow significantly more foreign trade as a normal part of Soviet economic activity.

Some of the foregoing has already been begun, such as the change of organization of the Soviet trading apparatus to encourage foreign trade and the enactment, through the new enterprise law, of legislation to allow individual industries to practice more foreign trade. Soviet and Western companies are investigating joint ventures as well, but these and other proposals are plagued by many Soviet problems, such as the lack of accurate statistics and an irrational pricing system (Ericson 1988; Feder 1988). Such difficulties slow the process of economic change and thereby jeopardize behavioral manifestations of a new view of national security which would include the strengthening of the Soviet economy through international trade.

Efforts to restructure the Soviet economy also contain contradictions in the national security arena which have yet to be resolved. Just one of the dilemmas involves rationalizing and managing the construction of a new generation of conventional weapons (as Soviet doctrine indicates might happen) when (1) the technologies for their fabrication and use are not yet available to the Soviets; (2) the military must compete for resources with basic areas of the Soviet economy, particularly machine-building industries and computer manufacturers; and (3) even if these dilemmas could somehow be resolved, new generations of highly sophisticated weapons will inevitably cost large amounts of money, drawing funds and other resources from numerous other efforts for economic change.

Perestroika of the national security system implies political problems for the current Soviet leadership. One of them, evident from the previous discussion, involves efforts to convince the Soviet military that it will continue to occupy a position of prominence in the Soviet socioeconomic structure even though it has to pay the price of waiting for fundamental restructuring to occur to receive modern, conventional weapons. The argument is telling that the fabrication of new conventional weapons is impossible until the basic industries that have to build them are modernized first. It takes no genius to agree with this logic, and Gorbachev has used it to justify allocating fewer resources to the military. He has also announced conventional troop reductions of about 10 percent, causing discomfort in military ranks (Gorbachev 1988b: 17–18; Tatu 1988). New definitions of national security are yielding fewer funds for the armed forces and a relatively diminished size and role for the military in spite of the projected production of new weapons. The Soviets seek to constrain and stabilize military modernization at the lowest feasible levels.

Far more fundamental, however, are the political problems resulting from the push toward a new process of decision making in the Soviet economy. A paradox of the current efforts at reform is that two of its major tenets—a shift of everyday management from the Party to the government and decentralization of economic decision making—has to be initiated from high Party levels. This simultaneously supports the traditional view of the CPSU as the highest and ultimate decision maker and propagates the new conception of local-level decision making independent of higher authorities. The tension these two notions generate has not yet been resolved and involves a struggle between orthodoxy (read Stalinism) and reform. If past history is a guide, orthodoxy may yet win, but some sort of amalgamation is possible and is being worked out through the new enterprise law whereby the role of the Party and

central ministries is to issue broad directives—called "control figures"—
leaving to the local enterprises the power to make decisions within that context (Ericson 1988).

In turn, new economic decision making has strong implications for the
entire process of decision making in other areas of Soviet life. The final
resolutions of the June 1988 CPSU Conference affirm Gorbachev's calls
for a new, more powerful role to be played by the local Soviets in managing
the everyday affairs of Soviet citizens (Gorbachev 1988a: 4; *Pravda* 1988:
1, 2). This involves nothing more than a change in the role of the Party
from political micromanager to general overseer. If Soviet citizens are to
be able to make economic decisions relatively independently, should they
not also have the training to make their own decisions about their own
lives at the local level? Gorbachev and his allies consider political reform
to be essential for economic and social restructuring to succeed. As the
final document from the Party conference states:

> The conference considers that top priority is to be given today to a
> fundamental reform of the political system. Precisely this system must
> open up new possibilities for the deepening of *perestroika* in every area
> of public life and guarantee that is it irreversible. (*Pravda* 1988: 1)

Certainly the Soviet Union does not need to become some sort of
democratic, multiparty system for significant or radical economic and
social change to result. The leadership's support for continuing Party
control plus the force of centuries of Russian culture and traditional
patterns of authority will weigh strongly against such a development.
Yet Gorbachev's restructuring necessitates Soviet citizens learning a new
process of decision making in economics and government that is removed
from the past patterns whereby, for example, unanimous votes were the
rule and public debate was shunned. The May–June 1989 meeting of the
new Congress of Peoples' Deputies provides a good model (the leadership
surely intends it to be that) for Soviet citizens to see how such discussion
and decision making can take place.

Perestroika encompasses, therefore, the incorporation of tenets producing a new Soviet political culture. It is likely to take generations to absorb
such change. Permanent alterations in Soviet national security policy and
behavior must necessarily take a long time because of their direct links to
economic change and the important relationship they maintain with the
development of Soviet political culture. And they will be fraught with
difficulties that include dealing with old ladies with shopping bags, who
might ruin everything.

Gorbachev's strategy in addressing the complex realities sketched in
this section is to approach change from the top with leadership change

holding the most immediate consequence, but including the related areas of changes in intellectual ferment and external conditions. He hammers constantly on the most difficult, most time-consuming, and, ultimately, the most crucial factor that will determine whether his regime will have long-lasting impact: economic change. As the process proceeds on all four levels at once, it implies changes in the objectives of Soviet national security policy and alterations in the nature of U.S. policy toward the Soviet Union. It is to these matters that the chapter turns.

Implications for Soviet Objectives

Given that Soviet national security policy is in a state of flux, it naturally arises to ask whether Gorbachev, if he succeeds in a significant or radical policy transformation, is really at base changing Soviet objectives. In other words, does change in Soviet policy signify a permanent transformation of objectives or merely tactical maneuvers while keeping basic objectives the same?

On one level the question is answered easily: the Soviet Union will still compete with the United States and other large nations to extend its influence internationally and to exercise power. In this sense objectives will not change; Western Europe, for instance, will be a focus of superpower interaction as the USSR attempts to woo European nations to its side.

But the answer is more complex than that. Objectives in foreign and national security policy are derived both from the ideological character of the Soviet Union as a Marxist-Leninist state with a particular history and from the capabilities, geostrategic position, and interests of the USSR as a great power. Changes in these can produce changes in objectives.

Ideology, the patterns of beliefs and attitudes used to interpret reality and to make projections about the future, is a first consideration. Soviet ideology from the days of Lenin has emphasized a number of different theses, including the irreconcilability of capitalism and communism, the inevitability of conflict between the capitalist and Communist worlds (even if, as developed under Khrushchev, the conflict need not be "inevitably" military), the emphasis on winning contests with the capitalist world, and the exploitativeness of capitalism that includes racism, discrimination against workers, crime in the streets, and, more recently, problems of homosexuality and drugs. All these elements and more have generated impressions of the United States as a nation to be feared and hated. As Philip D. Stewart and Margaret G. Hermann discuss in Chapter Three, the tenets of Soviet ideology are partly responsible for a security policy that has a strong military dimension, that emphasizes economic autarky, and that treats wishes for emigration from the USSR as a symptom of mental instability.

Immersed in this conflictual Marxist-Leninist outlook are notions emanating from traditional Russophile thought, particularly ideas about the superiority of the Russian lifestyle over that of the West. According to one observer, the "official" Soviet ideology (that is, the expressions of ideology most accepted by the government and Party) came more and more to incorporate Russophile thought during the 1970s and early 1980s as it became plain that the USSR could not surpass the United States in new technology (Shlapentokh 1988: 163). This meant that the United States was not a nation to be admired and emulated for its technological accomplishments (as in the past), but rather to be envied and distrusted even more than previously. Thus the 1970s and early 1980s produced an ideology that contained self-reinforcing propositions about conflict drawing from the strong traditions of Marxism-Leninism and Russophilism which, together with Soviet-U.S. conflicts of national interest, was bound to generate strong tensions with the United States. Under these conditions it is no surprise that the USSR was not predisposed to seek compromise and cooperation for resolving international conflicts.

This makes the "new thinking" in Soviet national security all the more interesting. For it demonstrates that official ideological tenets are changing, particularly the emphasis on the inevitability of international conflict and a "zero-sum" approach to international affairs whereby a nation wins only at the expense of others. Now, as we have seen in this work, the Soviets are conceiving of the requirements for security in a fundamentally different way. Ideas about political and economic security are beginning to displace the Stalinist fixation that associates security first of all with military power. Soviet Foreign Minister Shevardnadze formulates this view in the following way (1988: 10):

> The socialist states in the competitive struggle must realize their potential for self-development and, by their economic successes and higher individual and social labor productivity, show that socialism can provide man with more than any other sociopolitical system.
> This is our main national interest. The category of national security and all its aspects can and should be viewed solely in this connection.

The new ideology also contains another important element. Interdependence has become a key concept of Soviet foreign and national security policy. Soviet leaders refer to interdependence in two senses: the interaction between a nation's domestic and foreign policy and the relationships among the foreign policies of nation-states worldwide. Thus the Soviet leadership can claim that perestroika and democratization in the Soviet Union create strong preconditions for changes toward new thinking in Soviet foreign affairs and in the making of Soviet policy. Shevardnadze's July 1988 address at a conference of the USSR Ministry of Foreign Affairs contains this theme throughout. He also carefully argues that the interdependence among political systems of different types is the coming model for international politics. In rejecting the past Soviet models of "class conflict," he states that interdependence places a premium on cooperative relations among nations (Shevardnadze 1988: 10).

This argument leads Soviet leaders to claim that Soviet foreign policy has become "deideologized." As Gorbachev has put it, "The deideologization of interstate relations has become a demand of the new stage" (Gorbachev 1988b: 13). When applied to interstate relations, ideologies have caused conflict, according to Gorbachev, and have prevented the solution of critical world problems, such as hunger and disease. Shevnardnadze (1988: 4) has specifically criticized the "primitive ideologized approaches" of past Soviet foreign policy. In fact, the Soviet leaders are proclaiming a new ideology. The functions of the new way of thinking number at least two. First, the Soviet leadership uses it to promote a new image in the West, far from the "we will bury you" notions of Khrushchev (Shevardnadze 1988: 8) that the USSR had projected and toward the image of a much more reasonable actor in international relations. The ideological change displays a certain amount of traditional Russian utopianism about the future of the world system, in which the USSR can take a leading position. Thus the second function the new ideology serves is to make the Soviet leadership and population feel good about themselves, "to provide a positive image of the self" (George 1988: 3).

The technological accomplishments of the United States are more open for discussion and emulation. Russophile attitudes have been critiqued in the Soviet press by, for instance, *Pravda* commentator Vera Tkachenko, who notes the Soviet predilection for "the plebeian envy of other people born on more warm and abundant land" (quoted in Shlapentokh 1988: 163). The emergence of a new official ideology without some of its Russophile underpinnings has helped to make technological advance an acceptable major goal for the Soviet state and has assisted the development of foreign trade as a tool of Soviet national security policy. A rejection of the inward orientation that Russophilism has helped to produce is another of the major ideological changes of Gorbachev's administration.

Although a new official ideology is appearing, it is important to note that there are still strong elements of other ideological thought that compete with it and that are woven through it. As Franklyn Griffiths (1984) reminds us, many "tendencies of articulation" exist simultaneously in the

USSR, some of which can crop up as dominant in Soviet foreign policy depending in part on the exigencies of Soviet politics and the actions of the United States.

Objectives of Soviet policy relate to the pursuit of national interests as well as to ideology. The means by which national security interests are pursued—in other words, the "tactical" matters of Soviet national security policy—when accumulated over time, strongly influence objectives. They can change the ends themselves or make them more or less threatening to other parties. How a nation attempts to fulfill objectives is as important to success and to other nations' perceptions and responses as the stated objectives themselves. If, for example, the Soviet Union were to try to "expand" its influence only through economic means and were to eschew the exertion of influence via military means, the objective of gaining allies in the Third World might be more successful for the USSR, given that Third World nations are in such great need of economic support. This effort to expand might be simultaneously more acceptable to the United States because of relative American economic power and because the Soviets would be perceived as recognizing the limits to their military power. The objective of spreading influence remains the same but is colored by the means utilized and is less threatening. This may be true whether or not the Soviet leadership intends it to be that way. Thus the analysis of Soviet security policy need not rest on our notions of Gorbachev's intentions. Tactical changes cumulate to permanent changes.

How the means are decided is also important. If the process of decision making is more open and responsive to societal demands and problems, decisions about means in Soviet national security policy today might incorporate more impetus toward the resolution of Soviet economic and political problems (such as trade imbalances and human rights) than of military ones. The relative balance of means, then, might also shift. Decisions made on these bases might even change the nature of Soviet national security policy, transforming it into a policy more responsive to the limits of Soviet military power and considerably more willing to compromise on matters that are not deemed essential to maintaining the USSR's security.

The bases for change in Soviet national security policy are becoming stronger, yet predictions about future directions are always perilous. But the beginnings are mapped out and, if they reach fruition, could produce changes in the objectives and nature of Soviet policy. These include the changes in assumptions, policies, and behaviors discussed in the first section of this chapter. The result can be a Soviet policy that is much more sophisticated and less militarily dangerous yet which ultimately may be better able to compete with the United States for influence.

The road toward change will certainly be rocky and might present Soviet leaders with at least six important problems to resolve which touch upon important domestic and international issues. First, the continuation of a U.S.-centered global foreign and security policy may complicate Soviet efforts to extend vigorously the range of their diplomacy to multinational forums, such as the United Nations, and to nonaligned nations, given that both arenas could perceive themselves as simply battlegrounds of superpower competition and may not be receptive to Soviet advances.

Second, recognizing and dealing with a more pluralistic world conflicts with Soviet efforts to maintain control in Eastern Europe. Gorbachev will have to deal with a mighty tension between allowing or living with the pluralism that is developing in Warsaw Pact decision making, for example, and making clear what the limits of socialist pluralism may be. Otherwise Gorbachev may face another 1956 or 1968, when the only Soviet response to exercising Soviet hegemony was the least desirable one—military intervention. Use of the military in Eastern Europe would help to negate the changes in Soviet national security policy and to foster a return to more conservative principles.

Third, a greater emphasis on international trade, joint ventures with Western companies, and even, perhaps by sometime in the 1990s, trading the ruble in the international money market (Feder 1988) may generate threats to the broad government and Party control mechanisms over agriculture and industry envisioned under current Soviet legislation. The hectic and anarchic international trading arena, if allowed to operate in relation to the Soviet economy, might help to generate unemployment as it becomes obvious over which products the USSR holds the comparative advantage—and over which ones it does not. Economic disruptions like this are unwelcome and could lend force to arguments from conservatives who rail against dealing with capitalist powers and who are, in any case, opposed to any signs of capitalism in the Soviet economy.

Fourth, "democratization" and overall decentralization of decision making, the general destruction of Stalinist political patterns as part of radical economic change, not only may generate opposition internally but could also raise the expectations of Soviet citizens too high, hopes that could be shattered if controls are suddenly imposed as a result of too much glasnost'. As the dispute between Armenia and Azerbaidzhan over the governance of an Armenian section of Azerbaidzhan (Nagorno-Karabakh) demonstrates, domestic political instability can result from more freedom. This is the domestic political parallel to the Eastern European problem: how much pluralism is permissible, and under what conditions may it be fostered?

Fifth, arguments about new conventional weapons in Soviet doctrine may be seen as contrary to the demands of restructuring because they simply cost too much. Political problems with the Soviet military could result, as we have seen in the previous section.

Sixth and finally, the very admissions to economic weakness and to the poverty of the Soviet political decision-making process, while refreshing to many, may generate less appeal to nations of the Third World which are looking for models by which to stabilize their economies and to govern themselves. The Soviets have probably given up on their dreams for a broad scope of Third World operations and are entering a "thermidor" in their relations with the Third World. As Kolodziej and Kanet (1989) demonstrate, this could generate opportunities for more U.S. influence in the Third World, certainly an unwelcome development from the Soviet perspective.

The good news from the American vantage point of tendencies in Soviet national security policy deals not merely with the dilemmas that change will bring to the USSR. For the Soviet Union may be adopting emphases in its security policy in which the USSR will be competing with the United States in an area where the United States is enormously strong and holds a decisive and increasing advantage over the Soviets: international trade. The key area of high-technology trade is of special note; many nations not able or willing to produce advanced computers, for instance, look to the United States to provide them. As the Soviets restructure their economy to compete in international trade, important to Soviet economic security, the delays inherent in switching to new industrial processes will likely place the Soviets even farther behind the United States, continuing Soviet disadvantages in trade. The Soviets are beginning to behave in other ways that the United States should welcome: they have pulled troops out of Afghanistan, are very accommodating in arms control negotiations, and appear more responsive to the demands of their own citizens.

But the bad news for the United States is that if the Soviets do succeed, in the long run they will likely develop into a formidable competitor for influence worldwide because of the new breadth that Soviet security policy would encompass. Such a development might not happen until well into the next century, but given that it may occur, U.S. policymakers should weigh the implications of the good and the bad news. What should the United States do if the new tendencies of Soviet national security policy persist and the Soviets are able to manage the conflicts with which their policies present them? And can the United States prevent a reversion to "old thinking" in Soviet national security affairs?

Implications for American Policy

If significant or radical change occurs in Soviet national security policy, it could be a double-edged sword. On one hand, such change can be a disruptive element, and reacting to it can present dilemmas to the United States in dealing with the Soviet Union, U.S. allies, and nonaligned nations. On the other hand, it can present chances for the United States to respond and take its own initiatives to help create a substantially new and more harmonious bilateral relationship with the USSR and a more positive tenor and substance in relations with other nations. Although change in U.S. policy can be dangerous and fraught with unintended consequences, there is an equal or perhaps even greater risk in allowing all the initiative for change to come from the Soviet side: U.S. leadership could be weakened and creative policy options that could redound to the advantage of the West may not be explored. It thus seems that U.S. policymakers should deal actively with the emerging Soviet policy.

The challenge for American policy would be to manage the tension inherent in change: to maintain strategic and regional stability (for example, to continue military parity with the USSR globally and regionally and to prevent the emergence of governments hostile to the United States)—basic objectives of United States policy—while encouraging change in Soviet policy that is consistent with American interests (for instance, to reduce certain categories of nuclear weapons and actively to discourage nuclear proliferation). For it to succeed, a new U.S. policy must also present a somewhat reduced threat to the Soviet Union or risk a heightening of tensions and a possible return of past cold war patterns.

The task sounds like the squaring of the circle. But not to try would be to pass up a golden opportunity to explore the limits of change in Soviet national security policy and to assist a possible restructuring of international relations that could benefit most nations. The United States needs to move to reassess some of the main assumptions that have underlaid its policy toward the Soviet Union. A rethinking of these principles can introduce new (and less militarily dangerous) elements of competition and collaboration with the USSR and can build on the positive elements of change that have already taken place in Soviet policy. These assumptions number four. Since 1986 we can see change in some of them, but more decisive action needs to be taken.

First, the supposition that nuclear deterrence is the essential military underpinning of Soviet-American relations needs to be reassessed. Even under conditions of new conventional doctrines, nuclear weapons will likely maintain their importance in their deterrent role and should not be forsaken. But the nature of modern deterrence will change from one depending on nuclear weapons to one also relying on the maintenance of highly sophisticated conventional forces if the USSR decides to modernize its own. The United States does not want to be caught in the position of having to fight a nuclear war for lack of sophisticated conventional munitions. The choice of either nuclear war or submission is dangerous and robs American military planners of a more gradual ladder of escalation. U.S. resolve to construct conventional weapons is important to communicate to the USSR, as it will likely have a deterrent effect.

The potentially increased importance of conventional weapons in the U.S. and Soviet arsenals obviously generates competition on yet a new level and raises the threat of conflict. But it also generates new opportunities for cooperation, which American policymakers should investigate. Given that nuclear weapons may become relatively less important in the future for Soviet military strategy, the United States should encourage more discussions about the reduction of nuclear weapons, particularly strategic systems. Current proposals for a 50 percent reduction should be investigated thoroughly. The United States might also probe suggestions to eliminate the mightiest first-strike nuclear weapons, as Graham Allison suggests, "all land-based MIRVs that have hard-target capability," as a way of "testing Gorbachev" to see if an agreement can be reached in this sensitive area (1988: 23). In addition, given that a modern conventional arms race may ensue, new areas of cooperation in conventional arms control may be to the advantage of both superpowers. Limiting conventional arms growth could have the effects of cutting military costs in both nations significantly and of lending a much greater air of predictability to the emergence of new systems from both sides. It could make a "breakout" less likely and thereby reduce tensions. Conventional arms control negotiations, especially those that limit rapid-strike offensive systems (e.g., assault helicopters), could also help to encourage the tendencies of some Soviet military thinkers who are planning for a doctrine of the defense. All of these developments are in the American interest and could come about as a result of American initiative.

Second, the predilection of the United States to envisage regional conflicts as extensions of the U.S.-Soviet rivalry also needs to undergo thorough analysis. The Soviet Union has not lost interest in gaining influence in the Third World, but its commitments appear to have lessened, and the United States needs to recognize that. There may therefore be an even greater need for the United States to treat on a case-by-case basis Third World instabilities in areas of U.S. interest to ensure that there is reasonable evidence that the USSR is behind them. Assumptions about a Soviet imperial design for expanding Soviet interests ever outward (Brzezinski 1986: 30–75) need to be reassessed in light of current developments. There is ample evidence of efforts at Soviet expansionism from past history, and the USSR will still try to increase its power internationally, but the current time may represent a period of great change in Soviet policy including some retrenchment and a new perspective on international affairs. The Soviet debate over the future of its Third World policy demonstrates, for instance, tendencies for investigating more trade relationships with Third World nations—an element of competition with the United States—while, as Stewart and Hermann discuss, at the same time evincing more sensitivity than before about difficulties of alleviating the dilemmas of Third World economies, including world hunger, as a security problem. Given that U.S. foreign policy is also concerned with the latter issue, Soviet statements suggest a collaborative approach with the United States.

Of more relevance to military security in the Third World is another issue. Nuclear proliferation to Third World nations is not in the interest of either the United States or the USSR. Nuclear weapons in the hands of an unstable leader or a stable leader in an unstable region could produce catastrophe. If they were used by U.S. or Soviet Third World allies, the danger of a U.S.-Soviet nuclear standoff could be enhanced. A Third World nation could also develop the capability to attack one of the superpowers either directly or surreptitiously through terrorist organizations or. use nuclear weapons against U.S. or Soviet Third World outposts. It would be in the interest of the United States to initiate discussions leading to an agreement about how to handle nuclear proliferation and nuclear threats from the Third World. Such an agreement could deal with preventing proliferation to Third World allies/friends by, for instance, providing U.S. and Soviet security guarantees to nations that would obtain nuclear weapons to face a regional threat. The agreement could also deal with "outlaw" states and terrorist organizations by detailing the conditions under which the superpowers could deprive such nations or groups of their weapons. It is an area of strong common interest.

Third, American policy has been based on the assumption that the USSR is implacably hostile to Western values, particularly the notions of political and social pluralism and human rights. Moralism and ideology affect American foreign policy at least to the extent that the policy is less open than otherwise to creative directions for cooperation because of fundamental mistrust. Many respected commentators discuss this issue (Kennan 1972; Morris 1987; Parenti 1969). To be sure, the Soviet Union is not about to throw off centuries of inbred attitudes toward authority in just a few years. But as we have seen, the implications of changes in Soviet ideology and ideas about new patterns of decision making for the economy are profound for the development of new Soviet objectives and a new political culture in the long term.

The United States should be sensitive about the extent to which the USSR develops a more open society and should encourage it through, for instance, suggesting broad-ranging exchange programs in all spheres, from the religious to the military. A hopeful sign of change in the United States attitude bearing directly on military security is the six-day visit to the United States in July 1988 of Marshal Sergei F. Akhromeev, then chief of the Soviet General Staff. This marks the longest extended stay ever for a top-ranking Soviet military leader and has been reciprocated by Admiral William J. Crowe, Jr., chair of the United States Joint Chiefs of Staff. Over time, exchanges can have impact through, for example, the opportunity to discuss each others' military doctrine. This is a fruitful area for cooperation, and the United States should attempt to expand it to lower military levels.

Fourth, and finally, U.S. policy toward the Soviet Union is founded on Europe as the center of the United States-Soviet competition. Europe is likely to remain of great concern to the United States because it will continue to be an area of rivalry. As William Hyland (1987: 15) says,

> We must resist the periodic temptation to tinker with a successful alliance [NATO], to play with various forms and types of American involvement. . . . The balance of power could still be changed by shifts in this vital area. Preserving the European alliance must remain the cornerstone of American policy.

Though true, this does not mean (nor does Hyland suggest it) that the United States needs to continue to spend increasing funds for military preparedness in Europe. Soviet ideas about defensive doctrine and mutual security, in addition to their willingness to negotiate and sign an INF agreement in Europe to eliminate intermediate-range weapons, suggest that American policy should investigate more cooperative ways to limit European military confrontation, particularly through conventional arms reduction. Otherwise, given probable modernization programs in both nations, a conventional arms race could escalate to large proportions, possibly generating an atmosphere of greater conflict.

A dilemma for American policy in the NATO alliance is how to defuse military tensions through arms control, arms reductions, and doctrinal changes without also endangering U.S. influence in Europe, ruining NATO, and leaving the European continent much more open to Soviet political manipulation. A good number of European leaders and publics strongly approve of Gorbachev's European initiatives because they are based on less military confrontation and more diplomacy, leading, according to Robert W. Clawson in Chapter Ten, to the possibility of a vastly reduced U.S. military presence. The attitudes of alliance leaders and European public opinion may direct the United States to make decisions about reductions that it may not otherwise consider. The United States is not free to make unilateral choices about how to respond in the European context. In accepting Soviet arms proposals and pushing them further, will the United States actually be assisting in the large-scale diminution of American influence? Perhaps, but probably not.

The answer in part depends on one's view of the sources of U.S. European influence. Both culturally and economically the United States and Europe are strongly intertwined. These ties have at least as much to do with the strength of political relationships as the presence of the Soviet "bear." Even under a greatly lessened American military presence, the United States would retain influence in Europe, probably a significant amount. But the Soviets will keep a military presence on the continent for a long time, and the United States will maintain a large force in Europe, even under or perhaps because of conditions of arms control. The continuing existence of NATO as we enter the 1990s is not in doubt. U.S. influence is unlikely to be diminished by much in the future. In the longer term, of course, both NATO and the Warsaw Pact may become unraveled as political dynamics within each alliance play themselves out. But this may be largely out of the control of the superpowers.

Although the United States may demonstrate the needed policy flexibility toward the Soviet Union in the future (in some ways it already has), Americans need to recognize the limits of U.S. influence on the USSR. American initiatives and reactions to Soviet initiatives have to be received in a political context that is conducive to responding in a positive way. Thus the success of American policy, however benevolent it may be, depends on tendencies within the Soviet political context—and these are up to the Soviets themselves.

Of greatest immediate importance to currents of change within the Soviet political system, as this book demonstrates, is the composition of the Soviet political leadership. Who leads and how they lead makes a big difference and is a product of complexities in Soviet politics and society that are mostly beyond the reach of Americans. Nevertheless, American policy should make all attempts to encourage the development of leaders who espouse principles of national security that are in U.S. interests. As should be evident, some of those principles have been set forth under the Gorbachev administration. Such responses can involve engaging the Soviets in areas of mutual interest to the symbolic but nonetheless important gestures that recognize the legitimacy and importance of the current Soviet leadership to the U.S. future. Continuing summit meetings, as have taken place recently, are excellent and cooperative ways of lending prestige to Soviet leaders by demonstrating the reality of Soviet world power. This is not to say that the future under Gorbachev—or a compatible successor—would be solely cooperative. But relatively speaking, the competitive elements would take on a less military and conservative thrust and tend toward those areas dealing with economic competition and the search for influence. This would be a welcome development.

American policy is at a crossroads. Because of inbred Soviet conservatism, it would be far easier to drive the USSR back to old thinking than to encourage it forward to new patterns. The current Soviet political leadership is still vulnerable to challenge from within. Should the United States not respond positively to the current Soviet leadership and policy changes, it may face a USSR that reverts to some of the old assumptions, including the importance of military power in international relations.

A return of American policy to the days of containment would have predictable consequences for Soviet policy. Containment would assert notions of U.S. military superiority, question the legitimacy of the Soviet Union as a superpower, and, most important, impugn the changes that have taken place in Soviet national security policy, placing the U.S.-Soviet relationship in a context that is almost bound to provoke old thinking in Soviet policy: more confrontation than cooperation. Yet the complexities of Soviet domestic politics and economic change could lead to defeats for Gorbachev and a reversion to some of the principles of Brezhnev even under a more benevolent U.S. policy.

We return, then, to the theme of this chapter and book. Soviet national security policy bears a fundamental relationship to Soviet domestic affairs. The forces of economics and technology are important in this respect. Yet to a greater extent, change in Soviet national security policy depends on whether Gorbachev, or a successor with similar principles, continues to lead the Soviet Union.

References

Allison, Graham T., Jr. (1988). "Testing Gorbachev." *Foreign Affairs*, 67(1), 18–32.
Bogomolov, Oleg (1988, March 19). "Kto zhe oshibalsia?" *Literaturnaia gazeta*, p. 10.
Breslauer, George (1982). *Khrushchev and Brezhnev as Leaders: Building Authority in Soviet Politics*. Boston: Unwin Hyman.
Brzezinski, Zbigniew (1986). *Game Plan: A Geostrategic Framework for the Conduct of the U.S-Soviet Contest*. Boston: Atlantic Monthly Press.
Ericson, Richard E. (1988). "The New Enterprise Law." *Harriman Institute Forum*, 1(2).
Feder, Barnaby J. (1988, June 20). "Soviet Joint Ventures Face Obstacles." *New York Times*, p. 28.

George, Alexander L. (1988). Personal communication, November 7.

Gorbachev, Mikhail S. (1987a, February 17). As quoted in Philip Taubmann, "Gorbachev Avows a Need for Peace to Pursue Reform." *New York Times*. p. 1.

—— (1987b, September 17). p. 1.

—— (1988a, June 29). "O khode realizatsii reshenii XXVII s'ezda KPSS i zadachakh po uglubleniiu perestroiki." *Pravda*, pp. 1–7.

—— (1988b, December 8). "M. S. Gorbachev's Speech at the U.N. Organization." *Pravda*, pp. 1–2. Translated in Foreign Broadcast Information Service (FBIS), *Daily Report: Soviet Union*, December 8, pp. 11–19.

Griffiths, Franklyn (1984). "The Sources of Soviet Conduct: Soviet Perspectives and Their Policy Implications." *International Security*. 9(2), 3–50.

Hall, B. Welling (1987). "The Influence of Global Interdependence on Soviet Security Ideas and Assumptions." Presented at "A Third Revolution in Soviet National Security Affairs?" seminar sponsored by the Mershon Center, The Ohio State University, Columbus, Ohio, October 29–30.

Hewett, Ed A. (1988). *Reforming the Soviet Economy: Equality versus Efficiency*. Washington, DC: The Brookings Institution.

Hyland, William G. (1987). "Reagan-Gorbachev III." *Foreign Affairs*. 66(1). 7–21.

Keller, Bill (1988, June 17). "Secret Soviet Party Document Said to Admit Errors." *New York Times*, pp. 1, 6.

Kennan, George F. (1972). *Memoirs, 1950–1963*. Boston: Little, Brown.

Kolodziej, Edward A. (1989). "The Diffusion of Military Power within a Decentralized International System: Limits of Soviet Power." In Edward A. Kolodziej and Roger E. Kanet, eds., *The Limits of Soviet Power in the Developing World*. Baltimore, MD: Johns Hopkins University Press.

Kolodziej, Edward A., and Roger E. Kanet, eds. (1989). *The Limits of Soviet Power in the Developing World*. Baltimore, MD: Johns Hopkins University Press.

MacFarlane, Neil (1988). "The USSR and the Third World: Continuity and Change under Gorbachev." *Harriman Institute Forum*, 1(3).

Morris, Bernard S. (1987). *Communism, Revolution and American Policy*. Durham, NC: Duke University Press.

Parenti, Michael (1969). *The Anti-Communist Impulse*. New York: Random House.

Pravda (1988, July 5). "Rezoliutsii XIX Vsesoiuznoi konferentsii KPSS." Pp. 1–3.

Prokhanov, Aleksandr (1988, February 17). "Afganskie voprosy." *Literaturnaia gazeta*, pp. 1, 9.

Shevardnadze, E. A. (1988 August 12). "Shevardnadze Speech to July Conference Noted." *Vestnik Ministerstva Innostrannykh Del SSSR*, pp. 27–46. Translated in FBIS, *Daily Report: Soviet Union*, Annex, September 22, pp. 1–24.

Shlapentokh, Vladimir (1988). "The Changeable Soviet Image of America." *Annals of the American Academy of Political and Social Science* 497, 157–71.

Tatu, Michel (1988, December 20). "Soviet Military Voices Its Concern at Gorbachev's Troop Reduction Plans." *Le Monde*. Translated in *Manchester Guardian Weekly*, January 1, 1989, p. 14.

Triska, Jan, and David Finley (1967). *Soviet Foreign Policy*. New York: Macmillan.

Yevtushenko, Yevgeny (1987, Spring). Lecture presented at the Hudson Institute, Indianapolis, IN.

List of Contributors

Jan S. Adams was director of International Studies, The Ohio State University (1970–86), and is currently a faculty associate at the Mershon Center. She is author of *Citizen Inspectors in the Soviet Union: The People's Control Committee* (1977) and coeditor of *Transnational Approaches of the Social Sciences* (1983), and has published numerous articles on Soviet affairs. Currently she is completing a monograph on Soviet-Central American policy.

Robert L. Arnett is a specialist on Soviet military affairs with the Army Headquarters staff at the Pentagon. He has a Ph.D. from The Ohio State University and has published articles on Soviet military doctrine and Soviet views on arms control.

William J. Bishop is professor of political science at Denison University in Granville, Ohio, and a senior faculty associate of the Mershon Center at The Ohio State University. He has published in the *International Yearbook of Foreign Policy Studies* and in the *Mershon Quarterly Review*. He is currently working on a book about coalitions, cleavages, and leadership change in Soviet politics.

Robert W. Clawson is professor of political science, executive director of the Center for International and Comparative Programs, coordinator of the Soviet and East European Studies Program, and associate director of the Lyman L. Lemnitzer Center for NATO Studies at Kent State University. He has authored articles on Soviet-sponsored international

329

organizations and Soviet domestic politics and has contributed chapters on Soviet national security policy in several books of which he has served as coeditor. Most recently he edited *East-West Rivalry in the Third World* (1986).

Mary C. FitzGerald attended a Soviet high school in Moscow and has received a B.S., M.S., and M.A. from Georgetown University. Currently a Ph.D. candidate at Georgetown, she has published numerous articles on Soviet military affairs, as well as two monographs: *Soviet Views on SDI* (1987) and *Changing Soviet Doctrine on Nuclear War* (1989).

Margaret G. Hermann is associate professor of political science and research scientist at the Mershon Center, The Ohio State University. Her research interests focus on foreign policy decision making, in particular the effects of leaders' personalities on governments' foreign policy activity. She is editor of *A Psychological Examination of Political Leaders* (1977) and *Political Psychology* (1986) and is currently writing a book about how leaders shape foreign policy.

Hans Heymann, Jr., is distinguished professor of political economy at the Defense Intelligence College in Washington, D.C., and adjunct senior fellow of the Hudson Institute. He is a long-time student of Soviet defense economics, both as a senior economist at the RAND Corporation (1950–75) and as national intelligence officer for political economy of the National Intelligence Council (1975–83). He is currently studying the impact of the information revolution on Soviet society.

George E. Hudson is professor of political science at Wittenberg University and a senior research associate at the Mershon Center, The Ohio State University. Author of many articles and papers on Soviet foreign and national security policy, he has published works in *World Politics*, *Soviet Studies*, and *Crossroads*, as well as in a number of edited books. He is the recipient of fellowships from the Council on Foreign Relations and the National Science Foundation.

Richard W. Judy is director of the Center for Soviet and East European Research at the Hudson Institute. He is a former professor of economics and computer science at the University of Toronto. His recent publications on Soviet computer technology have appeared in *Soviet Economy*, *Gorbachev's Economic Plans*, *Advances in Computing*, and elsewhere. His research interests also include economic reform in the Eastern bloc countries and the emerging role of Germany in post-cold war Europe.

Roger E. Kanet is professor of political science at the University of Illinois at Urbana-Champaign. He is currently engaged in a project on superpower cooperation in managing regional conflict. He has published extensively on various aspects of Soviet and Eastern European foreign policy, including *The Limits of Soviet Power in the Developing World,* coedited with Edward A. Kolodziej (1989), and the edited volume entitled *The Soviet Union, Eastern Europe, and the Third World* (1987).

Steven Merritt Miner is assistant professor of Russian history at Ohio University. During the academic year 1988–89 he was a visiting research scholar at the Hoover Institution at Stanford University. His publications include *Between Churchill and Stalin: Great Britain and the Origins of the Grand Alliance* (1988).

Robin Alison Remington is professor of political science at the University of Missouri-Columbia. Her works on Soviet-Eastern European alliance politics have been published for twenty years. She is the author of *Winter in Prague: Documents on Czechoslovak Communism in Crisis* (1969), *The Warsaw Pact: Case Studies in Communist Conflict Resolution* (1971), and numerous articles and chapters on the Warsaw Pact, Soviet-Eastern European relations, and the political role of the Polish military in the 1980s.

Philip D. Stewart is professor of political science and director of the program in Soviet International Behavior at the Mershon Center, The Ohio State University. He is also task force coordinator of the U.S.-Soviet Dartmouth Program. His many articles have appeared in journals such as *American Political Science Review*, *American Journal of Political Science*, and *World Politics*.

John E. Tedstrom is an economist with Radio Free Europe/Radio Liberty, Inc. He is the author of numerous articles and chapters on the topic of Soviet economic restructuring. His major research interests include Soviet defense economics, Soviet economic privatization, and Soviet regional economics. He earned an undergraduate degree (economics) from DePauw University and a graduate degeree (economics) from Indiana University.

Index